Trade and Hemisphere

Trade and Hemisphere
The Good Neighbor Policy
and Reciprocal Trade

Dick Steward

University of Missouri Press
Columbia, 1975

Copyright © 1975 by The Curators of the University of Missouri
University of Missouri, Columbia, Missouri 65201
Library of Congress Catalog Number 75–8503
Printed and bound in the United States of America
ISBN 0–8262–0179–2

Library of Congress Cataloging in Publication Data

Steward, Dick, 1942–
    Trade and hemisphere.

    Bibliography: p.
    Includes index.
    1. United States—Foreign economic relations—Latin America.
    2. Latin America—Foreign economic relations—United States.
    3. United States—Commerce—Latin America.
    4. Latin America—Commerce—United States. I. Title.
HF1456.5.L3S83   382'.0973'08   75–8503
ISBN 0–8262–0179–2

To Dad, Buddy, and Walt

Preface

The original objective of my research was to analyze the economic aspects of the Good Neighbor policy. I soon discovered that the reciprocal trade agreements negotiated prior to and during World War II lay at the heart of this policy. Furthermore, I wondered if Roosevelt's political accomplishments, so often cited by diplomatic historians of the New Deal, had been matched in the field of trade and commerce. I soon came to the dual realization that the Good Neighbor policy needed serious revision because of its economic shortcomings and that studies in the area of United States-Latin American economic diplomacy needed greater amplification.

Further research led to the inevitable: The trade agreements and the host of related topics were far too complex to generalize. Negotiations differed with nations having competitive rather than complementary economies. Different policies were formulated for countries having larger direct or portfolio investments. The Open Door in commerce had no such corollary in the area of finance. The Administration formulated, therefore, a rational program if not a coherent policy. Cuba played a different role than Colombia; discussions in Brazil did not stem from the same demands as they did in Mexico. For this reason, I took a country-by-country approach in the majority of chapters. Questions of geopolitics, finance, personalities, philosophy, and the diverse nature of international capitalism also received consideration; the "country approach" was interrupted when warranted by these exigencies.

I am concerned mainly with a series of interrelated ideas. Because of the Great Depression the major diplomatic concern of the New Deal was the search for foreign markets; Latin America and the reciprocity negotiations played an early and vital role in this search. In the process of commercial expansion, Cordell Hull and the State Department, despite presidential, congressional, and business skepticism, enlarged the function of government responsibilities in areas long considered the purview of private capital; and finally, the trade precedents set by New Deal diplomats laid the ground rules for international capitalism in the years to come.

I have also tried to weave the reciprocity treaties into the context of the Great Depression, economic nationalism, isolationalism, the Axis menace, and the new sense of national mission manifested by men like Cordell Hull. This is an account of both achievement and failure. For the philosophy of liberal trade did not juxtapose American ideals and self-interests any more than it served as the economic arm of the Good Neighbor policy. Rather, it engendered the rhetoric of idealism and the diplomacy of imperialism. But one caveat is in order. Hull's brand of missionary capitalism did not exhibit the consistency of a *Weltanschauung* composed solely of big business interests and nurtured in the tradition of dollar diplomacy. This interpretation would be an injustice to the secretary of state's idealism. Although Hull was perhaps a gratuitous moralist, his imperial objectives were tempered by a profound belief that freer trade, to a large degree untested in the United States' experience, could promote recovery for economies as diverse as Guatemala and the United States.

Consequently, American economic diplomacy primarily enhanced the self-interests of the United States. It did not promote real economic recovery in Latin America. Frequently, the reciprocity agreements retarded industrialization, entrenched dictators, encouraged monocultures, stifled an incipient bourgeoisie, and put the region squarely within the trade orbit of America's Open Door empire. The agreements symbolized the secretary's dictum that the "political line-up followed the economic line-up" of nations.

Still, the fundamental weaknesses of the trade program belied its strengths. Despite American importunities, reciprocity could not check protectionism at home or economic nationalism abroad. Unable to sustain liberal momentum, the State Department resorted to such measures as export-import loans, lend-lease, stockpiling, and a cartel plan to accomplish these ends, as well as to blunt Axis designs on the political economies of South America. By the time of Pearl Harbor the reciprocity program with Latin America had ground to a standstill—incongruous in a world beset by conflict. However, Hull's philosophy survived. It emerged from the ashes of war with a new sense of national purpose to become the ideological fulcrum of international capitalism.

I am indebted to the staffs at the National Archives, Library of Congress, Houghton Library, Roosevelt Library, and the State Historical Society of Missouri for their patience, courtesy, and assistance.

In addition, my appreciation is extended to such readers as Lloyd Gardner, Jim Watts, Walter LaFeber, Harold Woodman, Louis Kahle, Win Burgraff, and Alan Millet for their insights, criticisms, and suggestions. Special thanks, however, must go to Walt and Marie Scholes, the finest team of scholars and friends I will ever have.

No acknowledgment would be complete without mentioning Roseann Rahn, Nancy Gage, and my wife Gloria who spent many long hours correcting my spelling and typing the manuscript.

D. S.
Jefferson City, Missouri
May, 1975

Contents

1

Cordell Hull and the Origins of Reciprocal Trade

The inauguration of Franklin D. Roosevelt did little to dispel the anxiety felt by many observers of American economic diplomacy. In the midst of depression, the United States in 1933 remained saddled with the 1930 Hawley-Smoot Tariff, which had raised barriers to import trade to record levels. But the liabilities of this legislation had yet to be demonstrated to an American public skeptical and frightened of any venture reminiscent of economic internationalism. Neomercantilism, the resort to economically narrow unilateral measures by public officials, pervaded not only the United States but the world. These powerful forces of economic nationalism, superpatriotism, and national self-containment had dominated international economics since the onset of the depression. The United States, as did the world, stood at an economic crossroads, perplexed but also indignant at an international system unable to harness the productive capacities of science and technology. Certainly international statesmen had cause for alarm, since few nations escaped the most colossal economic failure of modern history.[1]

The magnitude of the worldwide collapse was staggering. The quantity of world trade decreased 25 per cent from 1929 to 1932–1933. In terms of value, the decline was even more telling. Between 1929 and 1934 the value of world trade fell 66 per cent. But even more alarming to American economic analysts was the

1. F. W. Taussig, *The Tariff History of the United States* (New York: G. P. Putnam's Sons, 1931), p. 4. Also see Raymond A. Bauer, Ithiel de Sola Pool, and Lewis Anthony Dexter, *American Business and Public Policy* (New York: Atherton Press, 1963), p. 25; Lloyd C. Gardner, *Economic Aspects of New Deal Diplomacy* (Madison: University of Wisconsin Press, 1964), Chapter 1.

proportionately greater decline in United States foreign trade. Exports in 1933 accounted for only 52 per cent of the 1929 volume and only 32 per cent of the 1929 value. In 1929 total American export trade amounted to $5,240,995,000. By 1932 the value had plummeted to $1,611,016,000.[2]

The most disheartening factor in the foreign trade picture remained the continual shrinkage of world trade and the yearly reduction of the United States favorable merchandise balance. In 1929 the United States enjoyed 13.88 per cent of total world trade, but by 1932 this share had decreased to 10.92 per cent, while the gross tonnage of American vessels engaged in foreign trade declined by over 50 per cent from 1921 to 1934. The low point in quantum was reached in 1932; the low point in value was not reached until 1934. To a great degree the passage of the Hawley-Smoot Tariff stimulated as well as reflected the precipitous decline in foreign trade.[3] The causes for such failure were not difficult to discern.

One of these causes, found in Hawley-Smoot, was the principle of "equalization of costs of production" drafted in the "flexible provisions" of Section 336 of the 1930 Tariff Act. This equalization clause empowered the President to raise or lower tariff rates by up to 50 per cent to equalize production costs and minimize foreign competition. In short, Section 336 threatened to destroy all forms of international trade except items on the free list (goods exempted from import duties) and foreign specialties considered noncompetitive with American goods. While the clause stimulated foreign retaliation, it was also symptomatic of deeper problems that plagued the international economic community.

The mischief resulting from Hawley-Smoot showed up in other ways. In a neomercantile attempt to aid agriculture by higher tariffs, President Hoover initiated a log-rolling festival

2. Ethel B. Dietrich, *World Trade* (New York: Henry Holt and Company, 1939), pp. 13–15. *Operation*, June, 1934, to April, 1948, pt. 2, Summary (1948), pp. 7–8. *FTLA*, pt. 1, Report No. 146, 2d Series (1942), p. 36. All abbreviations and shortened expressions used in footnotes are expanded on the list on p. 302.

3. *FTUS*, 1932, TPS No. 151 (1933), p. iv. Dietrich, p. 15. U. S., Congress, House, *House Report No. 1000*, 73d Cong., 2d sess., 1934, 2:3. Abraham Berglund, "The Reciprocal Trade Agreements Act of 1934," *The American Economic Review* 25:3 (September 1934):415.

of vested interests that surpassed all bounds of economic reality.[4] (Parenthetically, ad valorem duties provide less effective protection in periods of depressed prices. However, Hawley-Smoot was initiated before the world collapse, although the cost differential was very difficult to apply.) Congressional committees found themselves overburdened and ill-staffed, while the fundamental issues and alternatives in tariff-making sought to correct but could not cure the fundamental defects of the process.

Vocal paralysis likewise infected the critics of ultraprotectionism in Congress and the business community. Political activity of economic groups was not uniform or universal. Equal stakes did not produce equal pressures. As one student of American tariff history remarked, "The protective tariff is well established because large areas of adverse interests are too inert and sluggish to find political expression."[5]

The history of Hawley-Smoot demonstrated that the responsibility of tariff-making, if it was to be a rational policy promoting the general welfare, could not be the sole prerogative of congressmen heavily influenced by lobbyists, pressure politics, and local vested interests. The tariff of 1930 proved to be one of the greatest of all omnibus measures, requiring an expertise far above the knowledge of most politicians. The passage of the Hawley-Smoot Tariff, therefore, amply supported the advocates of "scientific" tariff-making. It also reaffirmed the conclusion of many students of international economics that the United States still operated with a debtor mentality superimposed upon a position of economic dominance.[6]

Before World War I United States tariff policy had little effect on the international financial structure or the volume of world

4. Dietrich, pp. 52–53. For the equivalent ad valorem rates in the tariffs of 1922 and 1930, see TC, *The Tariff and Its History*, Miscellaneous Series (GPO, 1934), p. 84. Taussig, pp. 419–500, 502–5.

5. E. E. Schattschneider, *Politics, Pressures and the Tariff* (New York: Prentice-Hall, Inc., 1935), pp. 66, 163. Cordell Hull, *The Memoirs of Cordell Hull*, Vol. 1 (New York: Macmillan Company, 1948), pp. 132–34.

6. Schattschneider, pp. 283–87. Maxwell S. Stewart, "Tariff Issues Confronting the New Administration," *FPR* 9:2 (March 29, 1933):15. U. S. Congress, Senate, 73d Cong., 1st sess., *World Trade Barriers in Relation to American Agriculture*, Document No. 70: vii. Henry J. Tasca, *The Reciprocal Trade Policy of the United States* (Philadelphia: University of Pennsylvania Press, 1938), pp. 1–2.

trade. The war, however, catapulted the United States into the status of a creditor nation at the same time that rising tides of economic nationalism and protectionism swept across the continents of Europe, America, and Asia. American tariffs no longer served as a source of income but protected domestic industry and labor. Yet the structure of the American economy had basically changed. Cordell Hull had warned Congress in 1920 that high protective tariffs could put an end to American export trade and United States dominance in international finance and commerce. Few heeded his admonitions. The adoption by the Warren Harding Administration of the unconditional most-favored-nation clause in 1923 did little to initiate a more liberal trade policy, since the Fordney-McCumber Tariff of the preceding year set even higher tariff barriers.

Prior to 1923 United States tariff policy was based on the conditional most-favored-nation clause, which meant that American trade concessions were granted to nations that reciprocated with duty concessions to this country. Harding extended the clause in such a way as to grant automatically to all countries having most-favored-nation treaties the concessions given to any nation in the past or future. Although Harding's diplomats worked very hard to negotiate unconditional most-favored-nation agreements, they encountered stiff resistance from European competitors, skepticism on the part of domestic business, and international loan policies not conducive to tariff bargaining.

The effects of the tariff changes were negligible. Even so, Harding's diplomats claimed that concessions granted by one nation to another should automatically be given to the United States, since America too had theoretically adopted the procedure. In reality, Washington granted tariff concessions unconditionally to no one because it had raised rather than lowered duties.[7]

Neomercantilism thereby increased the instability of the post-

7. Francis B. Sayre, *The Way Forward: The American Trade Agreements Program* (New York: Macmillan Company, 1939), pp. 15–17. Hull, *Memoirs*, Vol. 1, pp. 106–7. League of Nations, *Equality of Treatment in the Present State of International Commercial Relations: The Most-Favored-Nation Clause*, League of Nations, II, Economic and Financial, 1936, II, B. 9 (Geneva: Series of League of Nations Publications, 1937): 12. Hereafter cited as *Equality of Treatment*. Also see *Operation*, pt. 1, p. 1.

war economic situation. As a creditor nation with a high protective tariff, the Republican administrations prevented foreigners from improving their trade balance through exports to the United States. A massive economic collapse was forestalled primarily through foreign lending by the United States in the 1920s. The importation of nondutiable goods into the country, American tourist spending abroad, immigrant remittances, and the transfer of gold to the United States also prevented the effects of American tariff policy from being acutely felt. For a short while, the U.S. had its cake and ate it, too. Debt payments to financiers and exporters flowed over the oceans and across the borders of the hemisphere.

The stock market crash in 1929 ended American credit to Europe, Asia, and Latin America. This contraction of international monetary credit in turn created a cycle of deflation. To protect themselves from falling prices, many nations, especially in Latin America, established a complicated set of barter arrangements, monetary devaluations, currency restrictions, higher tariffs, import licensing, quotas, and embargoes. Since many nations experienced problems with currency depreciation, there was a tendency to regulate exchange and impose quantitative restraints on imports. The cumulative effects of these measures reinforced the notion that the international economic variables operating to prevent the establishment of economic stability through a dependence on the interplay of world market forces were apparently insurmountable. Economic nationalism, disguised as temporary emergency measures, became an even more respectable standard of international economic conduct.[8]

The systematic discrimination against foreign trade manifested in the Hawley-Smoot Tariff was soon matched in foreign lands by a host of devices equally destructive to world trade. Exchange controls, probably the most hotly debated of these trade restrictions, appeared in 1931. In part because of the changed distribution of gold (much of which had flowed into the United States during the preceding decade) as well as the problem of reparations, war debts, speculations, a lack of liquidity, and un-

8. *World Trade Barriers*, p. 6. Stewart, p. 16. Henry L. Deimel, Jr., "Commercial Policy Under the Trade Agreements Program," *The Annals of the American Academy of Political and Social Science* 186 (July 1936): 16–17.

sound international lending, the postwar exchange parities did not remain in equilibrium. The fluctuating rates of exchange also hampered sound commercial transactions and prejudiced the liberal flow of goods and services across national boundaries.

Other monetary problems plagued the international economic system. The extensive use of the gold exchange standard greatly contributed to this problem. London in 1914 had been the center for European financial activity, but as the foreign exchange value of her monetary unit weakened during the 1920s, the outflow of gold and the exhaustion of foreign exchange resources became acute. Hence a lack of coordination due to London's abdication as the center for financial activity created an uncertain world financial structure. With the collapse of the Credit Anstalt of Vienna (the major banking house in Austria), and the suspension of gold payments by the United Kingdom, the tottering structure of world finance collapsed.[9]

Currency devaluation, initially begun in 1931 by England and other members of the sterling bloc, led to further quantitative restrictions on world trade. A tripartite commercial policy adopted by Great Britain included the Import Duties Act, designed to protect British producers; the Ottawa agreements, which safeguarded dominion producers; and the "new-model" trade agreements, designed to favor and safeguard Britain's best foreign customers. Other powers followed suit. The Japanese invasion of Manchuria and German activities in the political economies of Central Europe signaled the beginning of more flagrant attempts by the totalitarian powers to control the markets of weaker neighbors. The inextricability of political and economic factors in the new methods of commercial policy became a dominant characteristic of the 1930s.[10]

Although they were aware that exchange control and its concomitant, clearing agreements (bilateral arrangements whereby part or all of the commodity trade between two nations are kept

9. James W. Gantenbein, "The Causes and Effects of Governmental Control of Foreign Exchange," *AFSJ* 13:2 (February 1936):62–63, 92.

10. Arthur Feiler, "Current Tendencies in Commercial Policy," *The American Economic Review* 27: 1: Supp. (March 1937):31, 39. Ethel B. Dietrich, "The New Model Trade Agreements," *The Journal of Political Economy* 42:5 (October 1934):595.

balanced—a very common practice between Latin America and Europe) reduced the volume and value of international trade, numerous debtor nations, especially in Latin America, nevertheless resorted to these measures. These nations adopted exchange control to conserve the gold supply, to provide exchange for servicing the external debt, to prevent the flight of capital, to assure essential imports, to stabilize the exchange rates, to serve as a bargaining point in future trade negotiations, and to act as a regulatory instrument in a planned economy. Brazil, Argentina, Colombia, Bolivia, Uruguay, Chile, and Nicaragua adopted exchange control in 1931; the next year Costa Rica and Paraguay followed suit. Overlooked by all nations was the fact that artificial trade controls by their very nature contributed to even more counterproductive control measures that had the effect of further decreasing world trade.[11]

The reversal of the trend toward economic nationalism became a paramount aim of Hull's diplomacy. But the elimination of exchange control and the liberalization of trade necessitated the correction of the economic conditions that produced it. Here, then, was the need for the reciprocal trade program.

Reciprocity was also designed to dovetail national self-interests with the liberal ideal. Underlying the assumptions of Hull and other members of the State Department was the profound influence of Woodrow Wilson. In his *Memoirs*, Hull claimed that "Woodrow Wilson's victory was for me the opening of a new era." By 1916 Hull had embraced a trade philosophy that he never relinquished. Finally, he prided himself on the fact that his "broad international economic view" became the catalyst of Point Three of Wilson's Fourteen Points. Indeed, it would be safe to say that when revisionist historians such as N. Gordon Levin, Jr., described Wilsonian policy as the construction of "a stable world order of liberal-capitalist internationalism" com-

11. League of Nations, *Enquiry Into Clearing Agreements,* League of Nations, II, Economic and Financial, 1935, II. B. 6 (Geneva: Series of League of Nations Publications, 1936):10, 14–16, 24–25. Herbert M. Bratter, "Foreign Exchange Control in Latin America," *FPR* 14:23 (February 15, 1939) :274–77. See also, TC, *Regulation of Imports by Executive Action,* Miscellaneous Series (GPO, 1941). Dietrich, *World Trade,* p. 125. *Enquiry,* pp. 16–24. *Equality of Treatment,* p. 15.

bating "imperalism on the Right and the danger of revolution on the Left," they were not far from the essence of Hull's philosophy.[12]

Hull diagnosed the depression as political, economic, and social chaos engulfing the world and destroying ethical standards of moral conduct. "Truth, candor, law, and fair dealing had been banished from many chancelleries." Nation upon nation flouted treaty observances and succumbed to the rule of force rather than accept the rule of law. The peaceful settlement of disputes, disarmament, and economic cooperation went unheeded. "The world, in fact," lamented Hull, "never more nearly approached economic and financial catastrophe domestically, and anarchy internationally." The Wilsonian dream of a world guided by an ethical and moral consensus appeared to be transformed into a nightmare.[13]

To the idealist, the world of law, character, and morality, as well as the traffic of commerce and finance, had no political or territorial boundaries; these were *a priori* truths. Moral principles of individual liberty, truth, respect, justice, and mutual trusts, endemic to all men, transcended artificial political demarcations. Again recalling Wilsonian rhetoric, Hull's assistant secretary of state, Francis Sayre, remarked that "Truth does not change." The generic qualities of freer trade more than a strict construction of Adam Smith's laissez-faire fitted the same pattern of thought.[14]

But the world of Woodrow Wilson and the Fourteen Points had changed perceptibly since 1919, and the New Deal idealists realized it. Wilson's abhorrence of power politics and his basic misunderstanding of the balance of power in Europe led him to conclude that World War I had been waged on a Manichaean stage and played to perfection by the forces of democracy and totalitarianism. To Hull, however, the traditional reasons for conflict were no longer applicable.

Influenced by the enormity of the depression, Hull argued that

12. Hull, *Memoirs*, Vol. 1, p. 69, 81–82. N. Gordon Levin, Jr., *Woodrow Wilson and World Politics: America's Response to War and Revolution* (New York: Oxford University Press, 1968), p. vii.

13. Hull, *Memoirs*, Vol. 1, pp. 124–25, 136–37, 172.

14. DS, Francis B. Sayre, "Woodrow Wilson and Economic Disarmament," CPS No. 20 (1936), p. 1. Hull, *Memoirs*, Vol. 1, pp. 124–25.

the root cause of war stemmed from economic forces. Just as Wilson's idealism sensed a dichotomy between the rulers of a pernicious nation and the ruled, so too did Hull view a separateness between a nation's political and economic policies. Nations discarded the sanctity of moral and legal contracts and pursued political and territorial aggrandizement not because of chauvinistic, racial, or imperialistic impulses but because of corruption, blindness, and self-centered materialism, which characterized the international economic community.[15]

The abolition of power politics became a logical course for the economic determinist. Since there could be no victor in a modern war that would wreck the economic fabric of society, the justification for power politics proved illusory. True power became synonymous with economics. The panacea for world peace, therefore, lay in liberal trade. Hull never clearly perceived, however, that liberal trade might be as much the result of world peace as the cause.[16]

The Great Depression changed the emphasis of statesmen from politics to economics. As Franklin Roosevelt put it, the economic interchange of goods became "the most important item in our country's foreign policy."[17] Men began to doubt the effectiveness of political solutions to international problems. Ironically, both Hull and Roosevelt to some extent agreed with the Marxian concept that conflict among nations stemmed from economic forces. But for the Marxist, war arose inevitably from imperialism, while Hull, starting with many of the same assumptions, concluded that economic conflict could be diminished by economic cooperation among nations. Hull emphasized the elimination of power politics by freeing the economic channels of trade and investment, thereby redressing the uneven global distribution of natural resources. Reciprocal trade, the logical extension of the Open Door philosophy, was designed to prevent the im-

15. Hull, *Memoirs*, Vol. 1, pp. 172.

16. *CPS*, No. 20, p. 1. Also see Francis B. Sayre, "The Winning of Peace," *CPS* No. 38 (1937), p. 2–7. Sayre, *The Way Forward*, pp. 103–4. William R. Allen, "Cordell Hull and the Defense of the Trade Agreements Program, 1934–1940," in Alexander DeConde, ed., *Isolation and Security* (Durham: Duke University Press, 1957), pp. 130–31.

17. Robert H. Farrell, *American Diplomacy in the Great Depression* (New Haven: Yale University Press, 1957), Chapter 1. Franklin D. Roosevelt, *Looking Forward* (New York: John Day Company, 1933), p. 245.

perialistic impulse.[18] As Ethel B. Dietrich has stated, "When trade and investment are free, territorial possessions are of secondary importance. When trade and investments are controlled by governments and when the once open doors are banged-to, then the territorial possessions become important."[19]

By reversing the causal relationship of the Great Depression and the loss of world trade, Hull assumed that liberal trade was also the logical place to make a *démarche* from the economic and political strategy of the 1920s. He saw the Great Depression as a direct result of the loss of world trade through blind economic nationalism pursued by the United States and other great powers. In the secretary's mind, the depression was the effect of a shrinkage of world commerce, not the cause. Hull set out to prove the interdependence of the American economy and the world at large. Since economic policy had political ramifications, a wise United States commercial and financial program could go far toward the easing of international political tensions. Reciprocal trade seemed destined to increase American participation in world affairs.[20]

The trade agreements program also promised to perform several cathartic functions for the domestic economy. Schooled in the Wilsonian philosophy of New Freedom, Hull, Assistant Secretary Sayre, and other State Department officials denounced the growth of bureaucracy, economic self-sufficiency, and governmental regimentation. Economic self-sufficiency, Hull said, "would inevitably mean a fundamental and sweeping readjustment and reorganization of the whole domestic agricultural,

18. Roosevelt, *Looking Forward*, p. 245. Francis B. Sayre, "World Peace and Foreign Trade," *CPS* No. 31 (1936), p. 1–11. Francis B. Sayre, "The 'Good Neighbor' Policy and Trade Agreements," *CPS* No. 34 (1937), p. 13.

19. Dietrich, *World Trade*, p. 339.

20. Hull, *Memoirs*, Vol. 1, pp. 356, 176–77. Bauer, pp. 96–103. Bauer's study verified the connection between internationalism and free trade and isolationism and protectionism. Also see George N. Peek, *Why Quit Our Own?* (New York: D. Van Nostrand Company, 1936), p. 185. Some of the revisionist works on the 1920s have redefined isolationism because of aggressive economic policies. See Joan Hoff Wilson, *American Business and Foreign Policy, 1920–1933* (Boston: Beacon Press, 1971), especially chapters 3–7. See Wilson's *Ideology and Economics: U. S. Relations with the Soviet Union, 1918–1933* (Columbia: University of Missouri Press, 1974), pp. vii–xi.

industrial, commercial, and general economic structure." Although Hull might have admitted that economic self-sufficiency and governmental regimentation, if vigorously pursued, could produce limited economic recovery, the cure, he argued, would be worse than the disease.[21] Francis Sayre agreed: "National economic self-sufficiency would sound the death knell of civilization as we know it."[22] Because of his progressive temperament, Hull found it difficult to accept the growing tendencies of the New Deal toward paternalism, bureaucracy, and centralization. By allowing for the freer flow of market variables, liberal trade measures might serve as an alternative to governmental direction of the economy. Hull never fully comprehended the paradox that the reciprocal trade agreement program extended vast powers to the executive branch of government regardless of what function reciprocity might serve.[23]

The internationally coordinated restoration of commerce, shipping, and industry through liberalized trade measures also promised to purge the hedonism, reckless spending, and indolence that characterized the 1920s. Again Hull took the lead. The secretary described this "ten-year holiday" as an orgy of artificial prosperity and easy reward that vitiated the national character. The time, to Hull, had now come for America to return to what she did best. Hull symbolized most vividly the link between the work ethic and Christian morality as he celebrated the virtues of "hard work" as the principal ingredient in economic and moral recovery.[24]

Finally, the reciprocal trade agreement program rested on the assumption that excessive protection of American industry and agriculture hindered the efficiency of labor, thwarted specialization of functions, and discriminated against the consumer. Hull opposed government discrimination and regimentation and argued that market forces should determine, if possible, the flow

21. Cordell Hull, "Our Need for Foreign Trade," *CPS* No. 26 (1936), p. 5. Hull, *Memoirs*, Vol. 1, pp. 197–98.

22. Sayre, *The Way Forward*, p. 2. Also see Sayre's "American Commercial Policy: The Two Alternatives," CPS No. 23 (1936), p. 1–10.

23. U. S., Congress, *Congressional Record*, 73d Cong., 2d sess., 1934, 78, pt. 5:5630.

24. Cordell Hull, "Secretary of State Sends Message to the Foreign Service," *AFSJ* 10:5 (May 1933):168. Gardner, pp. 16, 39–40.

of international trade. To Hull, this assured the most efficient productive methods and the most potent means to increase labor efficiency. The stability of American capitalism, synonymous with freedom, necessitated a revision of extreme protectionism. Since Roosevelt and his Cabinet opposed a unilateral reduction of duty rates, the Hull trade program offered the best available method to effect a downward revision of the tariff.[25]

Secretary Hull, however, realized that domestic politics ruled out the possibility of free trade. His trade policy, therefore, espoused "liberal" rather than "free" trade. The program realistically avoided both extreme economic nationalism and extreme economic internationalism. In fact, members of the Department of State went so far as to argue that reciprocal trade was "a temporary measure" to deal with an "acute emergency." Hull stated on March 8, 1934, before the House Ways and Means Committee that the object of the trade program was to reopen and seek new outlets for United States surplus production; after the emergency there would be ample time to make a thorough review of the program. No one in the department, however, offered an alternative.[26]

With the exception of Assistant Secretary of State Raymond Moley, Cordell Hull received solid backing by the State Department. Nevertheless, he faced formidable obstacles to his trade program not only from other governmental agencies but in the ambivalence of President Roosevelt. The Tennessee senator's selection as secretary of state might very well have been a gesture on Roosevelt's part to solidify the Southern wing of the Democratic party or, at least, repayment for Hull's support at the 1932

25. Raymond L. Buell, *The Hull Trade Program and the American System* (New York: Foreign Policy Association, 1938), pp. 23–24. R. Walton Moore, papers, Franklin D. Roosevelt Library, Hyde Park, N. Y., Box 8, November 13, 1936. Also see William Phillips, diary, 1933–1936, Vol. 1, Houghton Library, Cambridge, Mass. December 13, 1933. Hull, *Memoirs*, Vol. 1, p. 374.

26. J. M. Letiche, *Reciprocal Trade Agreements in the World Economy* (New York: King's Crown Press, 1948), pp. 19–20. Cordell Hull, "American Foreign Trade Policies," *CPS* No. 24 (1936), p. 8. Frank W. Taussig, *Free Trade, The Tariff and Reciprocity* (New York: Macmillan Company, 1924), p. 1. William Diebold, *New Directions in Our Trade Policy* (New York: Council on Foreign Relations, 1941), p. 3. Leroy D. Stinebower, "Proposed Foreign Trade Agreements," *AFSJ* 11:4 (April 1934):196–97.

convention. Quite possibly Roosevelt narrowed the field to the least unattractive candidates and then selected Hull.[27] Nevertheless, the secretary accepted the position with a resolute mind and spirit, confident that the opportunity afforded him a chance to promote world peace through economic cooperation among nations. Hull did not doubt Roosevelt's sincerity. "We did not discuss foreign affairs to see whether we agreed in our attitudes toward them. . . . We thoroughly knew each other's views in the main."[28]

Hull's belief in Roosevelt might well have been reconsidered in the light of certain speeches delivered by Roosevelt in the 1932 campaign. On the question of trade, Roosevelt muddied the waters in an October 26, 1932, speech delivered at Baltimore. After a qualified endorsement of negotiated trade treaties Roosevelt added:

> Of course, it is absurd to talk of lowering tariff duties on farm products. . . . I know of no effective excessively high tariff duties on farm products. I do not intend that such duties shall be lowered. To do so would be inconsistent with my entire farm program.[29]

The President's March 4, 1933, inaugural address offered little encouragement to Hull's views. Roosevelt devoted only 54 words out of 1,800 to foreign policy, and these pertained to the Good Neighbor policy.[30] On the matter of foreign trade, Roosevelt said:

> Our international trade relations, though vastly important, are in point of time and of necessity secondary to the establishment of a sound national economy. I favor as a practical policy the putting of first things first.[31]

27. Graham H. Stuart, *The Department of State* (New York: Macmillan Company, 1949), pp. 309–13. Hull, *Memoirs*, Vol. 1, pp. 353.

28. Hull, *Memoirs*, Vol. 1, pp. 157–59.

29. U. S., Congress, *Congressional Record*, 74th Cong. 2d sess., 1936, 80, pt. 1: 863. For Hull's reaction to Roosevelt's Albany speech see Hull, *Memoirs*, Vol. 1, p. 150.

30. Stuart, p. 320. Frank Friedel, *Franklin D. Roosevelt: Launching the New Deal* (Boston: Little, Brown and Company, 1973), p. 103. Friedel believes that the recovery program was essentially economic nationalism.

31. Cited in Roosevelt, *Looking Forward.* Also see *The Public Papers and Addresses of Franklin D. Roosevelt,* Vol. 2 (New York: Random House, 1938), pp. 11–16.

But underlying Roosevelt's political caution on tariff matters was a basic trust in the ingenuity, enterprise, self-confidence, and shrewdness of the American businessman—a quality best exemplified by the exploits of the Yankee trader. The Yankee trader, because of his superior qualities, could outbargain, undersell, and far outstrip his nearest competitor. He was the epitome of dynamic capitalism, seldom taking cognizance of the interdependence that existed between himself and the nation he exploited. All the Yankee trader asked was that he be given equality of treatment, preferably on the unconditional most-favored-nation basis.[32] The President's faith in the capitalist system, however, proved to be both a strength and a liability to the negotiators of reciprocal agreements. The Chief Executive's confidence provided the State Department with the support necessary to implement the reciprocity agreements, but the assumptions of the Yankee trader bordered very close to economic nationalism. As Roosevelt wrote in *Looking Forward*:

> I have none of the fear that possesses some timorous minds that we should get the worst of it in such reciprocal arrangements. I ask if you have lost faith in our Yankee tradition of good old-fashioned trading? Do you believe that our early instincts for successful barter have atrophied or degenerated? I do not think so.[33]

Yet Roosevelt did not fully recognize the inconsistency in the assumption that liberal trade policies harmonized with Yankee trading. In the meantime American economic policy wavered between the domestic planners and the internationalists. Roosevelt's "last moment" decision in the spring of 1933 not to ask Congress for authority to negotiate reciprocity agreements left the United States without a definite trade policy.[34] Late in 1933, Under Secretary William Phillips remarked in his diary, "Every department, especially the Tariff Commission, was in a fog as to the foreign trade policy to be pursued."[35] In effect, Roosevelt,

32. Percy Bidwell, "The Yankee Trader in 1936," *The Yale Review* 25:4 (June 1936):702–5.

33. Roosevelt, pp. 187–88.

34. Phillips, diary, Vol. 1, December 28, 1933; December 21, 1933. Diebold, p. 6. Sumner Welles, "Trade Recovery Through Reciprocal Trade Agreements," *CPS* No. 29 (1936), p. 3–4.

35. Phillips, diary, Vol. 1, November 22, 1933. See also Cordell Hull,

for the time being, had placed the recuperative powers of capitalism into the hands of the domestic planners.

Probably the prime reason for the confusion in New Deal trade policy resulted from the passage of the National Industrial Recovery Act and the Agriculture Adjustment Act. These domestic reform measures committed the United States to economic nationalism. The philosophy of NRA and AAA was to attempt an increase in wages, costs, and prices in the United States, but these increased price levels left the nation vulnerable to foreign goods. To protect the domestic economy from a flood of cheaper imports, Roosevelt moved to stop freer trade.[36] Economic nationalism was in full swing—much to the dismay of Hull.

Section 3 (e) of NIRA empowered the Executive to use protective measures against foreign competition for domestic industries operating under codes of fair practice. Section 15 (e) of AAA also empowered the President to levy an equal compensating tax on agricultural goods subject to processing taxes. Under the provisions of NRA and AAA the United States placed import quotas on liquor, lumber, tobacco, potatoes, cotton, and sugar.[37] These measures illustrated the inherent conflict between price raising and production restrictions on the one hand and the aim of tariff reduction to benefit consumers, achieve production efficiency, and lower costs on the other. This dichotomy between a stabilized domestic economy and lower prices through freer international competition enhanced the possibility of a centrally planned economy through regulated import and export control.[38]

Since exporters were considered part of their respective industries, the NRA provided them wth no separate code. In other words, the blue eagle did not make any distinction between the

papers, General Correspondence, Library of Congress, Feis to Hull, October 9, 1933.

36. Laurence J. deRycke, "International Commodity Control," *Proceedings of the Institute of World Affairs*, 11th sess., 11 (Los Angeles: University of Southern California, 1934): 133–34. Hull, *Memoirs*, Vol. 1, p. 248, 318. Joe R. Wilkinson, *Politics and Trade Policy* (Washington: Public Affairs Press, 1960), pp. 1–2. Tasca, pp. 10–13, 21–29.

37. *The Tariff and Its History*, p. 85. Diebold, p. 36.

38. U. S., Congress, *Congressional Record*, 73d Cong., 2d sess., 1934, 78, pt. 4: 3680. David H. Popper, "Progress of American Tariff Bargaining," *FPR* 11:6 (May 22, 1935):68.

cars exported by General Motors and the ones listed for domestic productions. The deputy administrator of NRA, Malcolm Muir, opposed any export activities that required either lower prices and wages or increased hours of labor in order to compete for foreign markets.[39] The Department of State and the American Manufacturers Export Association both correctly feared the loss of American export trade due to increased prices. The codes likewise created difficulties for certain Latin American nations badly in need of American imports. On July 26, 1933, Under Secretary of State William Phillips called to the attention of Hugh Johnson, head of the NRA, the importance of "continued competition on the part of American manufacturers in the export markets." To ensure American exporters a fair share of the world market the State Department urged that NRA codes not contain clauses affecting import and export trade.[40] The State Department also asked Johnson to allow one of its own officials to help regulate NRA codes; Johnson, however, politely refused. Stephen Early, assistant secretary to the President, told Phillips that Johnson would cooperate with the State Department, but Johnson said, "It does not seem appropriate to put a State Department official on a code authority supervising an industry."[41] Department of State relations with AAA were less strained. Although a division of authority existed in the trade agreement program, Hull and Secretary of Agriculture Henry Wallace generally worked together to increase agricultural exports and to minimize administrative overlapping.[42]

The logic of economic nationalism, however, had not run its course with the adoption of NRA and AAA. At the London Economic Conference in 1933, Roosevelt again demonstrated his uninvolvement with international solutions to the depression. Acting on the advice of Raymond Moley, Roosevelt rejected the stabilization of international currencies as "artificial and unreal"

39. DS 811:50/210, NA, RG 59. Also see *American Manufacturers Export Association Newsletter*, July 22, 1933. *New York Times*, July 23, 1933, Business 4N. *FTUS*, 1934, TPS No. 162 (1935), p. 8, 32. DS 811.50/210; 612.1115/50; 611.2131/65, NA, RG 59.

40. DS 811.6511/8; 611.1831/10, NA, RG 59.

41. DS 811.113/363; also see 811.50/222; 611.1831/10, NA, RG 59.

42. DA, *Records of the Office of the Secretary of Agriculture: General Correspondence of the Office of the Secretary 1933–1939*, NA, RG 16, M. L. Wilson to Kizer, August 16, 1938.

measures that tended to hamper domestic recovery. The President had taken the country off the gold standard in order to devalue the dollar and to stop the spiral of deflation. By keeping the gold standard, many of the European banking houses hoped to stabilize world currencies and to avert further economic collapse. Roosevelt thought differently. The immediate problem, however, was that Hull, who headed the delegation from the United States, saw the London Conference as a golden opportunity to initiate "a definite program of sane, practical, international cooperation" necessary to stimulate business recovery. The secretary's functions at London revolved primarily around the question of tariff barriers. Matters pertaining to war debts and currency stabilization were left in the hands of the Treasury Department, Federal Reserve experts, and Raymond Moley. Perhaps Hull failed to realize fully that the continual fall in world prices helped to create the trade barriers he hoped to abolish. In any case, his lack of knowledge in these fiscal matters allowed Moley to undermine his policy of international cooperation, to steal the spotlight from the secretary, and to steer the nation toward economic nationalism. Nevertheless, it is doubtful if Roosevelt would have committed himself at this juncture to any form of liberal trade. While Hull was en route to London, Roosevelt informed him that pressing political demands at home ruled out the possibility of immediate tariff legislation. As a sop to Hull's pride the President endorsed the idea of negotiating reciprocity agreements with "several minor countries" subject to congressional approval. Hull quickly rejected the proposal. The memory of Hawley-Smoot and Congress' role in the debacle that followed lingered all too vividly in his mind.[43]

The story of the London fiasco need not be recounted in detail here. Roosevelt's hastily prepared note torpedoed not only the international stabilization of currencies but also the hopes and aspirations of many statesmen seeking to refurbish a spirit

43. Julius Pratt, *Cordell Hull: 1933–1944*, Vol. 1 (New York: Cooper Square Publishers, Inc., 1964), pp. 35–48, 108. "National Foreign Trade Council's Review of World Export Trade," *AFSJ* 10:1 (January 1933):11. Hull, papers, Hull to William Hard, June 27, 1933, and Moley to Roosevelt, July 4, 1933. Hull, *Memoirs*, Vol. 1, pp. 250–52, 350. Stephen Heald and John W. Wheeler-Bennett, eds., *Documents on International Affairs, 1933* (London: Oxford University Press, 1934), p. 44.

of cooperation among the nations of the world. On July 2, 1933, the President scolded the delegates for dealing solely with stabilization to the exclusion of "fundamental economic ills." Shortly after, the conference adjourned in disillusionment and bitterness. The London Economic Conference affirmed the facts so evident a few months later at the Geneva Disarmament Conference; namely, that the environment that would allow peaceful agreement among nations in both political and economic matters did not exist. "The outlook," regretted Hull, "for any sort of international cooperation is seemingly near its lowest ebb."

Roosevelt's July 2 "bombshell" message clearly indicated that the President's neomercantile outlook intended to achieve "a balance between exports and imports thus preventing material losses or gains of gold between nations." The aftermath of London also convinced Secretary Hull of the impracticality of multilateral tariff reductions due to the complexities of commercial barriers. The experiences at London reinforced the argument that bilateral agreements adopted on an unconditional most-favored-nation basis by presidential action provided the most practical means to achieve freer trade. With the procedure for future trade negotiations clarified, Hull awaited an opportunity to implement his ideas.[44]

But Roosevelt did not prove to be an easy man to second guess. Despite his actions during the London Economic Conference, the President appeared unwilling to go to the extremes of economic nationalism. The monetary policy of the Roosevelt Administration after the termination of the gold standard in the U.S. had been twofold in nature. Raising the domestic price level in order to relieve the internal situation became the primary concern, while strengthening the competitive power of American commerce in the struggle for world markets rated secondary consideration.[45] Roosevelt probably realized that nations with depreciated currencies, such as the United Kingdom, the United

44. Stuart, pp. 322–23. Hull, papers, Hull to Norman Davis, September 20, 1933; and Memorandum, July 5, 1933. George Peek, *Why Quit Our Own?*, pp. 159, 162. Sayre, *The Way Forward*, pp. 42–50; Pratt, 1, p. 109.

45. League of Nations, *Review of World Trade 1934*, II, Economic and Financial, 1935, II. A. 8 (Geneva: Series of League of Nations Publications, 1934) : 63. *Documents on International Affairs, 1934*, p. 212. Maxwell S. Stewart, "Tariff Bargaining Under the New Deal," *FPR* 10:6 (May 23, 1934): 70.

States, and Japan, did not suffer equal export losses as did nations with stable currencies like Germany, France, and Italy.

Roosevelt based his actions chiefly on the fear that currency stabilization would retard domestic recovery. The President did not reject the internationalists' concern for freer trade *in toto*; he merely wanted assurance that stabilization would aid the recovery program. On November 11, 1933, Roosevelt set up the Executive Committee on Commercial Policy to coordinate the foreign trade activities of the government. The following month the White House issued a statement that read in part: "Now the time has come to initiate the second part of the recovery program and to correlate the two parts, the internal adjustment of production with such effective foreign purchasing power as may be developed by reciprocal tariffs, barter, and other international arrangements." In December, 1933, the Seventh Inter-American Conference at Montevideo provided the United States with the opportunity to implement these goals.

The atmosphere for the conference did not appear to be promising. In Cuba, the repressive regime of Gerado Machado y Morales had come apart at the seams despite the efforts of United States diplomats, and the overall situation continued to deteriorate. In South America the Leticia and Chaco controversies still raged. Argentina remained recalcitrant toward inter-American cooperation. And, finally, the United States did not seem sufficiently motivated in the direction of implementing the rhetoric of the Good Neighbor. Under Secretary Phillips, therefore, urged the postponement of the conference until a more propitious time. Hull reluctantly agreed. Montevideo, at least for the time being, appeared to be a dead issue. Roosevelt, however, did not agree with the advice of his diplomats. In all probability the Chief Executive was more concerned with the appearance rather than the reality of activism in Pan-Americanism, as indicated to Hull: "We don't think you need to undertake much down at Montevideo. Just talk to them about the Pan American highway."[46] But national prestige had slipped badly after the London Conference, and Roosevelt regretted the worldwide implications. The aftermath of London indicated the shift in American foreign policy toward economic isolation. The United States' role as a cooperative partner in the community of nations had been

46. Pratt, p. 154. Phillips, diary, Vol. 1, October 30, 1933.

recast as a narrow economic nationalist void of world leadership.

FDR reasoned, however, that a spirit of international cooperation needed to be rebuilt on a foundation more suitable to domestic needs. The Seventh Inter-American Conference appeared the best opportunity to achieve these ideals. But the President was far more hesitant to make broad economic commitments than political ones. A November 11 press release stated that the White House had informed the American delegation at Montevideo "to forego immediate discussion of such matters as currency stabilization, uniform import prohibitions, permanent custom duties, and the like." On the day Hull introduced his economic resolutions at the conference, Roosevelt voiced skepticism of the benefits of tariff reductions. On December 8, 1933, the President repeated to Hull that liberal trade agreements had to take into consideration the exceptions of NRA and AAA. He also refused to support the negotiation of trade agreements without congressional approval.[47]

The limitations placed on Hull at Montevideo, therefore, hampered the secretary's ability to initiate a comprehensive economic program for the Western Hemisphere. His scheme for an inter-American tariff truce and the abolition of exchange controls met with disapproval from the President, although Roosevelt belatedly agreed to bilateral trade agreements based on the unconditional most-favored-nation clause. With these limitations spelled out, Hull began work on the trade problem. On December 16, 1933, the visiting delegations signed the Resolution on Economic, Commercial, and Tariff Policy incorporated as part (iv) of the Final Act. The resolution, which was aimed toward the permanent liberalization of commercial policy, pledged each signatory to reduce high trade barriers through the negotiation of comprehensive bilateral reciprocity treaties based on mutual concessions and equality of treatment.

On December 24, the delegations signed and incorporated into the Final Act the Resolutions on Import Quotas (v), the Import Prohibitions (vi), and the Resolution on Multilateral Commercial Treaties (vii). The State Department believed that each of these represented a shift in American policy away from

47. Charles A. Thomson, "The Seventh Pan-American Conference," *FPR* 10:7 (June 6, 1934): 89–96. Hull, *Memoirs*, Vol. 1, pp. 321–22, 331–32, 353. Wilkinson, p. 3.

economic nationalism. Hull had won a tactical victory. The political concessions made in the Declaration of the Rights and Duties of States might well have been interpreted as a victory for the proponents of hemispheric solidarity and unilateral nonintervention, but the progress toward economic cooperation achieved at Montevideo belonged largely to Hull. The Seventh Inter-American Conference proved to be the first step away from the philosophy adopted at London. It also produced the political climate necessary to implement the changes in American commercial policy toward Latin America envisioned in the Montevideo resolutions. United States foreign trade policy at last had begun to crystalize, much to the credit of Cordell Hull and to the satisfaction of American export interests.[48]

The rationale behind the reciprocal trade program with Latin America involved both diplomatic and economic considerations. The Administration viewed with little equanimity its deteriorating trade position in the hemisphere. As the Bureau of Foreign and Domestic Commerce pointed out, "From 1929 to 1932 the United States exports to this area showed a decline in value of 78 percent, the largest for any trade region except Oceania." In 1929 Latin America took 18.6 per cent of American exports, but by 1932 the figure stood at only 13.4 per cent. Import trade from Latin America declined from 1929 to 1932 by approximately 68 per cent.[49] If the political lineup of nations did indeed follow the economic lineup as Hull suggested, then the State Department had cause for alarm.

Equally foreboding to American policymakers was the fact that Latin American nations, states, and municipalities increasingly defaulted on American loans. Of the $5,000,000,000 invested in Latin America, over $1,500,000,000 represented bonds, the least secure. Bond defaults, however, merely exacerbated Latin America's economic problems, since they cut off

48. Franklin D. Roosevelt, papers, Franklin D. Roosevelt Library, Hyde Park, N. Y., Official File, 614–A, Trade, Harry Tipper to Roosevelt, December 16, 1933. Phillips, diary, Vol. 1, November 28, 1933; December 13, 1933. Edward O. Guerrant, *Roosevelt's Good Neighbor Policy* (Albuquerque: University of New Mexico Press, 1950), p. 92. *Documents on International Affairs*, 1933, pp. 487–92. Hull, papers, General Motors Export Company to Hull, June 6, 1934.

49. *House Report No. 1000*, p. 3. *FTUS*, 1936, TPS No. 174 (1938), p. 76–78.

further capital needed to stimulate export production. To balance national payments Latin America decreased her imports and initiated other trade restricting devices. American direct investment in Latin America, which totaled approximately $3,518,739,000 in 1933, likewise faced dangers. The Great Depression revived political revolutions in Latin America, the immediate effect of which was to retard economic development. It also enhanced the possibilities of confiscation and expropriation of American property, which tended to increase diplomatic problems.[50]

The decline in world commodity prices, especially raw materials and foodstuffs, continued to stifle Latin America's purchasing power. Heavy foreign debt obligations, the slower fall in the price of manufactured imports, and the artificial exchange rates adopted by European powers added to Latin America's trials. The League of Nations reported that the depreciation of the dollar also retarded a "tendency towards increasing production and lessened unemployment."[51] A Good Neighbor policy designed simply to minimize the political abuse of American power could hardly solve the difficulties of Latin America. A system of international economic cooperation formulated to retard the spread of economic nationalism was imperative. Both the League of Nations and the Royal Institute of International

50. DS 811.503132/8A NA, RG 59. Bratter, pp. 274–75. U. S., Congress, *Congressional Record*, 73d Cong., 1st sess., 1933, 77, pt. 2: 1707–8; Macy M. Skinner, "The Outlook for Inter-American Trade," *Proceedings of the Institute of World Affairs*, 11th sess., 11 (Los Angeles: University of Southern California, 1934): 106–7. Henry Chalmers, "The Depression and Foreign Trade Barriers," *The Annals of the American Academy of Political and Social Science* 174:Supp. (July 1934):90. BFDC, *United States Trade with Latin America in 1930*, TPS No. 124 (1931), p. 1–2. Gardner L. Harding, "American-Owned Imports Help Our Trade," *AFSJ* 9:12 (December 1932):481. Donald M. Dozer, *Are We Good Neighbors?* (Gainesville: University of Florida Press, 1961), pp. 9–12.

51. Chalmers, pp. 88–93. *FTUS*, 1936, TPS No. 174, p. 76. Bratter, pp. 274–75. J. D. Magee, "Some Aspects of Tariffs and Trade in South America," *The Tariff Review* 81: (January 1930):11. League of Nations, *Monetary and Economic Conference*, League of Nations, II. Economic and Financial, 1933, II. Spec. 1 (Geneva: Series of League of Nations Publications, 1934): 7–9; League of Nations, *World Economic Survey Fourth Year, 1934–1935*, League of Nations, II. Economic and Financial, 1935. II. A. 14 (Geneva: Series of League of Nations Publications, 1935): 7.

Affairs agreed that the lowering of tariff barriers and the adoption of unconditional most-favored-nation treatment were vital to world recovery.[52]

A first step in this new trade program envisioned the spirit of inter-American economic cooperation, which would be implemented through regional trade agreements or bilateral arrangements, and a downward revision of the United States tariff. Freeing the channels of inter-American commerce held forth the promise that new United States customers might be obtained in other parts of the world if reciprocity worked in Latin America. It was this reasoning that prompted Donald Dozer to state in *Are We Good Neighbors?* that "Pan American policy now occupied first place in the foreign relations of the United States." In a larger sense, however, the markets of the Western Hemisphere could not compare with the markets of Europe and Asia. As Lloyd Gardner has suggested, "State Department publicists constantly affirmed that trade agreements among industrial nations were of primary interest." Still, Hull realized America's greater bargaining strength with the Latin Americans. If these negotiations went smoothly and created no great domestic uproar, the secretary could begin the construction of a "united front" among the European industrial powers.[53]

Hull also saw the mutual reduction of tariff rates as a means of restoring a competitive economy, as well as aiding the consumer, through the principle of comparative advantage. It also ensured the procurement of vital raw materials needed for industrial efficiency. Again, Latin America's needs anticipated a larger policy. For example, over 80 per cent of United States imports from Latin America in these New Deal years were crude materials and foodstuffs. This increased specialization of Latin American labor and production made her welfare codependent

52. League of Nations, *World Economic Survey*, pp. 27–31. *Documents on International Affairs, 1933*, pp. 32–39.

53. Dozer, p. 39. Skinner, pp. 100–105. BFDC, TPS No. 124, p. vi. DS 811.50/181 NA, RG 59. Diemel, p. 16. Dozer, p. 25. Julian G. Zier, "Commercial Inter-dependence of the Americas," *Bulletin of the Pan American Union* 57:3 (March 1933):197–202. Guillermo A. Suro, "Trade Agreements Between the United States and Latin America," *Bulletin of the Pan American Union*, 58: 11 (November 1934):780–82. H. Gerald Smith, "Economic Ties Linking the United States and Latin America," *Bulletin of the Pan American Union*, 70:3 (March 1936):269–75. Gardner, p. 44.

with the United States. It therefore became mutually unproductive when approximately 40 per cent of Latin American imports to the United States were subject to custom duties or import excise taxes.[54]

Agriculture, as well as industry, relied extensively on foreign markets. Approximately 10 per cent of total United States production went abroad. American raw cotton production similarly depended on foreign markets. To that end, the trade program objectives included the stimulation of mutually profitable international trade and the removal of discrimination against American commerce. Artificial stimuli such as subsidies met with opposition by the State Department since these methods would only produce foreign retaliation through import quotas and licenses, along with antidumping laws. Export subsidies, bounties, and currency depreciation further enhanced the possibility of further exchange control. In 1933 less than 20 per cent of United States exports were subject to exchange restrictions.[55] The trade agreements were envisioned as a major way to impede that trend.

The June 12, 1934, Reciprocal Trade Agreements Act was undoubtedly designed as an emergency measure to increase American exports. What is generally not realized is that it was drafted by the State Department as an amendment to Hawley-Smoot rather than as a comprehensive tariff bill. One consequence of this is that the United States, having never repealed Hawley-Smoot, still operates under the highest tariff in its history.

Even more importantly, the act for the first time in United States history combined the unconditional most-favored-nation clause with the principle of active tariff bargaining through reciprocal agreements. It repealed the contingent duties (duties that vary in amount according to the duties placed upon American products) as inconsistent with the most-favored-nation clause.

54. George N. Peek, papers, Western Historical Manuscripts Collection, State Historical Society of Missouri, Box 13, Wallace to Peek, March 2, 1934. Buell, pp. 14, 25–29. Taussig, *Free Trade*, pp. 127–33. Francis B. Sayre, "The 'Good Neighbor' Policy and Trade Agreements," *CPS* No. 34 (1937), p. 1–4. *FTLA* pt. 2, p. 42. Harold B. Hinton, *Cordell Hull, A Biography* (Garden City: Doubleday, Doran and Company, Inc., 1942), Chapter 14.

55. Sayre, *The Way Forward*, pp. 3–8, 12–14. Hull, papers, Memorandum to Stinebower, June 2, 1934. *Operation*, pt. 4, p. 2.

The act, however, allowed for the imposition of countervailing duties to neutralize subsidies or bounties on products imported into the United States. As an extra safeguard, the architects of the trade program incorporated escape clauses into many of the reciprocal agreements that withdrew concessions to third countries should they obtain the major benefits, thereby causing "an unduly large increase" in the import article. The act also stated that the generalizations through reciprocal tariff bargaining excluded those nations discriminating against American commerce. Thus, for the first time in United States history, the nation adopted a multicolumn tariff, which is a tariff with two or more rates of duties on like products from different nations.

The President was empowered to raise or lower existing duties by 50 per cent. He could not transfer imported goods to the "free list," nor could he remove those existing imports on the free list. The reciprocity bill did give the Chief Executive authority to "bind" articles on the free list under legal restraint. Advance notice of the intention to negotiate reciprocity agreements signified that information from various governmental agencies such as the Tariff Commission (imports), the departments of State, Agriculture, Commerce (exports), and Treasury had been obtained. Lastly, the act expired in three years and was subject to renewal by Congress. It could not cancel or reduce foreign debts to the United States.[56]

The State Department realized that the basic objectives of reciprocal trade transcended the goals of enlarging American exports; but the policymakers, especially Hull, decided upon this line of attack. Hull's remarks to the Senate Finance Committee and the House Ways and Means Committee in 1934 consistently stressed this theme. Other Administration officials, such as Secretary Wallace and Commerce Secretary Daniel Roper, also emphasized the need for broader and more scientific economic plans in foreign trade policy to relieve domestic surpluses and

56. Pratt, pp. 110–11; Peek, papers, Box 13, Peek to Sayre, January 16, 1934. *Operation*, pt. 2, p. 8–9. Phillips, diary, Vol. 1, February 28, 1933. O. R. Strackbein, *American Enterprise and Foreign Trade* (Washington: Public Affairs Press, 1965), pp. 1, 30–39. William S. Culbertson, *Reciprocity* (New York: McGraw-Hill Book Company, Inc., 1937), pp. 12–13, 145–51, 171. Hull, *Memoirs*, Vol. 1, pp. 358–59. *House Report No. 1000*, pp. 16–17. Tasca, pp. 7, 32–33.

therefore promote internal recovery. Administration spokesmen from both inside and outside the Department of State
stressed the emergency nature of the Trade Agreements Act to
deal with a temporary economic crisis. The implications of these
statements pointed in the direction of increased presidential
power commensurate with the authority of other foreign executives to cope with any unforeseen emergency.

In the area of nontariff trade control (prohibitions, permits,
exchange control, quotas, monopolies, and milling and mixing
regulations) executive direction was nearly complete. The removal of tariff-making from congressional control and the increased government activities in foreign affairs marked a decisive
shift toward presidential power. The growth of executive power
during the formative years of the New Deal was not limited to
the domestic scene. Beginning with reciprocity agreements, the
New Deal broadened the horizons of governmental activity in
foreign affairs. To some degree these added responsibilities were
the outgrowth of economic necessity, but the rise of totalitarian
powers, which were trained in the art of political and economic
warfare, also necessitated greater responsibilities and duties in
the hemisphere.[57]

Latin America, therefore, fitted neatly into the overall trade
program, since it allowed Roosevelt to solve the apparent conflict between domestic and foreign trade objectives. First, Latin
America was a most likely place for the expansion of American
markets. American export trade relied extensively on triangular
trade. Any increased purchasing power for Latin America aided
domestic recovery if implemented by reciprocal trade and unconditional most-favored-nation treatment. Second, the United
States need not have feared industrial competition from Latin
America. As Lloyd Gardner has stated, reciprocal trade agreements combined with unconditional most-favored-nation treatment are normally proposals made by strong industrial nations
seeking to secure markets for a broad sweep of its products.

57. Culbertson, p. 101. Wilkinson, p. 6. *House Report No. 1000*, pp. 5–7,
12. Dietrich, *World Trade*, pp. 54–59, 77. James A. Robinson, *Congress
and Foreign Policymaking* (Homewood, Ill.: Dorsey Press, 1962), pp.
11, 59. TC, *Regulation of Imports by Executive Action*, Miscellaneous
Series (GPO, 1941), pp. 4–5. Francis B. Sayre, "How Trade Agreements
are Made," *CPS* No. 42 (1937), p. 1–5. Tasca, pp. 43–47.

"Only a great power," he wrote, "can afford to risk injury to some industries in order to obtain these larger markets."[58] Third, the United States trade program operated largely with non-competitive products. Latin America produced 90 per cent of world exports in flaxseed and 33 per cent of the world's market in cane sugar, cocoa, and castor seeds. Bananas, crude rubber, manganese, bauxite, and platinum likewise offered no competition to American enterprises. Fourth, reciprocal trade and the unconditional most-favored-nation clause were based on the principle of the chief or principal supplier. This principle purported that negotiations would be conducted only on those products from a country that constituted the chief source of supply. Therefore, tariff concessions protected domestic industry and agriculture from foreign dumping, since the Department of State limited the scope of concessions to a few nations. In most negotiations only a few countries were affected by the treaties and then only after negotiations with the nation that constituted the main source of supply had been completed.

Although the United States could ill afford a 33 per cent reduction in world trade resulting from international bilateral balancing, the Roosevelt Administration would not consider major tariff revisions. Bilateral agreements negotiated on the basis of the unconditional most-favored-nation clause therefore appeared as the safest alternative. In a letter to Raymond Moley in 1935, Roosevelt confessed:

> As to the bilateral treaties, do not get into your head that the most-favored-nation clause eliminates the bilateral features.
>
> In actual practice we are making bilateral treaties insofar as 99% of the articles affected are concerned.

In January, 1934, Roosevelt made his views explicit when he remarked to Francis Sayre that commercial bargaining should definitely increase United States exports by the approximate increase in imports.[59]

58. Gardner, p. 40.

59. Diebold, pp. 16–20. Berglund, pp. 417–19. Pratt, p. 115. *Review of World Trade, 1934*, p. 37. Elliott Roosevelt, ed., *F.D.R.: His Personal Letters, 1928–1945* (New York: Duell, Sloan and Pearce, 1950), p. 524. Roosevelt, papers, Official File, 20, Caffery to Howe, August 25, 1933; Official File, 313, Phillips to Roosevelt, December 4, 1933. Hull, papers, Chalmers to Hull, February 1, 1934. Roosevelt, papers, Official File, 614-A, Roose-

Finally, it must be remembered that reciprocal trade was not an anathema to all economic nationalists. As a debtor area it became essential for Latin America's total balance of trade to increase so that payment of debt service on United States obligations, plus the returns on United States capital investments and the payment for shipping costs and other services regularly purchased from the United States, could be met. The expansion of American markets in Latin America as well as loans and investments more closely integrated the hemisphere's economies and further eliminated the necessity of unilateral military intervention. Although World War I and its aftermath had eliminated all but the most remote possibilities of foreign intervention in the area, the State Department still needed the strategically vital areas of natural resources, communications, and investments secure and accessible. Without any sense of incongruity, Sumner Welles, certainly no economic nationalist, could remark that, "The day of 'dollar diplomacy' with all of its many vicious implications, is a thing of the past."[60] However, the trade agreements did seek to secure equitable allocations of foreign exchange from the debtor nations of Latin America. In this sense, reciprocity indirectly served to facilitate service and repayment of foreign debts.

Armed with the principle of "equality of treatment" and sharing a mystical faith in the Yankee trader, the economic nationalist went forth to search for market conquests. As Diebold stated, "Equality was a democratic ideal, a principle of laissez-faire capitalism, the basis of 'decent, honorable, and fair commercial relations'; for the United States it was also helpful, expedient and profitable."[61] The difference between equality of treatment and most-favored-nation treatment lies in the fact that the latter is contractual in nature while the former is given freely and independently of legal obligation. To the economic nationalist it was not reciprocal bilateral negotiations that aroused his ire but the fact that these concessions, through the unconditional most-favored-nation clause, were generalized to all nations with-

velt to Sayre, June 6, 1934. *FTLA*, pt. 2, p. 8. Stewart, "Tariff Bargaining Under the New Deal," p. 83. Dietrich, *World Trade*, pp. 218–19.

60. Summer Welles, "The Trade-Agreements Program in Our Inter-American System," *CPS* No. 22 (1936), p. 3.

61. Diebold, p. 25.

out corresponding pledges. "This may be a little realistic for the State Department to swallow readily," remarked one such nationalist, "but they might under pressure from the White House come around to it."[62]

The diplomatic assumptions underlying the Good Neighbor policy also entailed the performance of certain politico-economic functions by reciprocity agreements. In the first place, New Deal commitments toward Latin America were primarily negative in nature. For example, the pledges made by Hull in 1933 at Montevideo repudiated unilateral, armed intervention in the hemisphere by the United States. But this action, as well as Roosevelt's abrogation of the Platt Amendment in Cuba, held forth little or no constructive assistance for the basic problems of Washington's southern neighbors. The same situation was applicable in the withdrawal of American troops from Haiti, the elimination of American financial tutelage in Santo Domingo, the negation of the old canal treaty with Panama, and the abandonment of United States claims of free transit across the Isthmus of Panama. In short, the United States had made no solid, concrete, or constructive military or economic commitments for Latin America's welfare.

In this context the rhetoric of reciprocal trade agreements gave the Good Neighbor policy economic substance and a positive commitment to the welfare of the Americas. It made, wrote Bryce Wood, a "great contribution" to a "broader reciprocity."[63] In his memoirs, Hull recapitulated the political achievements of the Good Neighbor but qualified its success "if we had not been able to back them up with economic acts."

The ideal of Pan-Americanism couched in these terms signified

62. *Operation*, pt. 2, p. 9. Richard Carlton Snyder, *The Most-Favored-Nation Clause* (New York: King's Crown Press, 1948), pp. 6–11, 236, 241–43. *SAPFT*, NA, General Correspondence, Carter to Peek, August 30, 1934. *FTLA*, pt. 1, p. 54. Sumner Welles, "Trade Recovery Through Reciprocal Trade Agreements," *CPS* No. 29 (1936), pp. 3–4, 8. Charles C. Abbott, "Economic Penetration and Power Politics," *Harvard Business Review* 26:4 (July 1948) :410–24. For a different approach to Latin American policy during and after World War I, see Joseph S. Tulchin, *The Aftermath of War: World War I and U. S. Policy Toward Latin America* (New York: New York University Press, 1971), especially chapters 4–6.

63. Bryce Wood, *The Making of the Good Neighbor Policy* (New York: Columbia University Press, 1961), pp. 285–87.

no great departure from isolationism, yet it formally recognized an interrelationship among nations and assumed cooperation rather than conflict as the most effective form of international politics. In this sense, the Good Neighbor policy took a notable step in the direction of enlarging the community of nations. To Hull, inter-American cooperation became a prerequisite for wider international cooperation. "In carrying out our policies toward Latin America, it was never my wish to make them exclusively Pan-American." But the success of this program, in fact its very heart and soul, depended upon a wise economic policy on the part of the United States.[64]

64. Hull, *Memoirs*, Vol. 1, pp. 308–14, 321, 347–49. Dozer, p. 20. Cordell Hull, "The Reciprocal Trade-Agreements Program in War and Peace," *CPS* No. 73 (1943), p. 1.

2

The Dog House:
The Hull-Peek Controversy

Cordell Hull's trade program encountered numerous domestic obstacles as well as foreign complications during the formative years of the New Deal. Perhaps the most serious challenge came from the Office of the Special Adviser to the President on Foreign Trade headed by George Peek. The contest for interdepartmental control of the trade agreements program also stemmed from the lack of administrative coordination and design, the indecisiveness of the President, congressional opposition, and the powerful influence of American business. All of these factors created an environment conducive to the controversy.

In a larger sense, however, the trade battle centered around two distinct concepts of world trade. Unlike much of the New Deal experimentation, the story of Hull's trade program represented the triumph of idealism and theory over conservative and so called "realistic" methods for the promotion of international trade. Peek saw the catastrophic conditions that existed in world trade and decided to make the best of it. Hull rejected this brand of realism and sought to change the system; if his theory was incomplete, his idealism was nonetheless sincere. The Hull-Peek struggle also appears in retrospect as the most important interdepartmental attempt to limit the functions of the State Department in matters of trade and finance. In the process of promoting and protecting the reciprocal trade program, the State Department assumed new governmental functions and responsibilities that broadened the scope of its powers. Historian Carl Parrini, for example, has suggested that administrations from Wilson's to Hoover's rejected many of the guarantees offered to business by FDR.

Throughout the first year of the New Deal various departments dealt independently and with little deference to State Department guidelines in matters of foreign trade. Economic Adviser Herbert Feis later recalled "the continued chaos and conflict within the government about the nature and direction of our commercial policy." Under Secretary William Phillips singled out as the most culpable departments the Reconstruction Finance Corporation and the National Recovery Administration. Foreseeing the difficulties, both Hull and Phillips urged Roosevelt to set up a new interdepartmental organization for the coordination of all activities in foreign trade.[1] On November 11, 1933, Roosevelt established the Executive Committee on Commercial Policy, composed of the departments of State, Treasury, Commerce, Agriculture, NRA, AAA, and Tariff Commission representatives. A State Department official headed the newly formed organization. Secretaries Roper, Wallace, and Hull all appeared delighted with the prospects of increased departmental coordination in foreign trade matters.[2]

However, no one anticipated the advent of George Peek into a situation already marked by confusion and overlapping jurisdiction. A veteran of many farm fights, Peek was no stranger to the fisticuffs of national politics. In fact, his background as a past member of the War Industries Board and a director of the Moline Plow Company made him a leader of the farm capitalist bloc inside and outside the Administration. His opinions often represented the position of the powerful food and textiles industries. If Peek was not the spokesman of agri-business, it was not for lack of effort. Peek's overzealousness in the Department of Agriculture had prompted his resignation as head of AAA.

1. Herbert Feis, *1933: Characters in Crisis* (Boston: Little, Brown and Company, 1966), pp. 262–64. William Phillips, diary, 1933–1936, Vol. I, Houghton Library, Cambridge, Mass., November 2, 1933. Franklin D. Roosevelt, papers, Franklin D. Roosevelt Library, Hyde Park, N. Y., Official File, 614–A, Trade, Roper to Hull, November 15, 1933; Wallace to Hull, November 10, 1933. *SAPFT*, General Correspondence, NA, Peek to Donald Richberg, November 14, 1934. Cordell Hull, papers, General Correspondence, Library of Congress, Feis to Hull, October 9, 1933. Carl P. Parrini, *Heir to Empire: United States Economic Diplomacy, 1916–1923* (Pittsburgh: University of Pittsburgh Press, 1969), p. 10.

2. Phillips, diary, 1933–1936, Vol. I, November 13, 1933.

Roosevelt then suggested sending Peek as minister to Czecho-slovakia with the extra title of "Adviser to the President on Agricultural Imports and Exports with Europe." Unfortunately for Hull, Roosevelt agreed in December, 1933, to allow Peek to head a new organization promoting foreign trade. The President assured Phillips that Peek's position amounted to window dressing and that the special adviser would not interfere in State Department matters. The department was briefly reassured. Phillips remarked in his diary that the Department of Agriculture and especially Rexford Tugwell, who "hates the sight of Peek . . . is chuckling with the thought that he has foisted his adversary on the Department of State." Phillips, however, discounted Peek's persuasiveness and believed the department should "sit quietly," since the special adviser "will not be in the game very long."[3]

But Peek soon convinced both himself and others that he took his job in all seriousness. On December 30, Peek's "Proposed Foreign Trade Administration" suggested the shifting of vital trade functions of the State and Commerce departments to his administration. Wasting little time, Moline, Illinois' favorite son recommended to the White House that he, and not Francis B. Sayre, chair the Executive Committee on Commercial Policy. Peek also broached the question of setting up a corporation to finance exports and imports with himself as director. Secretary of Agriculture Henry Wallace at once recognized that Peek was up to his old tricks and predicted a hard road ahead for the State Department. Hull took the hint. On January 31, 1934, the secretary sent communiqués to Wallace; Jesse Jones, chairman of the Reconstruction Finance Corporation; and Daniel Roper, secretary of commerce, suggesting a meeting to discuss Peek's sudden onslaught.[4]

Much to the dismay of Hull, the initiative gained added momentum on February 26, 1934, when Roosevelt approved the establishment of two governmental banks headed by Peek to promote export trade; even more "tragic," the President agreed to a new trade organization that the department feared sup-

3. Ibid., December 4, 11, and 12, 1933.
4. Ibid., January 2, 1934. Hull, papers, Memorandum, January 8, 1934; Hull to Jesse Jones; Hull to Wallace; Hull to Roper; January 31, 1934.

planted many of its functions in foreign trade. Phillips called it the "biggest blow the State Department has ever received."[5] Peek neared the threshold of victory.

Roosevelt, however, seemed content with a balance of power, and without his support Peek's bid for control of the Executive Committee soon fell short. The President also undermined Peek's strength when on March 23, 1934, he gave him the title of Special Adviser to the President on Foreign Trade, "authorized to obtain, review, and coordinate the information, statistics, and data with reference to the foreign trade of the United States." Phillips remarked in his diary that the March 23 Executive Order settled the Peek challenge by limiting the scope of his activities. "The Department," wrote Phillips, "has won out again over a powerful adversary." Although the Department of State had once again encountered Peek's influence, it still underestimated his potential importance. Smarting under the provisions of the Executive Order, Peek conveyed his displeasure to Roosevelt. The restricted provisions of the act, Peek warned, could end "only in confusion and perhaps discredit to the administration."[6]

The special adviser's next power play came on June 12, 1934, with the passage of the Trade Agreements Act, which was to be implemented by an interdepartmental committee called the Committee on Foreign Trade Agreements. Although the act represented the sweetest victory in Hull's political career, Peek strove to gain control of its administration. The State Department's plan for the committee was that it be chaired by the department and subject to the Executive Committee. This proposal met with immediate opposition from Peek. Roosevelt wavered; not until June 28 did the President approve the State Department's plan. Peek thereupon sought equal representation on both the Committee on Foreign Trade Agreements and the Executive Committee. Peek insisted, to no avail, that the Com-

5. Phillips, diary, 1933–1936, Vol. 1, February 27, 1934.

6. Ibid., Vol. 2, March 19, 23, 1934. George N. Peek, *Why Quit Our Own?* (New York: D. Van Nostrand Company, 1936), p. 30. Julius Pratt, *Cordell Hull, 1933–1944,* Vol. I (New York: Cooper Square Publishers, Inc., 1964), p. 116. George N. Peek, papers, Western Historical Manuscripts Collection, State Historical Society of Missouri, Box 13, Peek to Roosevelt, March 17, 1934.

mittee on Trade Agreements be composed of six members, one each from the departments of State, Treasury, Commerce, Agriculture, the Tariff Commission, and the Office of the Special Adviser to the President on Foreign Trade. The actual make-up consisted of three votes for the State Department.[7]

From these early tests of strength, both Peek and Hull began to realize that the struggle for control of American foreign trade policy would not be an easy one. Peek's critique of the liberal traders became increasingly personal. The men in the State Department, Peek wrote to Louis Howe, a presidential adviser and confidant, were ill-suited for the tough trade negotiations ahead. "Trades are made by men, not machines." With his profound disdain for theorizers and academicians, Peek became a favorite of economic nationalists, protectionists, and commercial isolationists. Distrustful of idealists, Peek represented the epitome of economic realism. The world, in Peek's view, had changed, and the halcyon days of the Manchester liberals were history. American commercial and financial policy, Peek argued, had to recognize the world as it existed; wishing could not make it otherwise. As the coming years bore testimony, the pervasiveness of the special adviser's philosophy in and out of government circles rocked the State Department to its foundation and brought the trade agreements program to the brink of disaster.[8]

The passage of the June 12, 1934, Trade Act eliminated two alternatives for American trade policy, unilateral and multilateral tariff reductions, while the abortive 1933 reciprocity treaty with Colombia clarified the State Department's view that bilateral restrictive agreements did not serve the best commercial interests of the United States. The department believed the most effective trade policy for America and the world at large to be reciprocal trade agreements, incorporating the unconditional

7. Peek, papers, Box 15, Peek to Hull, June 25, 1934; Memorandum (R. C. Miller, director of Import and Export Relations, to Peek) , June 25, 1934. Phillips, diary, 1933–1936, Vol. 2, June 23, 1934. Gilbert Fite, *George Peek and the Fight for Farm Parity* (Norman: University of Oklahoma Press, 1954), p. 275.

8. Peek, *Why Quit Our Own?*, p. 246; for Peek's antiintellectualism see pp. 11, 21, 30–35, 191, 245. William S. Culbertson, papers, Library of Congress, Culbertson to J. W. Mailliard, Jr., December 19, 1934. Peek, papers, Box 15, Peek to Colonel Howe, June 30, 1934.

most-favored-nation clause.[9] Upon these grounds, the Department of State chose to do battle with the forces of economic nationalism. Peek quickly picked up the challenge.

Aided by such staff members as John L. Coulter, Henry Carter, and John Donaldson, Peek attempted to persuade Roosevelt and other department heads of the incompatibility of the unconditional most-favored-nation clause with reciprocal trade negotiations. Peek pointed to the Minority Report submitted by the House Ways and Means Committee on the Trade Agreements bill as the wisest course of action in the field of economic diplomacy. This report viewed a trade bargain between two nations as an exclusive agreement. Any automatic and unconditional extension of these arrangements did not serve the best interests of the United States.[10]

Peek also maintained that nations which operated with an unconditional most-favored-nation clause could survive only through the incorporation of "innumerable and extreme special bargains" in violation of the principles they supposedly affirmed. To the economic nationalists the clause failed to provide flexibility. The United States, Donaldson argued, must either "get around," "ignore," or "denounce" the unconditional clause or formulate trade agreements in broad, general terms supplemented by specific agreements covering specified exchanges of goods and services. "This would leave us freer to 'barter it out,' from quarter to quarter," he stated. Donaldson pointed to the War Trade Board of World War I as an excellent illustration of economic statesmanship.[11]

The economic nationalists, however, had little if any success in convincing Hull that the protection of American markets and the relaxation of restrictions on international trade lay in flexible, short-period, conditional most-favored-nation agreements. Peek deprecated the loss of American "bargaining power"

9. Edward O. Guerrant, *Roosevelt's Good Neighbor Policy* (Albuquerque: University of New Mexico Press, 1950), p. 93.

10. For tariff debate see U. S., Congress, House, *House Report No. 1000*, 73d Cong., 2d sess., 1934, 2. Also see *Operation*, June, 1934, to April, 1948, pt. 2, Summary (1948), pp. 8–9.

11. Peek, papers, Box 14, Donaldson to Peek, May 19, 1934; Box 15, Donaldson to Peek, June 1 and 5, 1934; Box 15, Carter to Peek, August 30, 1934.

through unconditional extension of concessions. Even more importantly, he believed the United States "will have proclaimed a general policy of tariff reductions without foreign adjustments of any kind, so far reaching as to block practically all later concessions on all commodities from all countries."[12] In regard to Latin American trade, he said, unconditional most-favored-nation treatment prohibited the United States from securing exclusive export quotas for its products.

In a memorandum to the Trade Agreements Committee on December 4, 1934, Peek elaborated these points and further stated that the unconditional most-favored-nation clause ruled out the practicality of barter arrangements, making it impossible to confine generalizations to principal suppliers. As Peek later put it, the idea of "principal supplier" was based on the fallacious premise that the world remained static. Attempts to expand the scope of tariff concessions based on the principles of unconditional generalization and the "principal supplier" would prove to be self-defeating, since the sources of American imports changed too rapidly, and many goods had no single chief supplier. Hull never convinced Peek that a reduction on tariff items from nations that were the main exporters did in fact limit the generalization of concessions and seldom weakened the United States' bargaining position. Nor, for that matter, did the secretary ever change Peek's attitude on the unconditional most-favored-nation clause. Peek labeled as overrated all multilateral arguments that tended to prove the importance of triangular trade.[13]

No doubt many of Peek's arguments against liberal trade rested on an abiding faith in a type of American isolation that emphasized individualism and self-reliance. To place the commercial welfare of nations upon more common grounds implied an interrelationship of economies, which impeded full economic sovereignty. Peek seldom failed to stress the fact that Hull's

12. Roosevelt, papers, Official File, 614–A, Trade, Peek to Roosevelt, October 31 and November 12, 1934. *SAPFT*, General Correspondence, NA, Peek to Hull, June 14, 1934; Coulter to Peek, November 14, 1934; Peek to Roosevelt, November 12, 14, 1934.

13. *SAPFT*, Memorandum (Peek to Trade Agreements Committee), December 4, 1934. Peek, *Why Quit Our Own?*, pp. 216–17, 253. Hull, papers, Peek to Hull, November 14, 1934.

trade program weakened America's potential for self-sufficiency. Roosevelt's special adviser envisioned world trade more in terms of a luxury rather than a necessity—manipulated, not freed, from the confines of rational state planning. Peek failed to see that the unconditional most-favored-nation principle (which to some degree implied a harmony of interests) better suited an industrial, creditor nation than bilateralism. Peek also failed to recognize that American commercial interests could best be protected from discrimination abroad by liberal trade practices rather than by retaliatory threats devised by economic nationalists.

To Peek and his staff the unconditional most-favored-nation clause departed from the sounder precepts of bilateralism. Only the League of Nations and the Pan-American Conferences (both un-American), a few foreign governments such as Japan (cheap labor costs), and the State Department (sentimentalists and academicians) favored the clause. As for American business, Peek's office found only the automobile industry susceptible to Hull's impractical schemes.[14] Peek persuasively argued that in a world racked with economic chaos and commercial dislocation, the multilateral policies of the State Department would encounter a difficult, if never-ending, road toward economic peace.

Sustaining a spirited offensive, Peek submitted a press release on June 9, 1934, entitled "Foreign Trade and Yankee Trading," that called for a return to "the old Yankee method of bartering— goods for goods, equal value given and received, a fair bargain on both sides."[15] The comment seemed a little out of character for Peek, since his model trader attempted more than an equal exchange. The nature of his endeavor was truly to win the trade game, not merely to break even. Yet Peek succeeded in transforming the economic nationalist into the Yankee trader incognito. Although State Department officials in the coming years vigorously attacked Peek's concept, they never fully understood the extent to which their own foreign trade assumptions harmonized with his.

Doubtless the problem to some degree was semantic. To the economic nationalist, Yankee trading implied the use of every

14. Peek, papers, Box 16, Memorandum (Carter to Peek), December 19, 1934.

15. *SAPFT*, Box 4, Press Release No. 2 delivered June 9, 1934.

available device to force other nations into granting exclusive and discriminatory trade preferences to the United States. To liberals, Yankee trading (although they rejected the terminology) implied that, given equality of treatment, the United States could outsell and outtrade all foreign competitors. In the process the liberal trader would provide other nations with the opportunity to save valuable exchange for the promotion of other worthwhile endeavors. The State Department's philosophy entailed a neat juxtaposition of the division of labor and capital with certain neomercantile overtones. Hull, however, hedged these harsher implications with the chimeric belief that American self-interests dovetailed with the liberal ideal.

Peek's trade philosophy was more explicit. The nations of the world that had made the greatest commercial advancement in foreign trade had done so not by the adoption of unconditional most-favored-nation treatment but by the employment of special trade agreements. In 1935 Peek could count over 202 exclusive bilateral understandings in which the United States had received no benefit. These agreements included such specifics as exchange control, clearing and compensation trade, balanced payments, barter, quotas, and tariff concessions. Peek cited Argentina and Brazil as excellent examples. In 1935 Argentina had bilateral arrangements with Belgium, Brazil, Germany, the Netherlands, Spain, Switzerland, and Great Britain. Brazil's exclusive agreements included Argentina, Chile, France, Germany, Greece, and Uruguay. In none of these cases did the United States receive benefits.[16] Why, Peek queried, must the United States squander priceless concessions through unconditional most-favored-nation clauses and render America's bargaining position increasingly weak? To some extent Roosevelt pondered the same questions.

Peek also urged the State Department, and Assistant Secretary of State Francis B. Sayre in particular, to participate freely in the policy of blacklisting nations that discriminated against American commerce. Not wishing to precipitate open trade warfare, the special adviser reasoned that if the United States made the black list "practically all-inclusive" (the plan envisioned almost all of Europe) then no one nation could take umbrage at Ameri-

16. Ibid., Memorandum (Weaver to Donaldson), January 11, 1935. Peek, papers, Box 17, Report to Peek, January 31, 1935.

can action. In essence, Peek's plan amounted to a return to conditional most-favored-nation treatment.[17]

Another of Peek's criticisms, and one might add a valid one, pertained to the State Department policy that matters of exchange control and payments for American goods should not become inextricable parts of the trade program.[18] The department's position remained firm; the revival of international trade would alleviate exchange problems much more simply than the inclusion of such provisions after costly and prolonged debate with each separate nation. With varying degrees of sophistication, both Hull and Peek assessed the problem correctly. Exchange control and clearing agreements did not promote trade, but they did help to ensure payment and protection to American exporters. The major handicap to world trade, Peek thought, lay not in high tariffs and quotas but in stifling exchange control provisions. Unlike Hull, Peek believed the only sound course of action would be that the United States act promptly in negotiating clearing agreements before the signing of any reciprocal trade accords.[19] Although the special adviser assessed the ills besetting international trade with a remarkable insight, his proposed solutions would have compounded an already complex situation.

Throughout 1934 Peek continued to harp on the inadequacy of statistics on American foreign investments and foreign investments in the United States. A letter sent to the White House on August 30, 1934, called for a tougher United States trade and investment position and described the lack of adequate bookkeeping in top level circles of government, especially in the Department of State. Herbert Feis, the economic adviser, referred to Peek's letter as "a rather second-rate job," since it omitted vital subclassifications of private investments and war debts. Ambassador to Chile William Culbertson called it a "misinterpretation of astronomical figures."[20] All in all, the letter showed how statistics could be manipulated to prove any point. Peek had

17. Peek, papers, Box 17, Peek to Sayre, February 8, 1934. *SAPFT*, Peek to Sayre, February 8, 1934.

18. Peek, papers, Box 15, Peek to Judge Moore, August 16, 1934.

19. Ibid., Peek to Hull, August 27, September 22, 1934.

20. William S. Culbertson, *Reciprocity* (New York: McGraw-Hill Book Company, Inc., 1937), p. 123. DS 811.503100/52, NA, RG 59.

become a worrisome gadfly, not simply because of his personal desire for power, but also because of the void that his office attempted to fill. In this sense the special adviser's power was essentially negative. If he could not direct policy he could nevertheless galvanize other departments into action if for no other purpose than to undercut the need for his existence.

The State Department at first did not take Peek's criticisms seriously. His challenges to control the Executive Committee and to administer the Trade Agreements Act had both failed. Engaging in a long-winded controversy with Roosevelt's trade adviser would only serve to give Peek extra attention and bring the entire trade program under closer scrutiny. Peek's relentless criticisms, however, forced the department's hand.

Hull and the department released barrages of economic facts and interpretations aimed at the bilateral theories. Peek's challenge provoked arguments that bilateralism produced added state planning and quantitative control over foreign trade. Economic nationalism, as defined by Hull, retarded the international specialization of labor and capital and failed to forestall competitive disadvantages in international trade. Bilateralism revived a neomercantile outlook in the community of nations and increased the propensity to use discriminatory trade practices. This kind of commercial blackmail, the secretary argued, was the prelude to armed conflict and the end of the free exchange of international goods and services. Furthermore, it blocked the exchange of commodities and capital while it stifled international lending. Bilateralism forced upon weaker nations the economic will of the stronger.

The State Department also refrained from taking an idealistic approach to its interpretation of the concessions granted under the unconditional most-favored-nation clause. The department reiterated its policy of automatically granting tariff concessions only to those nations that did not flagrantly discriminate against American commerce. The department also used, rather invidiously, Germany's attempts at bilateral balancing of trade to demonstrate that a planned economy often led to a fascist state.[21]

21. Culbertson, pp. 21, 103–4, 145–51. DS, Francis B. Sayre, "American Commercial Policy: The Two Alternatives," *CPS* No. 23 (1936). DS, Cordell Hull, "Our Need for Foreign Trade," *CPS* No. 26 (1936), pp. 1–7. Also

Peek's challenge to the State Department's supremacy in matters of foreign trade caused reverberations in other New Deal agencies that specialized in certain minor facets of the trade program. The Treasury Department, for example, collected the excise taxes (as distinct from tariff duties because excise taxes were not subject to changes in accordance with Section 336 of the 1930 Tariff Act), and the Bureau of Internal Revenue collected taxes levied on the processing of materials not produced in the United States. The Commerce Department provided detailed studies of American exports, the Tariff Commission on imports, and the Agriculture Department supplied data on both agricultural imports and exports. The Interior Department also had a stake in reciprocity agreements, since they affected American insular possessions.

The State Department, therefore, obviously did not possess complete sovereignty in the field of reciprocal trade. Hull needed to convince Roosevelt and other New Deal agencies of the value of his position.[22] Moreover, he needed the support of big business. In this endeavor Hull secured the support of the International Chamber of Commerce, the American Automobile Manufacturers Association, the American Manufacturers Export Association, and the National Foreign Trade Council. Business support, however, did not mean that Hull served only as a spokesman for certain economic interests; Hull was a capitalist in a pluralistic economy. But if he garnered business support it was because business could identify with the secretary's world view, not because Hull shaped his philosophy to serve the ends of big business.

Henry Wallace supported the Department of State. The secretary of agriculture shared many of Hull's convictions regarding the causes of the cataclysm in 1929 and the economic realities of the postwar era. Wallace accepted the connection between freer trade and political peace, and he subscribed wholeheartedly to the proposition that an international specialization of trade

---

see DS, Francis B. Sayre, "Reciprocal Trade Agreement," *CPS* No. 28 (1936), p. 1–12.

22. TC, *Imports, Exports, Domestic Production, and Prices* (GPO, 1937), p. iii. Pratt, p. 24. Cordell Hull, *The Memoirs of Cordell Hull*, Vol. 1 (New York: Macmillan Company, 1948), pp. 207–9. DS, Francis B. Sayre, "How Trade Agreements Are Made," *CPS* No. 42 (1937), p. 1–5.

and labor was essential to the progress of civilization. Unlike Hull, however, Wallace visualized the trade program, not as a step backward toward the classical economy of Adam Smith, but rather in terms of increased social control and rational planning.

In an article entitled "America Must Choose," Wallace set forth the alternatives for America's extrication from the thralls of the depression. Economic nationalism, economic internationalism, or a planned middle course of action appeared as the only American choices. The pervasiveness of economic nationalism (a phenomenon held in low esteem by the secretary) cancelled any immediate attempts to promote internationalism. Wallace said, "we must work to set our own land in order" and "learn to cooperate at home before we are fit to practice world cooperation in agriculture, trade, and the arts of peace." Production control and such emergency measures as the Agricultural Adjustment Act, argued Wallace, only sparred with the essential question. "Until the American people are ready to face [the] bare, distasteful facts" of international economics, the problem would not be solved. By such statements Wallace acknowledged the nationalistic implications of certain New Deal domestic innovations. He believed that a planned economy provided a necessary stepping stone toward world cooperation. To Hull, the most alarming aspect of Wallace's philosophy was his suggestion that a planned economy might serve as an alternative to trade liberalization.

Wallace viewed the religious and economic attitudes that lingered into the scientific and technological age as ill-equipped for the material abundance of the twentieth century. The "hard-driving profit motives of the past," Wallace lamented, dealt imperfectly with the problems of the modern world. America had to change its attitude on the nature of man and the nature of society. It must envision a cooperative objective broadened to encompass the international community of nations. Wallace believed that reciprocal trade rested upon such assumptions and consequently served as a golden opportunity for America to achieve a one-world concept. How very different from the ends sought by Hull!

Although both men perceived themselves as participants of a world community on the threshold of a new stage in the development of human civilization, Hull dreamed of a return to the bygone days of the Manchester liberal. In contrast, Wallace foresaw the budding development of international cooperation as the purification of political man operating within the narrow confines of the nation-state. Ironically, both men envisioned the trade program as a means to achieve an end totally divorced from the other's teleological concept of the world.

Although both the Wallace and Hull ideals looked to world peace and prosperity, they were clearly based on value systems worlds apart. While the secretary of agriculture stressed the necessity of replacing "the struggle for existence" with a "higher law of cooperation" and making the world in truth "one world" through the brotherhood of man, Hull pictured a planned society as synonymous with economic nationalism. To the secretary of state, Wallace's schemes amounted to a step away from political freedom and the values of the past. Wallace, unlike Hull, distinguished between the fallacies of economic nationalism and the merits of social control and planning, and he believed the latter best facilitated the internationalists' ideal. In the years to come Wallace became disillusioned with the trade program, but Hull never wavered in his conviction that reciprocity led to a prosperous and stable world.[23]

Throughout the early years of the New Deal, Wallace provided vital support for Hull's trade schemes against the onslaughts of George Peek. Many of the programs that had divided Peek and Wallace in the field of agriculture, such as production controls and a two-price system, now separated the men in the area of foreign trade. Wallace also maintained that the abandonment of the unconditional most-favored-nation clause destroyed triangular trade.

Wallace realized that many American agricultural products found a market in Europe only because these nations sold vast amounts of goods to Latin America and the Orient, which in turn sold much of their export merchandise to the United States. The adoption of bilateralism would upset the triangular arrange-

23. Henry Wallace, "America Must Choose," *AFSJ* 11:4 (April 1934): 182–204. For an engrossing and descriptive analysis of Wallace's personality and the roots of his intellectualism, see Arthur M. Schlesinger, Jr., *The Age of Roosevelt: The Coming of the New Deal* (Boston: Houghton Mifflin Company, 1959), pp. 28–36. For an early work quite sympathetic to Wallace's views, see Alonzo E. Taylor, *The New Deal and Foreign Trade* (New York: Macmillan Company, 1935), pp. 11–30.

ment and in the long run retard American agricultural exports.

M. L. Wilson and Mordecai Ezekiel of the Agriculture Department also opposed Peek's plans for export subsidies, barter, the dumping of excess agricultural products abroad, and loans to nations such as Germany to purchase American farm products. To strengthen its position, the Department of Agriculture also set up liasons with such independent organizations as the Foreign Policy Association, using these groups as a base of attack against the economic nationalists.[24] With the possible exception of Rexford Tugwell, undersecretary of agriculture, who once stated that he considered the trade program worthless and opposed any proposition smacking of laissez-faire, the Agriculture Department gave Hull unwavering support in his efforts to defeat George Peek.[25]

The Commerce Department also lined up solidly behind the Department of State in the trade battle. Henry Chalmers, in charge of trade negotiations for the Bureau of Foreign and Domestic Commerce, backed the internationalist point of view regarding foreign trade. Moreover, Secretary of Commerce Daniel C. Roper, in comments before the House Ways and Means Committee in March, 1934, provided a clue to the nature of his motives for promoting the trade program. "We hear a great deal about our agricultural surplus," said Roper, but the domestic products hardest hit by the depression were industrial goods made most efficiently at home. For Roper, the continued growth of foreign markets through the reciprocal trade program became imperative to the revitalization of American industry.[26] Although both secretaries Wallace and Roper spoke tactfully regarding the need to increase agricultural and industrial products respectively, one senses a certain anxiety over which area of domestic production would receive the greater benefits.

24. DA, *Records of the Office of the Secretary of Agriculture: General Correspondence of the Office of the Secretary, 1933–1939*, NA, RG 16, M. L. Wilson to Raymond Buell (president, Foreign Policy Association), August 7, 1934; Wallace to Roosevelt, November 7, 1934; Ezekiel to H. P. McCoy, January 10, 1934; Memorandum (Ezekiel to Wallace), November 26, 1935; Ezekiel to Karl Mitchell, March 6, 1934.

25. Phillips, diary, 1933–1936, Vol. 4, February 12, 1935.

26. *House Report No. 1000*, pp. 12–13. Peek, papers, Box 15, Robert F. Martin to Peek, September 24, 1934.

Meanwhile, Peek's office worked to establish contact with the departments of Agriculture, Commerce, Interior, State, Treasury, Justice, War, Navy, the Central Statistical Board, the Federal Trade Commission, the Tariff Commission, the NRA, and the RFC. Wayne Taylor represented the Special Adviser's Office on the Committee on Trade Agreements, John Lee Coulter on the Committee on Reciprocity Information, and James H. Edwards on the Committee on Country Negotiations for Brazil and other Caribbean nations. Peek himself sat on the Executive Committee on Commercial Policy. In an obvious attempt to emasculate the State Department's trade function, Peek also suggested that all foreign trade matters should go to Donald Richberg, executive director of the National Emergency Council, before taking effect. Richberg, however, shrugged the added responsibility and deferred to Hull. Again, the special adviser had fallen short.[27]

Checkmated at practically every turn, Peek's fleeting chance for victory rested on the bare hope that Roosevelt and his belief in the "Yankee tradition of good old-fashioned trading" would repudiate Hull's folly. The President lacked a deep comprehension of international economics; this in part explained his long retention of George Peek.[28] As late as July, 1935, Roosevelt described the Hull-Peek controversy to Jesse Jones as "one of detail and not of principle." On another occasion Roosevelt observed that Peek's barter schemes and Hull's reciprocity agreements "practically dove-tail into each other."[29]

Yet one is struck by the question as to why Roosevelt would allow open, internecine battles to rack his Administration. No doubt the President encouraged the political turmoil among policymakers vying for his approval. Even more importantly, Roosevelt was a political animal; it was, as the Belgium trade agreement so aptly demonstrated, the political repercussions of the reciprocity program that concerned him. In the President's

27. *SAPFT*, Office Memorandum No. 18, September 14, 1934; Special Office Order No. 1, July 30, 1934. Peek, papers, Box 16, Peek to Sayre, November 24, 1934; Peek to Donald Richberg, November 8, 1934.

28. See, Franklin D. Roosevelt, *Looking Forward* (New York: John Day Company, 1933).

29. Elliott Roosevelt, ed., *F.D.R.: His Personal Letters, 1928–1945* (New York: Duell, Sloan and Pearce, 1950), pp. 493–94. Peek, papers, Box 17, News Report, n.d.

way of thinking Peek represented powerful and dissident elements both in the farm bloc and the conservative wings of both parties. Although Secretary of the Interior Harold Ickes argued that "everyone wants to get rid of him," Roosevelt hesitated because of Peek's strength in agricultural areas.[30] The special adviser served as a counterweight to the idealism of Hull and provided the practical angle of trade favored by many western and southern conservatives.

Congressional criticism, especially Republican, had reacted as violently toward the June 12 trade bill as any measure yet initiated by the New Deal. Representative Allen Treadway of Massachusetts, the dean of archprotectionists, submitted a minority report on the bill that contained a scathing attack, listing twenty-four objections to the act. Congressional comments ranged from such absurdities as a charge of "absolute despotic authority" to the accusation that the trade bill signaled the failure of representative government in the United States. But Roosevelt's concern lay not in the quantity of the tariff debate but in the intensity.

The tariff, as demonstrated by the Seventy-third Congress' debate, remained one of the most divisive issues in American politics. The elimination of a possible conservative coalition utilizing the tariff as a political weapon became Roosevelt's prime concern. Since only two Republicans in the House and four in the Senate had voted for the Trade Act, it had most certainly become a partisan issue. If the President remained unsure of most of the intricacies of reciprocity agreements, one salient fact persisted—Roosevelt would not allow the New Deal to rise or fall on the tariff issue. Perhaps Peek's later remark that he may have been only an opiate to pacify the farmers and Congress did not miss the mark by much.[31]

Other critics of the trade program outside of Congress also

30. Harold L. Ickes, *The Secret Diary of Harold L. Ickes: The First Thousand Days, 1933–1936* (New York: Simon and Schuster, 1953), p. 360. For a discussion of the Belgium Agreement see William Phillips, *Ventures in Diplomacy* (Boston: Beacon Press, 1952), p. 162.

31. Peek, *Why Quit Our Own?*, p. 155. U. S., Congress, *Congressional Record*, 73d Cong., 2d sess., 1934, 78, pt. 5:5674; pt. 6:5843–44; 74th Cong., 2d sess., 1936, 80, pt. 1:863–66. *House Report No. 1000*, pp. 21–22. Joe R. Wilkinson, *Politics and Trade Policy* (Washington: Public Affairs Press, 1960), p. 9–11.

tended to dampen Roosevelt's faith in reciprocity agreements. F. W. Taussig, the leading tariff historian, had opposed as early as April, 1933, the unconditional most-favored-nation principle. Yet Taussig failed to escape from the inherent contradictions of his own trade philosophy. As opposed to economic nationalism as he was to free trade, he sought a workable alternative to the unconditional most-favored-nation clause. Only future events would demonstrate the futility of his search.

Although Taussig disliked bilateral balancing of trade, he stressed "separate arrangements for reciprocal reductions in duty" as the United States' best opportunity to increase foreign trade. In his classic 1924 work entitled *Free Trade*, Taussig had provided an excellent critique of those who bordered too closely to economic determinism. Taussig reversed the causal relationship between economic and political freedom.[32] He also contested the belief that commercial activity between nations led to peace. Trade, he remarked, played a large role in inciting war and the warlike spirit. Taussig also failed to share the idealist's view of man or the progressive's sense of optimism; instead he spoke of the "instinctive prejudices and the inherent selfishness of the everyday man" and warned of "evil days" to come. No classical doctrine of free trade would lead to nirvana. Even though the American tariff sage opposed most of Hull's assumptions regarding foreign trade, he offered little intellectual succor to the economic nationalists. He denounced bilateral balancing of trade and opposed commercial agreements such as the reciprocity treaty with Cuba. The benefits derived from reciprocity agreements, Taussig argued, did not accrue principally to American exporters but to the American consumer. Any increased foreign demand for American products without a planned economy would be met by increased domestic production offsetting the previous advantage.

Like Hull, Taussig sought to harmonize the liberal ideal with economic reality and, like Hull, he found the means for harmony in the policy of the Open Door. "Our democracy is idealistic; our international aims are idealistic; our trade policy should no less rest upon ideals." But Hull's unconditional most-favored-nation

32. Frank W. Taussig, "Necessary Changes in our Commercial Policy," *Foreign Affairs*, 11:3 (April 1933):397–405. Taussig, *Free Trade, The Tariff and Reciprocity* (New York: Macmillan Company, 1924), pp. 15–25, 95.

policy was too close to Taussig's abhorrence of free trade. In retrospect, Taussig's advocation of the principle of nondiscrimination in international trade, the Open Door, and equality of treatment appeared unlikely ends given the means that he purported to employ. Searching for an illusory compromise to the implications of unconditional most-favored-nation treatment, Taussig failed to keep pace with the times.

Yet his influence in academic, business, legislature, and administrative circles was far reaching, and his support of Hull's program would have been of immense value in the difficult times ahead.[33]

The trade program had also fallen under the scrutiny of one of America's most seminal minds of the 1930s. In 1934 and 1935, Charles Beard, in collaboration with G. H. E. Smith, published works of immense vitality and imagination; however, they were antithetical in many respects to Hull's visualization of the world. In *The Idea of National Interest,* Beard attempted to show the need for a redefinition of national interests. Unlike the Marxists, and in stark contrast with his usual brand of economic determinism, Beard criticized the myth of the surplus market and the capital export market; to counter the capitalist penchant for imperialism, he demanded a self-contained, planned economy. For Beard, a reassessment of American self-interests pointed in the direction of domestic planning independent of foreign outlets for surplus goods and capital.[34]

Smith and Beard's second work, which was published in 1935 and entitled *The Open Door at Home*, expressed, as the title implied, the best policy to attain the national interest. Beard defined *The Open Door at Home* as the quest for the most efficient use of domestic natural resources and the industrial arts of the nation while avoiding "wasteful, quixotic, and ineffectual" extensions of American interests and influence abroad.[35] In Beard's view, world history had witnessed the destruction of the deterministic mechanisms of theological assurance. Neither God nor "invisible hands" (an obvious dig at Adam Smith and Cordell

33. Taussig, *Free Trade*, pp. 30–33, 96–119, 130–33.

34. Charles A. Beard and G. H. E. Smith, *The Idea of National Interest* (New York: Macmillan Company, 1934), pp. 378–92, 438–39.

35. Charles A. Beard and G. H. E. Smith, *The Open Door at Home* (New York: Macmillan Company, 1935) , p. vii.

Hull) any longer directed the productive capacities of man. Man's rational nature had escaped the perils of superstition and blind faith to find refuge in the wonders of science. But the Great Depression had dispelled the inevitability of progress through science and technology. Since all "so-called laws or axioms of economy must always be conditional," the agrarian and industrial surplus market assumptions were also relative and uncertain. To Beard, the only position capable of meeting the dictates of both ideals and self-interests must first of all be predicated upon the principle of uplifting the American people. Beard admitted America's responsibility for the betterment of the outside world. Still, he declined to elaborate, perhaps for fear of contradiction. Hull's sense of idealism bordered too closely to nineteenth-century moral imperialism for Beard; besides, he wrote, these altruistic impulses could best be sublimated by aiding ethnic minorities at home.[36]

Beard also denied the idealist position that American commercial expansion could bring the liberal ideal and national self-interest into harmony. Beard wrote that trade expansion, especially with the underdeveloped world, carried with it "countervailing tendencies," which inoculate "the simple minds of colonial peoples with the equalitarian ideas of the Western world" and spread Marxist revolutions.

Beard also rejected the position that low tariff advocates represented national interests and high tariff proponents represented narrow, selfish interests. He suggested that one of the world's greatest free-trade experiments, the forty-eight states, did not succeed in preventing a catastrophic depression. For Beard, the analogy also held true when it applied to foreign lands. Consequently, Beard asked, who really spoke for the national interests?

Finally, Beard criticized Hull's trade philosophy for positing an economic view to the exclusion of national culture, loyalty, passion, race, religion, and political ideology. With the advent of science and heavy industry, Beard argued, classical economics became an anachronism. The idealist's assumption implied a static world void of imperial expansion, internal revolution, and rapid transformation.[37]

36. Ibid., pp. 1–54.
37. Ibid., pp. 54–59, 74–77, 112–17, 123–25.

Beard's searching critique of the trade program was not lost on Administration officials. Henry Wallace wrote to George Peek in December, 1934, that both of them could "well afford to ponder his viewpoint." Peek needed little convincing. Correspondence between Beard and the special adviser soon followed. By late 1934 Beard foresaw the direction of American foreign trade policy. Cordell Hull, he remarked to a Peek aide, did not live in the real world. To Beard, Hull personified a sentimental internationalist "lined up with powerful special interests in the United States" and "boggled up with Manchesterism and imperialistic delusions."[38] Possibly the key to Beard's later denunciations of Roosevelt-Hull diplomacy lay in their course of economic action, taken in the early years of the New Deal. These sentiments, it might be added, were shared wholeheartedly by George Peek.

Wooed but never wed to the doctrine of economic nationalism, Roosevelt appeared at times swayed by the persuasiveness of Peek. In a letter to Hull on November 9, 1934, Roosevelt suggested a compromise with Peek:

> Like most problems with which you and I have been connected during many years, there are two sides to the argument.
>
> In pure theory you and I think alike but every once in a while we have to modify principle to meet a hard and disagreeable fact![39]

Roosevelt seemed even more convinced of Peek's position after reading the criticism Peek's staff leveled at such trade agreements as the Brazilian treaty. "Why," pondered Roosevelt, "don't we insist on exercise of our rights and reciprocal advantages (?) corresponding under our M.F.N. clauses?"[40] But the President's confusion and indecisiveness did not provide the necessary leeway to sustain Peek's bid for control of foreign trade policy. The impasse created in the absence of definite guidelines by the White House put Peek at the mercy of a bureaucracy that he

38. Peek, papers, Box 16, Wallace to Peek, December 3, 1934; Beard to Gardner L. Harding, December 20, 1934.

39. Hull, papers, Roosevelt to Hull, November 9, 1934.

40. Roosevelt, papers, Official File, 614–A, Trade, Peek to Roosevelt, February 2, 1935. Roosevelt's reply to Peek can be found with this letter.

was powerless to control. Tenaciously, he clung to the hope that the tide would turn in his favor.[41]

However, Peek soon found other obstacles to his bid for power. Efforts to obtain pertinent trade dispatches from the Department of State and valuable data from other departments, such as Treasury and Commerce, met with rejection. By late 1934 the departmental lineup was complete. Peek had failed in his bid for bureaucratic support; the time for more radical measures had now come. "The whole question of foreign trade policy [is] coming to a head," wrote Peek. The State Department braced itself for the special adviser's final assault.[42]

The climax of the Hull-Peek controversy came in mid-December, 1934, as Phillips later recalled, "with a suddenness which was unexpected." For over a year the Office of the Special Adviser had worked for the negotiation of barter arrangements, especially with nations whose exchange difficulties handicapped trade. Peek's suggestions to the State Department in February, 1934, that the United States barter lard or cotton for German beer and wine was lukewarmly supported by Sayre, Phillips, and Fred Livesey, an international economic adviser. The Department of State agreed only to Peek's continuance of the matter without a formal commitment to approve it. At the same time, the department refrained from discussing the suggestions with other government agencies. Peek assured the State Department that Roosevelt had approved the plan. Besides, remarked Peek, the President also "had something of the New England trader in him." Peek favored initial negotiations by private American and German producers with later assistance by such governmental agencies as the Special Adviser's Office, the State Department, and the Export-Import Bank when necessary. In anticipation of the barter scheme, James D. Mooney, president of General Motors Export Company, arrived in Berlin to sound out the Hitler regime. "You realize of course," wrote Mooney to Peek,

41. John Dickinson, assistant secretary of commerce, explicitly stated to Hull that the Department of Commerce backed him against Peek. See Hull, papers, Dickinson to Hull, December 17, 1934. Peek, papers, Box 16, Peek to Roosevelt, December 12, 1934.

42. Peek, papers, Box 15, Peek to Feis, July 5, 1934; Box 18, Peek to Roosevelt, June 26, 1935; Box 16, Carter to Peek, December 5, 1934.

at the devalued dollar rate. The barter plan clearly ran
er to the principle of equality of treatment and prejudiced
ntire reciprocal trade agreements program. Brazil, for ex-
e, had already threatened to break off trade discussions if
United States violated a precept that she herself practiced for
rs.

rriving in Washington, Hull hastened to reinforce Sayre's
ments to the President. The secretary also stressed the ad-
e political repercussions of dealing with a regime as auto-
ic as Nazi Germany's. Hull's belated rejoinder clinched the
tter. Swayed by the logic of the department's arguments,
osevelt quickly retreated. The ebbs and tides of political for-
e once again broke over the hapless Peek.[45]

The remainder of Peek's career as special adviser to the Presi-
nt on foreign trade was anticlimactic. Peek's power play had
iled. Frustrated at every turn, his challenge now became open
arfare. In an initial barrage delivered at Quincy, Illinois, on
anuary 30, 1935, the special adviser openly attacked the uncon-
itional most-favored-nation clause. In a published letter to
he President on April 30, 1935, Peek attempted to prove statis-
ically that the United States continued to move closer to the
brink of financial and commercial disaster. A speech at Sea Island,
Georgia, on May 16, 1935, stressed the need for exchange regulations as a prerequisite for trade agreements. But the best was
to come.

In a speech delivered at St. Louis, May 24, 1935, Peek elaborated on practically every fundamental issue involved in American
foreign trade policy. The self-interests of the United States, he
exclaimed, necessitated a restoration of domestic prosperity,
which would benefit other nations as well. The stabilization of
currencies, argued Peek, would not eliminate special bilateral
agreements and, therefore, the United States must consider further manipulation of the currency. Peek again stressed the merits
of bilateralism and a policy of selective exports and imports directed by a permanent Board of Foreign Trade. The fundamental changes in the nature of international trade, said Peek,
necessitated resorting to these measures. High tariffs, quotas,

45. Hull, *Memoirs*, Vol. 1, pp. 372–74. Phillips, diary, 1933–1936, Vol.
4, December 13 and 14, 1934.

"that this matter was a little out of
have no ambition to be an unofficial

Throughout the summer and fall (
attracted little notice. But Peek's failt
foreign trade policy in the interim prob
move to circumvent Hull's program ii
The details of the barter plan were a.
Import Company would contract 800,00
cotton from American brokers during or
cent of the market price in dollars and 75
price plus a fixed premium in reichsmark
Bank would act as the agent for the Americ
sell the reichsmarks to American importer
prevailing value of the marks, in effect ma
change less than the official rate. The rei
exclusively used for the purchase of German
to say, the barter scheme clearly violated F
theories.[44]

On December 12, 1934, the White House ap
deal. Coincidentally, December 12 also found
from the nation's capital. Due to the secretar
Washington, Under Secretary Phillips persuad
postpone final agreement until Hull's return. Pl
Harry McBride of the State Department to Ch
brief Hull on the facts. Assistant Secretary of Stat
meantime, explained the ramifications of the bart
the President.

To facilitate the exportation of cotton, Sayre
United States would purchase subsidized German
place American exporters of other commodities th;
a disadvantage. The barter plan also discriminated a
nesses in gold standard countries who exported to

43. Hull, *Memoirs*, Vol. 1, pp. 371–72. Peek, papers, Box 18, F
to Peek, August 11, 1933, Memorandum (C. W. Dunning to Per
21, 1933; Box 13, Memorandum (Peek) , February 17, 1934; Box 1
to Peek, April 13, 1934. Phillips, diary, 1933–1936, Vol. 2, Jur.
Hull, papers, Phillips to Hull, December 13, 1934.

44. Peek, papers, Box 16, Memorandum (Interdepartment.
Agreement Committee), December 6, 1934.

barter, and exchange control throughout the world represented no temporary phenomenon. They would instead constitute a permanent change in the pattern of foreign trade.[46]

An unfortunate side effect of Peek's open attacks on the reciprocal trade program was the attention paid to it by the American press, much of which sympathized with the special adviser's position. Undoubtedly, Peek welcomed newspaper response, as it focused on Hull's so-called visionary and impractical schemes. Newspaper reaction, he reasoned, also served as an effective device to convince Roosevelt of the merits of bilateralism. As noted, the President's main concern in foreign trade policy was focused on a way to increase American exports with the least amount of adverse public reaction. Both Hull and Peek realized this fact, since both men were exceptionally keen to public sentiment.

Peek found support in the *Salt Lake Tribune*, the *Minneapolis Tribune*, the *New York Sun*, the *Philadelphia Inquirer*, and the *Davenport Times*. From cities as geographically diverse as Spokane, Cleveland, Memphis, Akron, Brooklyn, Washington, Dallas, and Boston came additional editorial backing. The *New York Times* on April 3, 1935, took cognizance of the differences in trade philosophies and came out in support of bilateralism. On May 19 the same newspaper called for a separate governmental agency to establish Administration policy in the area of foreign trade.

Hull also received widespread editorial endorsement. No simple geographical pattern or urban-rural breakdown was discernible here either. The *Chicago News*, the *Kansas City Times*, the *Newark News*, the *Birmingham Age*, the *Topeka Capital*, the *New York Herald*, and the *Washington Post* supported multilateralism. On May 18, 1935, the *Baltimore Sun* roundly condemned Peek's efforts to sabotage the reciprocity program.

> It is difficult to see why Mr. Peek or anybody else should be paid by the Administration for the apparently single purpose of jeering, upon inadequate evidence, at a considered policy of the Administration.

The secretary of state's sentiments were also voiced by the *Journal of Commerce*, the *Wall Street Journal*, and the *Export Ship-*

46. Peek, papers, Box 17, Peek to Beard, May 20, 1935; Peek to John Bassett Moore, May 7, 1935.

per. Not yet satisfied, Hull took to the road to explain and to defend department policy.[47]

In radio speeches on March 23 and May 22, 1935, as well as in numerous press releases and public addresses, the secretary and various subordinates struck back. On Herbert Feis' suggestion, the Commerce Department published trade and investment figures to act as a counterweight to Peek's April 30 letter. In a press release May 8, 1935, Roper hinted of Peek's culpability in statistical manipulation. The June 26 *Foreign Trade Letter* of the American Manufacturers Export Association published an article entitled "The Fallacy of Mr. Peek's Logic." The Twenty-second Convention of the National Foreign Trade Council, which met in 1935 at Houston, backed the reciprocal trade program and denounced bilateral balancing of trade and economic self-containment. *Foreign Affairs* in July, 1935, published articles by Henry Wallace and Herbert Feis debunking economic nationalism.

The State Department also received unexpected support from the Supreme Court in the May, 1935, Schecter decision, which destroyed NRA. This case also removed the legislative basis for the Office of the Special Adviser. Peek thereupon began the transfer of SAPFT employees to the Export-Import Bank, but he met with only limited success. Suffice it to say, Hull and other departmental heads gave the special adviser little if any assistance in the rearrangement.[48]

Peek enjoyed the turmoil he created. Dismayed but not distraught, he at times revealed the frustration, intensity, and sardonic humor nurtured in the wake of defeat. One illustration should suffice. In the general records of the Office of the Special Adviser an unpublished article entitled "The Generalization of

47. The newspaper accounts can be found in Peek, papers, Box 18.

48. Ibid., Box 18, Peek to Harry Tipper, executive vice-president, American Manufacturers Export Association, July 3, 1935; Box 17, Carter to Peek, May 28, 1935; Press Release by Roper, May 8, 1935. DS 811.503100/56, NA, RG 59. George G. Fuller, "Convention Commends Reciprocal Trade Agreements," *AFSJ* 13:1 (January 1936):12, 44. William S. Culbertson, "Wandering Between Two Worlds," *The Annals of the American Academy of Political and Social Science* 174:Supp. (July 1934):81–84. Henry Wallace, "The World Cotton Drama," *Foreign Affairs* 13:4 (July 1935):543–56. Herbert Feis, "The Open Door at Home," pp. 600, 611.

Concessions and the Policy of Unconditional MFN Treaties" found its way to Peek's desk. The article, prepared as a rebuff to his logic by a liberal trader, merited the special adviser's special condemnation. The article argued that bilateralism and the withholding of generalizations involved a double discrimination and invited retaliation by foreign powers. Peek's conditional system would require "perpetual negotiations" and no equality of treatment. Angered by the comments, Peek jotted down the following remarks; "Bunk," "Ridiculous sophistry and contrary to facts." But his choicest comments were yet to come. The article's defense of the generalization of concessions spurred the following reply from Peek, "Ha ha! Got under their skins." To the author's contention (possibly Henry Wallace) that "the major discrimination arises from the original concession to the chief supplier, not from the generalization to selected countries," Peek wrote "He is Nertz [*sic*]. . . . It would be useless to answer a crank." Certainly in keeping with his diminished prestige, Peek took comfort in his favorite poem, entitled "The Dog House."

> I love my little house because
> It offers after dark
> A pause for rest, a rest for paws,
> A place to moor my bark.[49]

On July 16, 1935, Peek tendered his resignation to the White House. Still, Roosevelt asked his recalcitrant adviser to reconsider his decision. A second letter by the Chief Executive prompted him to delay his departure from the Administration, but Peek's functions during his last months in public life centered mainly around the Foreign Trade Board bill, which was introduced by Senator J. Hamilton Lewis of Illinois and influenced heavily by Peek.

Peek hoped the board, if established, would limit unconditional most-favored-nation concessions only to nations not discriminating against American commerce. Matters of commercial and financial concern, he argued, should remain independent of diplomatic and political considerations. Peek also moved to enlist support from such figures as Senator William Borah of

49. *SAPFT*, General, Box 42, February 25, 1935.

Idaho; Charles Beard; E. P. Thomas, president of the National Foreign Trade Council; and Raymond Moley.[50]

When the Foreign Trade Board bill failed, Peek admitted the futility of working within the Administration to change policy. His attacks on Hull, and even the President, now increased in quantity and intensity. On November 11, 1935, they culminated with an article entitled "America's Choice." The article accused the New Deal of relaxation of immigration policy, reduction of tariffs, stabilization of international currencies, free export of capital and resumption of general loans, naval limitations by international agreements, dependence on foreign shipping and communication, participation in World Court decisions, and League collaboration. Incensed at Peek's audacity, Roosevelt forced his resignation.[51]

Lured by the siren's call of economic nationalism and political isolationism, Peek became one of the foremost critics of New Deal diplomacy. The logic of his assumptions led him to become active in such organizations as the Liberty League and the American Coalition. The latter organization, headed by John B. Trevor, was an isolationist group interested in the deportation of aliens. Peek also criticized the blacklisting of Nazi Germany by the State Department, arguing that the United States had thereby lost the opportunity to make some good business deals. Pogroms against the Jews in Germany, although deplorable, Peek remarked, should not be used as one of the justifications for breaking commercial contacts, because "primarily it was an affair of the Germans."[52]

In his efforts to discredit New Deal trade policy, Peek corresponded with Raymond Moley (who had broken with Roosevelt's foreign trade policy over the Canadian trade agreement), Father Charles Coughlin, and Milo Reno, leader of the Farmers' Holiday Association. He also returned to the fold of the Repub-

50. Peek, papers, Box 18, Peek to Roosevelt, July 16, 1935, July 18 and 29, 1935; Peek to Dowling, July 22, 1935; Roosevelt to Peek, July 17 and 25, 1935; Peek to Senator Lewis, July 30, 1935; Peek to Donaldson, August 23, 1935; Carter to Peek, September 9, 1935; Box 19, Peek to E. P. Thomas, October 30, 1935.

51. Peek, *Why Quit Our Own?*, pp. 33–35. Peek, papers, Box 19, Roosevelt to Peek, November 22, 1935; Peek to Roosevelt, November 26, 1935.

52. Peek, *Why Quit Our Own?*, p. 332.

lican party and worked tirelessly to keep the trade question a political football. As an alternative to both the liberal trade advocates and to the extreme protectionists, Peek sought, with little success, to steer the Republican party toward flexible tariff bargaining rather than prohibitive tariffs of the Hawley-Smoot variety. Here too, but for very opposite reasons, his advice was welcomed but never implemented.[53]

Utilizing such magazines as the *Saturday Evening Post*, Peek relentlessly criticized the reciprocity program. In 1936 Peek, in conjunction with Samuel Crowther, published *Why Quit Our Own?*, a scathing attack on the New Deal's conduct of foreign trade policy. Chapter 15, entitled "The Sell-Out," foreshadowed Roosevelt's political revisionists by a goodly number of years. William Culbertson and Francis Sayre promptly replied to Peek in like fashion. Innuendos such as "The Fairyland of Finance," "Economic Illiteracy," and "Peekinese Economics" dotted the pages of their works in defense of Hull. The State Department's *Commercial Policy Series* likewise reprinted numerous speeches given by department members in behalf of the trade program. The debate raged on, but history took a dim view of Peek's philosophy as each new reciprocity agreement pushed the United States closer to multilateralism. As Arthur Schlesinger, Jr., wrote, "Hull offered the multilateral doctrine in its nineteenth-century form; but what he offered could blend (under the ministrations of Herbert Feis and Alvin Hansen) with the new economics of Keynes; and Hull gave it unique moral force."[54]

Although Peek failed to discern the pitfalls of bilateralism and the profitability of triangular trade, the special adviser provided a trenchant examination of certain weaknesses in the trade program. Peek assessed correctly the inherent conflict between price control schemes such as NRA and AAA and the reciprocal trade agreement program. His pleas for detailed statistical analysis, coordination, and centralization of foreign trade and investment

53. Peek, papers, Box 19, American Coalition Letter, filed November 19, 1935; Box 20, Peek to Moley, December 26, 1935. Peek, *Why Quit Our Own?*, pp. 332–34.

54. Culbertson, *Reciprocity*, pp. 119, 123–31. Also see Francis B. Sayre, *The Way Forward: The American Trade Agreements Program* (New York: Macmillan Company, 1939); Sayre, "Our Problem of Foreign Trade," *CPS* No. 30 (1936), pp. 1–6. Schlesinger, p. 260.

activities did not go unheeded. Spurred on by Peek's encroachments on various departmental responsibilities, the New Deal bureaucracy greatly expanded its duties and functions in the field of international trade. And to some degree Peek's failure signaled the triumph of the intellectual and theorizer over congressional opposition and the narrow vested interests represented by the economic nationalists.

Yet Hull's program (and Peek quickly picked out the flaws) did not fully gauge the problems that plagued the unconditional most-favored-nation clause and the principle of equality of treatment. When foreign powers regulated foreign trade by other means than tariffs, liberal trade concepts had little curative power. Peek partially realized that the problems of foreign exchange control, quantitative limitations of trade, and other bilateral and exclusive agreements hampered the effectiveness of the unconditional most-favored-nation clause and equality of treatment. But instead of working to reduce these difficulties, Peek proposed to compound them through barter agreements, currency manipulation, quotas, and exchange controls. For all of Peek's political conservatism and fear of governmental power and responsibility, he never realized that the consequences of his own policies increased the regimentation that he later so violently condemned.[55]

Underlying Peek's philosophy of economic nationalism were his profound misgivings as to the course of world politics and international trade. Peek saw the "real" world as it was—not as it could or should be. He discerned, and probably correctly, that the chain of events that had produced a catastrophic depression and the nationalistic responses to cope with it could not be eliminated by pious and liberal rhetoric. Hitlerism and economic nationalism were not aberrations so easily dismissed. Yet Peek offered no constructive substitute for multilateralism. Roosevelt's special adviser failed to see that the implications of economic na-

55. League of Nations, *Equality of Treatment in the Present State of International Commercial Relations: The Most-Favored-Nation Clause*, League of Nations, II, Economic and Financial, 1936, II. B. 9 (Geneva: Series of League of Nations Publications, 1937), pp. 5–11. William Diebold, *New Directions in our Trade Policy* (New York: Macmillan Company, 1924), pp. 27–33. Richard Carlton Snyder, *The Most-Favored-Nation Clause* (New York: King's Crown Press, 1948), pp. 6–11, 236–243. Peek, *Why Quit Our Own?*, p. 249. Fite, pp. 300–301.

tionalism did not create commercial and financial security for the United States; instead there was the constant threat of retaliation.[56] Although Hull had probably misconstrued the causal relationship between trade and peace, Peek's error lay in the totally fallacious premise that bilateralism and economic self-sufficiency led to national security and prosperity. His exit from the stage of international trade came as a welcome relief to the advocates of reciprocity.

56. Peek, papers, Box 16, Memorandum (Conversation with Welles), October 12, 1934.

3

It Actually Costs Us Nothing

The New Deal did not represent the first attempt to negotiate trade agreements incorporating the unconditional most-favored-nation clause. In 1931 the State Department described its trade policy as one seeking to give equal commercial treatment to all nations and to secure for itself unconditional most-favored-nation treatment through the negotiation of such agreements. In this way, the United States sought to prevent sudden discrimination against American trade. The impetus behind these policy decisions can be found in the 1919 Tariff Committee Report, which suggested that the United States had reached the stage of financial and industrial maturity to merit reversal of her traditional commercial policy. In 1923 the Harding Administration implemented these recommendations by the incorporation of unconditional most-favored-nation treatment. However, the 1922 Fordney-McCumber Tariff and the 1930 Hawley-Smoot Tariff effectively cancelled most benefits. Section 338 of the Tariff Act of 1930 authorized prohibitive duty rates on many import commodities, thereby making the unconditional most-favored-nation clause "exceedingly embarassing in practice." The State Department suspended further negotiations.[1]

With the advent of the New Deal, the State Department again took up the cudgel for liberal trade. In taking advantage of Latin America's lack of export diversification, Hull and his staff carefully analyzed the economies of each state and pointed to the vulnerabilities inherent in a one-crop economy. What coffee was to Colombia and Brazil, nitrate was to Chile, sugar to Cuba,

1. DS 611.2131/15, NA, RG 59. For a brief summary of this chapter see Dick Steward, "It Actually Costs Us Nothing," in Walter V. Scholes, ed., *United States Diplomatic History*, Vol. 2 (Boston: Houghton Mifflin, 1973), pp. 127–34.

meat to Argentina and Uruguay, and so on down the list of monocultures. Armed with a plethora of vital statistics, the State Department moved the New Deal cautiously into the arena of world commerce. The story of the New Deal's first attempt at trade negotiations formally began during the London Economic Conference. At this time the passage of the Trade Agreements Act of June 12, 1934, appeared highly improbable. On the initiative of Franklin Delano Roosevelt, the State Department contacted several states concerning the possibility of tariff legislation. Assistant Secretary of State Jefferson Caffery referred to the trade schemes as a thoroughly researched program limited to Brazil, Argentina, and Colombia. The agreements were to be bilateral in nature, incorporating the unconditional most-favored-nation clause and a reciprocal reduction of tariff barriers, and were subject to Senate approval. The United States signed only one such treaty before the passage of the Trade Agreements Act, and this with the Republic of Colombia. The story of these negotiations nevertheless provides an important chapter on the philosophy and methods used by the State Department in the ensuing years.[2]

As early as April, 1933, the State Department began plans to obtain "the maximum possible advantage for American commerce" through a trade agreement with Colombia.[3] Congress, as well as most areas of American export business, was quick to realize the importance of the United States market to the Colombian economy. Walter S. Brewster, president of the Textile Export Association of the United States, compared Colombia's dependence on the United States to Argentina's reliance on Great Britain and intimated that America follow the British–Argentine example incorporated in the Roca-Runciman Agreement, which tied the economy of Argentina to that of Britain in such a way that the former had little economic chance to pursue liberal trade. The National Foreign Trade Council lamented the shrinkage of American export trade in respect to foreign com-

2. DS 621.113/21; 611.2131/31/136½, NA, RG 59.
3. DS 611.2131/19–19½, /89½; 821.61333/133, NA, RG 59. Also see BFDC, *The Coffee Industry in Columbia*, TPS No. 127 (1931), pp. 1–12. *Operation*, June, 1934, to April, 1948, pt. 7, Summary, p. 14. *FTLA*, pt. 2, Report No. 146, 2d Series (1942), pp. 142–45, 165. TC, *Regulation of Imports by Executive Action*, Miscellaneous Series (GPO, 1941), pp. 36–37.

petition and hoped to see the trend reversed.[4] The American Council of Foreign Bondholders also warned that Colombia's federal, departmental, and municipal debts could not be met without an increase in United States–Colombian trade.[5]

Probably the major factor that influenced the State Department in the beginning of its negotiations with Colombia was the strong bargaining position of the United States relative to the Colombian economy. In July, 1933, a seventy-nine-page memorandum prepared by the Bureau of Foreign and Domestic Commerce and entitled "Factors Affecting United States-Colombian Trade" reached the department's desk. The memo stated that the United States purchased over 80 per cent of Colombia's exports, while over 40 per cent of Colombia's imports came from the United States. These exports to Colombia in 1933 totaled only $14,600,000, while Colombian exports to this country, both dutiable and free, equaled $47,600,000. America's balance of payments in 1933 with Colombia (exclusive of its receipts on direct investments) stood at minus $30,000,000. Moreover, Colombia's economic position continued to deteriorate with each year of the depression, primarily because of the fall in coffee prices. Since 92 per cent of her coffee exports (which accounted for nearly 60 per cent of total export trade) found a duty-free market in the United States, a suspension of Colombia's coffee from the American free list would precipitate complete economic chaos. The report implied that the United States was in a position to drive a hard bargain with the Colombians (a fact that the State Department tactfully exploited).

The prospect of American economic pressure posed a real threat to the Colombian economy. Her coffee industry consisted of a large and politically powerful number of independent producers heavily dependent on mortgage and commercial banks to continue operations. The possibility of the imposition of coffee import duties by Washington (coffee having a very elastic price demand) enhanced the likelihood of the evaporation of badly needed foreign loans. Colombia's absence of a well-defined sys-

4. DS, 611.2131/23 NA, RG 59. Also see "Survey of the Financial and Trade Problems of Columbia in their Relation to the United States of America," *National Foreign Trade Council* 3 (1933) :5–8.

5. U. S., Congress, *Congressional Record*, 74th Cong., 1st sess., 1935, 79, pt. 2:1316–17.

tem of financing production was matched only by her poor transportation facilities for the transport of coffee to the world markets. The need, therefore, for economic overhead investment capital further increased Colombia's dependence on the United States.

In 1931 the Colombian government had taken complete control of foreign exchange operations, although it had not discriminated against the United States in the exchange allocation. The Colombian congress in the same year enacted a higher customs tariff in order to conserve dwindling gold reserves and protect infant industry. Duties on wheat, barley, cereals, rice, lard, fresh and canned fruits, cement, paper, cotton, silk, and woolen products all handicapped American trade. American exporters felt the squeeze from customs surcharges, excise and municipal taxes, and discrimination in transportation services. The shippers suffered because of difficulty in obtaining dollar remittances for export products shipped to Colombia.

The bureau's report detailed the decline in dollar value of Colombian exports from $130,520,000 in 1928 to only $67,067,000 in 1932 and traced this phenomenon to the fall in coffee prices. Even though Colombian coffee was both milder and of higher quality than that of her nearest competitor, Brazil, the price differential continued to slip because of the American consumer's shift to cheaper products. The trade figures for the year 1929 through 1933 bear witness to the export problem. In 1929 Colombia exported to the United States, duty free, $103,100,000 worth of products; in 1930 the figure slipped to $96,500,000. By 1933 Colombia's duty-free exports to the United States plummeted to a meager $42,200,000. Although America's direct investments in the production of Colombian coffee were slight, the indirect results of the fall in coffee prices adversely affected American interests, since approximately 70 per cent of the purchasing, marketing, and distributing of the crop was controlled by the United States.[6]

The realities of Colombia's political economy also increased Washington's bargaining position in the discussions. Traditionally, the oligarchs had maintained political and social prestige

6. Cordell Hull, *The Memoirs of Cordell Hull*, Vol. 1 (New York: Macmillan Company, 1948), p. 354. Hereafter cited as Hull, *Memoirs*. DS 611.2531/69, NA, RG 59.

at the expense of economic independence. A semifeudalistic infrastructure wedded to international capitalism, they reasoned, was a small price to pay for continued power. No doubt the Roosevelt Administration realized that in a confrontation between the oligarchs tied to the raw materials-producing sector of the economy and the emerging industrialists, the former would eventually emerge victorious.

Formal discussions with Colombia began in July, 1933. American hopes were high. Washington had everything to gain and almost nothing to lose; as one State Department memorandum put it, an agreement with Colombia "actually costs us nothing."[7] After some preliminary maneuvering, the talks began in earnest. First, President Enrique Olaya Herrera attempted to have the discussions conducted at Bogotá but received an unwelcomed response by the State Department. Hull contended that Washington must be the center for all future negotiations. Olaya did not press the matter. In August, 1933, he appointed Francisco Plata and Dr. Arturo Hernández to assist the Colombian ambassador, Fabio Lozano, in the coming negotiations. Washington's position on the trade agreements involved an examination of all principal items of trade between the United States and Colombia with tariff reductions on most American products. In return, Washington pledged that Colombian exports (a large percentage of which came to the United States duty free) would remain on the free list. But the United States held forth very little in the way of positive benefits for Colombia, since an agreement "actually" cost the United States "nothing."

The Olaya government, therefore, encountered a difficult problem. Washington gave little concrete assurance that freer trade held forth the prospect of increased commerce for all the Americas. In fact, many Colombians suspected that the American reciprocal trade program simply provided a rhetorical camouflage to disguise the aspirations of economic nationalists. Yet the consequence of commercial retaliation by the United States spelled the total collapse of the Colombian economy. Faced with mounting American pressure, Olaya's alternatives narrowed appreciably. To save her principal export market, Colombia might well have been forced to make sacrifices in domestic industry or

7. DS 611.113/21, NA, RG 59. This important memo came from the Treaty Division.

to delay the discussions as long as possible. Procrastination, it might be mentioned, was calculated on the premise that the United States would never resort to unilateral imposition of import duties. The United States had carefully phrased its dispatches in order to refrain from just such threats. But to run the gamut of commercial peril in order to save incipient manufacturing interests posed a grave risk for the Bogotá government.

In late August Allan Dawson, the American chargé in Bogotá, reported the suspicion prevalent among Colombians toward a trade agreement. Being singled out by the United States as the first nation to open reciprocal trade negotiations amounted to a rather dubious honor. Fear of possible United States duties on Colombian coffee and the abolition of Colombian exchange restrictions created a most unfavorable environment for discussion. *El Tiempo, El Espectador,* and *Mundo Al Día* echoed the discord from both industrial and agricultural circles in Colombia. The Colombian Agricultural Society and the Third National Agricultural Congress reflected the view that Colombia's agriculture must not be sacrificed to meet the demands of the United States. The National Federation of Industrialists voiced the same protectionist demands for their products.

The State Department, nevertheless, pressed forward, confident that comprehensive tariff reductions on both agricultural and manufactured products were possible. American pressure forced Olaya to a point of compromise. The Colombian president submitted that "the United States was trying to drive a hard bargain" and agreed to a series of tariff reductions on manufactured imports. In a communiqué to Hull in August, 1933, Dawson substantiated the fact that the Colombian manufacturing class, in a show of strength against the coffee interests, would be swept aside. Olaya, however, remained adamant against any duty reductions on foodstuffs, especially wheat, rice, flour, crackers, and biscuits. Clearly, Colombian agricultural interests predominated. Olaya also intimated that congressional authority enabling him to establish a system of maximum and minimum tariffs might be the best way to grant tariff concessions to the United States. In this way the reciprocal trade agreement might be put into effect without ratification by Congress.

Colombia, however, remained skeptical toward the reciprocity program. On August 22 the United States handed the Colombians a draft proposal that requested substantial industrial and agricultural concessions by the Olaya government. Colombia countered by a sharp reminder that American trade statistics did not convey "true reality," since the greater portion of profit from the sale of Colombian coffee, bananas, and petroleum went to United States citizens and companies. The following week Lozano continued the *démarche* by impressing upon the United States the importance of custom duties as the principal source of income for Colombia. The ambassador further proclaimed that Colombia would not sacrifice agricultural interests or essential industries to United States markets. With these points reaffirmed, Lozano submitted a counterdraft.[8]

The government in Bogotá also remained especially cool toward the United States' position on the unconditional most-favored-nation clause. The acceptance of the clause, argued the Colombians, might produce unforseen effects on Colombia's exports and would necessitate the renegotiation of existing trade treaties. Colombian officials offered an alternative solution that incorporated tariff reductions on exports from nations purchasing a certain amount of Colombian products. A memorandum by the Treaty Division of the Department of State on October 3 refused to countenance any deviation from unconditional most-favored-nation status, since the conditional clause offered no guarantee of equality of treatment. It afforded American exporters no assurance that Colombia would "not lower still further the reductions made in the agreement on their behalf, or reduce other products which may compete with theirs, and fail to accord to them corresponding reductions." The unconditional most-favored-nation clause was viewed as the legal embodiment of the principle of equality of treatment. The memorandum likewise insisted that Colombia must grant the United States substantial tariff reductions on agricultural products. In return, the United States might possibly broaden the scope of import reductions on Colombian products.[9]

8. DS 611.2131/24, /34, /45, /61, /67, /71, /77–78, /84, /88, /89, NA, RG 59. Also see *FR*, 1933, 5 (1952):217–20, 238–41, 226–34. DS 611.2131/105, /109, NA, RG 59.

9. DS 611.2131/82, /103, NA, RG 59. Henry J. Tasca, *The Reciprocal Trade Policy of the United States* (Philadelphia: University of Pennsylvania Press, 1938), p. 112.

Further trade difficulties included the Colombian proposal allowing municipalities and departments to have taxing power over imported articles. Colombia also wanted assurances that green coffee would not be subject to antidumping laws in the United States and further suggested that no restrictions be put on the volume of imports from one nation to the other (a move designed to strike squarely at NRA and AAA import regulations). The United States, however, proposed to limit the provision against prohibitions only on those specified articles in the schedules.

Colombia also insisted upon a larger oil quota from the United States, since she produced the third-largest volume of petroleum in Latin America. But her production capabilities suffered from the limited capacity of the pipelines to serve the oil fields. An increased oil quota might, therefore, serve as an incentive for attracting foreign investment capital to the country. American oil interests in Colombia likewise sponsored the idea. The State Department disagreed; it opposed Bogotá's demands largely because Colombia did not represent the principal supplier of oil imports. Any oil concession granted to Colombia in a trade agreement and extended unconditionally to all nations, especially Venezuela and Mexico in this hemisphere, increased the danger of adverse political and economic criticism at home.[10] The position of both nations appeared explicit and firm. The danger of an impasse measurably increased.

As a possible catalyst for trade discussions, a statement by Budget Director Lewis Douglas in early October, 1933, proposed a $.05 per pound tax on imported coffee.[11] Obviously distressed, Lozano urged that the United States reconsider. On October 26 Assistant Secretary of State Jefferson Caffery handed the American redraft to the Colombian minister. Douglas' veiled threat no doubt helped to speed up the trade discussions. In early December the United States and Colombia reached a final agreement.

The first agreement signed with Colombia on December 15, 1933, required congressional authorization. The minimum term

10. Franklin D. Roosevelt, papers, Franklin D. Roosevelt Library, Hyde Park, N. Y., Official File, 313, Phillips to Roosevelt, Dececmber 4, 1933. DS 611.2131/104½, /106½, /109, /114A–116A, /128, NA, RG 59. *FTLA*, pt. 3, p. 157.

11. DS 611.2131/105½, NA, RG 59.

of the agreement was two years. The United States agreed not to impose import duties, excise taxes, or prohibitions on a list of nine duty-free products set forth in Schedule II. These products included roasted and unroasted coffee, root of ipecac, bananas, emeralds, gutta balata, platinum, reptile skins, tagua nuts, and tamarinds. American antidumping laws excluded coffee. Colombia gave the United States concessions on 150 items of which half received customs reductions and the remainder assured of tariff treatment no less favorable than that enjoyed in 1933. American agricultural exports enjoyed limited reductions on hog lard, prepared cereals, potatoes, canned vegetables, fruits, milk, and hides. Each nation granted unconditional most-favored-nation status, a victory for United States commercial policy. Washington and Bogotá also reached the compromise position that all United States articles were to be exempted from state and municipal taxes other than those in force at the time of the agreement. The imposition of future taxes on import commodities could not exceed the maximum taxes in effect at the time of the agreement. These provisions only affected interstate commerce in the United States. Roosevelt also insisted that tariff concessions to Colombia did not affect American territorial possessions such as Puerto Rico, the Virgin Islands, and Hawaii.[12] The President reacted to the draft treaty with Colombia by giving it "an enthusiastic endorsement." A circular issued by the Colombian minister of finance said in part that "the proposed treaty . . . does not mar any national industries of importance nor any branch of agriculture."[13]

The final settlement appears in retrospect heavily weighted toward the American side. Edwin Wilson of the Division of Latin American Affairs remarked to Caffery that congressional ratification of both a Colombian and Brazilian treaty should be easy to obtain, since the United States made few, if any, substantial concessions. For extra insurance against the possibility

12. DS 611.2131/96, /136A, /194, NA, RG 59. Also see *FR*, 1933, 5:246–48. Roosevelt, papers, Official File, 614–A, Roosevelt to Welles, November 5, 1934. *Operation*, pt. 1, p. 41; pt. 4, p. 2. (For the text of the December 15, 1933, Reciprocity Treaty see *Operation*, pt. 4, pp. 249–54.)

13. William Phillips, diary, 1933–1936, Vol. 1, Houghton Library, Cambridge, Mass., December 6, 1933. DS 611.2131/166, NA, RG 59.

of violent reaction in Colombia, the text of the trade agreement was withheld until May, 1934.[14]

As to the question of Colombia's exchange control, the State Department adhered to the view that as long as no overt discrimination against the United States took place the practice was not a subject for negotiation. This policy continued to serve the department in future trade conversations. Operating on the assumption that the restoration of international trade alleviated exchange difficulties, the department failed to provide for a system of adequate dollar exchange. In other words, the department assumed that opening the channels of international trade would automatically solve the problem of other restrictive trade devices. In fact, this mistaken assumption later came to plague the proponents of increased foreign trade and provided much of the ammunition stored in the statistical arsenal of the economic nationalists.

The reciprocity treaty likewise set the precedent for future discussions involving nations in default of their external debts. The State Department feared that any attempt to link the trade agreement with a renewal of debt service seriously prejudiced the chances of increased trade activity. The goodwill necessary to implement reciprocity could not be jeopardized by crying over spilled milk. Payment to American bondholders, they reasoned, relied on increased international commercial prosperity, not pressure or coercion. Once again the restoration of international trade served as the panacea for the wide spectrum of commercial and financial ills. It also gave credence to the assertation, which will be later expounded, that the New Deal's primary concern in matters of economic diplomacy centered on the promotion of American trade rather than the protection and procurement of American loans and investments.[15]

But the New Deal's expectations that the success of the Colombian treaty promised an easy trade road ahead soon abated. Throughout the trade negotiations with Colombia a battle raged inside the Department of State as to the most workable procedure to put the reciprocity treaties into effect. The Treaty Division was able to argue persuasively for the executive agreements, since

14. DS 611.2131/120, NA, RG 59.
15. DS 611.2131/19, /152, /171, /181, NA, RG 59.

they did not need congressional approval, and the President's endorsement of the agreements seemed to ensure swift ratification. On the other hand, the Division of Latin American Affairs believed that executive agreements enhanced Colombian opposition, especially in the legislature, and did not provide for the same type of permanence that formal treaties possessed. The draft that was eventually presented to Colombia followed the advice of the Treaty Division and was based on the supposition that the quickest way to get results rested with executive agreements. Congress could later grant the President authority to negotiate further agreements. The Colombian trade treaty was therefore viewed as a matter requiring congressional legislation rather than the consent to ratification by the Senate.[16]

The imbroglio that followed resulted from Section 4 of the June 12, 1934, Reciprocal Tariff Act. The section stated that all persons wishing to present information relating to the effects of possible reciprocal tariff negotiations must be given an opportunity to present that information. Under the provisions of the act, a statement to the effect that trade negotiations were to be conducted required a thirty-day notice to the public. Obviously the trade agreement with Colombia failed to meet these standards and therefore necessitated renegotiation—an unwelcome prospect, since Colombia's agricultural concessions on lard in all probability would be lost. The Office of the Special Adviser to the President on Foreign Trade remarked that renegotiations meant the possibility of "substantial losses" for American commerce. What followed the abortive treaty of December 15, 1933, is a story of continued frustration and disillusionment as the State Department endeavored to salvage a semblance of victory from the Colombian trade rubble. Sumner Welles' prognostication that the United States would encounter only minor difficulty in future trade negotiations with Colombia proved to be as inaccurate as his previous forecasts on the Cuban situation.[17]

As early as February, 1934, "discreet inquiries" made of President Olaya's private secretary indicated that because of the

16. DS 611.2131/117–123, 611.3231/573, NA, RG 59.
17. DS 611.2131/193–197, /201–204, NA, RG 59. George N. Peek, papers, Western Historical Manuscripts Collection, State Historical Society of Missouri, Box 15, Miller to Peek, June 28, 1934. Also see DS 611.2131/234½, NA, RG 59.

Peruvian crisis (in 1932 Peru seized the region of Leticia from Colombia and threatened to engulf the two countries in war) the reciprocity treaty would not be submitted to the Colombian congress until July, 1934. August of the same year witnessed no change in the status of the treaty. The Department of State's tentative schedule had planned to give the public notification required under treaty between the United States and Colombia between October 1 and 15, 1934. The agreement was then to be quickly signed and the public simultaneously notified as to the trade negotiations with Brazil. By the end of December the State Department expected both the Colombian and Brazilian treaties to be ratified. The obvious reason for the department's attempt to bring the agreements into force at one time stemmed from the fear that America's pledges to retain coffee on the free list, when incorporated into a reciprocal trade agreement and granted unconditionally to all nations, lessened American bargaining power. "It is evident," remarked one diplomat, "that if we guarantee free entry to Colombian coffee we could not impose a duty on Brazilian coffee." Cordell Hull realized that the terms of the Colombian agreement, if made public, might jeopardize the success of the Brazilian discussions. To prevent such consequences, he expressed the hope that the Colombian congress would not openly debate the treaty.[18] It was a strange request. In light of the concessions granted the United States, however, it was perhaps a discreet move.

The timetable established by the State Department suffered further setbacks as the United States maneuvered to bring the provisions of the United States–Colombian treaty within the authority of the Trade Agreements Act. The department hoped only to give the thirty-day notification required by the act and then promptly re-sign the agreement with Bogotá. On December 10, 1934, Assistant Secretary Sayre handed the Colombian chargé, González-Fernández, the newly proposed reciprocity treaty. The assistant secretary prefaced his remarks by calling to the chargé's attention that the United States proposals signified no "radical changes" from the December 15 agreement.

Modifications in the treaty dealt only with antidumping provisions and state and municipal taxes. Matters pertaining to foreign exchange control were to be subject to a separate ex-

18. DS 621.113/21; 611.2131/176, /205–205B, /207, /234½, NA, RG 59.

change of notes entered into concurrently with the trade agreement. The department foresaw no serious exchange problem for American exporters because of the United States' strong trade position in Colombia, although Herbert Feis, the economic adviser, expressed the opinion that the United States might be better off avoiding a weak exchange provision with Colombia. American proposals to Colombia, wrote Feis, were very reasonable compared to the minimum exchange assurances and the continuance of debt service broached to Brazil.[19]

In Bogotá the American modifications of the December 15 treaty received a cool reception. Sayre remarked to Peek that American efforts to obtain greater agricultural concessions had been countered by Colombia's threat to break off trade discussions. The Colombian finance minister viewed the American changes as "very fundamental" in nature, while Dr. Hernández, chief of the Customs Tribunal, reacted with disgust to the United States elimination of antidumping laws. The anxiety and delay in commercial negotiations, reported the American chargé, had produced increased frustration and resentment toward the United States. Burdened with additional fiscal and monetary problems and smarting from the Rio Pact, which only had restored the 1924 boundary with Peru and failed to settle satisfactorily the Leticia controversy, the newly elected López administration faced formidable domestic opposition. Communist accusations of economic exploitation and Yankee imperialism resounded with an increasing fervor. In February, 1935, the American chargé in Bogotá predicted that the trade agreement could not possibly be signed until July of that year.[20]

By midsummer of 1935 Assistant Secretary of State Sumner Welles, obviously perplexed and frustrated, intimated to Francis Sayre his deep misgivings as to the course of the United States–Colombian trade discussions:

19. *FR* 1934, 5 (1952):71–82. DS 611.2131/282½–283, /293½; /297, NA, RG 59.

20. DS 611.2131/250, /260, /262–264, /272, /283, /290, /325, NA, RG 59. For an analysis of Colombia's attempts to break the dependency of a coffee monoculture and move toward crop diversification, see José L. Colon, "How Colombia is Improving Agricultural Production," *Bulletin of the Pan American Union* 68:1 (January 1934):51–59; Julio Caro, "Economic Progress in the Americas, 1935; Colombia," 70:2 (February 1936):180–83.

We commenced trade agreement negotiations with Colombia, I believe, in the autumn of 1933. During the past winter we have been making various requests for new provisions in the trade agreements and these new requests, as you know, have been misunderstood in Colombia, since the Colombian Congress is sure that there must be some 'nigger in the woodpile' every time we ask for a new provision. I cannot understand why we did not put in everything we wanted in the first trade agreement negotiated.[21]

The question concerned what, if anything, could be done by Washington to speed up the Colombian trade negotiations. The Division of Latin American Affairs, backed by the persuasiveness of Welles, argued that the United States should not interfere in the commercial policy of another nation. The division further recommended that mild reprobations drafted in the instructions to the American minister in Bogotá protesting Colombian trade agreements with Japan or Germany were equally improper. On July 11, 1935, the State Department went so far as to inform the Colombian government that any attempts on the part of United States private interests to obtain preferential treatment did not have the blessing of the department. In this manner the United States reaffirmed its stand for equality of treatment in conformity with the Montevideo Resolutions.

On September 13, 1935, the two nations at long last signed the illusory commercial treaty. The Colombian accord marked the sixth such trade agreement negotiated by the Roosevelt Administration, preceded by agreements with Cuba, Brazil, Belgium, Haiti, and Sweden. Twelve other reciprocity treaties were in the process of negotiation. Colombia acquiesced not out of commitment to free trade but because she had run out of delay tactics. More procrastinations, López reasoned, might force Washington to retaliate against coffee. Moreover, the signing of the treaty did not automatically ensure a speedy approval by the Colombian congress.

The final Colombian agreement eliminated the exceptions to the antidumping act to coffee, provided national treatment for federal internal taxes and transportation services, allowed for Colombia's canalization fee, exempted American territories from the bonds of the agreement, and reaffirmed the unconditional most-favored-nation clause. The agreement became ef-

21. DS 611.2131/320½, NA, RG 59. Also *FR*, 1935, 4 (1935):441–42.

fective thirty days after ratification by the respective executives on approval by the Colombian congress and continued in force for two years. The concessions granted in Schedule I and II remained basically intact. Colombia granted reductions or bindings on more than 150 tariff classifications covering 58 per cent of total United States exports. The United States granted reductions or bindings on 88 per cent of Colombian exports. The question of exchange control did not receive formal recognition. Colombia imposed no restrictions on the purchase of exchange in payments for the United States imports.

Colombia's trade practice now shifted to a multiple-column tariff incorporating a maximum column (the basic rate increased by 25 per cent) on nations that discriminated against Colombia or bought few of her products. The basic rate applied to nations that bought substantial amounts of goods from Colombia and did not discriminate against her goods. Finally, a minimum column was established for those nations signing unconditional most-favored-nation treaties.[22] On the matter of Colombian bond default, the agreement mentioned nothing. The State Department went to great lengths to postpone a public hearing on the debt situation, since it might have prejudiced ratification of the treaty.[23]

The State Department, however, had not reckoned with the ire of George Peek, special adviser to the President on foreign trade. Both Hull and Peek recognized that the Brazilian and Colombian negotiations "would shape the entire future course" of the trade agreements policy. Hull, however, refused to countenance Peek's policy of "immediate expediency," i.e., bilateral clearing arrangements and forced debt settlements with either Colombia or Brazil. Acts of economic nationalism, argued the secretary of state, might well prejudice future trade negotiations with Europe and Asia.[24]

22. DS 611.2131/330–332, /349–350, /373; 621.9431/15, NA, RG 59. *FTLA*, pt. 2, p. 142. For a survey of the various methods of valuation used as a basis for assessing customs duties, see, TC, *Method of Valuation*, 2d Series, Report No. 70 (GPO, 1933).

23. DS 611.2131/392, NA, RG 59.

24. George F. Peek, papers, Box 16, Memorandum (to Peek), October 12, 1934.

As early as November 2, 1934, Peek's office had presented a comprehensive examination of the proposed United States–Colombian agreement to the Department of State. The confidential study began with an introductory admonition, which stated in part:

> Since this Agreement (with the exception of the very special and distinctive case of Cuba) is the first one which the State Department proposed to conclude under the new program it is of strategic importance that we register our objections to it. A great deal that will happen in this entire program may hinge upon this first case.[25]

To Peek and his staff the draft agreement represented a "poor bargain" for the United States and was both "inadequate commercially and totally inadequate financially." To begin a new bargaining program that would in all probability limit American freedom of action was an "unfortunate precedent" signaling sheer folly. Peek maintained that the treaty gave greater benefits to Colombia than to the United States, since the devaluation of the peso put its actual worth at $.57 rather than the theoretical value of $.97 thereby increasing the relative price of American exports. It also failed to include provisions on defaulted debts and the reestablishment of an appropriate credit relationship for current transactions. The incorporation of an unconditional most-favored-nation clause, argued Peek, was "a paradoxical thing in a *special*, bargaining trade agreement" and nullified the United States' "*real* bargaining power with other countries." American pledges that coffee would remain on the free list eliminated the United States' most effective "bargaining weapon" against Brazil and other coffee-producing nations.

Peek's critical study did not stop with the preceding generalizations. The report analyzed step by step the specific provisions of the treaty and found most of them wanting. For example, the special adviser took exception to the United States antidumping exemption on unroasted coffee. The report suggested that no reservation adequately safeguarded the Roosevelt Administration in the imposition of internal processing taxes. Colombia's departments and municipalities might nullify tariff concessions

25. DS 611.2131/277, NA, RG 59.

through the imposition of higher taxes because of loopholes in the treaty. Peek also favored a shorter period than two years for the treaty to be effective.

Hull and the State Department, nevertheless, remained committed to their program. Peek's efforts to reformulate economic policy through the Executive Committee on Commercial Policy (an interdepartmental body concerned with the coordination of all aspects of American foreign trade policy) likewise met with defeat. Peek now faced three alternatives—either resign, work to circumvent the reciprocity agreement through barter and bilateral agreement independent of the State Department, or convince Roosevelt to change the course of American economic diplomacy. Eventually Peek utilized all three, working in reverse order.[26]

Throughout the latter months of 1934 and into the new year, Peek presented a relentless barrage of both economic facts and distortions to the White House. Peek reasoned, and no doubt partially persuaded Roosevelt, that the United States was in a strong position to require greater concessions from Colombia because of the United States' unfavorable balance of trade and Bogotá's position on bond defaults, blocked exchange, currency devaluation, and tariff hikes. The importance of American investment capital in Colombia and her dependence on the United States as a market for four-fifths of her coffee exports added more credence to Peek's case. By failing to achieve substantial concessions from Colombia, the United States lessened the likelihood of ever obtaining important tariff reductions from other nations. Peek's argument centered on the fact that the reciprocity agreements, combined with the unconditional most-favored-nation clause, enlarged the scope of American tariff concessions beyond the policy of principal supplier and thereby lessened America's bargaining position in future negotiations.[27]

Although Roosevelt remained somewhat less than ebullient toward Hull's direction of American economic diplomacy, the

26. Ibid. For the role of the Executive Committee on Commercial Policy, see Tasca, pp. 29–30, 48–49.

27. DS 611.2131/260, NA, RG 59. Peek, papers, Box 16, Memorandum (Peek to Roosevelt), November 14, 1934; Box 16, Peek to McIntyre, December 8, 1934. Roosevelt, papers, Official File, 614–A, Peek to Roosevelt, December 8, 10, 1934.

President refused to sabotage the Colombian agreement. The philosophy of economic nationalism had failed to displace the trade agreements program. Peek's first serious challenge to the authority of the State Department in the field of commercial and financial policy for the moment, at least, had been thwarted. Hull's achievement signified a sweet victory over domestic opposition. Only approval by the Colombian congress and formal ratification remained ahead. The prospects again brightened for the cause of reciprocity.

The State Department, however, had achieved only a semblance of victory. What had been hoped to be a speedy approval by the Colombian congress proved to be a source of continual frustration and delay. Although the Liberal government of President López did not fear conservative opposition to the trade agreement in Congress, the progress toward ratification was appallingly slow. By mid-November, 1935, chargé Dawson lamented "the inevitable delays of Colombian parliamentary procedure." Colombian newspapers such as *El Espectador* referred to the treaty as a "contract of slavery," while the American legation, under guard by two dozen police, braced itself for Communist demonstrations. The radical press *Tierra* urged popular fronts to organize a general strike against the treaty. Leftist demonstrations continued into December and tended to weaken the nerve of the moderate Colombian press to stand firm on the treaty.[28]

By January, 1936, a committee of the Colombian chamber of representatives finally submitted its report approving the reciprocity treaty. In a scathing attack the minority referred to the treaty as a "clear denial of the 'Good Neighbor Policy' " imposed upon a weak country by economic threats that would "harm [Colombia] materially and morally, economically and politically."[29] The *Anales de la Cámara de Representativos: Sesiónes Extraordinaria* recorded the tempo of political debates throughout the early months of 1936. Radicals and conservatives alike charged that the United States had adopted a new interpretation of the Monroe Doctrine designed to asborb the small economies of Latin America under the skillful ploy of nonintervention and

28. DS 611.2131/397–399, /406, /421, /427, NA, RG 59.

29. DS 611.2131/436, *Anales de la Cámara de Representativos: Sesiónes Extraordinaria*, Imprenta Nacional, serie 2.a, número 151, 28 de enero de 1936; número 155, 1 de febrero de 1936. Hereafter cited as *Anales*.

the equality of all states. When questioned by the chamber of representatives on February 8, 1936, Dr. Hernández admitted that the 1933 treaty had been more advantageous to Colombia than the one negotiated in 1935. Nevertheless, the chief of the Customs Tribunal supported the later agreement with the qualifications that "given the circumstances in which it was negotiated" Colombia would be wise to accept it. On February 14 the chamber of representatives passed the treaty on the third reading by a vote of 69 to 5.[30] The treaty had yet to pass the Colombian senate.

Throughout March, 1936, the debate continued in the senate. Views of America's commercial policy ranged from benevolent and idealistic to a "manifestation of the new expansionist modality of North American capitalism." One protectionist exclaimed that he had proof that Colombia had gone so far as to denounce commercial treaty with Japan in order to satisfy Washington.[31] The Colombian foreign minister, in reply to senatorial examination, defended the trade agreement as one of "imperious necessity," negotiated with the United States on a plane of absolute equality without pressure of any sort. The senate remained unconvinced. Dawson reported, "It is disappointing and disconcerting that at this stage and with so little time still before it, the Senate should treat in so casual a manner a measure urgently recommended by the administration."[32] The senate's delay forced President López to once again extend the life of congress.

In all probability, if the López administration had sincerely desired speedy approval of the treaty, it could have used more forceful means to pressure congress. Conservative voting strength in congress remained minimal. Moreover, Latin American governments traditionally had ways of short-circuiting obstinate legislators. The negotiations, therefore, appeared to move cautiously as much as a result of Bogotá's inaction as from any

30. DS 611.2131/455–456, NA, RG 59. *Anales,* número 157, 4 de febrero de 1936; número 161, 8 de febrero de 1936; número 163, 10 de febrero de 1936; número 164, 13 de febrero de 1936; número 165, 14 de febrero de 1936; número 166, 15 de febrero de 1936.

31. *Anales del Senado: Sesiónes Extraordinaria,* Imprenta Nacional, serie 6.a, número 266, 28 de marzo de 1936. Also see ibid., número 256, 16 de marzo de 1936; and DS 611.2131/471, NA, RG 59.

32. DS 611.2131/473, NA, RG 59.

ground swell of popular discontent. Coffee remained, sadly enough, the mainstay of the Colombian economy. If domestic manufacturing interests had to be sacrificed in order to propitiate the United States, then so be it. There was no doubt that the political economy of coffee reigned supreme. However, the Haitian government had already signed a reciprocity treaty with the United States incorporating the unconditional most-favored-nation clause and putting coffee on the free list. Colombia, therefore, had partially reaped the benefits of the treaty before ever signing with the United States, a fact no doubt fully recognized by the López administration. Quite possibly, Bogotá accepted the treaty and the unconditional most-favored-nation clause with the hope of opening avenues of trade with Europe that had been closed by Colombia's trade and fiscal policies.

On April 6, 1936, the Colombian senate passed the treaty for the third and final time. The exchange of ratification was accomplished on April 20 with the accord to become effective May 20, 1936.[33] Developments in the following months were carefully watched by the State Department in order to gauge the effects of the agreement. The first comprehensive report, a 150-page report entitled "Colombian Import Statistics Showing Effect of Trade Agreement," was submitted by the American legation to the State Department in February, 1937. The report produced an array of figures that amply proved that the agreement had been advantageous to United States trade interests. Chargé Dawson first analyzed imports into Colombia on articles subject to reduction in the trade agreement (Classification R) for June, July, and August, 1935, compared to the same period in 1936. The figures revealed that Colombian imports from the United States on those articles had increased from 891,149 pesos in 1935 to 1,798,153 pesos for the same period in 1936, or an approximate increase of 101.7 per cent. Interestingly, Colombia's imports from all other countries in Classification R declined from 344,496

33. For a sixty-three-page report by the Colombian government giving the text of the treaty and its defense see, "Proyecto de ley por la Cualse Aprueba un Convenio Comercial entre la República de Colombia y los Estados Unidos de América" (Bogotá: Imprenta Nacional, 1935). For the text of the Colombian law 74 dealing with the trade treaty see *Diario Oficial*, Imprenta Nacional, número 23186, 19 de mayo de 1936. DS 611.-2131/505–507, NA, RG 59.

pesos to 227,959 pesos, or by 34 per cent. Colombia's imports from articles bound under the trade agreement (Classification B) and exclusive of Classification R, for June, July, and August, 1935, totaled 2,644,579 pesos, of which 1,347,931 pesos worth of goods came from the United States. In 1936 Colombia's imports on products in Classification B equaled 1,721,264 pesos, or an increase of 27.6 per cent, while Colombia's imports on like articles from all other nations increased by only 12.3 per cent. Total United States exports to Columbia for the months June, July, and August in 1935 equaled 6,737,264 pesos. For the same months of 1936 the figures reached 9,842,877 pesos, or an increase of about 46 per cent. Colombia's import trade for the same period in 1936 from all nations excluding the United States measured an increase of 24.5 per cent over the months of June, July, and August, 1935. The report also showed that most American products showing substantial trade increases were machinery and manufactured products. American agriculture, with the exception of cotton goods, did not share proportionately in the resuscitation of American trade to Colombia. George Peek observed that "scarcely any reductions of practical value were made in the agreement" regarding agricultural products. These developments, it might be added, were not peculiar to Colombian trade. In 1936 nonagricultural products to South America made up 95.5 per cent of United States exports. It also marked a definite trend in the course of United States export trade with the world at large.[34]

In June, 1937, Dawson summed up the trade figures from the first year of operation for the trade agreement (June, 1936, to May, 1937, inclusive). America's exports to the Republic of Colombia had increased 56.8 per cent in value while Colombia's imports from all other nations increased by 29.2 per cent in value. Moreover, her exports to all other nations increased by only 11.8 per cent. "The competitive position of American exporters, in general, has improved since the taking effect of the agreement," reported Dawson.[35] By the end of 1938 the trend was nearly complete. Colombian export trade to the United States

34. DS 611.2131/540, NA, RG 59. Peek, papers, Box 16, Peek to Henry F. Grady, December 6, 1934. *FTUS*, 1935, TPS No. 166 (1936), pp. 1–7; *FTUS*, 1936, TPS No. 174 (1938), pp. 2, 20, 58.

35. DS 611.2131/549–550, NA, RG 59.

(excluding gold) for the years 1932–1934 compared to the average for 1937–1938 revealed a 2 per cent decrease, while American export trade to Colombia showed an increase of 154 per cent. United States balance of payments deficits with Colombia (exclusive of receipts on America's direct investments) fell from $46,000,000 in 1932 to only $17,200,000 in 1938.[36] Parenthetically, it should be noted that the trade agreement alone should not take full credit for the revival of United States–Colombian export trade. American trade to nonagreement nations also showed marked increase with world economic recovery. The year 1934, for example, witnessed the largest United States relative export excess since 1921, some $478,000,000—a phenomenon that cannot be attributed to the reciprocity agreements. This increase in the United States exports was due primarily to general economic recovery in most nations, a narrower range of fluctuation in exchange rates of various national currencies, the devaluation of the American dollar, and the resulting improvement in the competitive price position of United States goods.

Between the periods 1932–1934 and 1937–1939, average annual imports of dutiable goods to the United States rose from $538,000,000 to $964,000,000, an increase of 79 per cent. American exports for the same period rose from $1,774,000,000 to $3,159,000,000, an increase of 79 per cent. However, the average increase between 1932–1934 and 1937–1938 for American exports to trade agreement nations was 21 per cent greater than to non-trade agreement nations.[37]

The State Department, therefore, viewed its trade agreement program in general, and its Latin American program in particular, with optimism. The Colombian trade agreement, for example, adumbrated "a consistently greater increase in Colombia's imports from the United States than from other foreign sources of supply."[38] But the course of United States–Colombian trade simply manifested a larger phenomenon taking place throughout Latin America. The trade deficit with Latin America, which began to decline in the early 1930s, was completely reversed by

36. *Operation*, pt. 5, p. 14. *FTLA*, pt. 2, pp. 145, 159, 165. *Operation*, pt. 1, p. 53.

37. *FTUS*, 1934, TPS No. 162 (1935), pp. 1–8. *Operation*, pt. 1, pp. 55–56.

38. DS 611.2131/557, NA, RG 59.

1938. In that year, American exports to Latin America totaled $494,821,000, while American imports declined to $453,517,000. The geographic distribution of American export trade to Latin America also witnessed substantial gains. In 1932 United States exports accounted for 12.1 per cent of Latin American imports, but by 1939 the figure stood at 17.9 per cent. In 1936 the Bureau of Foreign and Domestic Commerce reported that, "the percentage increase in United States exports to Latin America was almost double the increase in our world trade in 1936."[39] World War II merely continued a pattern set in motion by the expansion of American markets in the early New Deal. If, indeed, as Hull asserted, "the political line-up followed the economic line-up," then the Roosevelt Administration, through the use of reciprocity agreements as one trade device, had succeeded in more closely integrating the economies of Latin America to the United States.[40]

The trade program was not so beneficial for nations like Colombia, as serious trade problems remained. Coffee continued to possess a stranglehold on this South American nation's economy. In 1937 attempts made by the leading coffee-producing countries to limit production by export quotas and crop reduction came to nothing. In an effort to maintain the volume of sales, Brazil thereupon abandoned coffee export controls. This action deprived Colombia of indirect price benefits from Brazilian export taxes on coffee while it created unbelievable coffee surpluses. The effects were predictable. The resulting fall of coffee prices forced Bogotá to institute provisions designed to stabilize and safeguard the Colombian currency.[41] In November, 1937, the López administration moved to restrict the issuance of exchange permits, to prescribe time limits for the delivery of newly mined gold to the Bank of the Republic, and to insure the utilization of all exchange licenses. These exchange regulations (a topic to be pursued later in detail) required delivery to the Central Bank at the official rate a specified percentage of the exchange arising out of exports of certain commodities, the remainder being available for disposal in the free market to holders of exchange permits. The exchange and financial developments of November 1937,

39. *FTUS*, 1936, p. 76; *FTUS*, 1934, pp. 47, 66. *FTLA*, pt. 1, p. 36.
40. Hull, *Memoirs*, Vol. 1, p. 365.
41. DS 611.2131/564, /568, NA, RG 59. *BFDC*, 351.1, NA, RG 40, Colombia, February 27, 1937.

remarked the American chargé, caused "a temporary situation that was close to a cessation of import trade. Exchange permits are now eight weeks in arrears." By 1938 partial exchange melioration allowed Bogotá to set up a free-exchange market, the selling rate of which closely approximated the official rate.[42]

Colombia's ability to buy American products rested upon other factors besides the export price of coffee. The procurement of needed exports, as well as the development of internal productive capacities, required vital foreign loans from both the private and governmental sectors of the United States economy. However, throughout the decade of the 1930s, Colombia's record for foreign debt payments deserved the dubious honor of being one of the poorest in all Latin America. Importunities by the State Department, private banking firms, and the semiofficial Foreign Bondholders Protective Council proved to be a series of endless frustrations as successive administrations of Colombian officialdom refused a compromise settlement. The State Department, therefore, refused to extend export-import credits to Colombia until such time as a satisfactory agreement might be reached. These delays in debt negotiations continued to retard the development of the Colombian market for American goods.[43] It also retarded the development of vital domestic industries, such as petroleum. Without American capital, Bogotá could not obtain the machinery and technological skills necessary to procure, transport, refine, or market crude oil. Throughout the 1930s Colombia's total oil exports (mainly crude) remained approximately 18,500,000 barrels. American tariff policies likewise retarded Colombian oil exports. It might be of interest to note that Colombia's exportation of crude oil to the United States in 1929 totaled 12,578,000 barrels, or 71.2 per cent of her total crude oil exports. By 1937 the figure had declined to only 431,000 barrels, or about 2.4 per cent of Colombia's total crude oil exports.[44] Thus, a potentially important segment of the Colombian economy withered on the vine of international capitalism.

The Roosevelt Administration also confronted numerous attempts by Colombia to modify the provisions of the agreement so

42. DS 611.2131/568, NA, RG 59. *FTLA*, pt. 2, pp. 141–43.

43. DS 821.51/2320, DS 611.2131/591, NA, RG 59. This topic will be given greater treatment in another chapter.

44. *FTLA*, pt. 2, p. 158; pt. 3, p. 165.

as to restrict the importation of American products. In May, 1939, Ambassador Spruille Braden informed Hull that President Eduardo Santos had requested alterations in the trade treaty permitting the raising of tariff duties on a specified number of American exports, the most important of which appeared to be cotton goods.[45] Hull's reply to Braden categorically denied the propriety of Bogotá's intimation:

> You should say that this Government would greatly regret the consideration of any backward step in the program of lowering tariff and other barriers to international trade which is such an important part of the foreign policy of Colombia as well as of the United States (e.g., the Lima declaration on the reduction of barriers to international trade).
>
> It will be realized that consideration of a change in any trade agreement item would require (under our trade agreements procedure) reopening of the agreement necessitating public notice and hearings in this country with inevitable attendant business uncertainty which in our opinion would not (repeat not) be to the advantage either of Colombia or the United States. Moreover, it would be extremely difficult, if not impossible, for us to justify the relinquishment of advantages obtained under the agreement for American textile exporters (who have already expressed to us their opposition to any change).[46]

Although the Santos administration was "disposed to move more slowly" on tariff revision after the Hull rebuff, it did not preclude the imposition of higher duties on certain agricultural imports. In 1940, for example, Colombia restricted rice and wheat imports. Cotton imports, too, felt the trade pinch as Colombia moved steadily in the direction of greater economic self-sufficiency during the war.[47]

Probably the New Deal's most serious external challenge for the control of the Latin American market came from the totalitarian powers of Germany and Japan, which will be given greater treatment in a subsequent chapter. One yardstick of success for the reciprocity program was its ability to checkmate fascist attempts to undermine the political economies of Latin America, which might have threatened the American Open Door empire.

45. DS 821.463/14, NA, RG 59.
46. DS 611.2131/594A, NA, RG 59.
47. DS 621.003/322; 611.2131/597; 621.006/42, NA, RG 59.

Measured in this way, reciprocity served a more useful role in Colombia than in most Latin American nations. In 1934 German exports to Latin America, less Argentina, equalled 180,000,000 reichsmarks; in 1936 the figure stood at 413,000,000 reichsmarks. In 1934 the percentage of Germany's total trade in Latin America was 4.3 per cent. In the next two years the figure had doubled. Japanese exports to Latin America likewise increased, although the gains were more absolute than relative. This was in large part because Japan did not purchase large amounts of Latin American staples such as coffee.[48]

In December, 1934, Colombia and Germany placed their export trade on an "informal compensation basis" due, in part, to German exchange restrictions. Approximately one year later, a formal compensation agreement was signed. Hull's reciprocity agreement no doubt helped partly to rechannel the Colombian market toward the United States and to retard substantial purchases of Colombian products by Hitler (American exports in 1938 were up 154 per cent over the 1932–1934 period). But the adverse trade balance suffered by Colombia in her trade relations with Germany remained the major reason Germany never succeeded in controlling more of this South American market. In 1936 the Colombian Exchange Control Board virtually suspended imports from Germany by limiting permits to raw materials and commodities urgently needed for Colombian industry. The following year a new agreement between the Hitler regime and Bogotá provided for a bilateral balancing of trade between the two nations. The trade statistics, however, pointed in the direction of diminished commerce. Between 1936 and 1937 the percentage of Colombian imports from Nazi Germany declined by 9.2 per cent. Concomitantly, American export trade to Colombia increased by 7.7 per cent. In 1936 Colombia exported to Germany 16.9 per cent of her total exports and 54.2 per cent to the United States. In 1937 Colombia shipped only 13.4 per cent of her export products to Germany and 55.9 per cent to the United States.[49]

Nevertheless, Colombia's dependence on her export trade

48. League of Nations, *Review of World Trade 1936*, II. Economic and Financial, 1937, II. A. 9. (Geneva: Series of League of Nations Publications, 1937), 37–43. DS 611.2131/568, NA, RG 59.

49. *FTLA*, pt. 2, pp. 143–57. DS 611.2131/568, NA, RG 59.

forced her to make concessions to feed the omnivorous war machine of Nazi Germany. By 1938 the pendulum again swung toward greater commercial intercourse between Colombia and Germany. Petroleum, platinum, hides, and oils, all essentials for the Germans, flowed steadily eastward across the Atlantic. This time the Roosevelt Administration did not rely solely upon reciprocity to come to the rescue.

As the Axis menace grew more alarming, the State Department began to view the developments more as a political and strategic danger rather than as a commercial one. The department maintained that American business, if given fair competition by the Latin American governments, could out-trade any of the Axis powers. But artificial trade devices designed to weld the economies of Latin America to the Axis powers seriously jeopardized the traditional Open Door policy. Spruille Braden, in 1941, echoed the apprehensions of many State Department officials as he recounted German and Japanese maneuvers to entrench themselves in the political economy of Colombia. "Once in, they [the Axis] will be evicted only with greatest difficulty if at all."[50] The United States Open Door policy in Latin America, which operated halfheartedly in commercial relations and seldom if ever in financial circles, underwent serious modifications. As Braden admitted in 1941, "The Department will recall previous efforts of Japan to obtain trade agreements have been checkmated largely by the Embassy's efforts."[51] By the late 1930s the reciprocal trade program in Colombia, as in the rest of Latin America, had lost much of its élan. New pressures, new incentives, and new programs would have to be implemented to offset the Axis threat. Questions pertaining to political cooperation in order to solidify the hemisphere against Axis activity, the development of Colombian industry, greater technical and military assistance, and the stabilization of currencies through such facilities as the Export-Import Bank would increasingly occupy the diplomatic stage.[52]

50. DS 621.9417/50, NA, RG 59.
51. Ibid.
52. DS 711.21/931, NA, RG 59.

4

Cuba and Economic Nationalism

Cordell Hull's economic liberalism did not apply to Cuba. Washington did not adhere to the unconditional most-favored-nation clause in Cuba's case, nor were tariff concessions granted to the United States automatically generalized to third nations. To rationalize this departure, the Administration employed a host of rhetorical devices. One phrase commonly used to justify Cuba's peculiar place in the American economy was that "geographical propinquity and historical considerations" dictated an entirely different course of action. The phrase, however, did not reveal the full impact of United States influence. With no other nation in the Western Hemisphere did the trade program border so closely on economic nationalism. Hull's remark that "Cuba was to be the kernel of our new and positive policy toward Latin America," appears tragically shortsighted in retrospect. For Hull failed to perceive the inherent dangers of economic forces beyond the control of American policymakers. The history of United States–Cuban economic relations during the period 1933–1939 recounts the pervasive influence of American business in the formulation of policy and the juxtaposition of American liberal rhetoric and economic nationalism. "In summation," Hull recalled, "if the case of Cuba was to be the focus of Latin American scrutiny of our acts and intentions, a happier one could scarcely have been chosen." On the other end of the economic spectrum, John Donaldson, adviser to Peek in the Office of Special Adviser to the President on Foreign Trade and an ardent economic nationalist, remarked with no sense of incongruity that the Cuban reciprocity treaty symbolized the type of "policy which we have constantly advocated."[1]

1. *SAPFT*, General Correspondence, NA, John Donaldson to Peek, May 13, 1935. George N. Peek, *Why Quit Our Own?* (New York: D. Van

Like the rest of Latin America, Cuba's trade with the United States following the crash declined sharply. In 1924 Cuba ranked as the sixth-best customer for United States exports, but by 1933 she had fallen to sixteenth. The decline related directly to the dependence of Cuba's purchasing power on sugar. As the United States Tariff Commission reported, Cuba's reliance on the exportation of sugar and sugar products had become the determining factor in the Cuban economy. Any decline in sugar prices "is directly reflected in the Cuban import trade, as well as in internal economic conditions." Moreover, the state of Cuban sugar export trade, the Tariff Commission admitted, depended greatly upon the sugar policy of the United States.[2] Although Cuba's sugar exports to the United States from 1924 to 1929 remained around 3,100,000 short tons per year, the price fell from $.04 to $.02 per pound. With the advent of the Hawley-Smoot Tariff the American duty on raw sugar imports increased from $.0176 per pound to $.02 per pound. By 1933 Cuban sugar exports had decreased to 1,495, 992 short tons. These declines, both in the price and volume of sugar exports, reduced the Cuban sugar income to 30 per cent of what it had been in 1929 and to only 12 per cent of the 1924 figure.[3]

The history of sugar and, therefore, the history of Cuba had been colored by the economic rivalry between the sugar cane interests (tropical and more efficient) and the beet sugar interests (temperate and lower yield per acre). The need for production control was imperative. However, interest groups were skeptical of international marketing schemes. American beet sugar interests no doubt preferred domestic tariff protection, while the more efficient Cuban interests opposed any international marketing agreement that threatened to stifle their competitive advantage. The failure to understand the necessity of international

Nostrand Company, 1936), pp. 262–64. Cordell Hull, *The Memoirs of Cordell Hull*, Vol. 1 (New York: Macmillan Company, 1948), pp. 342–44. Guillermo A. Suro, "Trade Agreements Between the United States and Latin America," *Bulletin of the Pan American Union* 68: 11 (November 1934): 780–89.

2. *FTLA*, pt. 2, Report No. 146, 2d Series (1942), p. 224; pt. 3, pp. 189–90.

3. Suro, pp. 786–87.

production controls spurred an increase in raw sugar output to offset the decline in the price level.[4]

The overproduction of raw sugar in Cuba, started by the United States Food Administration in World War I, was carried to fulfillment in the 1920s by American banking interests motivated by a desire to sell Cuba more sugar machinery and to promote the purchase of sugar stocks. Finally, in the wake of depression, Cuba agreed to a poor plan for production control. The Chadbourne Plan, signed in 1931 by Cuba, Java, and the sugar-exporting nations of Europe, sought to fix export quotas, to segregate surplus stocks, and to decrease sugar production. The plan was a complete failure. Moreover, the nations agreeing to the plan consisted of only 44 per cent of the world's sugar crop and only 70 per cent of the sugar entering the international market. Not privy to the plan, American insular possessions stepped up their production and offset the shortage. By June, 1932, the price of raw sugar fell to a record low of $.0057 per pound. As Charles Taussig commented, the Chadbourne Plan "was the culminating economic misfortune to Cuba." So catastrophic was the plan that by 1932 Cuba supplied the United States with a meager 28.2 per cent of her sugar, a figure approximately half the size of the 1922–1926 total.[5]

Nor was this the entire story. Efforts to diversify the Cuban economy and to escape the perils of monoculture met with lethargy in Cuba and reprobation and resistance in the United States. As early as January, 1930, Cuba stood ready to destroy incipient industries in return for larger sugar and tobacco markets in the United States. Rather than industrial and agricultural diversification, Cuba embarked on an orgy of public-works spending to bolster a sagging economy. This was the result of graft and corruption in the Cuban government and of American banking coer-

4. John C. deWilde, "Sugar: An International Problem," *FPR*, 9: 15 (September 27, 1933): 163–64. *FTLA*, pt. 2, p. 254.

5. deWilde, pp. 166–67. Raymond L. Buell, "The Caribbean Situation: Cuba and Haiti," *FPR* 9:8 (June 21, 1933):85. Paul R. Kelbaugh, "Recent Trends and Events in the Agriculture of Latin America," *Bulletin of the Pan American Union* 59:3 (March 1935):214–17. Charles Taussig, papers, Franklin D. Roosevelt Library, Hyde Park, N. Y., Box 37, Memorandum, March 14, 1933.

cion. The Central Highway, constructed for a cost of $80,000,000, and a marble capitol totaling $20,000,000 further bankrupted the government and destroyed Cuba's budding railroad program.[6]

But perhaps the greatest millstone hung around the neck of the Cuban economy involved the payment of interest and amortization to American bankers. In October, 1932, the American consul general estimated the Cuban debt at $179,357,460. Most of the foreign loans had been obtained from American sources and now were very much in danger of default.

The United States, nevertheless, maintained a firm grip on the political economy of Cuba. Despite his economic and political recklessness, Gerardo Machado y Morales, president of Cuba since 1925, tenaciously refused to default on American loans. In the face of mounting violence and revolution heightened by the depression, Cuba's dictator flaunted economic and political reform while attempting to maintain power by further borrowing. There would be no moratorium as long as Machado remained supreme. American bankers sighed in relief. Civil war in Cuba continued.

Economic chaos contributed to increased political conflict in Cuba. Violence and supression at the hands of the Machado dictatorship had become counterproductive. President Hoover and Secretary of State Henry Stimson, however, remained dedicated to both the status quo and nonintervention. Patiently they awaited the day when the Cuba imbroglio could be thrust upon a different administration.

American reciprocity negotiations with the Republic of Cuba, therefore, must be viewed from the backdrop of mounting civil disorder and its effects on American direct and portfolio investment in Cuba. The 1902 United States–Cuban Reciprocity Treaty had resulted in the rapid development of sugar production and the influx of United States capital into Cuba, both of which speeded up the process of agricultural specialization and increased Cuba's dependence on the United States. By the end of 1928, Assistant Secretary of State Francis White placed America's investments (direct and portfolio) in

6. DS 611.3731/358, NA, RG 59. Taussig, papers, Box 37, Memorandum, March 14, 1933.

Cuba in the neighborhood of $1,470,000,000. The statistical breakdown was as follows: government bonds, $110,000,000; sugar companies, $750,000,000; railroads, $150,000,000; public utilities, $150,000,000; manufacturing, $45,000,000; tobacco, $50,000,000; land, $100,000,000; merchandizing, $45,000,000; mining, $35,000,000; banking, $25,000,000; miscellaneous, $10,000,000. United States direct investment in Cuba ranked second only to Canada in the worth of American holdings outside the limits of the United States. But revolution and economic chaos in Cuba threatened the very lifeblood of these investments.

The Roosevelt Administration viewed the Cuban situation with special significance. Some of the reasons for this interest seemed quite obvious. Nearly 10 per cent of all United States portfolio investments in Latin America (equity and other security investments in foreign-controlled corporations and investments in security issues of foreign governments), as well as 24 per cent of all United States direct investments in Latin America, were in Cuba.[7] Historian Robert F. Smith has observed that three members of the "brain trust," Adolf Berle, Charles Taussig, and Rexford Tugwell, were officials in the American Molasses Company, while Secretary of the Treasury William Woodin, Daniel Roper, and Hull all had indirect connections with American business groups interested in Cuba. Although Smith's direct causal relationship between these private interests and public policy should not be made, it would be safe to assume that the trade program assumed vital importance to the extent that matters of reciprocity affected the future of American loans and investments in Cuba.[8]

The protection of its Cuban investments required political stability, which in turn necessitated economic prosperity to quell popular discontent. Reciprocal trade became one such avenue to promote economic recovery in Cuba (while at the same time benefitting American commerce), to alleviate political chaos, and to safeguard American investments. Besides, there was always

7. *FTLA*, pt. 2, pp. 228–29. US., Congress, *Congressional Record*, 73d Cong., 2d sess., 1934, 78, pts. 6 and 4: 6036–37; 3632–33.

8. Robert F. Smith, *The United States and Cuba: Business and Diplomacy, 1917–1960* (New Haven: College and University Press, 1960), pp. 141–43.

the intangible factor of prestige: If Washington could not maintain stability in its own backyard, how could it possibly sustain an empire throughout the hemisphere?

Judged by these standards, Machado had been found wanting. His administration, no matter how benevolent to American investors, had failed to perform the one function required by all United States factions, which was to maintain order. As Charles Taussig reported in early March, 1933, the United States through a "strong" ambassador must force Machado to resign, clearing the way for a provisional president and a gradual return to constitutional legitimacy. On May 8, 1933, Sumner Welles arrived in Havana as the new ambassador.[9]

The fall of Machado and the political actions of Welles' mission to Havana have been retold in numerous books and journals. But the inextricable role played by such economic forces as reciprocal trade in United States–Cuban diplomacy have not been given adequate treatment. Political reorganization of the Cuban government, revision of existing commercial agreements, and reconsideration of the Platt Amendment all vitally concerned the Roosevelt Administration as it sought to find solutions for the political and economic ills of Cuba. The resignation of Machado and the establishment of a government suitable to American interests became a *quid pro quo* for a revision of the 1902 Reciprocity Treaty. As the Division of Latin American Affairs put it, "In other words, the prospect of increased economic advantages is a plum which will not be granted until the Cuban Government has taken positive and satisfactory steps to conclude the present unrest."[10]

9. *FTLA*, pt. 2, pp. 227–28, 247. DS 811.503137/12, NA, RG 59. Graham H. Stuart, "Cuba and the Platt Amendment," *Proceedings of the Institute of World Affairs*, 10th sess., 10 (December 11–16, 1932) : 58. DS 837.51/1541, NA, RG 59. Also see George N. Peek, papers, Western Historical Manuscripts Collection, State Historical Society of Missouri, Box 15, Coulter to Peek, July 30, 1934. Taussig, papers, Box 37, Memorandum, March 14, 1933.

10. Franklin D. Roosevelt, papers, Franklin D. Roosevelt Library, Hyde Park, N. Y., Official File, 159–A, Memorandum, Division of Latin American Affairs, 1933. Buell, pp. 86–88. For full treatment of the Welles mission see Bryce Wood, *The Making of the Good Neighbor Policy* (New York: W. W. Norton and Company, 1961), chapters 2 and 3; also see Smith, pp. 144–57. For Welles' personal account, which understandably

Unlike the case with Colombia, both the United States and Cuba appeared anxious to conclude a new commercial pact. Administrations as early as William Taft's had maintained that the 1902 treaty made American goods competitive with German and English products. But a United States Tariff Commission Report published in 1929, entitled *The Effects of the Cuban Reciprocity Treaty of 1902*, presented the argument that the United States had gained little from the treaty: "The price premium on sugar," the authors of the report concluded, "conferred a unique advantage upon Cuba. The United States obtained no similar advantage from the treaty." The commission suggested that imports from Cuba increased more rapidly after the 1902 accord than did American exports to Cuba, although American exports to the rest of the Caribbean (with no trade agreements) increased at about the same rate. The United States, it was felt, could obtain a much better bargain in future negotiations. In other Tariff Commission reports, it was suggested that as a possible tariff concession to Cuba the United States could equalize the price of Cuban raw sugar with the continental United States and Hawaii by a 25 per cent reduction in the rate of duty on Cuban sugar.[11]

Cuban officials, such as Secretary of State Orestes Ferrara, also lamented the "useless and antiquated" 1902 treaty. Cuban benefits from the 1902 treaty were all but wiped out by Hawley-Smoot. Havana newspapers continued to denounce American tariff policy. Geographical proximity, close political relations, and a single banking and financial system all substantiated the Cuban plea for a new and special relationship between the United States and Cuba. Economic and political upheaval demanded the same.[12]

On March 30, 1933, the retiring United States ambassador to Havana, Harry Guggenheim, submitted a report urging the State

---

lacks objectivity, see Sumner Welles, *The Time For Decision* (New York: Harper and Brothers, 1944), pp. 193–200. For an article sympathetic to Welles, see C. A. Thomson, "The Cuban Revolution: Fall of Machado," *FPR*, 11 (December 18, 1935):250–60.

11. TC, *Sugar: Report to the President of the United States*, Report No. 73, 2d Series (1934), p. 1. *The Effects of the Cuban Reciprocity Treaty of 1902* (GPO, 1929), pp. 1–15.

12. DS 611.3731/382, /372, 611.373, Sugar/162, NA, RG 59.

Department to undertake reciprocal trade negotiations or to increase the preferential treatment for American products. Since 1927, when Cuba initiated a protective tariff, the American percentage of total Cuban imports had declined. Japanese rice, Canadian wheat, Argentine corn, Swiss watches, Belgian glass, Norwegian fish, British coal and coke, and Venezuelan oil now threatened America's commercial hegemony in Cuba. The ambassador further warned of German competition in iron, steel, and chemicals and Japanese and British competition in textiles.[13]

The Cuban Chamber of Commerce in the United States, an American institution representing over $1,000,000,000 in investments in Cuba, wrote Roosevelt that reciprocity negotiations would inspire "new faith and hope for the near future." Beside the restoration of "lost trade," a new commercial agreement represented an excellent safeguard for American investments. The State Department needed little convincing.[14] Throughout the early months of 1933 weekly and special reports by American commercial attachés in Havana chronicled mounting violent strikes and labor resistance in the sugar fields. The reports laid particular stress on the fact that the improvement in business conditions was predicated to a large extent on an early revision of the 1902 treaty.[15]

Financial reports from both private and governmental sources also warned of a possible Cuban moratorium on foreign debt. Shepard Morgan of the Chase National Bank informed Hull on March 14 of Machado's allegation that the banking situation in the United States made it impossible for Cuba to continue foreign debt service. Nonplused, Morgan said that the American bankers had done "everything possible to assist Cuba" to meet her debt obligations. Both Morgan and Assistant Secretary of State Francis White viewed Machado's threat as an attempt to get "into a bargaining position" on future political and economic negotiations. It was also possible that the Cuban dictator hoped to use

13. DS 611.3731/390, NA, RG 59.
14. *BFDC, NA, RG,* 40, *Weekly Reports of Commercial Attachés,* February 25, 1933; March 4, 1933; March 27, 1933; April 8, 1933; April 25, 1933; May 13, 1933; June 10, 1933; June 24, 1933. Also see *BFDC,* NA, RG 40, *Special Reports of Commercial Attachés,* March 24, 1933. DS 711.37/178a, NA, RG 59.
15. DS 611. 3731/398, /420, NA, RG 59.

the threat of debt default in such a way as to discourage American attempts to remove him from office.

The State Department was caught on the horns of a dilemma. Not wanting to induce the bankers to relieve the Cuban financial strain until a resolution of the political problem, the State Department nevertheless did not want to jeopardize American loans. Two of the more prominent loans, not including public works expenditures, included the Speyer loans of 1903–1904 and 1909 (the trustee being the Chase National), and the Morgan loans of 1914, 1923, and 1927 issued by J. P. Morgan, National City, Kuhn, Loeb and Company, J. & W. Seligman, Dillon and Reed, and Bankers Trust. The amount of their loans outstanding in January, 1933, totaled $56,480,500.[16]

On April 4 the *Official Gazette* promulgated the Cuban Mortgage Moratorium Law. It provided that railroads, national industries, and owners of sugar mill properties were relieved until July 1, 1935, of all payments on account of principal and interest due on mortgages secured by their properties. Mortgagors of rural property were relieved of interest payments above 2 per cent and city property above 4 per cent. Persons and entities benefiting under this law were required "to pay all taxes upon the unpaid interest which would have been due if the interest were being paid." Rentals on sugarcane lands were also reduced by 35 per cent under specified circumstances. The bill, of course, hurt American holders of mortgages but benefited American direct investors who had also suffered from the depression.[17] Machado, however, refused to default on the government loans. Although Cuban officials failed to receive salaries for five months, and "unparalleled poverty and distress" beset the island, Machado continued to pay American bankers. Welles reported the adverse effect on American prestige in Cuba and suggested a limited moratorium on the sinking fund charge due to American bankers. Since Machado refused to take the initiative, Welles urged Roosevelt and Hull to get American banking interests to call the moratorium. Predictably, Welles' plan met with a negative response.[18]

With financial relief nowhere in sight, revision of the 1902

16. DS 837.51/1544A, /1550, /1555, /1575, NA, RG 59.
17. DS 837.51/1545, /1558, /1563, NA, RG 59.
18. DS 837.51/1566, /1568, NA, RG 59.

trade treaty became even more imperative. No political reorganization of Cuba was feasible without also solving Cuba's economic ills. As Assistant Secretary Jefferson Caffery put it, Welles' "whole program in Cuba is predicated" upon the negotiation of a reciprocity treaty; failure to negotiate a treaty "will wreck his whole program." In mid-May, 1933, Welles undertook informal trade discussions with the Machado government. Roosevelt, embroiled in domestic recovery schemes, refused to prejudice New Deal momentum by asking for congressional authorization to negotiate reciprocal trade agreements. But since the Cuban negotiations involved only the modification of an existing treaty, Welles received permission to continue the talks. It might also be added that all important correspondence received by the State Department from American business concerns interested in trade with Cuba were forwarded to Welles.[19]

Throughout the summer months of 1933 diplomatic and consular officials, as well as interdepartmental committees, set to work analyzing United States–Cuban trade. The most influential examination of American commercial relations with Cuba was that of businessman-diplomat Philip Jessup. Paid by such industrial giants as Chrysler, DuPont, General Electric, National Cash Register, Pan-American Airways, Procter and Gamble, Remington Rand, Swift and Company, and the United States Steel Corporation to examine Cuba's economy, Jessup's private study indicated the lengths to which American business would go to corner this import market. Remarkably, Economic Adviser Herbert Feis called the Jessup report an impartial study that did not represent "the particular interests of any industry or industries." Feis' memorandum on the subject merits consideration.

> Mr. Jessup reports that minute study of a number of commodities indicates that for some lines of export trade an increased preferential would appear to be the best solution, for others a reduction in the Cuban tariff would also be necessary, for others only an increased Cuban tariff, or its equivalent in an import quota, with large preference for United States goods would suffice.

19. DS 611.3731/416½, /462, /502; 837.00/3514, NA, RG 59. Elliott Roosevelt, ed., *F.D.R.: His Personal Letters, 1928–1945* (New York: Duell, Sloan and Pearce, 1950), pp. 349–50.

Jessup explained that even with 100 per cent preferential on the present tariff the Japanese could still undersell American products. Therefore, the solution required an increase in the Cuban tariff plus a preferential for United States goods. When prices were out of the consumer's reach the United States should urge Cuba to lower her tariffs, while granting American goods a preferential. Jessup also suggested that Cuba might be willing to establish an import quota system giving the United States the major share. Feis commented that the report "obviously deserves careful study." [20] Perhaps it did; but the oddest feature of all was that no one seemed to question the impartiality of a report paid for by private enterprise. In retrospect, such examples as the Jessup study and the pervasive influence of American bankers demonstrate the extent to which the forces of economic nationalism shaped American policy toward Cuba.

In the meantime, Welles continued to work for an acceptance by all Cuban factions of his tender of good offices. The strategy included "keeping the negotiation of the commercial treaty as a leverage" until a political solution could be reached. [21] Unfortunately, a solution was not that simple. By August, 1933, Welles was thoroughly disillusioned by Machado's inability to preserve stability and stated to Hull, "There is absolutely no hope of a return to normal conditions as long as President Machado remains in office." If the Cuban president refused to step down, then the United States must consider the possibility of withdrawing diplomatic recognition. American armed intervention did not seem a remote possibility. The Cuban army, however, saved the day. On August 12 the ranking officers of the army informed Machado that he no longer commanded their allegiance. The following day, Carlos Manuel de Céspedes took the oath of office as President *ad interim*. [22]

The Céspedes government was short-lived. On September 5 the U. S. ambassador in Cuba reported a revolution by the army

20. DS 611.3731/466, NA, RG 59.

21. *FR*, 1933 5:325. For a brief history of United States–Cuban relations, see Lester D. Langley, *The Cuban Policy of the United States* (New York: John Wiley and Sons, Inc., 1968).

22. Langley, p. 344. Thomson, pp. 257–58. Also see Robert Smith's account on pp. 147–50.

and radical university elements "whose theories [were] frankly communistic."[23] Welles broached the subject of sending United States warships to Havana and Santiago to preserve order and strengthen Céspedes. Roosevelt refused. Céspedes fell, a victim of army, student and some labor agitation. On September 10, Dr. Ramón Grau San Martín became provisional president of the Republic of Cuba. Roosevelt, acting on Welles' advice, refused to grant diplomatic recognition. The events that followed remain a dark spot in United States–Cuban relations.

Mesmerized by the illusion of success in the Céspedes negotiations and piqued by the popularity of Grau, Welles dedicated himself to the overthrow of the new Cuban government. Throughout the remaining year, personal intrigue, intimidations, and outright prevarications by the ambassador failed to topple the Grau regime—a government supposedly without a popular base of support and ostensibly lacking the necessary characteristics to provide order and stability.

Welles shunned trade-agreement discussions, a slight that further handicapped Grau and created greater economic chaos in Cuba. The moratorium on the public debt, which in May, 1933, Welles had described as a dire necessity for Cuba, was now opposed with equal tenacity when suggested by Grau. Herbert Feis agreed; the State Department, Feis remarked, had "some measure of responsibility toward the American holder of Cuban bonds." Any action on the part of Cuba detrimental to American interests would set a bad precedent for the rest of Latin America.[24]

Some State Department officials such as Judge R. Walton Moore and William Phillips were becoming increasingly disillusioned with Welles; however, although urged by such men as Josephus Daniels to rectify past American inflictions upon Cuba, neither Roosevelt nor Secretary Hull showed much inclination to reverse the ambassador's policy.[25] On November

23. DS 837.00/3753, NA, RG 59.

24. DS 837.51/1612 ½, DS 837.00/4085, NA, RG 59.

25. Cordell Hull, papers, Library of Congress, General Correspondence, Daniels to Hull, September 18, 1933; Moore to Hull, November 27, 1933. William Phillips, diary, 1933–1936, Vol. 1, Houghton Library, November 6, December 9, 1933. Julius Pratt, *Cordell Hull: 1933–1944*, Vol. 1 (New York: Cooper Square Publishers, Inc., 1964), p. 151. Welles worked with

24 Roosevelt personally became involved. He issued a statement intimating that the Grau government had not "clearly possessed the support and the approval of the people." With his alternatives narrowing each day, Grau turned left. When the Cuban government threatened a takeover of certain independent electric light and power plants owned and operated in Cuba by American capital, it met with stern remonstrances from the department. All damages and expenses incurred by the companies as a result of governmental action "would be made the subject of diplomatic representations on the part of the Government of the United States at the proper time."[26]

The *coup de grâce* for the hapless Grau came three days after the suspension of foreign debt service. American pressure increased, and Grau resigned in defeat. On January 18, with Fulgencio Batista's approval, Carlos Mendieta became provisional president. Welles' chicanery, the pressure of business and America's lack of understanding of Cuban life combined to quell a potentially viable economic and social reform movement. On January 30, 1935, Representative Fred L. Crawford of Michigan cited an investigation by the Commission on Cuban Affairs. Bank ownership of the Cuban sugar mills, the commission reported, was extensive. The National City Bank and the Royal Bank of Canada, for example, each owned at least nine mills. The Chase National Bank owned three, the National Shawmut Bank of Boston controlled the Macarend sugar mill, and Armour and Company owned two mills. The commission condemned Welles for his activities against Grau and suggested that "the recent change in the commercial policy of the United States may tend to resurrect the old economic and political system which the revolution attempted to overthrow." Ambassador Josephus Daniels, writing from Mexico, also voiced his disgust with "the old school of diplomats." To Daniels, Grau represented a demo-

---

Taussig as an intermediary and also had a direct line to Roosevelt. See Taussig, papers, Box 37, Welles to Taussig, December 8, 1933.

26. DS 837.6463/10, NA, RG 59. Also see E. David Cronon, "Interpreting the New Good Neighbor Policy: The Cuban Crisis of 1933," *Hispanic American Historical Review* 39:4 (November 1959) :538–67. Cronon gives ample credit to Josephus Daniels in averting military intervention in Cuba but does not give adequate treatment to American economic coercion in the island.

cratic reformer supported by the majority of the Cuban people. The United States, he said, must put an end to diplomats who exploited Cuba. On the subject of dictating the Cuban government, he warned, "We made the mistake of imposing Céspedes on Cuba."[27] As Daniels and the coming years attested, America's diplomatic triumph in Cuba was a Pyrrhic victory.

On January 23, 1934, the Roosevelt Administration granted speedy recognition to the Mendieta regime. Jefferson Caffery, the newly appointed ambassador, arrived in Cuba in time to sift through the diplomatic rubble left in the wake of Welles' capers. On April 11, 1934, Mendieta decreed a moratorium on amortization but not interest payments on the external debt to ease Cuba's financial straits. What had been considered an anathema for Grau San Martín was now tolerated by the Roosevelt Administration. Roosevelt likewise authorized the Treasury Department to provide immediate financial assistance to the incoming administration. Also, the Administration established the second Export-Import Bank to grant credits to promote American export trade only in Cuba.[28]

Caffery now took up the reciprocity discussions with marked enthusiasm. Since the negotiators of the trade agreement never contemplated the extension of American and Cuban concessions to third nations, the impetus toward economic nationalism intensified. The reason why no real disagreement surfaced between the economic nationalists like Peek and the State Department was because both agreed in principle as to ends and means in the reciprocity agreement. The department refused to recognize that the bilateral arrangement offered to Havana might conflict with the principles of liberal trade and set a dangerous precedent for future negotiations. Washington's tentative schedule of proposed concessions on United States agricultural products listed preferentials ranging from 20 to 50 per cent. The case of lard is a telling example. The Cuban rate on lard, set at $20.21 per hundred kilos, virtually prohibited lard imports. Henry Wallace

27. DS 837.00/4176, NA, RG 59. Hull, papers, Daniels to Hull, July 10, 1934. U. S., Congress, *Congressional Record*, 74th Cong., 1st sess., 1935, 79, pt. 2:1281–83.

28. DS 102.81 Habana/574; 837.51/1615A, NA, RG 59. Edward O. Guerrant, *Roosevelt's Good Neighbor Policy* (Albuquerque: University of New Mexico Press, 1950), p. 100.

and the Department of Agriculture initially insisted that the Department of State press for a reduction to $3.21 with a 25 per cent United States preferential. Later, he backed down to $5.00 per hundred kilos.

A touch of economic nationalism infected other departments as well. The Treasury Department suggested that United States rate reduction on sugar would deprive the treasury of $23,000,000 per year and agreed to this reduction only if it could be partially made up by additional revenue derived from the profits of such export products as lard. The chief of the Division of the American Republics, Laurence Duggan, suggested that these demands "will probably raise a storm of criticism." Also, he added, such a reduction would destroy the Cuban lard industry.[29] Since Henry Wallace represented a vital cog in the reciprocity scheme, Hull deemed his support essential. Every effort was made to include Wallace's demands. Hull could ill afford a Peek–Wallace rapprochement.[30] Cuba's incipient industry rated secondary consideration.

By early spring America's policy regarding preferentials had crystalized. The United States would seek increased preferentials on items for which she possessed a competitive advantage or enjoyed a substantial share of the Cuban market. Hull considered a 50 per cent preferential desirable only to stabilize the Cuban market or to thwart foreign competition. In this way, suggested Welles, the United States could save real concessions for the more important products.[31] On the question of raising Cuban tariff rates on third nations as suggested by the Jessup report, Assistant Secretary Francis Sayre wrote:

> The Department considers that the general rule should be to seek no increase of rates of duty on importations from foreign countries.
>
> The above stated principle is one which the Department wishes strictly to follow in all ordinary circumstances and conditions.

29. DS 611.3731/559, /925; 611.3731/614A, NA, RG 59. For the importance of lard in American agricultural export trade, see TC, *Hogs and Hog Products*, Report No. 143, 2d series (GPO, 1941).

30. Peek, papers, Box 15, Coulter to Peek, July 13, 1934.

31. DS 611.3731/552, NA, RG 59. Hull also appeared very interested in abolishing Cuba's 30 per cent surtax. Also see DS 611.3731/631, /777, NA, RG 59.

He went on to equivocate: "It may be that in regard to some of the items in question it will be found advisable to depart from the general principle laid down above."[32] Herbert Feis appeared even more uncomfortable. Feis saw increased tariff rates on such nations as Japan as a way of enabling the United States to forestall competition more effectively.[33]

Commercial attachés Albert Nufer, Walter Donnelly, and Harry Turkel in Havana likewise barraged the Department of State with grim predictions of Washington's inability to compete successfully in the Cuban market without both substantial preferentials and increased tariff rates on all competitors. They proposed that the United States prevent Cuba's tariff duties from becoming so high that they encouraged the establishment of new industries in Cuba.[34]

Visibly lacking in the rhetoric of both the economic nationalists and the liberals was the confidence and buoyancy of the Yankee trader. The economic nationalist never shared the faith and security of American commercial superiority. In essence, far from being the catalyst for economic nationalism, the myths and assumptions of the Yankee trader found greater equanimity in the polemics of liberal trade. But ironically, in America's commercial relations with Cuba, even the liberal trader was not immune to temptation. In July, 1934, Hull reversed American policy on the question of preferentials and ordered a reexamination of all products for which the United States needed more than a 50 per cent advance. Hull viewed "the continuance of conditions with no end in sight, which have severely handicapped our trade in certain highly competitive items" as ample justification for his proposals.[35] American commercial attachés responded with alacrity. Harry Turkel reported that the United States needed a 60 per cent preferential in rayon textiles to forestall "the possibility of the manufacture of such textiles in Cuba in the near future."[36]

Laurence Duggan also demonstrated American commercial fears in Cuba when he suggested that the United States shift the

32. DS 611.3731/581A, NA, RG 59.
33. DS 611.3731/593, NA, RG 59.
34. DS 611.3731/577, /587, NA, RG 59. Also see *FR*, 1934, 5:129–34.
35. DS 611.3731/732A, NA, RG 59.
36. DS 611.3731/893, NA, RG 59.

unit of measure on certain American exports such as razor blades from weight to quantity and increase the general rate. These manipulations would thereby give the United States an ad valorem advantage of 200 per cent in the Cuban market. "Although this appears excessive," remarked Duggan, "Mr. Nufer states that it is necessary if we are to retain our share of the market."[37]

Other trade matters remained unsolved. On the subject of bindings (specified rates that each nation obligates itself not to increase), the department favored implementation only on specified items and not on all tariff products listed in the treaty. With the exception of Feis, the department rejected a binding of the absolute preference (the dollar spread between the general and United States rate) "since it is not in a position to make a similar concession to Cuba." Welles and Hull also agreed that to bind Cuban duties on third powers opened the United States up for criticism. On the question of exchange control, the Treasury Department, the Office of the Special Adviser to the President on Foreign Trade, and Herbert Feis believed that the United States needed an exchange control agreement to safeguard American trade. Hull and Welles disagreed. Nor did the Treasury Department seem anxious to push the matter, since they did not want to impair Washington's ability "to impose such foreign exchange regulations as it considers necessary."[38]

Hull also remained adamant in his desire that no quantitative restrictions be placed on American or Cuban products with the exception of sugar and tobacco. On these commodities the United States would lower the duty rate but maintain the quota. The Cubans feared that the prevailing rates on sugar and tobacco might terminate with the agricultural adjustment program and, therefore, wanted a guarantee of the maintenance of these rates throughout the life of the reciprocity treaty.[39]

American commercial experts Nufer, Donnelly, and Turkel also opposed a Cuban export tax on sugar, arguing that an increased United States preferential would diffuse more profit throughout the island if it went to the sugar producers rather than the government. The export tax, they argued, "would probably be spent in a series of social experiments, the political

37. DS 611.3731/612A, NA, RG 59.
38. DS 611.3731/609A, /684, /733, /879, NA, RG 59.
39. DS 611.3731/817, /875, NA, RG 59.

expedience of which would doubtlessly outweigh their economic usefulness." The commercial attachés also opposed Cuba's administration of the export duty, believing that Cuba could not be counted upon to do it properly. The suggestion amounted to a deprivation of Cuban sovereignty. Still, it caused few misgivings in the department. It was also a sad commentary on the United States' resistance to social change in Cuba. And, there was still another reason for this truculence. Underlying the department's opposition to Cuba's export duty plan was the fear that Grau San Martín might possibly return to power and utilize the revenue.[40]

On the question of the most efficient method with which to effect the Cuban Trade Treaty, the American negotiators favored a decree-law rather than the more complicated executive agreement. The decree-law also had the advantage of appearing to be an autonomous act by Cuba. Also, where Cuba's increases in the general duty affected third nations, "they would be only indirectly attributable to the United States."[41]

On matters of fiscal and commercial policy in Cuba, America's interests sometimes appeared to conflict. As Ambassador Caffery intimated to Hull, if Cuba granted the United States trade concessions she would have to find new ways to make up the deficit. Higher taxes were certainly out of the question. "I do not know" said Caffery, "how the Government is going to meet the situation." What American commercial interests urged, American financial interests feared. A loss of revenue from tariff concessions might well have stimulated Cuban fiscal irresponsibility and prejudiced American financial interests. On August 14, 1934, Cuba imposed a complete moratorium on the payment of the debt principal until 1942. The moratorium was mainly designed to protect the reorganization of the sugar industry. Grosvenor Jones, chief of the Finance and Investment Division of the Department of Commerce, severely criticized the decree and urged the State Department to shorten the moratorium. J. Reuben Clark, president of the Foreign Bondholders Protective Council, likewise importuned the department for redress. Special adviser to the President on foreign trade, George Peek, stressed the fact that

40. *BFDC*, NA, RG 40, 344 Cuba, Nufer, Donnell, and Turkel to Caffery, June 21, 1934.

41. DS 611.3731/620, NA, RG 59.

$32,000,000 of bonds held by American investors were in complete default as to interest. The State Department's position, however, remained firm. Increased commercial activity would be "of indirect benefit to the bondholders."[42] Commercial activity also enhanced the protection of America's direct investments in Cuba.

American–Cuban trade negotiations continued throughout the summer months of 1934. The abrogation of the Platt Amendment, the removal of Machado, and the overthrow of Grau San Martín had eased political friction between the United States and Cuba. Now, reasoned Hull, the United States must begin to stimulate Cuba's economic rehabilitation through reciprocal trade negotiations. Only through economic prosperity would the Pearl of the Antilles ever find political stability.[43]

On May 9, 1934, the Jones-Costigan Act placed sugar as a commodity under AAA restrictions. The law apportioned a fixed quota on Cuban and insular sugar imports to the United States with the proviso that "upon the termination of the Jones-Costigan sugar legislation and in the absence of any similar legislation providing for quotas," duties on products classified under paragraphs 501 and 502 would automatically be restored to the prevailing rates less the preference of 20 per cent. Cuba received a quota of 1,902,000 short tons and a reduced duty from $.02 to $.015 per pound. The impetus for this action seems to have come not from the Tariff Committee but from the State Department.[44] With the Cuban sugar market safely limited as to quantity exported to the United States by the quota system, real tariff bargaining began in earnest.

On July 3, 1934, a press release stated Washington's intention to negotiate a reciprocity treaty with Cuba. On August 8 Caffery sent Hull the tentative concessions, which totaled nearly 300 pages. Obviously it ranked as one of the most detailed trade analyses concluded by the department. The treaty bound rates against future Cuban increases and internal taxes. Because of

42. DS 837.51/1695, /1704–1707 4/6; 611.3731/576, /800, NA, RG 59. This subject will be taken up in greater detail in a future chapter.

43. See Hull's rather lengthy communiqué to Caffery on July 26 in DS 611.3731/841A, NA, RG 59.

44. United States, Congress, *Congressional Record*, 73d Cong., 2d sess., 1934, 78, pt. 8: 8399–8400. DS 611.3731/841A, NA, RG 59.

the special category created by concessions to Cuba, the United States adopted a "limited third column of tariff duties." America replaced its traditional single-column autonomous tariff with a multiple-schedule tariff. The treaty would remain effective for three years or until denounced with six months notice.

On the American side, Washington allowed unlimited entry of manganese. Avocados received the same treatment from June to September of each year. American concessions on sugar (the duty reduction from $.015 per pound to $.009 per pound increased the preferential from 20 per cent to 52 per cent), pineapple, and rum were acceptable to the Cubans. No concession was made on other kinds of alcohol.

On the other hand, the United States gained important concessions on meats, lard, vegetable oils, wheat flour, rice, potatoes, lumber, iron, and steel products. Havana, however, vigorously attacked requests on hog products and a quota on Cuban tobacco. The Cuban government also opposed the removal of consumption taxes on wheat and lard imports as well as reductions of import duties on oils, which would ruin the palmiche and peanut oil industries of Cuba. Washington, in any case, kept up the pressure. In dismay, one Cuban official remarked to Caffery, "Are you trying to force this treaty down our throats?"[45] On August 24 Havana swallowed the agreement.

The signing of the treaty prompted the *Diario de la Marina* on the same day to carry an article by Roberto A. Netto, chairman of Cuba's technical delegation. The article stated that the Cuban cabinet and not the technical staff surrendered to American pressure. Netto also predicted the ruination of Cuba's lard and oil industries.[46]

The United States–Cuban treaty, because of its bilateral and exclusive nature, extended tariff reduction to no third nations either with or without unconditional most-favored-nation status. Roosevelt had taken a giant step away from the principles of the

45. DS 611.3731/836, NA, RG 59.
46. DS 611.3731/554, /814, /836, /841, /857, /1024, /1006, /1054, NA, RG 59. Tasca, p. 42. For the text of the treaty see DS, *Reciprocal Trade Agreement Between the United States of America and the Republic of Cuba* (GPO, 1942); or the Spanish text in *Gaceta Oficial de la Republica de Cuba: Edicion Extraordinaria*, No. 79, 30 de agusto de 1934. For a listing of the Schedule see *Gaceta Oficial de la Republica de Cuba*, número 54, 1 de septiembre de 1934, tomo III.

Open Door that had been espoused in other negotiations. To no one's surprise, the Office of the Special Adviser favored the extension of the Cuban exemptions to the whole of Latin America. Peek believed the Cuban example represented the model to follow in all future negotiations. Nonetheless, Peek realized the unconditional most-favored-nation clause was not dead but "merely stunned" for the moment by the Cuban negotiations. He was particularly pleased by a memorandum from the Division of Latin American Affairs that clearly indicated the State Department's cognizance of certain illiberal features of the reciprocity agreement. "The trade agreement provided for increased preferences on all of the items supplied by Japan which are of interest to the United States except for the coarser grades of textiles." Welles remarked to Duggan that to eliminate Japanese competition in certain textile lines might make it necessary for Cuba to double the United States preference to 60 per cent. Peek, no doubt, supported the proposal.

Even Hull and Secretary Wallace, who believed that United States duty reductions should be made on products whose cost of production appeared "unduly high in comparison to those in more favored areas," disavowed their own principle when they artificially tried to stop foreign competition in Cuba. As Hull remarked to Roosevelt, "exceptional concessions" for American products were sought in the Cuban agreement to offset low prices and reduced cost of production by our competitors.[47] Most definitely this kind of American benevolence did not build economic stability in underdeveloped societies.

Business optimism increased with the Cuban treaty. The Rubber Manufacturers Association, the General Motors Export Company, the Automobile Manufacturing Association, and the Manufacturers Export Association among others sent their congratulations to Hull for work well done. Sizeable orders for American products, both industrial and agricultural, were placed. Orders for American products included over one million pounds of lard, one million pounds of pickled meats, and 5,000 automobile tires. The United Fruit Company's cargo shipments to Cuba were the largest on record since 1920. Press releases by the State Department throughout September and October glee-

47. Peek, papers, Box 15, August 15, 1934, Robert F. Martin to Peek. DS 611.3731/1156½, /1201A, /1215, NA, RG 59.

fully reported the revivification of American export trade to Cuba. Throughout 1934, Caffery sent to the department an abundance of documents verifying individual business gains in the Cuban trade.[48]

In fact, American optimism at times went beyond the bounds of propriety. Understandably American press releases, which showed enormous gains for American commerce, adversely affected the Mendieta regime, since these reports prompted Communists and other leftist elements to attack the reciprocity treaty. With tongue in cheek, Laurence Duggan said that their grounds for criticism "may be ill-founded." On November 23, Welles ordered a State Department report pointing to the mutually advantageous effects of the trade agreement program.[49] However, a Department of Commerce release on December 4, 1934, suggested at length that America had made a good bargain with Cuba. American trade had increased, but more importantly, "Imports from Cuba declined sharply from the September level and were lower in value than in October 1933." Havana newspapers quickly picked up the theme of commercial disparity. On December 22 the State Department, obviously disturbed by these developments, reprimanded the Commerce Department's tactlessness. Welles advised Roper to provide "a most careful scrutiny of interpretative comment in primarily statistical studies" because of "the extreme political sensitiveness of Cuba today." "I am not, of course," clarified Welles, "suggesting the suppression of factual data, but merely that any opinions expressed be entirely warranted and fully supported by the facts." Needless to say, the Commerce Department took the hint.[50]

Another interdepartmental problem that taxed the State Department was Cuba's threat to American insular possessions. Blanton Winship, governor of Puerto Rico, probably best explained his country's concern. Puerto Rico, he argued, competed for the American market with Cuba and any concession to Cuba worked to the detriment of his island. Lacking a responsive ear in the State Department, Winship turned to the Interior Department for solace. On October 13 Assistant Secre-

48. Phillips, diary, 1933–1936, Vol. 3, August 28, 1934. DS 611.3731/1000, /1034, /1079, /1046, /1148, NA, RG 59

49. DS 611.3731/1216, NA, RG 59.

50. DS 611.3731/1195, NA, RG 59.

tary of the Interior Oscar L. Chapman denounced the Cuban reciprocity treaty in a letter sent to the State Department. Puerto Rico, he said, "was grossly discriminated against and treated as a foreign territory." Henry Grady of the Trade Agreements Division, obviously ruffled at Chapman's assertiveness, exclaimed that the letter "might well have originated in Republican Campaign Headquarters rather than another governmental department presumably committed to the same policy. We will have a good deal of this sort of thing from the Department of Interior." That department, however, did not retreat. Their next proposal suggested that any changes contemplated in United States tariff rates should be submitted to the Department of Interior. The State Department rejected the idea on the grounds that it gave the Department of Interior the right to veto any tariff concessions considered adverse to American territories. Under Secretary Phillips replied to Interior Secretary Harold Ickes that the Chapman letter was both "incorrect and unwarranted." To Ickes' dismay, State Department lines held firm. The departments of Commerce, Agriculture, and Treasury refused to break with Hull. The Interior Department begrudgingly retreated.[51]

As to the actual United States–Cuban trade statistics, America's agricultural exports accorded concessions by Cuba revealed an increase of 174 per cent during the first year of the agreement, while nonagricultural products granted concessions increased by 86 per cent. On the other hand, leading United States products not accorded concessions increased by only 33 per cent. Cuban agricultural exports to the United States that had been granted concessions increased by 281 per cent, but when sugar was excluded the increase diminished to a paltry 17 per cent.

Monoculture, not viability, was the chief result of the treaty. The proportion of United States total export trade taken by Cuba increased from 2.1 per cent in 1934 to 2.7 per cent in 1936, while the proportion of American merchandise in Cuba's total import increased from 56.2 per cent in 1934 to 58.3 per cent in 1935 and to 64.4 per cent in 1936. In 1933 the United States exports to Cuba totaled $22,674,000, and Cuban exports to the United States tallied $57,112,000. By 1938 America exported to Cuba $75,152,000 worth of products and imported $108,363,000 of Cuban goods. Even as late as 1938, when the value of American

51. DS 611.3731/1080½, /1145½, /1146, NA, RG 59.

exports to Cuba witnessed its first decline since the passage of the trade agreement, the competitive position of the United States improved. In 1938 the United States balance of payments with Cuba witnessed the third year in a row during which the American deficit had shrunk even without tabulating the return from American direct investments in Cuba. The reciprocity agreement and the Jones-Costigan Act also halted the decline in Cuban sugar exports to the United States. No doubt the benefits, both direct and indirect, accorded the United States from the reciprocity agreement far outweighed the concessions granted Cuba. In 1934 the United States received 24.6 per cent of her total consumption of sugar from Cuba; in 1935, 30.7 per cent; 1936, 29.8 per cent; 1937, 31.7 per cent; 1938, 29.1 per cent; 1939, 24.8 per cent; and 1940, 27.9 per cent.[52]

Certainly some of the indirect results of the reciprocity agreement contradicted many of the liberal precepts that constituted, as Hull so vigorously argued, the only alternative to economic nationalism. The Open Door did not apply in Cuba. An import-control law in March, 1935, as well as other surtaxes, applied discriminatory treatment to Japanese textiles. The decree-law of April 4, 1936, provided for import surtaxes on rice and other basic commodities and introduced an import-quota system applied in such a manner as to favor nations such as the United States. Cuba also failed to promote the principle of the most-favored-nation clause, even going so far as to denounce her obligations with Portugal, Japan, and Italy. In 1938 only Great Britain, France, and Spain received most-favored-nation treatment from Cuba. The record of America's Caribbean protegé in the promotion of liberal trade principles fell far short of the standards set by the United States for the rest of Latin America.[53]

The agreement with Cuba impeded further business disorganization in Cuba. (Amusingly, Under Secretary Phillips recalled in his diary the "somewhat unusual procedure" of the Roosevelt Administration when it defrayed the expenses of a delegation of visiting Cuban businessmen who came to express their appreciation of the reciprocity agreement.) But the real problems of mass suffering and deprivation in Cuba remained

52. *FTUS*, 1936, TPS No. 174 (1938), pp. 82–83. *FTLA*, pt. 2, pp. 236, 253, 266; DS 611.3731/1391½, /1710, NA, RG 59.

53. *FTLA*, pt. 2, pp. 230–34.

unsolved. The benefits of the trade agreement, as Vice-Consul Hernan C. Vogenitz reported in 1935, passed largely into the hands of American sugar interests. He warned prophetically that "while a few American corporations might gain larger profits through such a program, the policy will most certainly lead to internal disorders in Cuba," which would result in either American intervention or a "social and economic program perhaps still more radical than that carried out by Mexico."[54] To an extent, American increased preferentials on sugar represented a rather subtle method of keeping Cuba in economic colonialism, since United States capital, looking for the best and most remunerative investment, again went back to sugar and retarded Cuba's efforts to escape the perils of monoculture. As Cuba's ex-secretary of agriculture, Amedeo López Castro, stated in *Noticiero Mercantil* May 20, 1939, the trade agreement "was entered into with sugar interests in view, sacrificing certain incipient experiments and even some sectors of national production which began to convert themselves into sources of real wealth."[55]

As a historian rather than a propagandist, one is wary of efforts to take historical circumstances and weave them into a rational and conscious conspiracy. Policymaking, especially in the U.S. Department of State, hardly if ever follows a consistent pattern, much less the oneness and sense of purpose conceived in terms of economic colonialism and exploitation of the Latin American continent. To believe this is to do injustice to the idealism of such men as Cordell Hull. The error lies in their conceptualization of the role and function of the diplomat. The best interests of the United States and the promotion of national security in terms of the protection of American lives and property abroad, as well as the promotion of American trade and investment, is the shared view of the businessman. And, more often than not, the men in the higher echelons of decisionmaking come from the world of business. As the history of United States–Cuban relations attests, this juxtaposition of men and ideas was a harbinger of disaster. The years preceding World War II offer a classic example of how the State Department defined the national interests in traditional concepts and how this definition failed

54. Phillips, diary, 1933–1936, Vol. 5, August 2, 1935. DS 611.3731/1217, /1570, NA, RG 59.

55. DS 611.3731/2038, NA, RG 59.

to promote the economic and social transformation of Latin America. With these observations in mind, one can begin to examine the remaining decade of United States–Cuban relations.

Unfortunately, Cuba's financial condition following the trade agreement steadily worsened.[56] In February, 1935, Cuba's public debt amounted to $149,477,280; some $50,000,000 of which made up the external debt, while the public works debt totaled $80,000,000, the sugar stabilization plan accounted for nearly $10,000,000, and miscellaneous debts came to nearly $10,000,000. Cuba, hard pressed to make domestic ends meet, received a continuous barrage of complaints from the Foreign Bondholder's Protective Council (established under the tutelage of the State Department) and American banking concerns to resume debt payment. The State Department also applied pressure. Throughout the summer of 1936 Shepard Morgan, vice-president of the Chase National Bank, and D. G. Munro, representative of the Foreign Bondholder's Protective Council, tried without success to negotiate a favorable debt settlement. What made the problem all the more serious for Havana was the fact that these importunities influenced policymakers such as Duggan and Welles to forgo export-import credits to Cuba. On June 6, 1938, Duggan stated the United States position. Because of Cuba's default on its public works obligation, "The Department consistently maintained that as a matter of policy it would not be wise for the Export-Import Bank to participate in credits to the Cuban government or departments thereof." Furthermore, export-import credit to finance the purchase and coinage of silver by the Cuban government was also to be stopped.[57]

Cuba's financial problems also prolonged necessary readjustments in the United States–Cuban reciprocity treaty resulting from the unconstitutionality of the Agricultural Adjustment Administration. AAA had granted concessions on tobacco, Cuba's second greatest export commodity. The restoration of duties

56. For an excellent and detailed analysis of many aspects of Cuban economic and financial life, see, Wyatt McGaffey and Clifford R. Barnett, *Twentieth-Century Cuba: The Background of the Castro Revolution* (Garden City: Doubleday and Company, 1965).

57. DS 837.51/1772, /1782, /1889½, /1898½, /1909½, /1975, /2040½, /2105A–2106½, /2141, /2151–2153, NA, RG 59. For the debt negotiations see Chapter 6. For Export-Import Bank discussions see Chapter 8.

on tobacco on March 17, 1936, would have a very adverse reaction in Cuba, Caffery warned. Nevertheless, from mid-March, 1937, to December 22, 1939, Cuba's preferential on tobacco exports to the United States remained suspended.[58]

Cuba became even more alarmed over the prospects that her sugar exports might also fall within the jurisdiction of the United States Supreme Court. With the invalidation of the Agricultural Adjustment Administration processing tax in early 1936, and the soon-to-expire Jones-Costigan Act, Cuba began to urge renegotiation of the commercial treaty. The State Department, however, opposed opening up the trade discussions again because of powerful domestic interests, the United States' reduced bargaining position, and the increasing independence and nationalism of the Cuban people. A memorandum by Walter Donnelly of the Division of the American Republics urged "sitting tight at this time and letting well enough alone." J. Butler Wright, the newly appointed ambassador to Havana, agreed. In 1937 Congress passed the Sugar Act, which again granted Cuba approximately the same quota on raw sugar, but the act decreased the direct consumption quota on processed sugar.[59]

The Havana government refused to be satisfied with American generosity. Colonel Fulgencio Batista y Zaldivar, chief of staff of the army from 1934 to 1940 and the dominant personality on the Cuban scene as well as of more dissident political elements throughout the island, increasingly challenged Roosevelt's tutelage. Washington's line, too, hardened. Cuba had to be taught fiscal responsibility and respect for American investments. Batista's response was to challenge United States economic supremacy by building a popular base of support far left of what Washington deemed as wholesome to American interests. Matters appeared on a collision course.

Cuba's efforts in 1938–1939 to negotiate a supplementary trade agreement, in the hope of further sugar reductions from $.09 per pound to $.075 per pound, and to restitute her tobacco market became the immediate issues around which more substantive matters revolved. In October, 1938, Batista intimated his intentions to pay off bonds held by United States investors requisite to a

58. *FTLA*, pt. 3, pp. 209–12. 611.3731/1404, 1613½, NA, RG 59.
59. DS 811.6135/301; 811.6131/370; 611.3731/1589, /1598, /1607, /1633, NA, RG 59.

State Department announcement regarding an intention to negotiate a supplemental trade agreement. The department, obviously pleased but suspicious at these overtures, refused to move until after the November elections. But the department had other problems that were more pressing. In January, 1936, a Cuban Decree Law Number 522 distributed to the sugar mills a production allotment available to Cuba under American legislation. This decree, Duggan noted, resulted largely from discussions and negotiations within the industry itself and provided for maximum protection for Cuba's large sugar mills (mostly owned by United States interests) as distinguished from the smaller mills (owned primarily by Cubans). The decree would expire in 1941. Batista had to be told that in order to keep his sugar quota and obtain a supplementary trade agreement, the essence of the 1936 law had to remain in effect. American-owned companies that produced direct consumption sugar and syrup in Cuba (such as the Hershey Company) had to be protected. Duggan's proposal, remarked State Department official Henry Deimel, "is a question of protecting American investments abroad rather than of the protection and promotion of our foreign trade" and represented "a departure from the established policy of dealing only with matters relating more strictly to our foreign trade in negotiating trade agreements." Either Deimel had been fast asleep throughout the early New Deal negotiations with Cuba or else he mistakenly believed that the essence of reciprocity agreements with other Latin American nations was identical in purpose with Cuba.[60]

By late 1938 the Department of State had begun a searching review of its policy toward Batista and his coterie. Batista's flirtations with the left were matched by his inability to establish economic order. As a department memorandum by Duncan White put it, "The monetary, banking and fiscal difficulties of Cuba appear to be approaching a comparatively critical stage." Batista's financial irresponsibility created a critical economic situation with internal political repercussions. Without an extensive national capital market, Cuba could not finance budget deficits in the same manner as financially mature countries. Cuba

60. DS 837.51 Public Works Debt/133; 611.3731/1659, /1878, /1883; 837.61351/2131, NA, RG 59.

tried inflating the currency, securing foreign loans, and the accumulation of a floating debt of unpaid bills as means of covering the deficits. Loans to Cuba would only prolong the problem. As White's memorandum confessed, "In the long run the burden of present Cuban policies can be expected to fall to a major extent upon existing private investment in Cuba. . . . Unless the United States Government has some especially strong political motives in regard to Cuba," the present government should be allowed to fall.[61]

America's suspicions of Batista seemed confirmed when the Cuban leader sponsored a mortgage revaluation scheme in the fall of 1938. Batista hinted that America's failure to grant extra concessions on sugar and tobacco through a revision of the trade agreement necessitated a stringent mortgage revaluation plan. All mortgages contracted prior to 1930 would be scaled down 50 per cent and mortgages contracted between 1930 and 1934 by lesser amounts. Total Cuban mortgages equalled approximately $450,000,000, the American share of which approximated $150,000,000.

Privately, the department reacted in horror to this new kind of economic independence. "Dangerous in the extreme" and "confiscatory" uttered Ellis Briggs and Emilio Collado. Publicly, Hull's men worked to scale down mortgages to a predetermined proportion of the present value of the property. While maintaining that a mortgage readjustment constituted a legitimate prerogative of the Cuban government, the department also believed that it should be fair to both creditors and debtors. The American bankers were also reminded that a "rigid attitude" on their part only exacerbated matters. If a formula could be reached that circumvented confiscation, then the department would not interfere in the mortgage situation.[62]

The American position quickly hardened. Under Secretary Welles stated unequivocally that Cuba must come to an economic settlement with the United States prior to further assistance. No longer would the Export-Import Bank extend credit to assist the Cuban government in the coinage of additional silver pesos. Warren Lee Pierson, president of the Export-Import Bank, ar-

61. DS 837.51/2168, NA, RG 59.
62. DS 837.51/2115, /2221, /2224, /2277, NA, RG 59.

rived in Cuba to relay the message. In addition, he added that Cuba's mortgage revaluation plan justified the Export-Import Bank's resistance to finance new public works projects. But, stated Pierson, export-import credits were also contingent upon Cuba's payment of the Public Works Debt held in large part by the United States.

At first glance Pierson's actions may now appear strange. As president of a separate government agency one might expect a more independent line. Such was not the case. He was a hand-picked State Department man, and the Export-Import Bank (as will be shown later) by the late 1930s utilized its capital resources for more than the promotion of American exports.[63] The bank, in fact, became one of the most powerful weapons in the department's diplomatic arsenal to combat foreign competition and Latin American nationalism.

Pierson's threats did not deter Batista. He, too, reached deeper into his bag of tricks. Seemingly because of a decline in the sugar industry, Cuba enacted a decree on June 10, 1939, which required sugar exporters to turn over 20 per cent of the foreign exchange produced by their exports in return for debased silver currency. America's sugar interests in Cuba, as expected, caused a clamorous reaction. On July 19 Welles instructed Ambassador Wright to inform the Cuban government that, added to American financial claims and the credit moratorium, the June 10 monetary law must also be changed before American economic cooperation would be forthcoming. The same day, the State Department considered suspending negotiations for a supplemental trade agreement with Cuba.[64]

Anxiety and bewilderment characterized the department's attitude toward Cuba. The halcyon days of 1934, when officials joyously predicted an end to political and economic chaos in Cuba, seemed a cruel joke. Reciprocal trade no longer appeared to be the cheap panacea for Cuba's ills. Frustrated, the department turned on its own henchmen. Even the American bankers (the National City Bank of New York and the Chase National, in particular) fell from favor. The American banks, chided Collado, have "failed to provide adequate banking facilities to meet

63. DS 837.51/2234A, /2261, NA, RG 59.
64. DS 837.51/2364, /2410–2411, /2424, NA, RG 59.

the needs of the Cuban economy." Only the sugar industry, he added, had received adequate banking facilities.[65]

Batista, undismayed at the furor he created, refused to buckle under American pressure. Violating the confidential nature of the trade negotiations, the Colonel leaked America's proposed concessions to Cuba. Cuba, maintained Batista, had not received "real reciprocity." A department memorandum prepared by Philip Bonsal reported that, "The Cuban Communist party, which supports Colonel Batista, has gone on record as opposing the supplemental trade agreement [since] pro-Fascist reactionaries headed by Mr. Welles" had drawn it up. Cuba was drifting ever closer to economic independence. The department had had enough. Trade developments, conditioned by Cuba's discharging of United States debts, the monetary law, and the mortgage moratorium had to materialize by August 31, 1939. If by that time Washington did not have satisfaction, Hull would terminate negotiations for a supplemental trade agreement.[66]

The department's threat fell on unresponsive ears; Batista did not appear impressed. Washington tactfully retreated. Hull extended the deadline to September 9, but with no effect. The secretary decided that the political implications of a suspension of trade negotiations did not merit such action. As a counter-move, on September 12, 1939, the Roosevelt Administration suspended the Cuban sugar quota and immediately raised the import duty on sugar to $.015 per pound, leaving the way open for discussion of a supplemental trade agreement. Ambassador J. Butler Wright reported that the news came as "a great shock" to Batista, who was now belatedly coming around to the United States position.[67]

The department took fleeting encouragement from the course of political events in Cuba. President Federico Laredo Brú, a protegé of Batista, opposed the severity of the moratorium legislation. Rumor had it that Brú would veto the measure in order to propitiate the United States. It would also allow Batista to save face. This happy arrangement prompted State Department official Ellis Briggs to remark, "Everyone will be converted into

65. DS 837.51/2457½, NA, RG 59.
66. DS 611.3731/2048½, /2059, /2108, NA, RG 59.
67. DS 837.51/2469A; 611.3731/2126, NA, RG 59.

one big happy family."[68] [My emphasis.] Batista, however, thought differently. Cuba, born out of the wedlock of war and suffering and the pains of political and economic illegitimacy, would not return home a prodigal child.

As confidently predicted by the department, President Brú in October, 1939, vetoed the mortgage revaluation bill. If the entire episode had been merely a political ruse by Batista designed to show his independence from the United States, then the Cuban leader could now retreat gracefully. However, the Colonel immediately undertook plans to override Brú's veto and "flaunt" the United States. Batista threatened to retain the pay of the Cuban house of representatives unless the mortgage bill was sustained. He also moved to solidify his power with both the military and leftist groups. "Would we prefer," queried Bonsal, "to be flaunted or flouted" by Batista?[69]

One of the most important communiqués that attempted to explain the meaning of Batista's actions came from Ambassador Wright in November, 1939. The Cuban leader, maintained Wright, had made it clear that he intended to follow a cooperative line with the United States in international affairs but complete independence in internal affairs. Therefore, the mortgage bill, as Batista saw it, was purely a domestic measure. Batista had patterned his course of action after Lázardo Cárdenas of Mexico. The Colonel's base of support shifted ever increasingly toward labor unions such as those sponsored in Mexico. Batista was "actually fostering the Communist party," upon which he depended more and more for support.[70]

Necessity, however, often breeds strange bedfellows. Ambassador Wright's telegraph, delivered to Hull in mid-November, predated the supplementary trade agreement by approximately one month. One can only surmise to what extent the diplomatic and economic pressure exerted by the department produced the desired effects. Cuba, without the United States sugar market, floundered. The United States, without a friendly Cuba, remained strategically vulnerable to Axis activity. A marriage of necessity, if not convenience, was imperative to both sides. Batista's bid for a large measure of economic independence in

68. DS 837.51/2480, NA, RG 59.
69. DS 837.51/2488, /2502, /2508, NA, RG 59.
70. DS 837.61351/2212, NA, RG 59.

the final analysis proved incapable of the ideological commitment necessary to sustain itself. The Colonel reluctantly gave in to American pressure. On December 18, 1939, Cuba signed the Supplemental Trade Agreement with the United States.

The agreement restored the reduced duty on sugar and granted concessions to Cuban tobacco. The supplemental treaty made no mention of Washington's preconditions to Havana, but the implications were palpable to all concerned. Although minor difficulties over debt payment and moratorium legislation remained, the Roosevelt Administration had succeeded in blunting the cutting edge of Cuba's economic program. Many American creditors worked out voluntary readjustments with their Cuban debtors, and the department also worked to have interest rates raised to reduce amortization periods and to exclude obligations contracted after the 1934 moratorium. Debt service on the public works obligations resumed, and American sugar interests remained more or less undisturbed. By 1941 export-import credit flowed freely to Cuba. The same year also witnessed a further American tariff reduction on sugar to $.0075 per pound.[71] By 1942 lend-lease credit filled the coffers of Batista if not the Cuban treasury. Militarily speaking, admitted Duggan, no justification existed for additional lend-lease to Batista, but it could be used to give the Cuban leader political support if and when he needed it.[72]

In retrospect, Ambassador Wright's analysis of Batista was overly alarming. The dictator in 1939 was searching for an ideology. He doubtlessly saw the wave of the future: the potent forces of nationalism and communism. Still, his country did not imitate Cárdenas' Mexico, nor did it avert Castro's Cuba. Economic independence required an end to the peonage of commercial and financial debt to the United States. Yet this was impossible without a radical restructuring of the Cuban political economy to offset American retaliation. These kinds of vast structural changes in turn required an ideology that Batista did not possess in the early years of World War II. Therefore, his bid for economic independence, regardless of his motives,

71. For a description of the 1939 Supplementary Treaty see DS, *The Department of State Bulletin* 1:26: Publication 1417 (December 23, 1939): 729–31. DS 837.51/2437, /2642, /2783; 837.011/404½, /417A, NA, RG 59.
72. DS 837.51/2872, NA, RG 59.

proved abortive. In the end, Batista took the path of least resistance. He made his peace with the capitalist interests, took their aid, lined his pockets, and oppressed his people. Today, in a hemisphere filled with political and ideological acrimony, Batista's bid for leftist support appears as a brief aberration hardly noticed and even less explained. One can only surmise what course Cuban history might have taken had Batista in all earnestness formed a viable leftist coalition. But then, conjecture has always been more sporting than history.

5

Smoking the Brazilians Out

In 1943 a Department of State memorandum revealed that the department's reciprocity agreement had adversely affected both Brazil's industrial development and her balance of trade. The outcry from Brazilian private and official sources to revise the trade treaty in their favor, the author of the memo remarked, should be quickly laid to rest. Washington must "smoke the Brazilians out on this whole problem." The curious feature of the memo, however, lays not so much in its counterrevolutionary position as in its admission that the failure of the New Deal trade program was, paradoxically, its very success. Such was not always the case, as "smoking the Brazilians out" took more time and effort throughout the 1930s than the Department of State had imagined.[1]

During the early 1930s a solution to the continued loss of American trade and investment opportunities in lands south of the Rio Grande severely taxed the energies and resources of the State Department. Brazil was a case in point. Throughout the 1930s, New Deal trade advisers became particularly concerned with the deterioration of trade between the United States and the largest nation in South America. In 1929 the United States imported duty free $203, 200,000 worth of Brazilian goods and $4,500,000 worth of dutiable goods, while exporting $108,500,000 worth of products to Brazil. By 1930 American exports to Brazil decreased by $53,700,000, and Brazilian exports to the United States declined to approximately $130,900,000. The United States balance of payment deficit with Brazil for the same year soared to a record $132,900,000. The year 1931 wit-

1. DS 611.3231/1462A, NA, RG 59. This November 8, 1943, memorandum should not be confused with an Acheson to Caffery note with the same code number.

nessed further reduction in exports; American export trade to Brazil plummeted to $28,500,000, while Brazil's exports to the United States fell to $110,200,000.[2]

Coffee, cane sugar, and crude rubber (in that order) ranked as the three leading imports during the New Deal period. Brazil, of course, exported sizeable quantities of each. The Tariff Commission reported that Brazil placed second only to Argentina as the most important trading nation in Latin America. She also ranked as the fifth-largest supplier of United States imports in the world, supplying 60 to 65 per cent of United States coffee imports.

Brazil was very important financially. As late as 1938, estimates of American holdings of Brazilian dollar bonds having a par value of $298,000,000 gave Brazil the dubious honor of possessing the world's third-largest debt to United States creditors (Canada and Germany ranked first and second, respectively).[3] Direct investments in this nation of the Amazon also ranked of the first order and deserved top official attention.

Unlike Colombia, and to a far greater degree than Cuba, Brazil represented a sizeable export market for American products and a vital source of imports. But unlike Cuba, where America's economic policy waivered between the influence of American sugar investments, financial concerns, and commercial interests, the New Deal's economic policy regarding Brazil primarily revolved around the quest for import and export markets and the elimination of German competition in the political economy of Brazil. As historian Frank McCann, Jr., has suggested, Washington realized that the Open Door in Brazil was the best possible way to ensure America's economic supremacy.

Unlike Colombia and Cuba, the history of American–Brazilian commercial relations during the 1930s witnessed a far more intensive effort, especially on the part of Germany, to control the export-import markets of Brazil for political purposes. And, as the stakes increased, so too did the implications for United States

2. *FTLA*, pt. 2, Report No. 146, 2d Series (1942), pp. 101–4. *Operation*, June, 1934, to April, 1948, pt. 5, Summary, p. 11.

3. *FTLA*, pt. 2, pp. 73, 95, 104; pt. 3, p. 37. *FTUS*, 1935, TPS No. 166, p. 42; 1936, TPS No. 174, p. 98–99. Frank D. McCann, Jr., *The Brazilian-American Alliance, 1937–1945* (Princeton: Princeton University Press, 1973), p. 149.

strategic, military, and diplomatic considerations on the South American continent. Quite naturally, Secretary Hull and his department gained valuable knowledge of the nature of political economy from the Brazilian experience. The department also obtained insights into the limitations of reciprocity agreements as a means to achieve political, ideological, and economic ends.

Brazil, as did most Latin American nations, suffered from a lack of heavy industry. From the days of independence until 1844, Brazil had remained an economic adjunct of the British Empire, tied to a commercial treaty which limited Brazilian duties on English manufacturers to 15 per cent. The dominance of the slave system until near the end of the nineteenth century further retarded the development of a viable economy. Relying primarily on the exportation of agricultural products for market subsistence, Brazil floundered under the pressure of deteriorating prices and increasingly unfavorable terms of trade caused by numerous depressions. Although Brazil could not accurately be described as a monoculture, the country was nevertheless divided into regions concentrating to a large extent upon single products: São Paulo in coffee, Pernambuco in sugar, Bahia in cocoa, Paraná in herva maté, Santos in bananas, and Pará in rubber. These regional monocultures exhausted both soil and men, exposed the finances of both the planters and government to uncontrollable price fluctuations, retarded the growth of industry, and contributed to an unstable social system.[4]

To some degree the Getulio Vargas revolt in 1930 represented the loss of unlimited power by São Paulo and the coffee interests in Brazil. It also strengthened the influence of the military and hastened Brazil along the path of economic nationalism. But if coffee had lost some of its political power, it had not lost its economic power. In March, 1929, the price of Brazilian coffee stood

4. George Wythe, "Brazil: Trends in Industrial Development," in Simon Kuznets, Wilbert E. Moore, and Joseph J. Spengler, eds., *Economic Growth: Brazil, India, Japan* (Durham: Duke University Press, 1955), p. 34. Horace B. Davis, "Brazil's Political and Economic Problems," *FPR* 11: 1 (March 13, 1935) :1–6. José Jobim, *Brazil in the Making* (New York: Macmillan Company, 1943), p. 93. Henry W. Spiegel, *The Brazilian Economy* (Philadelphia: Blakiston Company, 1949), pp. 126–28. Also see the Niemeyer Report submitted by British economic exports in 1931. Lincoln Gordon and Engelbert L. Grommers, *United States Manufacturing Investment in Brazil* (Boston: Center for International Affairs, 1962), pp. 1–3.

at $.248 per pound. By October, 1931, the price had declined to a meager $.076 per pound. Vargas had to react. His attempts, however, at coffee export taxes, crop diversification (mainly through wider use of cotton), and crop destruction (the government destroyed 32 per cent of the 1931–1932 coffee crop and 65 per cent the following growing season) failed to curtail production effectively or to halt the decline in prices.

To meet the crisis, Brazil in 1931 initiated a three-year moratorium on practically all national, state, and municipal debts. Vargas also imposed limited exchange control requiring foreign exchange to be conducted through the Banco do Brasil. Exporters were required to sell a certain percentage of their export bills to the *banco*, the remainder of which could be sold on the free market at a lower value of the milreis. (Because of the lower value of the milreis in the free market, the percentage of export bills deposited with the *banco* realized fewer milreis per unit of foreign currency.) Throughout the remaining decade of the 1930s, Brazil's foreign trade fluctuated greatly because of the use of exchange control, debt service obligations, compensation arrangements, currency depreciation, import controls, tariff charges, and export duties. As Hull would quickly discover, these barriers to freer trade did not vanish with the negotiation of the United States–Brazil treaty but were of such a complex nature as to threaten the very essence of reciprocity itself.[5]

The American Chamber of Commerce for Brazil on May 12, 1931, reported that Brazil had failed to meet payment on its commercial arrears, frozen American capital investment in the sum of $30,000,000, discriminated against the United States in the granting of exchange cover, and imposed excessive tariff and port duties on American exports. The report suggested a bilateral conditional most-favored-nation reciprocity treaty with Brazil granting the United States a guaranteed exchange policy and the payment of American creditors from the proceeds of Brazil's export tax of coffee. If Brazil failed to comply with the United States' demands, then a duty should be placed on Brazil's coffee.

5. Henry W. Spiegel, "Brazil: The State and Economic Growth," in Kuznets, p. 420. José Maria Bello, *A History of Modern Brazil 1889–1964* (Stanford: Stanford University Press, 1966), pp. 279–95. Davis, pp. 8–9. *FTLA*, pt. 2, pp. 73–78; pt. 3, p. 41. Gordon, pp. 3–4.

The State Department, at this juncture, was not opposed to certain suggestions of a bilateral nature. President Hoover and Secretary of State Henry Stimson would try most anything. Their efforts to circumvent trade restrictions met with quick rejection, however. The Brazilian minister of finance refused to grant special exchange facilities or preferences to American exporters, and the Bureau of Foreign and Domestic Commerce failed to consummate a coal-coffee barter deal. These efforts to implement bilateralism ran counter to Hull's later official declarations.[6]

The Roosevelt Administration's first move toward reciprocity discussions came in the summer of 1933. Brazil, Colombia, and Argentina were given top priority. "We believe," remarked Assistant Secretary of State Jefferson Caffery, "that if we attempted more than these Latin American countries at the beginning we would probably find that we would make very little progress with any of them." Of these initial negotiators only Colombia had signed an agreement prior to the June 12, 1934, Trade Expansion Act.

Although the Colombian negotiations progressed rapidly throughout 1933, the Department of State had just reason for including Brazil. The liberal trade resolutions adopted at Montevideo seemed destined to failure. Great Britain had extended the tentacles of neomercantilism far beyond the bounds of the Ottawa Agreements. In May, 1933, the Roca Convention with Argentina tightened Britain's hold on one of Latin America's most powerful nations. Germany, France, Japan, and Italy likewise initiated neomercantile programs. Special compensation agreements, blocked accounts, and special trade and financial devices (including the United States bilateral agreement with Cuba) appeared to be multiplying at an alarming rate. If the State Department could bring Brazil into the reciprocal fold, it could possibly check the tide of economic nationalism and increase export markets for American traders.[7] Since the chief export of Colombia and Brazil was coffee, the department feared

6. DS 611.3231/505, /508; 832.5151/140, NA, RG 59. *BFDC*, 351.1 Brazil, June 14, 1933, NA, RG 40.

7. Samuel Flagg Bemis, *The Latin American Policy of the United States* (New York: Harcourt, Brace and World, Inc., 1943), pp. 295–304. DS 611.3231/520; 611.2531/69; 811.5831/63, NA, RG 59.

that Congress would fail to ratify the Colombian treaty because of the most-favored-nation clause unless the Roosevelt Administration also put before it a treaty with Brazil.

Pressure as well as polemics emanated from Washington as the Roosevelt Administration sought to convince the Vargas government that a reciprocal trade agreement served the best interests of both nations. The department's position as outlined by the Treaty Division was to "avoid any appearance of trying to get something for an inadequate return" while asking for low duties. Rio was also to become sufficiently cognizant of the United States' ability to impose an import duty on coffee.[8] The American chargé in Rio de Janeiro commented that the Brazilian government was fully aware of potential American duties on coffee but hoped that the United States would not resort to such a "powerful recourse." An editorial published in *Correio da Manhõ* on July 26, 1933, urged the Brazilian people to forget the "lyrics of continental fraternity" and wake up to economic realities. The editorial especially cited Brazil's dependence on the American market for both imported and exported products.[9]

The Brazilians could well ponder Washington's strong bargaining power. Approximately 95 per cent of Brazil's exports to this nation came duty free, while approximately the same percentage of America's exports to Brazil were dutiable. Brazil enjoyed an unusually large favorable balance of trade with the United States but, nevertheless, imposed exchange control on American commercial concerns. The Office of the Special Adviser to the President on Foreign Trade especially stressed the disparity in United States–Brazilian commercial relations. From 1914 to 1933 the United States trade deficit amounted to $1,751,700,000. American loans and investments to Brazil for the same period (minus interest and earnings from bonds), combined with the trade deficit, equaled $2,065,000,000. Peek's office emphasized the fact that coffee equaled 85 per cent of the value of Brazil's exports to the United States, thus rendering the Brazilian economy peculiarly vulnerable to American pressure.[10] On the other hand, countries such as France and Italy imposed rather high duties on imported coffee but also received equal

8. DS 611.3231/535, /571, NA, RG 59.
9. *FR*, 1933, 5:14. DS 611.3231/534, NA, RG 59.
10. DS 611.3231/539, /566, /612, NA, RG 59.

commercial treatment from Brazil and special financial considerations. Few analysts mentioned the profitability of Brazilian coffee to American domestic enterprises after it had been imported, processed, and distributed.

On August 29, 1933, Washington and Rio de Janeiro held the first informal conversation on reciprocity. The initial American proposals incorporated the unconditional most-favored-nation clause modeled after the report of the Economic Committee of the League of Nations and extended to quantitative restrictions. The department proposed reductions on American export products ranging up to 35 per cent. Duties were to be computed on the ad valorem basis with surtaxes not to exceed 10 per cent. The American proposals also suggested a clarification of Brazilian taxes and fees and "administrative" orders, all designed to trick American exporters. The department espoused the right to appeal fines as well as to obtain more orderly diplomatic representation in cases under dispute. The United States also desired national treatment for American exports. If Brazil or the United States established quota systems, the proposed American treaty guaranteed an equitable share of the trade and equality of treatment in matters of exchange control (a point belabored by such organizations as the National Foreign Trade Council, the Office of the Special Adviser, and the American Exporters and Importers Association). The department, however, reserved the right to discriminate in favor of its possessions. (United States customs territories included Alaska, Hawaii, and Puerto Rico but not the Philippines, the Virgin Islands, Guam, or Samoa.)

Generally speaking, the department proposals foreshadowed the suggestions later outlined in a report submitted by the Committee for Reciprocity Information. As if to prod the Brazilians into trade negotiations, Hull reminded Ambassador Lima e Silva of the "recurrent efforts" to tax coffee and tea imports by American domestic interests. The secretary, however, made no direct threat. The Brazilian ambassador countered with a request for a $50,000,000 loan to stabilize the milreis and to provide exchange for United States goods. Hull remarked that the Reconstruction Finance Corporation lacked the necessary authority to affect the loan.[11]

11. U. S., Committee for Reciprocity Information, *Stenographer's Minutes of the Hearing Before the Committee for Reciprocity Information in*

No substantial progress concerning the commercial treaty was made during the remainder of the year. Brazil, confessed Ambassador Hugh Gibson, remained willing to readjust her duties but not to the extent suggested in American proposals. Substantial reductions, advised Gibson, would deprive her of revenue and inflict damage on her industry. In addition, Brazil paid for imports from the United States in cash, while many of her important exports such as cotton, wool, and fruits were not purchased extensively by this country. Brazil also hedged on the unconditional most-favored-nation treatment, since the Vargas administration wanted to maintain a bargaining position in respect to such nations as France. With prospects for an early agreement slim, Washington and Rio de Janeiro slowed the tempo of the discussions.[12]

The State Department also encountered resistance of a sort from such powerful business concerns as the Associated Coffee Industries of America. This association insisted that since coffee represented America's best economic weapon, they should be allowed to participate in the trade discussions. The industry further maintained that numerous trade fiascoes, such as the 1931 coffee-wheat barter arrangement (which led to the complete cessation of American flour exports to Brazil for over a year), might well have been avoided through previous consultation with the Associated Coffee Industries.

Unlike in many past cases, the department seemed overly impressed with the power and persuasiveness of the coffee industry. A memorandum dated October 12, 1933, by the Division of Latin American Affairs suggested that the Department of State " 'play ball' with the Association." The department's position as formulated by Henry Grady, Francis Sayre, and Sumner Welles contemplated no action on the question of coffee until confirmation

---

Connection with the Negotiations of a Reciprocal Trade Agreement with Brazil, Guatemala, Nicaragua, El Salvador, Honduras, and Costa Rica, Vol. 1, October 22, 1934 and October 27, 1934. George N. Peek, papers, Western Historical Manuscripts Collection, State Historical Society of Missouri, Box 15, Memorandum (Martin to Peek) July 28, 1934; Box 17, Peek to Roosevelt, February 8, 1934. *FR,* 1933, 5: 23–28. DS 610.1131/79; 611.3231/548, /571, /614½, /750, NA, RG 59.

12. DS 611.3231/578A, /580, NA, RG 59. McCann, p. 162.

by the major importing interests represented by the Associated Coffee Industries of America.[13]

The connection between the Commerce Department and the Associated Coffee Industries was even more involved. William F. Williamson, manager of the association, continually stressed the need for a special trade commissioner at São Paulo to represent the coffee interests. Williamson's suggestion that his association would defray part of the expense for the mission met with the disapproval of Dr. C. T. Murchison, director of the Bureau of Foreign and Domestic Commerce. Still persistent, Williamson appealed over the head of Murchison to Ernest Draper, assistant secretary of commerce. In October, 1935, "due to very heavy pressure from the coffee and foodstuffs industries," the Commerce Department relented. A special trade commissioner "acceptable to those industries" and sharing "the major portion or possibly all of the expenses to be incurred" would be established. Draper made no mention of a possible conflict of interests between a bureau representative paid and selected by private coffee concerns.[14]

The Department of State viewed the entire scheme with a jaundiced eye. The department argued that the consulate general at São Paulo could provide ample information and services for the coffee industry. Williamson, backed by the Commerce Department, refused to budge. In March, 1936, William Phillips agreed to the plan. Draper reassured the State Department that the coffee interests represented a "special case. In no sense does it constitute a precedent."

American commercial attachés in Brazil criticized the plan, since a particular commodity represented by a special trade commissioner and allowed to exert such an obvious preference was a transgression of all standards of propriety. Such a plan violated the maintenance of complete control by the Bureau of Foreign and Domestic Commerce. The bureau, however, caustically referred to the criticism as "inspired" and continued the operation. Throughout the coming years, the bureau supplied the Associat-

13. DS 611.3231/553, /566 3/4, /694, NA, RG 59.
14. *BFDC*, 351.1 Brazil, NA, RG 40, May 29, 1935; August 17, 1935; September 12, 1935; October 1, 1935; October 2, 1935; November 7, 1935; November 14, 1935; November 25, 1935.

ed Coffee Industries of America with confidential material transmitted by American Consuls in Brazil and received via the State Department.[15]

Also of particular interest to the State Department were private reports from such sources as A. E. Taylor of the Food Research Institute at Stanford University outlining possible guidelines in the trade negotiations with Brazil. Taylor suggested that a duty on coffee would not decrease American consumption as much as it would make American consumers turn to cheaper sources of coffee, such as Brazil. Therefore, the threatened tax might not have the desired effect on Brazil as much as it would on countries such as Colombia. Parenthetically, it might be added that the June 12 act prohibited the President (not Congress) from transferring any article between the dutiable and free lists. This fact compounded United States difficulties in exercising economic coercion against Brazil. Taylor's report also opposed the use of the United States' bargaining power to force Brazil to earmark the balance of dollar exchange for coverage of payment of service charges on dollar bonds and other American investments (as Great Britain employed in the Roca Agreement). This would force Brazil to pay foreign debts rather than buy American products, prejudice the entire idea of reciprocity, and create more pressure for bilateralism. Taylor's logic reaffirmed the department's position. Hull and his department, because of the depression psychosis, seemed more anxious to promote American foreign trade with Brazil than to protect American loans and bonded indebtedness.[16]

On August 31, 1934, Roosevelt announced Washington's intention to negotiate a foreign trade agreement with Brazil. Hull tentatively planned to bring the Brazilian accord into force simultaneously with the Colombian agreement. He ordered the terms of the Colombian agreement to remain secret until after the Brazilian signature, since Brazil might possibly stall the discussions pending the end of the other negotiation.[17]

15. Ibid., March 13, 1936; March 16, 1936; August 31, 1936; September 11, 1936. Dates where confidential material was given to Williamson can be found in October, 1936, through June, 1937, from Rawls, chief of the Foodstuffs Division.

16. DS 611.3231/590, NA, RG 59.

17. DS 611.2131/205, /205B-207. Also DS, Press release, August 31, 1934, DS 611.3231/618, NA, RG 59.

Throughout the remainder of 1934 the department labored in the face of many adversities to complete a commercial treaty with Brazil. Foreign competition, especially German, threatened the very essence of reciprocity. In 1933 Brazilian imports from Germany increased by 93 per cent, while imports from the United States decreased by 3 per cent. By October, 1934, Germany intensified her attempts to force Brazil into a compensation marks agreement by threatening to cut back on coffee purchases. The terms *compensation* or *aski marks* referred to special currencies that Germany used in its export trade. Instead of purchasing imports with regular marks, Hitler and Hjalmar Schacht, acting minister of the German economy, paid for the goods with these currencies, which could only be used by the exporting country to purchase specified German goods. This practice limited international trade by inducing an artificial demand for products otherwise secured more cheaply by other competitors.

The department, wrote Donald Heath of the Division of Latin American Affairs, must do "everything we properly can to prevent Brazil from concluding the compensation agreement with Germany." German compensation agreements, remarked Heath, amounted to "petty exchange grabbing" and would help Brazil's balance of trade vis à vis Germany. Heath believed that if Germany failed to buy Brazilian coffee and turned to other markets, the Vargas government could easily capture the vacant coffee market. If all other alternatives failed, the State Department would have preferred that Brazil implement exchange control and/or tariff revision before the nation succumbed to compensation agreements.[18]

For Hull, the principles of commercial liberalism could best be achieved by turning "the tide toward greater freedom in worldwide commercial policy." Compensation agreements and other such arrangements led to excessive importation of nonessential commodities, the artificial diversion of trade from normal economic channels, and an increase in exchange control. But the attempts to convince Rio of the efficacy of a liberal declaration of economic policy met with failure. Resistance to a declaration emanated from such domestic sources as the Office of the Special Adviser as well as from Dr. Oswaldo Aranha, chief negotiator for the Brazilian delegation. Aranha believed that

18. DS 611.3231/654½, /659–660, NA, RG 59.

questions of exchange control, coffee export schemes, and the foreign debt precluded any immediate declaration. He further stated that without American credit it would be necessary for Brazil to initiate even more stringent exchange-control measures. Aranha argued that only American credit could preclude the taking of funds off of the commercial market in order to maintain debt service. In other words, Brazil could not continue to buy large quantities of American goods and repay their loans at the same time without more United States credit.

The Brazilians also shared little faith in Hull's belief that tariff reductions led to a more prosperous international community. Brazil's tariff had remained static for twenty years, yet her trade had fluctuated greatly. Prosperity, argued the Brazilians, depended upon many factors other than tariffs. Questions of transportation, postal and telegraph facilities, public and private credit, and guarantees to commerce, capital, and labor remained of higher priority. Obviously unmoved by Rio de Janeiro's logic, the State Department on October 30, 1934, informed the Vargas administration that the espousal of such clearing and compensation agreements might well force the United States likewise to adopt such measures. Although the department reassured Rio de Janeiro of its intention to free the channels of international commerce, the threat to adopt such illiberal trade doctrines was implied.[19]

Brazil, despite misgivings, accepted the German compensation system. The State Department, therefore, refrained from pushing for a liberal declaration of economic policy. Hull hoped to accomplish results through an exchange control provision with Rio that would either abnegate the special agreement with the Nazis or circumvent it by pledging "to accord the same treatment to American trade." Both Feis and Welles intimated to the Brazilian authorities that the adoption of the department's plan would go far to facilitate American credit to Brazil. The department mistakenly believed that the unconditional most-favored-nation clause, together with an exchange control provision,

19. William Phillips, diary, 1933–1936, Vol. 3, Houghton Library, Cambridge, Mass., October 11, 1934. *FR*, 1934, 4:549–54. DS 611.3531/265; 611.3231/648, /668, NA, RG 59.

would effectively forestall serious German competition in Brazil.[20]

On November 24, 1934, Hull submitted the draft of the Reciprocal Trade Agreement to Brazil. Articles I through III dealt with the ordinary exemptions from customs duties in excess of the said schedules and prohibited all national or federal internal taxes, fees, charges, and exactions higher than those in effect on the day of the signature of the agreement.[21] Article IV dealt with the prohibition of import licenses, customs quotas, and other forms of quantitative restrictions except those specifically stated in the agreement. Article V pertained to "sympathetic consideration to all representations" by either government with respect to alleged discriminations by government monopolies. Article VI concerned pledges to grant unconditional most-favored-nation treatment in exchange allotments, while Article VII pledged unconditional most-favored-nation treatment in matters of customs and tariffs and pledged the United States to prevent the imposition of excise duties on Brazilian coffee. Article VIII pertained to custom classifications, fines, and appeals and was an attempt to deal with the long-standing Brazilian fine industry. Article IX dealt with arms control. Article XI exempted the Philippines, the Virgin Islands, American Samoa, Guam, and the Panama Canal Zone from the provisions of the treaty. Article XII supplanted the 1923 commercial treaty; the new agreement would become effective thirty days after proclamation by both governments and would remain in effect for two years. The Department of State also enclosed a joint declaration of policy with respect to clearing and compensation agreements that pledged both nations to "discourage the multiplication of agreements of this character [so long as] any other solution" remained feasible. The department, however, refused to consider the trade negotiations as a means to force Brazil into resuming payment of defaulted bonds.[22] All in all, the State Department's draft to

20. *FTLA*, pt. 2, p. 77. *FR*, 1934, 4:557. DS, 611.3231/686, NA, RG 59.

21. For the list of tariff concessions requested by the United States see DS 611.3231/674, NA, RG 59. Also see *FR*, 1934, 4:554–55, dealing with reductions, freezes, and reclassifications.

22. For the memorandum and draft of the reciprocal trade agreement with Brazil see *FR*, 1934, 4:558–68; 557. DS 611.3231/686, /729, NA, RG 59.

Brazil represented one of the most comprehensive trade agreements in the history of Hull's program.[23]

The department, of course, faced the usual outcry of condemnation from the special adviser to the President on foreign trade. Peek criticized the absence of a provision providing for the funding of blocked balances. Peek proposed to liquidate these obligations by forcing Brazil to issue new bonds with long maturity at 5 per cent through call provisions, serial retirement, or sinking fund operations; the indenture would contain a provision giving the trustee a lien on Brazilian coffee importations sufficient to maintain complete debt service, including principal in case of default. The Export-Import Bank would then offer to purchase these bonds from their bona fide holders at face value. The department opposed Peek's plan on the grounds that Brazil's default did not constitute permanent default but merely a question of delay. Peek's plan, in addition, prejudiced American interests in nations where the United States had no effective means of securing equality of treatment for American interests.[24]

Peek also believed that the "country by country and commodity by commodity" approach to reciprocal trade constituted the best means of tariff bargaining. The special adviser relentlessly argued that the unconditional most-favored-nation clause was tantamount to "unilateral economic disarmament," and little basis of fact existed for the principles of triangular trade and principal supplier. Although Peek failed to convince either the State Department or the Executive Committee of Commercial Policy, his criticisms forced the department to inform Roosevelt at every step of the way in the Brazilian negotiations. Peek's efforts to rechannel the direction of American commercial policy failed to solicit Roosevelt's categorical approval. Quite possibly in his efforts to discredit Hull by the December, 1934, barter scheme with Germany Peek saw an opportunity to sabotage the Brazilian agreement. Rio informed the Roosevelt Administration that the proposed cotton deal with Germany seriously prejudiced the commercial treaty with the United States. Had Peek's

23. Edward O. Guerrant, *Roosevelt's Good Neighbor Policy* (Albuquerque: University of New Mexico Press, 1950), p. 94.

24. Peek, papers, Box 15, Coulter to Donaldson and Taylor, October 9, 1934; Box 16, Peek to Welles, November 23, 1934; Peek to McIntyre, October 29, 1934. DS 611.3231/696–698A, /709, /718, NA, RG 59.

barter scheme prevailed, it appears certain that United States–Brazilian trade negotiations would have been further delayed.[25]

On December 18, 1934, the Brazilian ambassador, Oswaldo Aranha, a staunch supporter of United States policy abroad, informed Herbert Feis that although Brazil sympathized with American efforts "to eliminate from commercial practice all and every expedient involving a derogation from the so-called liberal policy," economic realities forced Brazil to retreat from an "inflexible liberal policy." Brazil, therefore, had to adopt those measures necessary to sustain her foreign trade while the state of international economics remained in transition. Although the State Department refused to subscribe to such reasoning, it recognized that "American tariff policy has been one of the underlying reasons forcing the world to resort to such expedients."[26]

Nevertheless, Hull remained adamant. The Brazilian agreement had to include minimum exchange safeguards, either as an article of the treaty (Feis' position) or through an exchange of notes contemporaneous with the treaty. Although the Roosevelt Administration encountered certain difficulties regarding tariff concessions on American leather, flour, soap, cotton textiles, steel manufacturers, and tires, the crux of the problem centered around Washington's attempt to vitiate the German-Brazilian agreement. The Department of State's ploy was to eliminate exchange control provisions and to secure adequate payment of foreign debts.[27]

The final agreement, signed on February 2, 1935, did include an exchange of notes whereby Brazil pledged to provide both full and prompt coverage of foreign exchange due to American imports and additional exchange to liquidate gradually existing deferred commercial indebtedness. Brazil also agreed to accord most-favored-nation treatment in the allotment of exchange on profits, dividends, and expenses incurred by foreign commercial enterprises operating in Brazil. Rio de Janeiro would continue

25. DS 611.3231/685, /691, /701–702, /710, NA, RG 59. Peek, papers, Box 16, Memorandum (Peek to Roosevelt), November 14, 1934; Peek to McIntyre, December 8, 1934; Franklin D. Roosevelt, papers, Franklin D. Roosevelt Library, Hyde Park, N. Y., Official File, 614–A, Trade, Peek to Roosevelt, December 8, 10, 1934.

26. *FR*, 1934, 4:571–74. DS 611.3231/717, NA, RG 59.

27. DS 611.3231/705, /762, NA, RG 59.

the payment of frozen credit notes issued in June, 1933 (which will be discussed in Chapter 6). Action, however, speaks louder than rhetoric. As the State Department soon discovered, the Brazilian exchange market had yet to be controlled. This was because the exchange clause permitted Vargas to engage in various practices inimical to American interests. The most important loophole was the compensation trade with Germany. Although the "free" exchange market was to assume a major role in the financing of Brazil's imports, chargé George Gordon reported on February 8 that "neither a resumption of official exchange allotments nor assurances with respect thereto have been forthcoming."[28] The battle was far from won.

As to the actual schedules, the trade agreement gave the United States reductions on sixty-seven agricultural and industrial products and bound thirty-nine others. The United States in turn bound Brazilian coffee and eleven other products on the free list, which comprised about 90 per cent of Brazil's exports to the United States, and reduced duties on seven other commodities. Congratulations to Hull and the department came from such organizations as the American Manufacturing Export Association, the Foreign Policy Association, the Associated Coffee Industries of America, the National Foreign Trade Council, the American Brazilian Association, and the Council on Inter-American Relations. Shipping lines such as the McCormick Steamship Company likewise expressed satisfaction over the treaty.[29]

At first, Brazil likewise appeared pleased with the commercial treaty. As one military attaché's report so simply put it, "They [the Brazilians] are more convinced than ever that they have a loyal and fair friend in their big brother up North." Chargé Gordon reported "no single instance of editorial criticism of the treaty"; a none-too-startling fact, since Vargas kept a tight rein on most of the press.[30]

28. DS 611.3231/756, /780, NA, RG 59. League of Nations, *Review of World Trade, 1934*, II. Economic and Financial, 1935, II. A. 8. (Geneva: League of Nations Publications, 1934) :50. Davis, p. 10.

29. TC, *Digest of Trade Data with Respect to Products on which Concessions were Granted by the United States in the United States-Brazilian Trade Agreement* (GPO, 1925). *FTLA*, pt. 2, p. 75. DS 611.0031/1356, /1381; 610.113/130; 611.3231/774, /784, /795, /827, NA, RG 59.

30. Military Attaché Report No. 1393, February 8, 1935, DS 611.3231/921; /808, NA, RG 59.

Criticism from home soon suppressed the optimism of the first days of the treaty. Representative Allen Treadway called the Brazilian treaty "another link in the chain of the present administration to destroy American industry." George Peek and other representatives of farm interests criticized the scarcity of tariff concessions for American agricultural products. As Under Secretary Phillips confided in his diary, "Almost everyone had the jitters." The domestic outcry of such lobbies as manganese, Phillips said, had greatly discouraged Hull in his efforts to push reciprocal trade agreements. The secretary, he wrote, now believed it best to slow down the program in order to placate domestic fears.[31]

Obviously distraught at the criticism engendered by his trade program, Hull, with the aid of Herbert Feis, defended the essence of multilateralism in a detailed memorandum to President Roosevelt. Bilateralism, barter, and all other forms of economic discrimination, Hull wrote, represented "the greatest menace today to international relationships." Multilateralism implemented by the most-favored-nation policy was the best solution for the recovery of foreign trade. Each commercial agreement contemplated increased domestic production and employment, not the ruination of American industry. But to Hull, reciprocity agreements represented "only a step in the direction of broader movements and methods of trade development." The secretary envisioned (and the postwar years fulfilled) a simultaneous reduction of trade barriers through multilateral conventions. The tone of the memorandum, however, resounded more with the realism of Herbert Feis than the idealism of Tennessee's favorite son.

Hull promised to use "every method of restoring commerce" notwithstanding unilateral, bilateral, regional or multilateral solutions. To implement the goals envisioned at Montevideo, Hull proposed sound loans and investments to the stable but underdeveloped nations of Latin America as any such "hardheaded businessman would approve." Hull further stated:

Experience teaches without qualification that nations with surplus capital and surplus production beyond their ability to con-

31. U. S., Congress, *Congressional Record*, 74th Cong., 1st sess., 1935, 79, pt. 3: 1473. DS 611.3231/785, NA, RG 59. Phillips, diary, Vol. 4, February 11, 1935.

sume at home or to sell for cash abroad, have found it profitable to supply other countries with credit and to engage in investments deemed sound from every business standpoint.

This quotation aptly demonstrates little or no concern for either uplifting the masses of Latin America through the use of U.S. funds and investments or building viable economies. If American capital contributed to the betterment of Latin America (as Hull believed it would) the goal was merely ancillary to the protection and extension of American capitalism under the aegis of the Open Door.[32]

Hull agreed that "an increase in our exports is dependent entirely upon our getting paid for them." Yet the United States, he said, must also provide sufficient funds through loans on foreign purchases. As to the exchange of notes with Brazil over exchange control, Hull defended it as the best the United States could possibly receive. "To have sought more far-reaching terms than these, might well have embittered our relations with Brazil."[33] Sufficiently impressed by Hull's logic and seldom-employed forcefulness, Roosevelt decided to retain the trade program and again postponed the day of reckoning with Peek.

But just as Hull had experienced frustration over Bogotá's delay in ratification, the same problem occurred with the Vargas government. Under Secretary Phillips informed the American chargé at Rio de Janeiro that Brazil's lethargy was having adverse repercussions on the general sentiment toward reciprocal agreements throughout the world. Preoccupied with the Chaco affair, the Brazilian foreign minister paid little heed to American importunities. In April, 1935, the Brazilian congress expired without approving the treaty. Further delays also gave Brazil's industrial interests, as well as America's private interests, the opportunity to rally opposition against the treaty. The São Paulo industrialists using the newspaper *O Jornal* attacked the commercial treaty as a compromise of national sovereignty. *O Jornal* suggested that the United States helped exacerbate the hardships of the Great Depression that in turn stimulated economic nationalism. But, the publication suggested, the United States then realized that the effects of economic nationalism stimulated economic independence and thereupon dedicated itself to the

32. DS 611.3231/803, NA, RG 59.
33. Ibid.

destruction of "artificial industries" in Latin America in order to preserve its market for manufactured goods. The trade treaty seemed to threaten Vargas' control over the Brazilian populace.[34]

The Brazilian outcry came from sources other than the press. The 1934 constitution, for example, based on class as well as district representation, allowed for more vocal criticism than Ambassador Hugh Gibson deemed favorable to American interests. Although Gibson realized the adverse effect on certain Brazilian manufacturing interests, the United States, he warned, must take "immediate and energetic measures to counteract this influence" or face the "definite possibility of nonratification." On August 27 Getulio Vargas agreed "to take all possible measures" to ensure early ratification. Class deputies representing Brazilian industry, such as Envaldo Lodi, soon found it exceedingly difficult to exercise freedom of speech. Vargas' *Estado Novo* had done its work well. As Gibson none-too-remorsefully reported, "Various other leaders of the opposition to ratification have been dealt with by one means or another." Brazil's newspapers, such as *Diario de Noticias, Correio da Manha, Diario Carioca, Jornal do Brazil*, and *A Nação*, quickly endorsed the reciprocity program. On December 2, 1935, the United States and Brazil exchanged ratification of the commercial treaty. Vargas had weathered a menacing storm.[35]

Washington had initiated the unconditional most-favored-nation clause in 1923. Automatically, it extended tariff concessions to all nations not overtly and singly discriminating against American commerce. Brazil, on the other hand, had followed no such policy. In fact, the treaty with the United States represented the extent to which Brazil subscribed to unconditional most-favored-nation treatment. The government at Rio de Janeiro referred to the American agreement as one of "contractual reciprocity." Vargas' plans, devised by the chief of the Commercial Section of the Foreign Office, Sebastiaõ Sampaio, called for the eventual renunciation of all commercial agreements prior to January 1, 1934, (excepting the United States, Portugal, Uruguay, France, and Argentina) looking toward renegotiation with

34. DS 611.3231/964, /976, /993A, NA, RG 59.

35. Cordell Hull, papers, General Correspondence, Library of Congress, Gibson to Hull, September 20, 1935. DS 611.3231/970–971, /989, /991, /997, /998, /1000, /1010, /1020, NA, RG 59.

provisional agreements to be signed pending renegotiation. Hull, fully cognizant of Brazil's unwillingness to extend duty concessions granted to the United States to third nations, informed Ambassador Gibson to refrain from the subject, since "this is a matter to be determined solely by the Brazilian government." Since the likelihood of successful Brazilian negotiations with Europe seemed difficult, the department reasoned that "the ultimate effects on the adumbrated Brazilian policy will be somewhat more favorable to American trade." It was one of many cases in which the policy of the Open Door worked to inhibit American competition in Latin America.[36] It was also a telltale sign that neither ethics nor consistency necessarily had to stand in the way of self-interests.

Brazil, therefore, became Washington's early if not somewhat recalcitrant ally in the promotion of liberal trade. Vargas, however, had no intention of further lowering Brazil's duties in future negotiations. He merely sought to free Brazil's commerce from administrative and special foreign restrictions that impeded her exports. Nevertheless, Gibson predicted that American commerce "will be the gainers from the general condition which the new agreements will bring about." The ambassador awaited future Brazilian attempts to readjust the German compensation marks difficulties with anticipation. Little did Washington realize the potency of Nazi Germany's threat to stifle American efforts to open the potential markets of Latin America to freer commercial intercourse.[37]

It did not take long for Hull and his economic advisers to realize the seriousness of the German threat. Although the Vargas government now permitted the prompt remittances on commercial obligations, the department became increasingly perplexed by the alarming increase in German export trade to Brazil. In 1934 Germany exported 14 per cent of the value of Brazil's total imports; in 1935 the figure rose to 20.7 per cent, and in 1936 Brazilian imports from Germany equaled 23.5 per cent of the value of her total imports. On the other hand, American export trade remained static. The percentage of Brazil's total

36. *FTLA*, pt. 2, p. 75. DS 611.3231/1102A–1105, NA, RG 59.

37. Ethel B. Dietrich, *World Trade* (New York: Henry Holt and Company, 1939), pp. 324–25. DS 611.3231/111, /1115, NA, RG 59. For aski marks see McCann, p. 150.

exports to the United States and Germany from 1934 to 1936 remained at approximately 38 per cent and 13 per cent respectively. However, Germany by no means felt committed to remain in such an inferior trade status in Brazil. U.S. Ambassador to Berlin William Dodd conveyed Nazi intentions, especially by Dr. Hjalmar Schacht, to preempt Brazilian exports and thereby discredit Hull's program in Latin America. Germany, reported chargé Fay Des Portes, was "conducting a well organized and astute campaign . . . to discredit in every way possible American efforts on this continent." The political, strategic, and military ramifications of such German economic activity were not lost on the State Department.[38]

Although vitally concerned with American export trade, the department realized that German inroads in the Brazilian market were not entirely at the expense of American trade. For example, the Nazis by late 1936 had replaced Great Britain as the chief supplier of Brazilian coal. In accounting for the loss of American export trade to Brazil, the German compensation mark system (inaugurated in the closing months of 1934) could not be considered the major factor in the decline of American exports to Brazil. German subsidies (created by the system of exchange control imposed by Hitler) had created the price differences that contributed to the underselling of American products.[39]

The United States also had to contend with some other rather complex monetary manipulations by the Banco do Brasil. Under the auspices of the pro-German finance minister, Souza Costa, the *banco* allowed German banks to carry overbought positions up to 500,000 marks. These currency reserves enabled German importers to quote prices on the Brazilian market in milreis rather than in marks, thereby eliminating exchange risks on the part of Germany. American free currency enjoyed no such advantage.

Combined with German subsidies and exchange advantages, the compensation marks agreement provided the Hitler regime with untold trade advantages over American competitors. A German compensation marks agreement with a nation with which

38. *FTUS*, 1936, pp. 97–98. DS 711.62/116; 611.3231/1153½, /1162, /1218, NA, RG 59.

39. DS 611.3231/1149, NA, RG 59. German economic activities will be discussed in greater detail in Chapter 8.

she enjoyed an unfavorable balance of trade necessitated the purchase of an ever-increasing quantity of German products or the accumulation of useless compensation marks. The compensation agreement forced the sale of German goods to absorb the volume of marks created by German purchases whether sufficient demand existed or not. Such a bilateral balancing of trade precluded the use of exports to Germany as a means of debt services and other external payments in countries other than Germany.[40]

The United States also found herself with increasing competition from Brazilian industry and from foreign competition in agricultural exports. In 1926, 26 per cent of Brazil's wheat imports came from the United States. A decade later United States wheat exports amounted to only .01 per cent of the total value of Brazil's wheat imports. Argentina had effectively captured the market.[41]

Since Hull refused to countenance a duty on Brazil's coffee imports designed to subsidize American exports to Brazil, the State Department worked for a revision of the trade agreement with Brazil. The Interdepartmental Subcommittee on Monetary and Exchange Problems urged the department to convince Brazil that Germany must pay for a part of her imports in international exchange and "further restrict the quotas which already apply to sales of certain commodities to Germany on a compensation basis." In July, 1937, discussions with Souza Costa achieved limited success. Rio de Janeiro pledged that imported goods would not be favored by any "direct" subsidy from the government of exporting countries; the government also agreed to restrict compensated currency to ensure against the dislocation of commerce and to protect free international currency. Mixed committees were also to be established in New York and Rio de Janeiro to facilitate trade. The United States, for its part, agreed to sell $60,000,000 worth of gold that could then be used as collateral for short-term credit to promote exchange equilibrium. The same month, however, Vargas extended the German–Brazilian compensation marks agreement for three months.[42]

German–American competition in Brazil (which will be ex-

40. DS 600.0031 World Program/123; 632.6231/224; /611.3231/1060, /1149, /1176, /1182, /1195, /1206B, NA, RG 59.

41. DS 611.3231/1171, NA, RG 59.

42. DS 611.3231/1172, /1187, /1197, NA, RG 59.

amined more closely in Chapter 8) approached a stalemate. In 1938 Brazil received 25 per cent of her imports from Germany, 24 per cent from the United States, and 10 per cent from Great Britain. Such an existing state of affairs was injurious to the security of the Western Hemisphere. Examples of German activities in the political economies of Central Europe spurred alarm that the same methods might be tried in Brazil. Stalemate in Brazil, therefore, not only meant the failure of Hull's trade policy with the largest and potentially the richest nation in Latin America but an opening wedge of Nazi subterfuge and subversion in the hemisphere. An economic stalemate in Brazil, in short, became a harbinger of disaster.[43]

The close cooperation between the Hitler regime, German producers and trade organizations at home, and the German Chamber of Commerce abroad "reached a technical proficiency in coordinated production, propaganda, and distribution." In the exportation of certain leading non-trade agreement items, such as iron and steel sheets and wire, coal, aircraft, electric dynamos and generators, iron tubes, pipes and joints, hand tools, internal combustion engines, copper, spinning and weaving machinery and photographic dry plates, Germany far outstripped her American competitors. Germany, like the United States, also put pressure on Rio de Janeiro by threatening to stop purchases of Brazilian coffee.

The availability of credit by German exporters, the compensation marks, and further Brazilian exchange restrictions in December, 1937, adversely affected American export trade. Germany in early 1938 possessed a favorable balance of 17,000,000 marks from which payments could be made for Brazilian imports from Germany. Brazil, the American consul general, William Burdett, remarked, had not shown "a very encouraging approach to the basic purposes and objectives of the trade-agreements program of the United States."[44]

The United States, for its part, relied heavily upon the excellent distributing facilities of American firms operating in Brazil. Although the trade agreement had not produced the desired

43. Alton Frye, *Nazi Germany and the American Hemisphere, 1933– 1941* (New Haven: Yale University Press, 1967), p. 75; *FR*, 1936, 5:249.

44. *BFDC*, 351.1 Brazil, NA, RG 40, January 13, 1939. *FTLA*, pt. 2, p. 93. DS 611.3231/1231–1233, /1332, NA, RG 59.

effects in increased trade activities, it did prevent the enactment of measures palpably discriminatory against American interests. A 2 per cent ad valorem pension tax on imports in 1936 exempted American trade agreement items, as did the consumption taxes of 1938. The difficulties in obtaining deliveries from Germany, the fear of a European war, and the gradual advance in the selling rate of the compensation mark negated Germany's ability to corner the Brazilian market. Germany was further hampered by the ever-present danger that Vargas might curtail the German compensation marks trade. The Reich's war preparations also resulted in a cutback in her ability to sell abroad. One should also remember the fact that an ever-increasing number of American factories shipping autos, tires, and machinery to Brazil were located in Canada and thereby escaped United States trade statistics.[45]

The State Department likewise viewed with helpless alarm the resurgency of economic nationalism in Brazil. As Latin American nationalism and Axis subversion increased throughout the hemisphere, economic matters no longer played a minor role in shaping political and strategic decisions.[46] In early 1938 Vargas turned rather suddenly against foreign capital. Foreign insurance companies and banks, it was feared, might soon come under the nationalizing provisions of Article CXLV of the new Brazilian constitution. In April, 1938, Vargas began the process of nationalizing the petroleum industry and moved to curtail remittance abroad of earnings on foreign capital invested in Brazil. On November 10, 1938, the Brazilian dictator declared that foreign capital that sought exorbitant profits or attempted to exercise tutelage over the national life would not be tolerated. No "formal protest," opted a Division of the American Republic memorandum, should be made by the department at this time.[47]

The major development regarding the American–Brazilian reciprocity agreement from mid to late 1938 revolved primarily

45. DS 611.3231/1217, /1233, /1262, /1396, NA, RG 59.

46. A recent study by David Green entitled *The Containment of Latin America* (Chicago: Quadrangle Books, 1971) documents the Nazi attempts to infiltrate the airlines of many South American countries.

47. DS 832.00/1077, /1165, /1233; 811.503132/19, NA, RG 59. *FTLA*, pt. 2, p. 74.

around the delay in providing exchange for American goods. The granting of preferential exchange treatment on May 23, 1938, only partially relieved the exchange situation. For its part, Brazil denied that the bank of Brazil actually possessed adequate exchange due to the adverse trade balance, the servicing of the notes of the various unfreezing arrangements, the rearmament program, and the depressed price of coffee sales receipts. The Brazilian exchange backlog, because of Brazil's private obligations to United States interests, ranged from estimates of $10,000,000 to $40,000,000. A backlog likewise existed on interest and dividends due American investments. On the outstanding dollar debt of $357,000,000, Brazil made no payment of service. [48]

Internal revenue taxation on imported products and isolated instances of customs difficulties likewise marred the trade picture. On the whole, Brazil's commercial policy showed little enthusiasm for the basic purposes and objectives of the trade program. A Special Subcommittee on Brazilian Exchange Treatment reported that although the United States supposedly received equality of treatment from Brazil, "there are different varieties of equal treatment. What we are getting (with the exception of Germany) is equally bad treatment with the other countries exporting to Brazil." The subcommittee recommended "a firm and determined statement" for Brazil to "put its house in order." If Brazil assented, then Export-Import Bank credits might be utilized to assist Brazil in complying with American requests.[49]

The beginning of the end of Germany's thrust for control of the Brazilian market came with surprising swiftness in March, 1939, and was finally laid to rest with the autumn blitzkrieg on the plains of Poland. The reasons were threefold. First, the Vargas regime by early 1939 had cause for economic alarm. What had amounted to a favorable balance of trade in 1936 totaling nearly $75,000,000 had by 1938 plummeted to a meager $159,451. The decline in coffee and cotton prices was the most important reason for the disaster. Second, the compensation marks system retarded balanced internal and external growth. Third, lured

48. DS 832.5151/1218, 611.3231/1294A, /1312, NA, RG 59.
49. DS 832.515/1255, 611.3231/1263, NA, RG 59.

by the possibility of substantial American financial assistance
and spurred by the economic realities of a European war, Vargas
agreed to discuss outstanding economic problems with Washington as well as matters of general economic policy.[50] Lost in
the intrigue was Vargas' inability to use the Nazi menace as
leverage against Washington. By 1939 the scheme as well as the
Brazilian pocketbook was bankrupt.

In February, 1939, the pro-American foreign minister and
former ambassador to Washington, Oswaldo Aranha, arrived in
the United States to discuss Brazil's restrictions on American
enterprises and investments, Brazil's banking laws, proposed
Brazilian nationalization of insurance and power companies,
and a solution to the foreign debt problem. For the better part
of a month Aranha and a team of Brazilian economic experts
negotiated with Welles, Feis, Briggs, Collado, and Hull. On
March 9, 1939, an exchange of notes signaled the end of Brazil's
prodigal economic courtship with Nazi Germany. In return for
pledges of a free exchange market, a resumption of debt payments, and equitable treatment for American investments, the
United States provided Brazil with export-import credits totaling
$19,200,000 to go toward the payment of American exports to
Brazil through the establishment of acceptance credits for the
bank of Brazil's exchange operations. Washington promised to
grant long-term credit through the Export-Import Bank to finance the purchase of economic equipment in the United States
that would aid Brazil's transportation and industrial development and to provide American agricultural technicians to Brazil. The Treasury Department also agreed to finance a
$50,000,000 loan for the establishment of a central reserve bank
in Brazil. What the reciprocity program had long been unable
to achieve through liberal trade pronouncements, the economic
muscle of the United States accomplished without considerable
delay.

The use of such credit certainly marked a new era in Hull's
economic diplomacy; and, in geopolitical terms, the price tag
was cheap. William Phillips commented from Rome that fascist

50. Great Britain, Department of Overseas Trade, E. Murray Harvey,
Report on Economic and Commercial Conditions in Brazil (London: His
Majesty's Stationery Office, 1939) , p. 32. DS 611.3231/1358, NA, RG 59.

editorials denounced the March 9 agreement as tantamount to the destruction of German industrial supplies from Brazil.[51]

Although the department had good reason for viewing the Aranha Agreement as a step toward greater financial and commercial activity with Brazil, some questioned the efficacy of further import credits to a nation in default on its foreign indebtedness (partial debt service resumed, however, on April 1, 1940). The Aranha Agreement also did not deter the Germans from continuing to pressure American competitors. Nevertheless, the direction of Brazil's economic policy—and indirectly the direction of her political alignment—now veered increasingly toward the United States. Brazil even began to negotiate other reciprocity agreements. Aranha referred to the United States–Brazilian agreement as the model to be emulated by the nations of South America.[52]

What the Aranha Agreement started, World War II completed. A December, 1940, consular report from Pernambuco commented that German compensation trade remained "practically at a standstill with German exporters inactive." Competition with American products remained practically nonexistent. Brazil's commercial policy also remained "unquestionably pro-American." By the end of 1939 Brazil sustained for the first time in her modern history an unfavorable balance of trade with the United States. By mid-1940 the deficit was running nearly $2,000,000 per month. American non-trade agreement items both dutiable and free, for the first time unhindered by German competition, increased at a greater rate than trade agreement items.[53] As a memorandum from the Division of the American Republics put it, the "potential American bargaining weapon" vis à vis Brazil no longer existed. To offset the deficit further, export-import loans to American exports needed for the development of the Brazilian economy, especially in economic overhead investment capital, were soon forthcoming. A $25,000,000 re-

51. DS 033.3211–Aranha, Oswaldo/60; 832.51/1406; 832.5151/1481; 611.3231/1337, /1351, /1353, /1362, /1369, NA, RG 59. *FTLA*, pt. 2, p. 105. TC, *Regulation of Imports by Executive Action*, Miscellaneous Series (GPO, 1941), p. 27.

52. DS 462.00 R 296 b.i.s./631; 832.00/1253; 611.3231/1379, NA, RG 59.

53. DS 611.3231/1404, NA, RG 59.

volving credit fund was also granted to Brazil in the hopes of forestalling any unfavorable developments in exchange matters. As foreign economic coordinator Dean Acheson remarked to Jefferson Caffery in March, 1943, the State Department should also consider "the development of new export industries in Brazil."[54]

The war, however much it orientated the Brazilian economy toward the United States, further stimulated the forces of economic self-sufficiency. As the war progressed, American prices and conditions of sales steadily worsened. Luiz Aranha, brother of the foreign minister, referred in July, 1940, to the great obstacle to Pan-Americanism created by "the commercial methods used by American businessmen." The loss of the German market likewise galvanized Brazilian industrialization. By 1943 department officials became increasingly concerned that Brazil would soon drastically modify the provisions of the 1938 treaty.[55] Although diplomatic dispatches since the first months of 1935 had denied any injury to Brazilian industry caused by the reciprocity agreements, Allan Dawson of the Division of American Republics became sufficiently cognizant of the problem to make the following comment:

> It is thoroughly realized that the Brazilians may ask for a number of concessions (in the new trade agreement) we cannot make and that they will in all probability wish protection for part of their domestic industry which will not be to our interest and that the negotiations will consequently be most difficult.

The United States, remarked Dawson, should "smoke the Brazilians out on this whole problem."[56]

By January, 1944, Vargas authorized the Brazilian Foreign Office to enter into negotiations for a new trade agreement as Brazil speeded up the process of industrial diversification of her economy. Although Vargas had never wholeheartedly endorsed Hull's programs, Brazil's rejection (along with the Argentine and Chilean problems) might well indeed have destroyed the

54. DS 832.5151/1551; 611.3231/1398, /1426, /1428, /1435, /1462A, NA, RG 59.

55. DS 611.3231/1431, /1441, /1447, /1453, NA, RG 59. Also see Warner Baer, *Industrialization and Economic Development in Brazil* (Homewood, Ill.: Irwin, 1965).

56. DS 611.3231/1462A, NA, RG 59.

essence if not the existence of reciprocal agreements in Latin America. If reciprocal trade did not disprove Hull's theory that the political lineup followed the economic lineup, it did prove the invulnerability of special German trade devices in the face of liberal trade rhetoric. Only the promise of extensive American capital investment and the economic consequences of the war in the long run destroyed Nazi economic influence in Brazil. Although the rhetoric of reciprocity allowed the United States to partake in the liberal creed, it proved singularly ill suited to the broader policy goals that the department advocated. By the advent of World War II, the idealism of reciprocal trade agreements had been sobered and tempered to a large extent by the Brazilian experience.

6

A Conflict of Interests

As the preceding chapters have indicated, the primary interest of the State Department in the formative years of the New Deal was the promotion of American export trade. Latin America played a vital role in this economic philosophy because it was to be the testing ground for the wider program. Brazil became more important than France; Cuba more than Holland; and Colombia took on even greater immediate significance than Sweden. This was mainly because of the geopolitical and economic leverage that America could exert in this hemisphere. No matter how difficult the Latins might become, Washington, in the end, would give less and take more in these negotiations than with the industrial nations of Europe. Once Hull could check protectionism—which was more virulent than he suspected—by initiating reciprocity with Latin America, he could move on to bigger markets. But if he failed on the Amazon, he would surely fail on the Rhine. In the area of foreign trade, therefore, the Administration formulated, if not a coherent policy, a nonetheless rational program.

Questions of policy, however, arose over three fundamental issues. This chapter primarily will deal with these problems. The department first had to decide which group of American interests, financial or commercial, deserved a priority in the allotment of foreign exchange by the nations to the south. The second problem was that neither U.S. commercial nor financial interests could agree among themselves as to end and means. The third issue revolved around the changing concepts of the Open Door. In other words, would the United States undertake a multilateral approach in the realm of finance as it had in the field of commerce?

The need for department guidelines in all three problem areas was imperative. Large commercial firms, for example, were represented by the National Foreign Trade Council and used their influence to discriminate against the smaller export firms represented by the American Manufacturers Export Association. In the realm of finance, the bondholders themselves could not agree on policy. The large banking concerns, represented by the Foreign Bondholders Protective Council, and the small bondholders, represented by a multitude of independent organizations, were suspicious of each other. Rivalry and confusion, therefore, existed not only between financial and commercial interests but also within each group.

In the first years of the New Deal, the State Department's actions and inactions benefited American commercial interests. But as the 1930s progressed, the department stepped up its efforts to secure payment on American loans and bonded indebtedness throughout Latin America. This pursuit posed a difficulty in economic diplomacy. Should Washington cooperate with European nations, such as Great Britain and France, in an attempt to procure payment of debts or pursue the same objectives unilaterally? By the late 1930s the answer was clear. Economic liberalism operated only in foreign commerce. The United States would undertake no multilateral efforts in financial matters. European attempts at cooperation with Washington in the area of debt settlements, amortization schedules, etc., found the doors at Foggy Bottom slammed tightly shut to any such *détente*.

The most immediate problem faced by the department was the intense rivalry between American financial and commercial interests for the limited exchange available for foreign remittance. By freezing all or part of its exchange, a country could prohibit its currency from being converted into other currencies. This policy often was used because of a scarcity of foreign exchange resources caused by balance-of-payment difficulties. The problem of exchange control was particularly acute in Latin America and greatly enhanced the contest for available exchange among the capitalist institutions in the United States. No doubt the entire economic picture was much more complex. Bankers, large and small manufacturers, shippers, exporters, importers, plus competing public bureaucracies promoting their own philosophies and special interests all had conflicts. Still, the major protagonists were the financiers and the traders.

With the advent of the Great Depression, private capital from the United States ceased to be available in great quantities.[1] The total net nominal amount of publicly offered foreign securities sold in the United States from March, 1921, to February, 1933, totaled $9,287,000,000. From March, 1933, to December, 1939, it amounted to only $143,854,000. This lack of capital resulted from the rash of defaults in Latin America and the disruption of banking procedures in this country. Without foreign capital, Latin America no longer had the necessary resources for the production of her exports.[2]

The region also faced the adoption of artificial exchange rates, blocked currencies, and bilateral clearing agreements by many European powers. The initiation of the Hawley-Smoot Tariff added to Latin America's economic woes. Nor could Washington's southern neighbors take much comfort from their favorable balance of trade with the United States and Europe. The credit side of Latin America's balance of trade proved deceptive because it overstated the amount of exchange made available by the amount of profits earned by foreign enterprises.[3] Furthermore, the area faced a rapid decline in raw material prices, the slower fall in prices of manufactured imports, and the pressure

1. Harry C. Hawkins, *Commercial Treaties and Agreements: Principles and Practices* (New York: Rinehart and Company, Inc., 1951), p. 188. Henry J. Tasca, *The Reciprocal Trade Policy of the United States* (Philadelphia: University of Pennsylvania Press, 1938), pp. 229–31. For background information on interest group conflict from 1916 to 1923, see Carl P. Parrini, *Heir to Empire: United States Economic Diplomacy, 1916–1923* (Pittsburgh: University of Pittsburgh Press, 1969).

2. *BFDC*, 640 General, NA, RG 40, Amos Taylor to Senator Lee, May 4, 1940. United Nations, Department of Economic and Social Affairs, *Foreign Capital in Latin America* (New York: United Nations, Department of Economic and Social Affairs, 1955) and reprinted in part in Marvin D. Bernstein, ed., *Foreign Investment in Latin America* (New York: Alfred A. Knopf, 1966), pp. 29–65.

3. *FTLA*, pt. 1, Report No. 146, 2d Series, p. 55. Gardner L. Harding, "American Owned Imports Help Our Trade," *AFSJ* 9:12 (December 1932): 481.

of heavy foreign debt obligations (the burden had increased with the decline in prices).[4]

Latin Americans turned to various commercial and financial expedients to halt further deterioration of their economies. Two of the more widely used procedures included the suspension and/or default on American loans and bonded indebtedness and the regulation of foreign exchange. The latter method prohibited the conversion of foreign holdings of its own currency into other currencies. As Henry Tasca stated in his book, *The Reciprocal Trade Policy of the United States*, "The foremost problem in the administration of exchange controls from the standpoint of foreign trade is the allocation of exchange."[5]

The guidelines established by Latin American states for the allocation of exchange on the basis of priorities created a major problem for New Deal officials engaged in matters of economic diplomacy. American financial interests urged the State Department to exert pressure on Latin American nations to allocate the limited amount of exchange available for foreign remittance to cover debt service as the first priority. To the American bank-

4. *FTLA*, pt. 2, p. 142. Herbert M. Bratter, "Foreign Exchange Control in Latin America," *FPR* 14:23 (February 15, 1939) :274–75. Henry Chalmers, "The Depression and Foreign Trade Barriers," *The Annals of the American Academy of Political and Social Science* 174:Supp. (July 1934): 88–93; Henry L. Deimel, Jr., "Commercial Policy Under the Trade Agreements Program," 186 (July 1936) :16–17. James W. Gantenbein, "The Causes and Effects of Government Control of Foreign Exchange," *AFSJ* 13: 2 (February 1936) : 62–63, 92. Ethel B. Dietrich, *World Trade* (New York: Henry Holt and Company, 1939) , pp. 48–54, 104–8, 121–25, 148. TC, *Regulation of Imports by Executive Action*, Miscellaneous Series (GPO, 1941) . League of Nations, *Remarks on the Present Phase of International Economic Relations*, League of Nations, II. Economic and Financial, 1937, II. B. 9 (Geneva: Series of League of Nations Publications, 1938) :13–15; League of Nations, *Enquiry into Clearing Agreements*, League of Nations, II. Economic and Financial, 1935, II. B. 6 (Geneva: Series of League of Nations Publications, 1936) : 10–17, 24–25. Hereafter cited as *Enquiry*. League of Nations, *Equality of Treatment in the Present State of International Commercial Relations: The Most-Favored-Nation Clause*, League of Nations, II. Economic and Financial, 1936, II. B. 9 (Geneva: Series of League of Nations Publications, 1937): 5–15. Hereafter cited *Equality of Treatment*. Wendell Gordon, *The Political Economy of Latin America* (New York: Columbia University Press, 1965) , Chapter 6.

5. Tasca, pp. 229–30.

ers and bondholders, the climate for increased trade depended primarily upon Latin American solvency and payment of debt obligations. To this end, several banking firms and investors urged certain nations on the South American continent to impose quotas on imports, thereby permitting more exchange for debt services, earnings, and dividends.[6]

American commercial interests, on the other hand, argued persuasively that increased trade opportunities stimulated prosperity and, consequently, enhanced the possibility of resumption of Latin American debt service. A letter by E. P. Thomas, president of the National Foreign Trade Council, to the Bureau of Foreign and Domestic Commerce in 1935 urged a priority on foreign exchange relating to the purchase of American goods. Thomas' letter and the basic assumptions of American commercial interests graphically demonstrated a wide divergence of opinion from financial interests. As Thomas put it, "commercial indebtedness resulting from exports of American products takes precedence over the service of bonded debt."[7]

Undoubtedly, Hull and his advisers, in their quest for foreign markets, failed to comprehend fully the friction between American financial and commercial enterprises. Hull's studies in the philosophy and art of tariff legislation had acquainted him with only a few of the complex issues of foreign trade. The Trade Agreements Act itself reflected this myopia, for the department's legislation failed to establish equally systematic guidelines for matters relating to the protection of American loans and investments, if and when these interests conflicted with the abetment of American export trade.

It was not long after Roosevelt's inauguration that Hull and his advisers encountered the rivalry for exchange. Their position, that it was improper for the government to promote or to regulate the competition for foreign exchange, satisfied no one. In the absence of such dictates by the department, American business interests found it necessary to compete vigorously with one another for influence both within domestic and foreign governmental circles. The odds, however, were heavily weighted in favor of American commercial enterprises—a fact not altogether

6. DS 832.5151/132, NA, RG 59. *BFDC*, 640 Brazil, NA, RG 40, Donnelly to Gibson, July 7, 1938.

7. *BFDC*, 640 Brazil, NA, RG 40, Thomas to Dunn, April 5, 1935.

unrecognized by New Deal diplomats. The reasons for this policy came directly from the debacle of 1929.

The advent of the Great Depression laid bare the myth that foreign loans and investments could circumvent necessary readjustments in the American debtor mentality and the infrastructure of the domestic economy. Before World War I the United States, as a debtor nation with a favorable balance of trade, could allow major European states to handle with some degree of assurance the more important problems of international economics. But World War I not only made the United States a net-creditor nation with over $17,000,000,000 invested abroad, it also greatly stimulated American export industries. The United States had become, in the matter of a few short years, an economic giant.

But America shrugged its responsibilities as recklessly as it flaunted its power. Instead of lower tariffs, Congress passed higher and more prohibitive duties on imports. Rather than use wise commercial and fiscal policies abroad and economic reforms at home, the Harding and Coolidge administrations postponed economic collapse by unsound foreign lending. The blame, furthermore, was not altogether the Republican administrations'. Hoover and Hughes, for example, both tried to reverse the unsound loan policies of the private bankers but with no success. As a result, the Republican administrations could not circumvent any great contraction of overextended industry and agriculture at home and, at the same time, buttress unstable economies abroad. Excess corporate profits during the 1920s that had not gone into Wall Street speculation were in many cases carelessly plowed into foreign loans and investments with little regard as to the soundness of the operation. Foreign bonds, as recklessly floated as they were invested, lured thousands of American citizens to seek illusory profits in overseas speculation. In 1929 the bubble burst. Throughout Europe and Latin America suspension or default on American loans and bonded indebtedness became an established method for dealing with the economic crisis.[8]

8. Herbert Feis, *The Diplomacy of the Dollar* (Baltimore: Johns Hopkins Press, 1950), pp. 5, 16. For a brief examination of Hull's commercial philosophy as implemented by the Department of State see Cordell Hull, "Assistance Rendered to American Commercial Interests by the Department

The disaster of 1929 not only spelled the defeat of the Republican party; debt default also created a legacy of suspicion toward the bankers and financiers who had masterminded the strategy now so utterly in ruins. Congress, the American people, and the State Department in their collective search for scapegoats blamed the pernicious influence of Wall Street and the Republicans. A sixty-three page comprehensive policy memorandum entitled "American Diplomatic Policy in Its Relation to the Recent Growth of American Trade and Investment in Latin America" was submitted by the division of Latin American Affairs to Secretary Henry Stimson in January, 1931. A masterpiece of economic diplomacy, it blamed the Republican administrations for a lack of circumspection regarding the chicanery of American financiers in their careless pursuit of profit.[9] No doubt connections between American financial circles and the confusion over World War I war debts, as portrayed by the Nye Committee, further exacerbated tensions between the public at large and the moneyed class.

When President Roosevelt remarked in his inaugural address that "the money changers have fled from their high seats in the temple of our civilization," he probably was not referring principally to international banking activities. Nevertheless, his statement symbolized the New Deal's unwillingness to promote wholeheartedly any policy that smacked of financial complicity. The Administration saw no incongruity in rejecting dollar diplomacy while promoting commercial expansion, since the latter did not entail the use of marines to bail out incautious financial speculators. Both policies, granted, led to politico-economic control of Latin America; yet the means of liberal trade assumed far less military and diplomatic risk. One incident that revealed Roosevelt's hostility toward speculation occurred during the visit of Dr. Hjalmar Schacht, future German minister of economic affairs and president of the Reichsbank, to Washington in May, 1933. Schacht later recalled that when he informed President Roosevelt that Germany would soon cease payment of the interest on the American loans, the Chief Executive gleefully

---

of State and Its Foreign Service," *CPS* No. 39, pp. 1–5. Also see Henry Wallace, "America Must Choose," *AFSJ* 2:4 (April 1934):182–204.

9. DS 811.503110/30, NA, RG 59.

remarked, "Serves the Wall Street Bankers right!" Although re-
tracted the following day, the statement serves to illustrate Roosevelt's bitterness toward the large banking circles in the United
States. This antagonism toward American bankers worked to
the advantage of American commercial interests. In its hesitancy
to give strong support to these American bankers and bondholders during the initial New Deal years, the Roosevelt Administration, consciously or unconsciously, pursued a course of
action in the best interests of American commerce.[10]

The June 12, 1934, Trade Agreements Act best signified the
Roosevelt Administration's preoccupation with the promotion
of American export trade. New Deal foreign trade experts believed that a restoration of international trade and, consequently,
goodwill, would create an environment propitious to American
trade, finance, and investment. The key to understanding New
Deal economic diplomacy in Latin America (with the exception
of Cuba, where the interests of trade, finance, and investment
conveniently juxtaposed) can be found in Hull's effort to free the
international channels of trade and reinvigorate the Open Door.
This was, he believed, the approach that would best protect
American loans and investments and promote the national interests. Indirectly, the trade agreements sought to secure equitable treatment in the allocation of foreign exchange from debtor
countries by the liberalization of international trade. The department rationalized that increased prosperity to both debtor and
creditor nations would facilitate service and repayment on
foreign debts.

The United States Tariff Commission also agreed with the
direction of American economic diplomacy. In its report on the

10. Cordell Hull, papers, General Correspondence, Library of Congress,
Daniels to Hull, August 17, 1934 and September 19, 1935. Cordell Hull,
The Memoirs of Cordell Hull, Vol. 1 (New York: Macmillan Company,
1948), p. 126. U. S., Congress, *Congressional Record*, 73d Cong., 1st sess.,
1933, 77, pt. 5: 4747–49. George N. Peek, *Why Quit Our Own?* (New York:
D. Van Nostrand Company, 1936), pp. 200–211. Philip S. Fogg, "Interna-
tional Implications of the War Debts," *Proceedings of the Institute of
World Affairs*, 11th sess., 11, December 10–15, 1933 (Los Angeles: Uni-
versity of South California, 1934): 149–54. Stephen Heald and John W.
Wheeler-Bennett, eds., *Documents on International Affairs, 1934* (London:
Oxford University Press, 1935), pp. 195–96. Hjalmar Schacht, *My First
Seventy-Six Years* (London: Allan Wingate, 1955), pp. 309–10.

Trade Agreements Act, the commission stated, "To make possible service on or repayment of foreign debts owed the United States likewise was not among the ends set forth in the act."

In the initial negotiations, Hull refrained from any overt actions in support of American bankers and bondholders that might have jeopardized the trade treaties. The department, for example, opposed public hearings by the Securities Exchange Commission on bond default in such cases as Colombia for fear that the hearings might prejudice ratification of the trade treaty.[11] Although Assistant Secretary of State Sumner Welles deprecated discrimination against holders of bonded indebtedness and short-term creditors, he too refused to lodge a formal protest to the Colombian government over the matter. Josephus Daniels expounded this policy as succinctly as possible in a letter to Hull dated August 14, 1934. "Why," Daniels queried, "jeopardize larger trade in these countries by helping to collect money due private parties?"[12]

Secretary Hull agreed with Daniels' position. Against George Peek's advice, provisions concerned with debt service were not written into the trade agreements. As Welles told the special trade adviser, the problem of foreign debt service was not so much one of "permanently blocked funds" but only a question of delay. Any attempt by the United States, Welles argued, to use its unfavorable balance of trade to secure financial advantages might seriously endanger American interests in nations where the United States did not have "effective means of securing equality of treatment for American interests."[13] Much to the displeasure of Herbert Feis, the economic adviser, the department refrained from linking the exchange question with the trade agreements. This left the matter squarely in the hands of competing American financial and commercial interests and foreign governments.

Left to fend for themselves, American financial concerns, as well as a number of bondholder committees, grew increasingly alarmed at the prospects of obtaining equitable treatment in the allocation of exchange. Their fears were probably justified. In

11. DS 821.51/1942; 611.2131/392, NA, RG 59.
12. Hull, papers, Daniels to Hull, August 17, 1934.
13. DS 821.5151/184; 821.51/1711; 611.3231/698A, NA, RG 59.

1934 an Advisory Committee of Exporters and Importers comprised of commercial organizations such as the National Foreign Trade Council, National Federation of Foreign Trade Associations, American Manufacturers Export Association, Export Managers Club of New York, National Association of Credit Men (Foreign Department) and the Council on Inter-American Relations hired Fred I. Kent as consultant. Kent had previously been appointed chairman of the Federal Reserve Board of New York on March 14, 1933. Kent became an object of controversy, however, after it was discovered that when selected by the Advisory Committee of Exporters and Importers, he also happened to be the consultant for the American Bankers Association Committee—a point not altogether overlooked by the Advisory Committee when they made their selection. The incident revealed the intense rivalry existent among the various private financial and commercial factions. Kent, with knowledge and previous experience in financial circles, could use this information to great advantage for the Advisory Committee of Exporters and Importers.[14]

Espousing the liberal trade doctrines of Cordell Hull, for their own interests, various other export agencies set themselves to the task of liberating frozen U.S. commercial credits. "The country must frankly face the fact," exclaimed the Foreign Policy Association, "that its foreign loans cannot be paid except by goods and services, and that, if the United States does not wish to accept such goods and services, it must be prepared to wipe out its foreign investments." American commercial interests, represented by Fred I. Kent and General Palmer E. Pierce, chairman of the Council on Inter-American Relations and assistant to the president of Standard Oil of New Jersey, sought Reconstruction Finance Corporation loans to Brazil in order to unfreeze commercial arrears and further American sales to Brazil. Although the State Department refused the request on the grounds that no government agency had the authority, Pierce and Eugene P. Thomas, president of the National Foreign Trade Council, negotiated frozen commercial credit arrangements in Brazil

14. George N. Peek, papers, Western Historical Manuscripts Collection, State Historical Society of Missouri, Box 16, E. P. Thomas to Peek, November 14, 1934.

totaling $25,000,000.[15] The agreements were made without financial assistance from the government.

In December, 1933, Argentina likewise signed an agreement freeing $40,000,000 to $50,000,000 of commercial credit. The National Foreign Trade Council also looked toward the possible release of some $10,000,000 worth of foreign exchange in Colombia. Bubbling with enthusiasm, Fred I. Kent looked toward further negotiations with Chile and other South American republics in the hope of unfreezing commercial exchanges that totaled $60,000,000. Both Kent and Thomas believed that frozen commercial credit agreements, handled through private business channels and signed prior to reciprocal trade agreements, enhanced the possible success of the State Department's negotiations.

Although the National Foreign Trade Council kept Secretary Hull's department informed on the entire proceedings, Hull and Under Secretary Phillips would express no official opinion on the transactions. Nevertheless, the department did nothing to discourage such agreements. As Ambassador Hugh Gibson reported from Rio de Janeiro, "In Kent's authority to control exchange we have a very powerful instrument for securing proper treatment for our nationals." Proper treatment for nationals protected by Fred I. Kent, however, implied protection primarily for American commercial interests.[16]

The activities of Kent and the National Foreign Trade Council in Latin America, combined with criticism by Senator William Borah, prompted Under Secretary Phillips to call to Roosevelt's attention the conflict of interests between American financial and commercial interests in the allotment of exchange. Phillips no doubt recognized the consequences of inaction by New Deal foreign trade officials; "An important question of economic policy is presented for immediate determination." By staying out of the exchange matter, Phillips said, the Administration aided one group of American creditors at the expense of another. Roosevelt, however, replied with his customary hesitation in matters of economic diplomacy, "Am not clear as to

15. Ibid., Box 13, Foreign Policy Association to Peek, February 26, 1934. DS 832.51/797; 832.5151/166, NA, RG 59.

16. DS 835.5151/162; /208A; 611.3231/976; 832.5151/146; /187; 832.51/835, NA, RG 59.

what this is all about and can therefore give you only snap judgment." The President's reply suggested no change in policy.[17]

American financial interests also suffered from the abandonment of the gold standard. Although certainly not conceived in terms of a vendetta, this piece of New Deal domestic legislation considerably reduced the worth of American loans to foreign powers and caused great consternation among American bondholders. A department report from Buenos Aires in July, 1933, quoted estimates from the Argentine minister of finance that the saving on the service of the external debt to United States interests would run approximately 10,000,000 pesos for the second half of 1933.[18] On June 10, 1933, the New York *Journal of Commerce* stated that the apparent aim of the Roosevelt Administration "will be to pay commercial creditors first in their own exchanges and long term bondholders only after imports had been fully paid for."[19]

The State Department gave no official reply to this statement. Rather, no written priority of lien for American creditors in exchange matters was issued. To some extent this policy also helped to explain the department's reluctance to become too deeply involved with exchange provisions in the negotiation of reciprocal trade treaties. A memorandum by E. C. Wilson of the Division of Latin American Affairs to Assistant Secretary Jefferson Caffery summed up this policy.

> There is obviously a conflict of interest between different groups of American creditors in regard to exchange control, and this is all the more reason why this Government should keep clear of the matter as regards the commercial treaty discussions.[20]

No doubt American commercial interests in Latin America magnified the problem of exchange by underestimating the amount of remittance obtainable through the bootleg market and foreign government sources. Nevertheless, a real problem existed. Any attempt to push the interests of the bondholders too aggressively might well be interpreted as a slap at American commercial interests, and yet the department could not afford

17. DS 832.5151/149A, /150, NA RG 59. *FR*, 1933, 5:60–61.
18. DS 835.51/923, NA, RG 59.
19. DS 832.5151/178½, NA, RG 59.
20. DS 832.51/780; 821.5151/165, NA, RG 59.

to combine the commercial and financial debt situations. As early as April 7, 1933, the American ambassador at Rio de Janeiro urged "a separation between 'frozen' exchange relating to merchandise, and 'frozen' exchange arising from accumulated milreis" on Brazilian bonds.[21] His opinion was shared by Rudolf Cahn, American vice-consul at Rio de Janeiro, who called the exchange problem "a question of imports versus loan service." "Thus," he said, "one or the other must suffer."[22]

The conflict of interest and the intense rivalry for exchange did not end here. As early as June, 1933, Feis quipped to Jefferson Caffery, "It may add a little piquancy to your reading" to learn that E. P. Thomas and the National Foreign Trade Council offered to sponsor and finance the Foreign Bondholders Protective Council (an organization formed under the guidelines of the Department of State).[23] Naturally, the department declined such a generous offer. Thereafter, Thomas continued the search for a formula agreeable to the exporters, the bondholders, and the Export-Import Bank in the hope that the actions of one group would "not nullify the actions of another." The competing interests reached no such agreement.[24]

It appears from this evidence that the State Department's position in regard to the allocation of exchange for American interests in Latin America was in fact to take no position at all. Yet inaction favored the commercial interests. Left to fend primarily for themselves, American financial interests, in the face of debt default by many Latin American governments, could not effectively compete with American commercial interests. This statement is, of course, open to exception. In the case of Cuba, American banking interests pervaded both the Cuban government and American sugar investments (see Chapter 3). An American–Cuban reciprocal trade agreement thereby enhanced the possibility of additional American exports to Cuba and vice versa. But even more importantly, because of United States control of the political economy of Cuba, it earmarked Cuban commercial profits (after American sugar interests received their share) to American financial interests.

21. DS 832.5151/129, /134, NA, RG 59.
22. DS 832.5151/132, NA, RG 59.
23. DS 832.5151/178½, NA, RG 59.
24. DS 832.5151/351, NA, RG 59.

On the other hand, in a case such as Argentina's, in which debt payments had been met, the department became extremely reluctant to prejudice the status quo, not so much for fear of alienating the American bondholders, but for fear that any additional exchange would find its way to British interests rather than to American exporters or stockholders.[25] A communiqué dated July 8, 1933, from Under Secretary Phillips to Fred I. Kent illustrated the Administration's point of view. After discouraging Kent from further meddling in blocked funds in Argentina, Phillips went on to suggest the reasons for such actions.

> It seems that government debt service to Americans accounted for about one-half the allocation to American interests and that the rest represented nearly 10% of the total exchange granted by the Exchange Control Commission although exports to the United States comprised only about 3.4% of the total exports.[26]

Any frozen exchange agreement, therefore, that changed the Argentine allotment of exchange to favor commercial interests could only jeopardize American financial interests without any appreciable benefit to American export interest. The reason for Phillips' concern was obvious. Any cursory examination of the Argentine situation revealed the strength of Great Britain in the political economy of Argentina.

The Roca-Runciman Agreement between Argentina and Great Britain in May, 1933, had contributed greatly to American difficulties. The agreement earmarked all necessary exchange derived from British imports to the service of loans held by British investors. It thereby eliminated the greatest source of foreign exchange for American products. Since Argentina also continued to maintain debt service on American loans, the burden on American commerce intensified. "The possibility of conflict," reported Willard Beaulac of the Latin American Division on October 20, 1933, "between the interests of exporters and holders of foreign bonds must also again be taken into consideration."[27]

Although the State Department did nothing to jeopardize

25. DS 835.5151/141, NA, RG 59.
26. Ibid.
27. DS 835.5151/189½, NA, RG 59.

United States dollar bonds in Argentina (the aggregate interest receipts of which represented the largest debt service in Latin America), certain department officials recognized the difficulties inherent in such a policy. As Ambassador Alexander Weddell reported from Buenos Aires in September, 1935:

> The situation illustrates admirably how foreign loans floated in the United States may redound to the distinct disadvantage of American manufacturers and exporters.[28]

For the most part, however, the activities of the trade organizations, through the negotiation of frozen commercial credit agreements, gave American commercial interests a decided advantage in the struggle for exchange control in Latin America.

Few official declarations of exchange policy were ever made. Those policy statements in regard to the exchange problem merely reflected the majority opinion of the Administration and the exporters. Fred I. Kent, for one, consistently maintained that "payments of bond service rank inferior to almost all other demands on the international exchanges." Kent even went so far as to suggest that the transfer of foreign earnings from American direct investments, as well as commercial indebtedness, deserved "clear priority" over bond payment. The economic adviser, Herbert Feis, readily agreed. "That the demands for current necessities must take priority over payments on old debts everybody recognizes."[29] A memorandum by Herbert Feis in 1937 pointedly inquired as to the "definitely established priority for the allocation of exchange for commercial purposes over servicing of external obligations." Feis received no official reply. He hardly needed (nor, one suspects, actually expected) a definition. The first problem, if not solved, had at least been successfully tabled.[30]

The State Department, however, faced other administrative vexations besides the rivalry between traders and bondholders. A second problem that called for governmental guidelines concerned the friction that existed within the ranks of both commercial and financial interests. Neither commercial nor financial concerns united solidly behind their respective interests. As a

28. *FTLA*, pt. 2, p. 40. DS 611.3531/357, NA, RG 59.
29. DS 832.51/824, NA, RG 59.
30. DS 832.51/1245, NA, RG 59.

result, confusion and internal dissension mounted. Nevertheless, the State Department refused to become too deeply involved in these regulatory functions, also for fear that its actions might unduly favor one group over another. Consequently, the competition for foreign exchange within commercial and financial circles, as well as between them, intensified.

Brazil serves as a case in point. In 1933 a dispute broke out between the large and small export associations. The trouble began with a transfer agreement negotiated by the National Foreign Trade Council, which discriminated not only against American bondholders but small American exporting interests as well. The American Manufacturers Export Association complained bitterly to the State Department that American firms in Brazil not having at least $50,000 in frozen credits "would have to be satisfied with whatever exchange might be left after the needs of the large firms had been met." Two months later, in August, 1933, the American Manufacturers Export Association again complained that since the Brazilian transfer agreement, no exchange had been forthcoming for small United States export firms. Much to the dismay of E. P. Thomas and the Council of Inter-American Relations, the American Manufacturers Export Association initiated plans for separate exchange agreements with other Latin American nations. Thomas' complaints to the State Department fell on deaf ears. Hull refused to become involved in the matter.[31] Any regulations of foreign exchange earmarked for American commercial interests might well be taken as an official affront to American financial interests. Hull and his advisers, therefore, walked a diplomatic tightrope. While paying lip service to each American interest in Latin America, the department carefully avoided entanglement with any single group.

The department's position of "benign neglect" (to borrow a Nixon Administration phrase) successfully avoided being involved in a conflict of interests between commerce and finance. The department likewise succeeded in staying clear of involvement in the allotment of exchange priorities between rival commercial organizations. However, by the mid to late 1930s, the Department of State assumed some responsibilities of a regula-

31. DS 832.5151/169, /170, /172; DS 835.5151/148, /172, NA, RG 59.

tory nature for American bondholders. The reasons for this were twofold. First, in the area of finance there existed too many bond-holder organizations. These groups frequently undercut one another and worked at cross-purposes. Secondly, Hull and his advisers slowly came to the conclusion that without government assistance, resumption of debt service throughout much of Latin America appeared unlikely.

Although the Department of State continued to deny any "implied assent" in the sale of Latin American bonds in the United States during the 1920s, Secretary Hull and his economic advisers believed that American national interests, as well as a sense of responsibility to the American bankers and bondholders, dictated some degree of protection for their investment. The problem centered upon which organization to support and how far the support should go.

For example, in the Colombian negotiations the department encountered the Independent Bondholders Committee for the Republic of Colombia, the American Council of Foreign Bond-holders, and numerous independent banking firms. Faced with the prospects of numerous bondholders committees, each com-peting independently for a favorable debt settlement, the depart-ment helped to organize the Foreign Bondholders Protective Council (FBPC), with former Under Secretary of State J. Reu-ben Clark as president. The department hoped, of course, to establish a more united front against foreign governments in debt negotiations and to make a more positive contribution to-ward their settlement.

Department efforts, however, were not successful without a considerable degree of arm twisting both at home and abroad. The elimination of the divisions and strife that plagued the bondholders became the first order of the day. This task could not be accomplished only by the establishment of the FBPC. For example, Laurence Hoover, the secretary of the Independent Bondholders Protective Council, refused to cooperate with the Clark organization in many of the negotiations, including those with Colombia. Hoover argued that the Foreign Bondholders Protective Council was organized by the major banking concerns, which would quickly sacrifice private bondholders in order to procure short-term loans to various departments and municipali-ties. The accusations contained an element of truth. The National City Bank of New York, which held short-term loans to Colombia, continued to be paid, while both commercial creditors and long-term bondholding interests failed to secure payment. Colombian municipal and departmental bonds likewise were in default, but national government bonds were met. As Freeman Matthews, a member of the Division of Latin American Affairs, explained in a memorandum dated May 9, 1933, "There was a direct conflict of interest between several American classes of bondholders."[32] But as the Bureau of Foreign and Domestic Commerce pointed out in 1935, "The great bulk of the blocked funds in Colombia pertain to investments." The amounts of frozen funds in commercial transactions seemed trivial in comparison with unremitted earnings on investments.

In an effort to blunt the criticism aimed at the Foreign Bondholders Protective Council and to buttress its sagging prestige, the State Department in April, 1935, urged Joseph P. Kennedy and the Securities Exchange Commission to investigate the question of protective committees. In particular, the department directed its attack against Laurence Hoover and the IBPC. The hearings, directed by Judge James Landis of the commission, dragged into 1937 but uncovered some startling facts. For one, they revealed a definite conflict of interests between large investors and short-term creditors of the Colombian government and the bondholders, the long-term creditors. Two members of the Independent Bondholders Council, for example, were found to be employed by Standard Oil of New Jersey. When questioned before the Landis committee, Colonel Edward F. Hayes, a director of the board of Standard Oil, admitted that in a conflict of interest between the oil company and the bondholders his allegiance would be to the former. By December, 1937, several members of the Hoover council had resigned, the organization thoroughly discredited.[33]

On the other hand, the department's connections with the Foreign Bondholders Protective Council were, according to Under Secretary Phillips, "excellent"; and the department in cases

32. DS 821.51/1634, NA, RG 59.
33. William Phillips, diary, 1933–1936, Vol. 5, Houghton Library, Cambridge, Mass., April 11, 1935. DS 832.51/866; 821.5151/174; 821.51/1882, /1889, /2087, /2088, /2156, NA, RG 59. *BFDC*, 640 Brazil, NA, RG 40, Jones to Thomas, April 19, 1935.

such as the Brazilian negotiations suggested to its embassy in Rio de Janeiro that the Vargas regime be informed that the council "was itself a product of Government initiative." But Hull, acting with the approval of Roosevelt, refused to identify too closely with the bondholders council. Although the government had helped initiate the council and had an "excellent" working relationship with it, the department did not want to jeopardize the success of the trade negotiations. Obviously perplexed at Hull's decision, Ambassador Hugh Gibson argued that the bondholders represented "the most important American interests in Brazil." The department's instructions, Gibson exclaimed, had been of such a "perfunctory" nature that little assistance could be rendered to American bondholders. Gibson further warned that unless "positive steps" were taken to safeguard American bondholders the consequences would be lamentable. Nevertheless, the department, and in particular Assistant Secretary Sumner Welles, refused to consider any working partnership with the council. The following years would witness drastic modifications in the policy—for without administrative guidelines, the prospects for a united front by American bondholders seemed remote. And without the department's backing, the chances for success in the Latin American debt negotiations appeared equally distant.[34]

Changes in administrative policy nevertheless occurred. Slowly, the department began to take a more aggressive role both in actively promoting the interests of bondholders and in assuming more directional control over the Foreign Bondholders Protective Council. The reasons behind these subtle shifts in policy were not altogether obvious. Mounting pressure from the financial community and the department's growing connection with the FBPC partly explained the change. Also of importance was the fact that by the late 1930s the department no longer assumed that increased trade would automatically solve other nations' allocation of exchange problems. Brazil again illustrated this fact.

In 1937 Vargas again suspended the remission of funds destined to the service of the external debt and called for new nego-

34. Phillips, diary, Vol. 4, March 16, 1935. DS 832.51/811, /850, /862; 821.51/1569, /1713, NA, RG 59.

tiations. The suspension did not include the obligations assumed for the liquidation of commercial credits in arrears. The United States share of the defaulted bonds totaled approximately $370,000,000. The State Department estimated that perhaps as many as 120,000 American bondholders had a stake in the Brazilian negotiations. Although J. Reuben Clark and the bondholders expected aggressive action by the State Department to force Vargas into reconsideration, Welles refused to follow such action on the basis that any coercive measures might "seriously prejudice the operation of the Brazilian–American commerical agreement."[35]

Throughout 1937 and 1938, Clark, president of the protective council, and his successor, Francis White, refused to agree to any permanent debt settlements as suggested by Brazil and Colombia until the price of coffee had stabilized. The council's relations with Brazil remained static until the March 9, 1939 Aranha Agreement in which the Vargas regime, against strenuous opposition from the Brazilian army, agreed to resume debt payments. Dana G. Munro, chief negotiator for the council, prepared to depart for Rio de Janeiro. Welles urged the Brazilian government to defray Munro's expenses, which amounted to $7,500, with the proviso that upon completion of the agreement the council (under State Department directives) would reimburse Brazil.

To speed the negotiations, Hull and his advisers applied pressure on both parties. The department, for example, intimated that export-import funds for the construction of a Brazilian steel plant required a debt settlement. Nor did the department take a passive role regarding the claims espoused by the Foreign Bondholders Protective Council. In fact, the department pressured the council tremendously in the Brazilian negotiations, virtually coercing Francis White into an acceptance of the final settlement. The department made it clear to the council that without the assistance of the foreign minister, Oswaldo Aranha, the chance for success in the negotiations appeared impossible. They further explained that growing opposition from the Brazilian army had made Vargas extremely skeptical of the merits of a debt settlement. For these reasons, Aranha and the State Department de-

35. DS 832.51/1196, /1199, /1216, /1222, NA, RG 59.

manded that the council accept a compromise solution. Under pressure, the council agreed to a longer amortization period and a lower rate of interest on its long-term bonds.[36]

In the Colombian debt negotiations, the State Dpartment assumed an even more didactic role toward the Foreign Bondholders Protective Council. Attempts by Munro to affect a temporary debt settlement with Bogotá collapsed in the fall of 1937. Throughout the following year, Francis White continued to handle the Latin American negotiations in such a truculent fashion as to render settlement impossible in many cases. With the Colombian negotiations stalled, Chile and Costa Rica likewise threatened to circumvent the council by a direct appeal to the bondholders, who they believed would be more susceptible to a compromise settlement. Obviously distressed at the council's failure, Under Secretary Welles dictated the following guidelines to Laurence Duggan: "I think we have come to the point where if the Foreign Bondholders Protective Council continues to expect our help and active interest, they will have to abide by our recommendations as to policy."[37]

The State Department also assumed a harder line toward the Colombian government. Herbert Feis informed Bogotá that the department expected debt negotiations to be handled through the Foreign Bondholders Protective Council and no other organization. Warren Lee Pierson, president of the Export-Import Bank, reluctantly agreed to the State Department's policy that no export-import loans would be considered until Colombia met her debt obligations. However, in 1939 the bank modified its policy to rule out only credits for official purchases; private concerns in Colombia received credit considerations.

Administration policy remained inconsistent. While Pierson and the State Department discriminated against the Colombian government for its financial recalcitrance, the Peruvian and Brazilian governments, both of which had likewise defaulted on externally funded obligations, received credit consideration.

By 1940, partly for political and economic reasons, the department found the question of Colombian debt obligations increasingly embarrassing. Under the sponsorship of Sumner

36. DS 832.6511/79; 832.51/1152, /1241, /1244, /1406, /1480, /1491, /1520, /1522, /1530, /1831, NA, RG 59.

37. DS 821.51/2221; 832.51/1831, /2217, NA, RG 59.

Welles, the department negotiated a settlement much to the dissatisfaction of the council. Dana Munro later recalled that the entire episode smacked somewhat of a double-cross to the bondholders. The terms of the agreement, as well as the manner of the negotiations, far from satisfied the council. Yet the State Department would exert no further pressure on the Colombian government. The final debt settlement with lower interest and longer amortization periods was a compromise weighted in favor of the Colombians. But a salient feature of the sequence of events lay in the extent to which the State Department, by the late 1930s, had assumed a quasi-public responsibility in matters of financial importance long considered the domain of private enterprise.[38]

The third issue that called for administrative guidelines arose in the late 1930s, after the department adopted a more aggressive role in the protection and procurement of American loans. But a policy of increased aid to American financial interests still posed a problem of mechanics. In short, should the United States cooperate with the major European creditors to effect joint debt settlements in Latin America or pursue a unilateral course of action? The essence of reciprocal trade agreements implied a harmony of interests among exporting nations that could best be realized under liberal trade doctrine. No such philosophy existed in the realm of finance. In fact, by this late date, Hull had good reason to believe that no such harmony of interests existed in the commercial sphere as well. The number of exclusive bilateral agreements and special commercial and financial privileges had not diminished with the passage of the Trade Agreements Act in 1934. Hull, therefore, decided against multilateral ventures in the payment of foreign debts.

The department soon came to accept the fact that the Open Door in matters of commercial relations (equality of treatment for all nations with special bargaining favors for none) had no such corollary in matters of finance. Throughout Latin America, British financiers, backed by the prestige and pressure of Downing Street, vigorously competed with American financial interests for exchange available for foreign remittance. Although the United States supplied a major share of the loans to the Carib-

38. Personal interview with Dana G. Munro, January 29, 1968. Also see DS 821.51/2106, /2240, /2264, /2315, /2344, /2352, /2353, /2383, /2401½, /2413, /2425, NA, RG 59.

bean area and the western regions of South America, Washington encountered strong European competition on the Atlantic seaboard of the southern continent. In Argentina the Roca-Runciman Agreement, which was signed in 1933 and renewed in 1936, provided ample proof of London's intention to use every available means of pressure to attain desired financial and commercial ends. As a result of such agreements, the department became increasingly bold in its attempts to protect American financial interests from British discriminations. The department no doubt had cause for alarm. British financial interests, with the aid of the foreign ministry, did not limit themselves to Argentina.[39]

In Brazil, for example, as a result of the failure of American bankers (but not the British) to finance the Vargas revolution, the latter's banking interests first secured their loans. Rothschild and British accounts continued to be paid, while American financiers stood in line. The Niemeyer plan, devised in 1934 by British interests, weighted Brazilian foreign debt payments for 1934–1937 against the United States. The schedule of payments and the priority given to federal rather than state and municipal bonds all worked to Great Britain's advantage.[40]

In 1935 the Department of State had pushed for a bilateral financial settlement with Brazil to be negotiated by the Foreign Bondholders Protective Council at the expense of British, French, and other foreign interests. Little headway had been made. Not until 1938–1939 did the Foreign Bondholders Protective Council, abetted by the good offices of the State Department, succeed in regaining the initiative. The upcoming Aranha negotiations greatly served to create this newly found leverage. The British interests, represented mainly by the Rothschilds, as well as the French financial interests, decided at this juncture to join with the American group in arriving at a debt settlement with Brazil. The State Department, however, would hear nothing of the plan, since as Under Secretary Welles put it,

39. Rudolf A. Clemen, "Economics in Latin-American Relations," *Proceedings of the Institute of World Affairs*, 14th sess., 14, December 13–18, 1936 (Los Angeles: University of Southern California, 1937):134–37. See also Bernstein, pp. 3–26.

40. DS 811.503132/8A; 550.51/639; 832.51/752, /757, /800 3/4, /889; 832.5151/132, /139, NA, RG 59.

the Brazilian government had "repeatedly informed us that they would reach an agreement with the Americans but were not interested in reaching an agreement with the Europeans." The danger of a European war also lessened the likelihood for successful negotiations by the British and French bondholders. The State Department, therefore, remained cool to any suggestion by London or Paris for joint negotiations.[41]

Intense Allied rivalry, even during the war against the Axis powers, did not abate. Great Britain had tremendous cause for alarm, as approximately one-half of her investments in Latin America were liquidated during World War II. Problems over foreign debt settlement in Latin America continued to plague Allied diplomacy. As late as 1944, the major financial powers had not yet reached agreement in regard to the Brazilian debt. A March 1, 1944, memorandum by Laurence Duggan referred to one British financial scheme "as a means by the British of ruining Brazil's credit in the United States in order to force Brazil to secure Government loans in Great Britain."[42] Not until the "Paris" and "Hague" clubs of the postwar era did Washington agree to joint United States–European sponsorship of debt settlements in Latin America. These "clubs" were agreements by the major European and American banking concerns, sponsored by their respective governments, to scale down interest payments and amortization periods.

In conclusion, Hull's department consistently resisted pressure to undertake a multilateral approach to the Latin American debt problem. The Administration's Open Door policy in Latin America (incorporating the reciprocal trade agreements as the cornerstone) pertained only to the quest for import and export markets. No similar multilateral undertakings were launched in the field of Latin American finance. If "invisible hands" were indeed at work in the international economy, they appeared less able to erect an edifice of international finance solidly grounded on multilateral principles than to construct nationalistic policies much narrower in scope.

41. DS 832.51/1360, /1496, /1550½, /1568, /1640, /1673, /1714, NA, RG 59.
42. DS 832.51/2331, NA, RG 59.

7

Argentina and the Failure of Reciprocity

The domestic opposition to Hull's trade schemes was mild in comparison with the rancor created in Argentina. In 1935 the *American Foreign Service Journal* optimistically predicted that "Argentina is becoming one of the most confident cooperators with the United States in seeking the solution of all major inter-American problems." Less than a half a decade later the United States ambassador to Buenos Aires, Nelson Armour, sadly predicted to Secretary Cordell Hull that Argentina was fast becoming the "outpost of the Rome–Berlin Axis" in the Western Hemisphere.[1] What had gone wrong? Had American policymakers in the early New Deal deluded themselves into a false sense of euphoria, or had American political and economic relations with Argentina in 1940 floundered on the rocks of more contemporary suspicion and intrigue? No doubt Argentina's long standing intellectual, political, cultural, and economic ties with Europe fostered a degree of independence and sensitivity that rebelled at the slightest hint of United States hegemony in the Western Hemisphere.[2] But were the flames of nationalistic sentiment in the Pampas kindled by New Deal statesmen ill-suited or possibly ill-equipped to deal with the problem? An examination of the reciprocal trade negotiations provides some of the answers.

The cultural and intellectual dichotomy between the hemisphere's chief protagonists found little solace in the similarities

1. John W. White, "Secretary Hull Wins South American Good Will," *AFSJ* 12: 7 (July 1935) :408. DS 611.3531/1558, NA, RG 59.

2. For the better general works on United States–Argentine relations see Arthur P. Whitaker, *Argentina* (Englewood Cliffs, N. J.: Prentice-Hall, Inc., 1964) ; Harold F. Peterson, *Argentina and the United States, 1810–1960* (Albany: State University of New York, 1964) ; Aldo Ferrer, *The Argentine Economy* (Berkeley: University of California Press, 1967) .

of climate and agricultural exports. Competitive rather than complementary in the nature of productive resources and economic organization, United States trade relations with Argentina witnessed the greatest fluctuation in both value and volume of trade in all of Latin America.[3] From 1929 to the end of 1932 American exports to Argentina plummeted from $209,900,000 to $31,000,000—a greater decline than to any other large United States market in South America. American imports from Argentina showed an appreciable decline. In 1929 Argentine exports (dutiable and free) to the United States amounted to $117,-600,000. By 1932 the Argentinean trade figures had fallen to a meager $15,800,000.[4] To a great degree the 1930 Hawley-Smoot Tariff was to blame for this decline in trade, since it raised the duties on fresh, frozen, and canned beef to $.06 a pound. Also a sanitary embargo on South American beef impeded a major source of income for Argentina.[5]

Argentina, for her part, went off the gold standard in December, 1929, and in October, 1931, initiated exchange control. In November, 1933, Argentina established a dual exchange market with the *prior permit* system for the purchase of foreign exchange, in which an importer applied for a permit to obtain the official rate and, if refused, turned to the higher prevailing rate in the free market. Quota allocations, invidious methods of valuation, and a host of previously mentioned devices stifling the flow of international goods likewise characterized Argentina's attempt to remain economically solvent. She did not, however, default on foreign debt obligations and remained fiscally responsible throughout the decade of the 1930s—a record matched by few Latin American republics.[6]

3. League of Nations, *Considerations on the Present Evolution of Agricultural Protectionism*, League of Nations, II, Economic and Financial, 1935, II. B. 7 (Geneva: Series of League of Nations Publications, 1936) : 8–33.

4. *FTLA*, pt. 2, Report No. 146, 2d Series, p. 29. *FTUS*, 1934, TPS No. 162, p. 79. *Operation*, June, 1934, to April, 1948, pt. 5, Summary, p. 20.

5. Ethel B. Dietrich, *World Trade* (New York: Henry Holt and Company, 1939) , p. 291. *FTLA*, pt. 3, p. 121.

6. *FTLA*, pt. 2, pp. 8–11; TC, *Regulation of Imports by Executive Action*, Miscellaneous Series (GPO, 1941) , p. 20. Herbert M. Bratter, "Foreign Exchange Control in Latin America," *FPR* 14:23 (February 15, 1939) : 278–79.

Argentina contended with some justification that American tariff acts in 1921, 1922, and 1930 created "insurmountable" barriers to trade. In 1919, 18.9 per cent of Argentina's total exports came to the United States; by 1932 only 3.4 per cent of her total exports found a market in the United States. Defensive measures aimed at protecting the exchange situation in Argentina therefore followed rather than preceded American tariffs. No doubt depression alone would have magnified Argentina's exchange problem, but combined with American tariffs and sanitary embargoes on meat, the results were staggering. The ratio on American ad valorem equivalents in 1932, as compared to more liberal trade years, ranged from 300 per cent on canned meats to approximately 570 per cent on flaxseed and casein.[7]

Although the chances for successful negotiations with Argentina did not appear bright, Hull realized the futility of the broader implications of reciprocal trade unless the singularly most important nation in the South American continent also espoused the multilateral doctrine. Nevertheless, the history of United States–Argentine reciprocity negotiations demonstrated the timidity and fear on the part of Roosevelt and the State Department to pursue basic ideals in the face of domestic political and economic adversity.

Argentina, like numerous Latin American states, appeared at the onset of the State Department's commercial *détente* generally receptive to Hull's trade ventures. As Donald Dozer wrote, "The gradual drying up of Latin American markets in Europe under the system of economic nationalism" increased the desire of Latin American nations for enlarged export outlets in the United States. Buenos Aires, however, refused to espouse any Pan-American ideal that smacked of United States tutelage. A basic reorientation of Latin American policy toward political and economic connections with the United States and the adoption of regional or hemispheric solidarity grounded on a rejection of involvement in European affairs failed to engender warm response from such nations as Chile, Peru, Uruguay, and Argentina. Politically, Argentina's espousal of the Saavedra Lamas Anti-War Pact, although not recognized by American diplomats at the 1933 Montevideo Conference, demonstrated her disdain

7. DS 611.3531/199, NA, RG 59.

for hemispheric unity. The pact was not so objectionable for its content as for its intent, which was to stall the diplomatic momentum of Roosevelt's and Hull's overtures.

Economically, Argentine acceptance of the May, 1933, Roca-Runciman Agreement signaled Buenos Aires' reluctance to adopt inter-American solutions to economic problems. The Roca Agreement, which was signed in order to protect Argentina's meat markets in Great Britain from the Ottawa Agreements, limited the exchange available to American interests and thereby denied full equality of treatment to the United States in exchange matters. These decisions charted the course of Argentine political and economic history toward the viscissitudes of European economic nationalism rather than the ideology of the Roosevelt Administration.[8]

Argentina, however, did not make her choice rashly. Hopeful of supplying the United States with 1.5 per cent of its meat supply and increasing linseed, casein, hides, wool, extract of quebracho, and fruit exports to the United States, Argentina as early as January, 1933, agreed to reciprocity negotiations with the incoming Roosevelt Administration. The *Buenos Aires Herald, La Prensa,* and *La Nación* on March 24, 25, and 26, 1933, respectively, echoed government optimism and enthusiasm for reciprocity. Both Washington and Buenos Aires refused to examine basic economic difficulties without first putting on rose-colored glasses. Delayed first by the London Economic Conference, Argentina's ambassador, Felipe Espil, was thereupon informed that trade negotiations during the remaining summer months of 1933 appeared unlikely. Espil refused to give up so easily. "Pressing the matter" of a reciprocity agreement, he appealed directly to Roosevelt. Out of deference to American interests in Argentina, the State Department agreed to include Buenos Aires in the "exploratory" studies. The Commerce Department quickly followed suit. The Latin American Committee

8. Whitaker, pp. 92–93 DS 835–5151/116A, /130, /232½; 835.51/976½, NA, RG 59. Donald M. Dozer, *Are We Good Neighbors?* (Gainesville: University of Florida Press, 1961), pp. 25, 48. Stephen Heald and John W. Wheeler-Bennett, eds., *Documents on International Affairs, 1936* (London: Oxford University Press, 1937), pp. 544–47. Cordell Hull, *The Memoirs of Cordell Hull,* Vol. 1 (New York: Macmillan Company, 1948), p. 349.

of the Inter-Departmental Advisory Board on Reciprocity Treaties, the Agriculture Department, and the Tariff Commission likewise initiated studies. The following day, July 13, 1933, Chile, Canada, and Uruguay asked to be considered in reciprocal trade negotiations. The department refused the requests.[9]

Under Secretary of State William Phillips conveyed to Ambassador Espil the hard facts of Roosevelt's and Hull's fear of substantive trade agreement discussions with Argentina. Talks with an agricultural competitor such as Argentina, stated Phillips, only aroused congressional opposition and prejudiced the entire trade program. Hull later suggested that a reciprocal agreement limited to only a small number of commodities might gradually be extended to encompass more substantive products. The move would thereby circumvent domestic opposition. The department made no mention of the Roca Agreement. Unimpressed with the department's procrastination, Espil communicated a veiled threat that if the United States failed to negotiate a trade agreement she must suffer the consequences.

Cognizant of both President Agustín Justo's continuance of interest and amortization payments to American bondholders and investors and British attempts to stifle the Argentine market for American automobiles and other manufactured goods by earmarking 30 per cent of Argentina's exchange, Roosevelt sought to increase purchases from Argentina on linseed, tin, corned beef, and wine. In this way the New Deal trade advisers sought to increase Argentina's exchange for the purchase of principal American export items such as cotton and silk manufactures, cordage, automobiles and auto parts and accessories, rubber, lumber and petroleum products, and agricultural machinery.[10] Nonetheless, the Roosevelt Administration stalled reciprocity discussions. On December 1, 1933, Secretary of Agriculture Henry Wallace informed Roosevelt and the State Department that a report by the Bureau of Agricultural Economics concluded that a reciprocity treaty with Argentina would amount to a net loss to American agriculture. Any real concessions granted in the reciprocity agreement, the report argued, should be forthcoming from American industrial goods. For months the de-

9. DS 611.3531/126, /130, /133, /143–146A, /153; 611.2531/70; 611.3331/28, NA, RG 59.

10. DS 611.3531/142, /161, /169, /174–175, /196; 800.51/887, NA, RG 59.

partment avoided Argentine trade experts sent to Washington for the negotiations.[11]

On December 27, 1933, Assistant Secretary of State Francis Sayre laid out the fundamental problems of policy inherent in the Argentine trade negotiations to President Roosevelt. Did Administration trade policy desire substantial tariff reductions or "a series of shadow treaties?" "The real question," remarked Sayre, "is as to political expediency." The granting of real concessions to Argentina "which are not radical nor unduly injurious to American producers" became the illusory goal of American policymakers.[12]

Throughout 1934 the State Department shied away from any written commitments to Argentina that might have limited American freedom of action in matters of commercial policy. Although Argentina extended certain nonobligatory tariff reductions to the United States granted in the Roca Agreement and continued to maintain foreign debt service, all indications pointed to further European inroads into Argentina's commerce. Bilateral exchange agreements similar in nature to the Roca Agreement were signed with Germany, Switzerland, the Netherlands, Belgium, and Spain. A 20 per cent surcharge on American imports brought pleas for relief from Chrysler Corporation and the Automobile Manufacturers Association. But as Alvin Hansen observed, the failure of a trade treaty could hurt the United States very little, since Argentina vitally needed American petroleum, electrical, industrial, and automotive products.[13]

The Great Depression and economic nationalism also affected Argentine exportation of meat. On January 1, 1927, the United States prohibited the importation of Argentina's meat from contaminated regions because of an outbreak of foot and mouth disease. The rationale behind the act lay in the fact that the viruses lived in the bloodstream of both frozen and fresh carcasses before external lesions were perceptible. Only the destruction of such animals, both live and slaughtered, precluded the spread of the disease. Section 306(a) in the 1930 Hawley-Smoot Tariff Act established a sweeping sanitary embargo that

11. DS 611.3531/221, NA, RG 59.

12. DS 611.3531/229, NA, RG 59.

13. DS 835.5151/415, /423; 611.3531/227, /269, /314½, /318–320, /325, NA, RG 59.

required the Department of Agriculture to exclude nations, rather than specified regions, from meat imports other than cured meats if found to contain foot and mouth disease. Although due care was in order, the measure was a purely protective device, not designed to give protection from disease but from Argentine competition.

By widening the provisions of the 1927 act to include countries rather than regions, Argentina's mutton and beef exports to the United States dwindled to insignificance. (Uruguayan meat was not impeded by the sanitary embargo. However, the Hawley-Smoot rates effectively barred most of Uruguay's export trade.) Argentina's newspapers faithfully relayed to their readers congressional opposition in the United States to any modification of the 1930 provision. American livestock associations, in an effort to justify their own existence to the cattlemen and sheepmen throughout the country, added to the cacophony. By building ill will between the hemisphere's most powerful nations, the livestock associations, and one might add the American Farm Bureau, attempted to build membership and increase dues by creating an illusory enemy in the Argentinean.[14]

In May, 1935, the United States agreed to a Sanitary Convention allowing for freer access of Argentina's meats into the United States. In a sense, this gesture of reciprocity by the Roosevelt Administration became an integral part, not only of the Argentine–American trade agreement, but also of the Good Neighbor policy. In an attempt to strengthen hemispheric unity at the 1935 Pan-American Commercial Conference at Buenos Aires through the improvement of political and economic relations and the promotion of freer trade, the passage of the Sanitary Convention became an acid test of United States sincerity. To the dismay of the State Department and numerous trade organizations, however, the Senate Foreign Relations Committee refused to report the bill out of the committee. The failure of ratification likewise caused serious embarrassment at the 1936 Inter-American Peace Conference, also held in Buenos Aires. More-

14. *BFDC*, 400.0 Argentina, NA, RG 40, American Manufacturers Export Association to Roper, October 20, 1935. Franklin D. Roosevelt, papers, Franklin D. Roosevelt Library, Hyde Park, N. Y., Official File, 614–A, Trade, Box 2. DS 835.5151/579, 611.3531/138, /362, NA, RG 59.

over, the failure of the Sanitary Convention not only reaffirmed Argentina's economic commitment to Europe but rendered even more difficult the negotiations for a reciprocity agreement with the United States.[15]

The sting of the Senate's rejection, however, was temporarily mitigated by the agricultural drought that severely hit the western farming states in 1935–1936. Consumption demands and the need to restock dwindling domestic cattle herds stimulated Argentina's exports. In these years 32.6 per cent of Argentina's exports to the United States consisted of meat and meat products. As a result of the drought, Argentina's imports increased by 122 per cent in 1935 and remained high the following year. For the first time in recent history Argentina enjoyed a favorable balance of trade with the United States, amounting to $23,398,000. The United States, however, because of a continuance of Argentina's debt service, maintained a favorable balance of payments. Because of an increase in American imports, Argentina also relaxed its exchange provisions, which operated to the detriment of American commercial interests.[16]

The negotiations of the reciprocity treaty with the pride of the Pampas were also postponed until after the 1936 presidential election. The State Department envisioned further delays in the amendment of trade negotiations with Argentina to be caused by impending battles over the renewal of the June 12, 1934, Trade Agreements Act. Politics also played a leading role in the trade discussions after the Supreme Court's Schechter and Butler decisions, which ended both the NRA and the AAA, respectively. Consequently, Roosevelt was left with only the shambles of a farm and industrial program. Shortly after these defeats, Roose-

15. Papers such as *La Nación, The Buenos Aires Herald, La Prensa,* and *Libertad* continually stressed the United States Senate's opposition to beef imports and helped fan the flame of anti-Americanism. *BFDC,* 400.0 Argentina, NA, RG 40, Sevey to Moody, February 2, 1938. C. A. Thomson, "Toward a New Pan-Americanism," *FPR* 12:16 (November 1, 1936) : 202–10. "Pan American Commercial Conference," *AFSJ* 12:9 (September 1935) : 507.

16. *FTUS,* 1935, TPS No. 166, p. 57; 1936, TPS No. 174, p. 93. United States, Congress, *Congressional Record,* 75th Cong., 1st sess., 1937, 81, pt. 1: 832–37; 3d sess., 1938, 83, pt. 6: 6477–78. DS 611.3531/393, /409, NA, RG 59.

velt began to plan new appointments to the Court. Henry Wallace saw a way out. He again informed Roosevelt of the impossibility of attaining both a reciprocity agreement with Argentina and judiciary reform. Roosevelt needed little convincing. Once again domestic concerns and timorous support for the reciprocity program engendered added frustration and bitterness in the Argentine nation.[17]

Circumstances somewhat beyond Argentina's control further handicapped prompt negotiation of a commercial treaty with the United States. Although exchange difficulties lessened throughout 1935–1936, the United States' position remained firm. The distribution of available exchange should be adjusted to the natural volume of trade and not based on the theory of equal exchange for imports versus exports. The State Department certainly had justification for assuming such a position. Nevertheless, it created serious problems. For example the British, although they renewed the Roca Agreement in 1936, continued to use the threat of decreased meat imports in favor of its imperial preferences. Any United States–Argentine agreement that gave trade concessions to Washington or relaxed exchange control to the detriment of the pound sterling might well have meant disaster to the Argentine economy.[18]

Other serious barriers to negotiations included the possibility of major tariff concessions on Argentine flaxseed imports, which in turn would have increased exchange available for American exports. But the Agriculture Department and the Agricultural Adjustment Administration became "most uncooperative," disapproving practically every proposed agricultural concession. Attempts to go over Wallace's head also met with failure and forced Hull to settle for an unsatisfactory arrangement. America would make no substantial concession on flaxseed.[19]

The department also prejudiced the negotiations by condi-

17. Roosevelt, papers, Official File, 614–A, Trade, Wallace to McIntyre, March 13, 1937; Wallace to Roosevelt, July 10, 1936. DS 611.3531/407, NA, RG 59.

18. James R. Scobie, *Argentina: A City and a Nation* (New York: Oxford University Press, 1964), p. 188. DS 611.3531/326, /407; 835.5151/564, NA, RG 59.

19. DS 611.3531/468, /470, /496–497, NA, RG 59.

tioning the talks upon a British reciprocity agreement. Sayre informed Ambassador Espil on October 1, 1937, that without London in the trade fold an agreement with Buenos Aires would not be forthcoming. Sayre did not elaborate on the connection between the British and Argentine reciprocal trade negotiations. Herbert Feis, in conjunction with the Division of Latin American Affairs, also stalled the commercial discussions by urging the incorporation of a protocol (similar in nature to the Roca Agreement) protecting American investments in Argentina against national expropriation. If the Roosevelt Administration signed a reciprocity agreement with Argentina prior to guarantees for American investments, argued Feis, then the United States would lose its "only real bargaining power." Although Feis and members of the Division of Latin American Affairs did not truncate commercial discussions with Argentina, they no doubt further dampened the negotiations.[20]

State also delayed the negotiations by stressing to Ambassador Espil the need for informal discussions designed to reach a tentative agreement before public announcement of the formal negotiations. Sayre believed that this gesture of good faith by both nations entitled the United States to full equality of treatment with respect to exchange allotments and rates on the day of public notice of intention to negotiate a trade agreement with Argentina. By this device, the department hoped to exclude the exchange question from the trade discussions and thereby eliminate Argentina's most potent bargaining weapon. Argentina recognized the ploy and agreed only to a partial amelioration of the exchange difficulty with the formal announcement. Full equality of treatment in exchange matters would be forthcoming after the conclusion of the trade agreement. Any such action prior to the conclusion of a reciprocal trade agreement, argued Espil, would be "exceedingly difficult" because of the Argentine–British relationship.

The basic problem remained. With Argentine exchange policy limited by the Roca Agreement and United States agricultural interests opposed to any agricultural concessions, how could Buenos Aires expect to acquire the necessary exchange to grant full equality of treatment to the United States in exchange mat-

20. DS 611.3531/491, /493, /495, /529, NA, RG 59.

ters, to comply with British demands, and still to remain a solvent state? Argentina, therefore, by partiality as well as by predicament, could not accede to American demands for either equality of treatment or the unconditional most-favored-nation clause.[21]

By early 1938 the possibility of successful trade negotiations brightened. The incoming Argentine president, Roberto M. Ortiz, removed Carlos Saavedra Lamas from the foreign ministry and replaced him with Ramon Cantilo, a man considered more sympathetic toward the United States. On January 29, 1938, Argentina also reduced the surtax on American products from 20 per cent to 10 per cent as a sign of good faith in the coming discussions. The basic Argentine problem of finding sufficient exchange to grant the United States unconditional most-favored-nation treatment while meeting the demands of the Roca Agreement remained unsolved. On January 7, 1938, *La Prensa*, considered moderately sympathetic toward the United States, cited Argentine exchange control, the Anglo–American trade negotiations, and Argentina's desire for the inclusion in the announcement of formal negotiations of a pledge by the United States government concerning the Sanitary Convention as the basic stumbling blocks in the discussions. Secretary Hull for his part refused any compromise on the exchange principle. The United States, he demanded, must have unconditional most-favored-nation treatment in regard to exchange. Hull issued a *sine qua non* that before any preliminary announcement of a trade agreement would be made, Argentina must agree that "under the trade agreement official exchange will be granted for all United States exports irrespective of the status of Argentina's trade balance with the United States." Unless President Ortiz subscribed to such a policy, Hull believed the adverse effects in the United States would not merit the risks involved in prolonging the negotiations.

The department's position, in effect, would strain Argentine–British relations by limiting official exchange for remittance on British investments and create a strain on the Argentine official market. Hull refused to accept any solution of the exchange problem except "the most complete application of the unconditional most-favored-nation principle." To allow Argentina

21. DS 611.3531/541, /547–548A, /553½, /555; 711.359–Sanitary/405, NA, RG 59.

to deviate, Hull maintained, would create a bad precedent for future undertakings.[22]

For its part, Argentina continued to distinguish between "unconditional" most-favored-nation treatment (granting automatically to third powers all trade advantages without compensation) and "unlimited" most-favored-nation treatment (allowing no leeway on matters of official exchange and exchange balance). The Ortiz government also never fully accepted Washington's explanation that Cuba stood in such a historically peculiar situation as to merit exceptionable treatment, while the United States continued to push Argentina into a total commitment to the unconditional most-favored-nation policy. Trade negotiations, argued *La Nación*, consisted in realizing the practical and real, not the blind adherence to doctrine as personified by Secretary Hull. To this end, Buenos Aires proposed to grant the United States either complete exchange coverage on specified items or a definite proportion of Argentine exchange.[23]

The State Department counter-proposed that Argentina grant to the United States official exchange proportionate to American exports in a representative period. Although Argentina accepted the American idea (to the department's dismay), no "representative" period could be found suitable to both nations. Efforts by the State Department to obtain Argentine approval to control imports on a commodity basis rather than a country basis also met with failure. Negotiations between Herbert Feis and Alfredo Louro, chief of the exchange bureau, and the pro-German Dr. Irgoyen, a financial attaché in the foreign office, failed to find a basis of agreement. On March 28, 1938, Sayre informed Ambassador Espil that the time for reciprocity discussions had passed. It was impossible, Sayre explained, to accept the Argentine proposal without abandoning "basic principles."[24]

Argentina, however, refused to revamp its exchange policy to fit United States designs. By mid-1938 her exchange situation had become critical. Exports had decreased by nearly one-half the 1937 figure, while the Argentine exchange bureau further re-

22. DS 611.3531/585, /589–591, /593A, /604–606, /608, NA, RG 59. Also see *FR*, 1938, 5:279–80, 283–86.

23. DS 611.3531/604A, /612 2/3, /615, NA, RG 59.

24. *FR*, 1938, 5:287–90; 611.3531/623, /626, /630, /632, /670, NA, RG 59.

stricted United States products available on the German and British market. Only American agricultural machinery, automobiles, lumber, and a few miscellaneous items received official exchange. Practically all commercial trade was forced into the free market, thus creating a spread between the official and free exchange market of about 20 per cent.[25]

With the extension of the prior permit system in November, 1938, Argentina took a further step toward complete government control of trade along bilateral lines. Under the prior permit system, imports, with few exceptions, were subject to prior exchange permits that entitled the holders to buy official exchange at one of two official rates. Whether or not exchange is granted at either of the two official rates depends not only on the type of commodity imported but also on the country of origin. Germany, noted a May 24 consular report, had become Argentina's second-best customer. The influence of the German system continued to mount in early 1939 with an Argentine wool and wheat barter deal for German machinery. Buenos Aires also negotiated a clearing agreement with the Mussolini regime similar in nature to the Nazi agreement.[26]

By late 1938 all indications pointed to Argentina's continued resistance to Hull's program. To the Argentines, commercial liberalism held little appeal other than academic. Hull's reciprocal trade negotiations had failed with Italy and Germany, nations important to Argentine prosperity. And the agreement with Great Britain, the nation most vital to Argentina, had not yet become effective. For Buenos Aires to forsake such bilateral arrangements as the Roca Agreement prejudiced the economy without the slightest assurance that Washington could or would change its policy in such vital areas as canned and fresh meat.[27]

In fact, American commercial policy seemed destined further to injure the Argentine economy. The Agriculture Department's prohibition of Argentine beef at the New York World's Fair (the United States' decision was made shortly before the opening of the fair) appeared as a senseless act of discrimination aimed at discrediting Argentine beef before a world audience. The Agriculture Department, with State Department acquiescence,

25. DS 835.5151/797, /822, /945; 611.3531/633–634, NA, RG 59.
26. DS 611.3531/635, /672, /853, /956; 835.5151/897, NA, RG 59.
27. DS 611.3531/664, NA, RG 59.

also threatened the Argentine economy through the negotiation of a wheat for Brazilian coffee barter scheme financed through the Export-Import Bank. American wheat exports to Brazil spelled the end of one of Argentina's most important wheat markets. Only after Argentine threats of open economic warfare and a threatened boycott of the Lima Conference did Washington agree to suspend the barter negotiations.[28]

By mid-1939 Argentine–American economic relations had reached such a low ebb as to threaten political and diplomatic relations as well. Argentine newspapers called United States the greatest economic enemy to increased international trade. Argentine commercial policy meanwhile moved closer to the European orbit. By 1939 American automobile sales in Argentina had decreased in sales by one-half over the previous year. Washington, for its part, adhered to its tough line on exchange, and Roosevelt personally refused to consider any tariff concessions on Argentine canned beef. Argentina countered by threatening the imposition of a quota system on American products. By late summer 39 per cent of all American products were embargoed for the remainder of 1939. Only 4 per cent of Great Britain's products and 3 per cent of Germany's commodities suffered a similar fate. A full-scale trade war between the hemisphere's most powerful nations appeared likely. The effects of such an action would spell a telling blow to the Good Neighbor policy and, it was argued, irrevocably lose Argentina to "the totalitarian, bilateral trade orbit."[29]

The history of American commercial relations with Argentina throughout the years prior to World War II points to impracticality and poor diplomacy by both sides. Argentina contributed to the misunderstanding by a semi-controlled anti-American press blustering to the tune of bellicose Argentine nationalism, an arbitrary allocation of official exchange, and an unrealistic view of American agricultural protectionism. Washington's rigidity on both the exchange problem and tariff concessions, combined with "traditional reserve and bureaucratic red tape" and a timorous defense of the Argentine negotiations before the press and Congress, further aggravated the situation. Clearly the re-

28. DS 611.355/165; 611.3531/743, /752, /937, /1277–1279, /1282, /1301, NA, RG 59.

29. DS 611.3531/797½, /829, NA, RG 59.

ciprocal trade program as the economic arm of the Good Neighbor and the harbinger of American commercial prosperity (and thereby the safeguard of American loans and investments) throughout the Western Hemisphere had failed.[30]

Disillusioned by the Argentine negotiations, Washington searched for an alternative program to the trade agreement. Henry Wallace, for example, turned toward such schemes as export subsidies. In a conversation with a State Department assistant, Alger Hiss, Secretary Wallace reportedly "treated the trade agreements program in rather a cavalier and unsympathetic manner, as though it merited little serious consideration for the future." To undertake the Argentine negotiations, Wallace argued, meant "an immediate end to the trade agreements program [and assured] a violent death to the program which was hardly preferable to a slower form of extinguishment."[31] Wallace's attitude toward reciprocal trade, noted Under Secretary Welles, was "very depressing."

Other proposals that circumvented the trade program with Argentina came from within the Department of State. Laurence Duggan of the Division of American Republics urged the extension of export-import credits prior to reciprocity negotiations. Duggan argued that such credit would increase American sales to Argentina, help to ameliorate exchange difficulties, and "drive a considerable wedge" into the bilateral system. Even though he realized that export-import assistance to the Ortiz government might lessen the imperativeness of a reciprocity treaty, Duggan pushed for such a policy. The department, however, refused any wholesale reevaluation of the program.[32]

Welles and Hull remained committed to the trade program. To them the political rather than the economic implications of a trade program with Argentina assumed overriding consideration. A United States–Argentine agreement, Welles remarked to Roosevelt, would "buttress and solidify the good-neighbor policy," retard totalitarian influences, and promote American trade. Welles likewise urged Roosevelt to impress

30. Voluntary Consular Report No. 206 found in DS 611.3531/853; also see DS 611.3531/851½, NA, RG 59.

31. DS 600.1115 /1117, /NA, RG 59.

32. DS 833.51 Bank of Uruguay/12; 835.5151/1031, /1039; 611.3551/837, NA, RG 59.

upon Secretary Wallace the need "to cooperate wholeheartedly in defending the agreement."[33]

The advent of World War II changed the complexion of United States–Argentine trade negotiations. Although the belligerence expressed toward the United States at the Lima Conference by the Argentine foreign ministry, coupled with Argentina's support of Nazi activities in Patagonia, Brazil, and Uruguay, revealed the political predilections of Ortiz, he was willing to mend economic fences with the Roosevelt Administration. Argentina's consumer problem had increased greatly with the coming of war, since Europe could no longer supply commodities such as coal, fuels, iron, steel, and numerous manufactured products deemed vital to the war effort. Exchange restrictions on American products had increased the price of many commodities, causing widespread discontentment among the populace. Ortiz could not afford to lose Radical support, most of which appeared to favor the reciprocity treaty with the United States.[34]

But the war also compounded exchange difficulties with the United States. Although dependent on Argentine products, Washington refused to make substantial tariff concessions on them or extend export-import aid prior to a trade agreement. Great Britain added to the vexation by her refusal to allow Buenos Aires to utilize favorable exchange balances from British markets for the purchase of American goods. Powerful pro-Axis forces inside the Ortiz government, such as Raúl Prebisch, president of the Central Bank of Argentina, Cantilo of the foreign office, Louro, chief of the exchange control commission, and financial expert Dr. Irigoyen all retarded efforts to break the nexus of bilateralism.

The realities of a European war, nevertheless, channeled Argentine import trade toward the United States. It also alleviated to some extent the urgency of a reciprocity treaty in the commercial sphere. Still, Hull sensed the political and diplomatic necessity of the treaty. The semblance, if not the substance, of continental solidarity assumed a higher priority in the face of

33. DS 611.3531/896A, NA, RG 59.

34. Gino German, "Transformation of the Social and Political Structure," pp. 120–22, and John J. Johnson, "The Argentine Middle Sectors on the Political Defensive," pp. 132–37 in Joseph Barager, ed., *Why Péron Came to Power* (New York: Alfred A. Knopf, 1968).

totalitarian pressure. Toward that end the State Department again tried to negotiate a trade agreement with the Ortiz government. Hull also made a concerted but unsuccessful effort to modify the discriminating provisions of the Roca Agreement through pressure on Great Britain.[35] He made it clear to Buenos Aires that the Roosevelt Administration would not prolong the reciprocity negotiations after the opening of Congress in January, 1940. Roosevelt, under no circumstances, would risk battle with congressional opponents of the trade agreements program (which came up for renewal in 1940) in order to ensure the success of the Argentine negotiations. If by January 5 Argentina and the United States had not agreed to terms, then Washington would be obliged to suspend the talks. On August 23, 1939, the State Department gave public notification of the Argentine negotiations. The events that followed pointed again to the lack of diplomatic sagacity that marred American and Argentine negotiations. The failure of the hemisphere's most powerful protagonists in the commercial sphere also heightened existing political and diplomatic tensions and prejudiced the very future of hemispheric solidarity.[36]

Hull's tactics in the Argentine negotiations envisioned the total elimination of all bargaining points in the hope of expediting discussion. In other words, the Department of State would make its best and last offer—no deals, trade maneuvers, or bargains. Ortiz would have only the option of accepting or rejecting the entire package. As a result, Hull agreed to compromise on such questions as quotas and exchange control, but staunchly maintained that American tariff concessions in Schedule II (concessions granted to Argentine imports) represented the United States' final offer.[37]

Argentina, on the other hand, continued to think in terms of

35. DS 611.3531/1291; also see 611.3531/1223, /1241–1244, /1304, NA, RG 59. Also see William Diebold, *New Directions in Our Trade Policy* (New York: Council on Foreign Relations, 1941), pp. 63–64. J. Fred Rippy, *British Investments in Latin America, 1822–1949: A Case Study in the Operations of Private Enterprise in Retarded Regions* (Minneapolis: University of Minnesota Press, 1959), pp. 76–77. For evidence of pro-Axis sympathies in Argentina, see DS 610.1131/322; 611.3531/829, /1496, /1558; 832.51/1458, NA, RG 59.

36. DS 611.3531/1159, /1404A, NA, RG 59.

37. DS 611.3531/1174A, /1317, /1496, NA, RG 59.

horse trading and refused to believe that Hull's concessions represented America's final offer. To complicate the problem, Argentina in December, 1939, agreed to earmark the proceeds of her exports to Britain and France solely for purchases and debt servicing within those countries. Throughout the trade discussions, British economic policy in particular worked to thwart all efforts by the United States and Argentina to reach a commercial *détente*. Thus, two-fifths of Argentina's exchange derived from exports remained blocked. Since the United States concessions in Schedule II failed to provide Argentina with the necessary exchange to meet Hull's essentials, Buenos Aires mistakenly surmised that Washington was merely angling for a better bargaining position. Without greater concessions by the United States, argued U.S. Ambassador Nelson Armour, Argentina would continue to impose a rigid exchange and quota policy against the United States.[38]

On January 2, 1940, Hull sent a final offer to Ortiz prefaced by the remark that the United States had reached the "absolute limit" in regard to tariff concessions; concessions that had been weakened by stringent quotas on Argentine canned meat and linseed. Hull's offer required a reply by Cantilo and the foreign office no later than January 5. If by that date Argentina had not complied with the American position, then Hull reserved the right to suspend negotiations. Argentina, unfortunately, persisted in the belief that the State Department would eventually moderate its tariff policy. To a disconcerted Argentine audience, Hull on January 5 terminated the trade negotiations "with no plan or understanding as to their renewal." Although Hull eventually disavowed the latter phrase, the insult enraged Argentina and created a reservoir of suspicion and ill will.[39]

Ambassador Armour continued to push the State Department into providing Argentina with "an economic alternative" to European bilateralism. In a communiqué dated June 24, 1940, Armour vigorously stressed the fact that in the final analysis economic considerations would determine Argentina's alignment in the impending struggle with fascism. Armour urged the extension of export-import credit or the purchase of additional Argentine products. The maintenance of a policy of drift

38. DS 611.3531/1420, /1467, NA, RG 59. Rippy, p. 84.
39. DS 611.3531/906, /1422A, /1447, NA, RG 59.

enhanced the possibility of "economic and perhaps political domination" of Argentina by the Third Reich.[40] Four days after Armour's warning, the ambassador again urged Secretary Hull to reconsider the consequences of American commercial policy with Argentina. Unless the United States reversed its policy, said Armour, Argentine minister of finance, Dr. Pedro Groppo, would not aid in the economic phases of the continental defense plan. The message, however, failed to be transmitted to the proper channels until valuable time had elapsed. Laurence Duggan confessed to Herbert Feis that the delay in transmission would "remain one of the great mysteries of all time." Duggan went on to lament:

> This Division has not been noted for its nesting habits, but it is just possible that the dispatch may have been used to block a hole in a chair or keep wind from blowing through a crack in the windows. In any case, we will try and do better.[41]

Although the political deterioration caused by United States inactivity in the field of commercial and financial policy continued, Washington also faced increasing attacks on American investments (primarily oil), trade, and loans in Argentina. An adherence to such a policy, calculated to propitiate vested and protective interests at home, promised a complete default on American loans by the Argentine government. Notwithstanding, powerful domestic forces seemed intent on blocking such a *détente*. Congressional criticism voiced the opinion that the 1940 renewal of the Trade Agreements Act had envisioned no reciprocal agreement with the Argentine government. Even within the ranks of the Administration, opposition to reciprocity remained intense. Raymond B. Stevens, chairman of the United States Tariff Commission, vigorously opposed any substantive concessions to Buenos Aires, while Henry Wallace and the Department of Agriculture continued to work for the subsidization of agricultural exports, a policy inimical to Hull's program.[42]

Partly as a result of crosscurrent opinion concerning reciprocity with Argentina, as well as the political and economic consequences of inaction, the Department of State preferred to stall

40. DS 611.3531/1533, NA, RG 59.
41. DS 611.3531/1548, NA, RG 59.
42. DS 611.3531/1539, /1584, /1607½–1609½, NA, RG 59.

the trade negotiations in deference to the extension of export-import credit. In June, 1940, Warren Lee Pierson, president of the Export-Import Bank, extended $20,000,000 to the Argentine government in the hopes of forestalling any precipitous action by Argentina deemed detrimental to American financial or commercial interests. But the effectiveness of American loans fell far short of State Department expectations. Prompted by the Argentine government's belligerence at the Havana Conference, Ambassador Armour with some degree of candor referred to America's chief protagonist in the Western Hemisphere as the "outpost of the Rome–Berlin Axis." Armour continued to stress the importance of increased American purchases of Argentine products as the only solution to protracted friction.[43]

By the spring of 1941 Nazi victories in Europe and increased subversive activities in Latin America pointed to the need for hemispheric solidarity. The assumption of political power in mid-1940 by Vice-President Ramon S. Castillo also pushed Roosevelt into more positive economic steps regarding Argentina. With the Trade Agreements Act renewed and the 1940 elections past history, the President once again felt confident enough to initiate reciprocal trade conversations with Argentina. In May, 1941, (after the passage of the Lend-Lease Act) Washington announced the intention to negotiate a reciprocity agreement with Buenos Aires. The impetus for such a decision stemmed primarily from political considerations. Export-import credit, for example, had forestalled any danger of default on American loans. In April, 1941, Argentina established separate foreign exchange procedures for certain United States products. By July, 1941, Castillo had abolished the Argentine exchange control commission and no longer required prior exchange permits for essential United States imports. Clearly the necessity for a reciprocal agreement stemmed from more important considerations than commercial or financial.[44]

During the course of the negotiations, the United States made substantial concessions in the vital area of meat imports. For example, Washington agreed to cut in half the $.06 per pound duty on prepared and preserved meats and agreed to the proposition prohibiting restrictions on the importation or sale of

43. DS 611.3531/1534–1535, /1558, NA, RG 59. *FTLA*, pt. 2, p. 42.
44. *FTLA*, pt. 2, pp. 11–12.

any product listed in the schedule of reciprocal concessions. The State Department thereby made a vital concession to Argentina on canned beef, a product previously considered sacrosanct to American domestic livestock producers. It was also assumed that these concessions would automatically be extended to Uruguay. Argentina, for its part, modified her exchange control regulations and agreed to apply the principle of nondiscriminatory treatment in the area of quantitative limitations on all export products. Satisfied with Argentina's minor adherence to liberal trade principles, Roosevelt and Hull accepted the treaty. On October 14, 1941, after eight years of political acrimony, the United States and Argentina signed the agreement. It was to become provisionally effective November 15, 1941.[45] But Argentina's continued flirtation with the Axis powers soon dispelled whatever ebullience Secretary Hull might have entertained for his trade program as the harbinger of solidarity between the two powers. As solid as any marriage built on a courtship of suspicion and misunderstanding, United States–Argentine relations in 1941 could not overcome the depths of ill will that had developed the previous decade. Sadly, the efforts of the Administration to amend the economic grievances of Argentina were too little and too late to change the course of the latter's diplomacy.

Disgusted by Castillo's lack of cooperation in hemispheric defense measures, the State Department opposed formal ratification of the agreement in an effort to demonstrate visibly Washington's displeasure. Argentina, however, continued to move ideologically closer to fascism. Unable to deter her right-wing predilections by nonratification of the reciprocal agreement, the United States with "a minimum of publicity" relented on December 9, 1942.[46] Formal ratification only minimally affected Argentina's attitude toward the United States and the Allied powers. As the following years bore striking testimony, the road toward reconciliation was a rocky one.

Most assuredly the political and economic aspirations of Hull's trade program in Argentina had not met with marked success. The secretary had ample justification for disillusionment. Yet, a considerable degree of the failure lay within rather than outside

45. DS, *Bulletin: Trade Agreement with Argentina* 5:121A:Supp. (October 18, 1941):1–44.

46. DS 611.3531/2086, NA, RG 59.

of the Administration. Hull's own timidity combined with Roosevelt's concern for domestic priorities could not overcome powerful protective interests in time to rechart the course of Argentine–American relations. The secretary was incapable of promoting either American commercial interests or retarding bilaterialism in Argentina. Nor did the failure of the trade program pertain solely to Argentina. Other Latin American nations, whose principal export commodities competed with rather than complemented the United States economy, likewise found stern resistance by vested interests in the United States and only lukewarm support from New Deal officialdom. The Administration, as late as the attack on Pearl Harbor, had not made trade agreements with Chile, Uruguay, Peru, Bolivia, Paraguay, and Mexico.

8

The Others

Detailed examinations of United States trade negotiations with Brazil, Colombia, Cuba, and Argentina have been made in this study because of their unique importance to the understanding of inter-American history. This chapter will give an overview of other trade discussions, both successful and unsuccessful, for they too contributed to the interpretation and revision of the Good Neighbor policy. Discussion of these other nations will begin with Mexico.

The long and tedious trade negotiations with America's neighbor south of the Rio Grande finally culminated with an agreement on December 23, 1942.[1] The discussions demonstrated the limitations of Hull's economic diplomacy. For a Good Neighbor policy that could not come to terms with one of its foremost Latin trade partners for nearly a decade had little reason to be congratulated. The history of these negotiations especially in the late 1930s and early 1940s, would be remiss, however, if the reciprocity agreement was removed from the overall context of United States–Mexican relations in the tumultuous years that preceded them.

Mexican appetites for increased trade with the United States were first whetted in the summer of 1934 by the Cuban reciprocity agreement. Mexican exports to America had been seriously impaired by the 1930 Hawley-Smoot Tariff, and badly needed imports from her northern neighbor had also been curtailed by the New Deal's NRA codes. Now, the possibility of a

1. For the text of the agreement see DS, *Executive Agreement Series,* No. 311. For an analysis of the agreement see DS, *Bulletin,* December 26, 1942, pp. 1033ff.

reciprocal arrangement with the United States along the lines of the Cuban treaty offered new hope.[2]

The Cuban treaty mistakenly brought forth the prospects of duty reductions in vegetables and live cattle under 700 pounds within the provisions of a limited agreement. The Mexican government was especially anxious to complete the deal before Lázaro Cárdenas assumed the presidency. Washington would have no part of it. Chief of the Division of Mexican Affairs Edward Reed, and the assistant chief, R. C. Tanis, as well as Sayre and Hull, opted for "a more comprehensive trade agreement" with Mexico that would take "a normal place on the schedule" of negotiations.[3]

Mexico's second revolution of the twentieth century began on December 1, 1934, with the inauguration of Cárdenas. Almost immediately, Roosevelt and Hull faced a brand of revolutionary nationalism that was to test the mettle of the Good Neighbor policy. The revolution had a duality of purpose. At the heart of the matter was Cárdenas' desire for the social and economic improvement of the Indian masses. To accomplish this goal he implemented Article XXVII of the 1917 constitution, the most sweeping agrarian reform in the history of his nation. But for Cárdenas, progress for the masses entailed much more than land. He therefore set out to free his country from the shackles of colonialism. The new nationalism, as historian Charles Cumberland suggested, bred a "pathological xenophobia" toward foreigners in general and Americans in particular.[4]

Cárdenas' conflict with the United States pervaded every major aspect of Mexican economic life: American land was to be nationalized; subsoil deposits were to be protected; mining policies were to be in conformity with labor benefits granted by Article CXXIII; American business interests were obligated to educate the people and to construct schools. Even some American clerical groups found themselves in violation of Articles III and CXXX. Collectively, these economic conflicts became the acid test of Mexico's power and will to achieve real independence.

2. DS 612.1115/50, NA, RG 59.

3. *FR* 1934, 5:387, 398.

4. Charles Cumberland, *Mexico: The Struggle for Modernity* (London: Oxford University Press, 1968), p. 307.

United States–Mexican relations were complicated in June, 1934, when the Mexican leader nationalized the railroads of his country not already under government supervision. The same year, Mexico placed "special burdens" on American exports to offset the disadvantages incurred in her trade with this country. This action was taken, said Ambassador Josephus Daniels to Hull, to raise revenue and not to be in a better bargaining position with the United States in trade negotiations. Hull remained unconvinced.

By 1935 trade negotiations had taken a back stage to these and other more immediate problems. In fact, the *Foreign Relations Series* of 1935–1940 did not even include specific material on reciprocity. The major questions concerned American agrarian claims and a general revision of petroleum concessions. (Cárdenas opposed confirmation of many United States applications for oil concessions.) The plot thickened in 1935 when Mexico's supreme court reversed its 1932–1933 decision and henceforth allowed subsoil rights to flow directly to the Mexican government. The agrarian question came to the forefront the following year when the Department of State made heated representations concerning the November 23, 1936, Mexican expropriation law. The department urged Cárdenas to refrain from expropriating lands owned by United States citizens until authorizations for payment had been made.[5]

The most sensational scene was yet to come. On March 18, 1938, Mexico made its greatest leap toward modernity by expropriating foreign-owned oil companies valued at nearly a half billion dollars. From that moment on, nationalization overshadowed all other trade questions.[6]

5. TC, *Comercio Exterior de la America Latina,* primera parte (GPO, 1931), p. 8. For a short factual analysis of Mexican economic policy see *FTLA*, pt. 2, section 17, pp. 19–28. Also see Cordell Hull, papers, Personal Correspondence, Library of Congress, Daniels to Hull, March 25, 1937.

6. The best accounts of the oil controversy can be found in Bryce Wood, *The Making of the Good Neighbor Policy* (New York: Columbia University Press, 1961), chapters 8–9; Howard F. Cline, *The United States and Mexico*, Rev. ed. (New York: Atheneum Press, 1963), chapters 11–12. For earlier controversies see *FR*, 1935, 4:768–69. Also see William Diebold, *New Directions in Our Trade Policy* (New York: Council on Foreign Relations, 1941), p. 71. Also see background material in Robert F. Smith, *The United States and Revolutionary Nationalism in Mexico, 1916–1932* (Chicago: University of Chicago Press, 1972).

Nature as well as politics hampered the normalization of commerce before the Second Revolution. Petroleum had always been a bone of contention between the two nations because of the oil lobby's power in the United States. In addition, Mexican competition in copper, zinc, livestock, agricultural products, vegetables, fruits, and handicrafts made commercial discussions difficult. Politically, neither FDR nor the State Department had a penchant for martyrdom—a fate they expected if they aroused the protectionist sentiments of the mighty oil and agricultural interests in the Southwest and their spokesmen in Congress.[7] Even New Deal legislators, who ardently defended the reciprocity program in the 1930s (such as Representative Frank Buck of California), hedged on the question of Mexican agriculture and promised that the Administration contemplated no action at the expense of domestic interests. Roosevelt, too, fully realized the political consequences of close economic ties with a government supposedly indulging in religious persecution of Catholics. Throughout these years of Mexican reform, the *Congressional Record* of the United States contained numerous resolutions and joint resolutions, sponsored in large part by the Knights of Columbus, admonishing the Mexican government for its lack of religious toleration. All in all, Roosevelt and Hull saw the political risks of a trade agreement far outweighing the economic benefits.[8]

The reluctance of FDR and his Good Neighbor diplomats to push vigorously for a commercial *détente* with the Cárdenas administration demonstrated more than their hostility to revolutionary nationalism.[9] It also showed that the United States had little compunction to honor the ideals of the Good Neighbor

7. See Hull's 1940 testimony as well as other comments in U. S., Congress, House, *Extension of Reciprocal Trade Agreements Act: Hearing Before the Committee on Ways and Means*, 73d Cong., 3d sess., 1940, 1–3; U. S., Congress, Senate, *Extension of Reciprocal Trade Agreements Act Before the Committee of Finance*, 76th Cong., 3d sess., 1940. Hull, papers, Personal Correspondence, Daniels to Hull, January 22, 1938.

8. U. S., Congress, *Congressional Record*, 74th Cong., 1st sess., 1936, 79, pt. 3:2578–80. For resolutions typical of Knights of Columbus propaganda in 1935 see H. R. 283, H. R. 194, H. R. 277, and H. Concurrent.

9. The author is indebted to David Green, *The Containment of Latin America* (Chicago: Quadrangle Books, 1971) for amplification of the term revolutionary nationalism.

when they conflicted with the realities of national self-interests.

A closer scrutiny of United States–Mexican economic relations should prove the preceding observation. As the American commerical attaché in Mexico City pointed out to Secretary of Commerce Daniel Roper in 1938, American trade with Mexico had increased every year since 1933 without any trade treaty. From a low of $31.6 million in 1932, American exports had risen to $105.8 million by 1937, while Mexican exports to the United States stood at $37.4 million in 1932 and only $55.3 million in 1937. In fact, the United States trade balance had grown so rapidly that it forced Mexico into the adoption of additional customs duties to stem the tide of United States goods.[10]

U.S. dominance of the Mexican market, therefore, predated the New Deal. Beginning with the 1930 Hawley-Smoot Tariff, the United States effectively blocked foreign inroads into its domestic market. Mexico, on the other hand, did not retaliate with the same ferocity. In addition, Mexican duties remained *specific* (constant and independent of the price of imported products) while American duties were mainly *ad valorem* (customs charges fluctuating with the price of the imported article). In a period of depressed prices, such as the 1930s, the United States gained a considerable advantage. Also contributing to the overall Mexican trade deficit was the decreased value of Mexican currency in relation to the American dollar, which, as one Mexican official put it, meant that "Mexican tariffs have amounted to an actual, increasingly smaller charge against American products by Mexico." By the time Cárdenas, in 1937–1938, moved to counter United States trade gains (an action that under other circumstances might have prompted the Roosevelt Administration to take action), both countries had become locked in a larger and more important struggle over oil and the future course of the Mexican Revolution.[11]

The expropriation controversy of 1938 stirred a hornet's nest inside and outside the Roosevelt Administration and delayed the reciprocity program. Especially virulent was the reaction of the major oil companies. For some time they had found the Department of State susceptible to the argument that access

10. *Operation*, July, 1934, to April, 1948, pt. 5, p. 24. Hull, papers, General Correspondence, Lockett to Roper, June 29, 1938.

11. *FR*, 1942, 6: 498–99.

and procurement of petroleum in foreign lands was vital to the national interests. The bonds of this partnership seemed in 1938 to be coming apart. Pressure, importunities, and cajolery were all applied to various public officials in the hope that it would encourage the "hard liners" to take more aggressive actions, such as the rupturing of diplomatic relations, an economic boycott of Mexican goods, and a suspension of all credit to the revolutionary government.

The chief protagonists were Hull and presidential counselor Bernard Baruch on one side and Secretary of the Treasury Henry Morgenthau and United States Ambassador to Mexico Josephus Daniels on the other. American big business waited impatiently on the sidelines for Roosevelt to declare a winner. Baruch unequivocably believed that the nationalization of oil was a prelude to even greater efforts to destroy United States investment in Mexico. Nothing less than the safety of American capitalism was at stake if these rash measures spread to other lands. The expropriation, he claimed, would directly affect the United States by hurting its standard of living and by allowing hostile powers to move into these strategic areas of investments. For his part, Hull interpreted Mexico's action as a slap in the face of the Good Neighbor. Moreover, there was no way of telling just where or how far the expropriation disease might spread. More than the Bolivian expropriation of Standard Oil in March, 1937, the Mexican move signaled the greatest challenge to United States hegemony in the Western Hemisphere.[12]

Confronted by the scope of the Mexican Revolution, the Department of State closed ranks; that is, all but Josephus Daniels. Chief of the Division of the American Republics, Laurence Duggan, Economic Adviser Herbert Feis, and the president of the Export-Import Bank, Warren Lee Pierson, all agreed that until the oil controversy and the question of agrarian claims were resolved, the Export-Import Bank would cease financing Mexican projects. The department also urged the secretary of the treasury

12. Green, pp. 27–28, 33. A brief account of the oil controversy can be found in Edwin Lieuwen, *U. S. Policy in Latin America: A Short History* (New York: Frederick A. Praeger, 1965), pp. 65–66. Samuel F. Bemis, *The Latin American Policy of the United States* (New York: Harcourt, Brace and World, Inc., 1943), pp. 214–18, 345–50. Richard Barnet, *Roots of War* (Baltimore: Penguin Books, Inc., 1972), p. 203.

to suspend the monthly purchase of 5,000,000 ounces of silver from Mexico. After some hesitation, Morgenthau resumed the purchases for fear of driving Mexico into Hitler's waiting arms. Morgenthau also realized, just as Hull reluctantly had to admit, that Cárdenas might also expropriate United States mining interests valued at nearly a half billion dollars if pushed too far. Still, there were other lines of attack open to the secretary of state.[13]

When the United States and Venezuela signed a reciprocal trade agreement, Hull took sweet revenge by establishing import quotas on Mexican oil. By such efforts, Washington circumvented the spirit of the unconditional most-favored-nation clause by not extending the oil concession to Mexico. Henceforth, Venezuela received 71 per cent of United States oil imports, and Mexican purchasing power decreased.

American sales to Mexico decreased while recriminations increased. Trade across the Rio Grande dipped to lows not experienced since the initiation of Hawley-Smoot. The trend that had begun in the early 1930s toward increased trade between Mexico and the United States now ceased. In short, it would be safe to say that the oil problem, along with its other ramifications, nearly set off a full-fledged trade war.

There also ensued an escalation in the tone and harshness of Hull's diplomatic notes to Cárdenas. Fortunately, Daniels tempered the secretary's words before passing them on to the Mexican officials. The secretary, furious over these diplomatic improprieties, prompted Daniels to respond with some personal and unprofessional correspondence. Ironically, the ambassador's overtures may have calmed Hull down.

In a series of letters to Hull that spanned the months of March to October, Daniels expressed his true feelings and sympathies for the Mexican Revolution. On March 22, 1938, he wrote to Hull, "If there must be real and serious strain between our Government and Mexico, I pray it may not be over oil . . . the trail of oil here has been a slimy one." The ambassador spoke of

13. Wood, pp. 223–27. For Daniels' account of the Mexican episode see his *Shirt-Sleeve Diplomat* (Chapel Hill: University of North Carolina Press, 1947). Also see Cordell Hull, *The Memoirs of Cordell Hull*, Vol. 1 (New York: Macmillan Company, 1948); Duggan to Pierson memo in DS 812. 75/94, NA, RG 59; *FTLA*, pt. 2, section 17, p. 17.

American oil interests pushing for armed intervention under Woodrow Wilson and now threatening Mexican national sovereignty once again. American oil and other big business interests, he continued, "go to bed every night wishing that Díaz was back in power." Daniels admitted that Cárdenas' action was rash and even economically unsound. He further believed that the department should aid the oil companies in their efforts to secure compensation. But the effort should be made, he added, not so much out of justice, but because of the ineptitude of the companies themselves.

Daniels, however, never tired in his warnings to Hull that oil should not be the cornerstone of diplomacy. On March 31, 1938, he remarked to Hull that the United States was "walking on quicksand." In a beautifully written letter two days later, Daniels described the tragic history of this Latin nation from Díaz to the revolution. The theme was the worsening position of the Mexican masses and the partial guilt of the American oil companies for their fate. Even at this late date, he warned, the companies were trying to foster a counterrevolution against Cárdenas. Daniels, too, had some very unkind words for American diplomats and their complicity in these matters.

In concluding this April 2 letter, the ambassador called upon Hull to transcend vested self-interests and to make the Good Neighbor policy a reality. Throughout the spring and early summer months, Daniels vainly strove for a *rapprochement* between the neighbors of the Rio Grande. In later personal correspondence, Daniels suggested that American direct silver purchases should not be linked to the oil question, although he remained adamant on the subject of just compensation for agrarian claims. Finally, as the dust of controversy began to settle in the fall of 1938, Daniels struck his heaviest blow in behalf of Mexican economic independence. In an October 18 letter to Hull, Daniels unveiled his true feelings and sympathies for the Mexican Revolution. Incongruous as it may appear, this North Carolina statesman had become very much a part of the revolution. A moralist, a man of principles, a prohibitionist, and an isolationist—Daniels was also a Wilsonian idealist with more than a touch of realism. And yet, he was a man whose humanitarian and antiimperialist spirit pervaded his almost every thought. To Hull, on that October day, he wrote that the British and French empires were the examples that Germany and Italy were emulating. Therefore, it behooved the United States to strike out in an opposite direction from the path of empire. To create hemispheric solidarity, he stressed, entailed sacrifices (oil) that the United States must be willing to make.

Hull never answered the impudent ambassador with the type of ringing defense that his rhetoric was capable of mustering. He was polite, prompt, and always professional in his replies. Yet the sting of economic loss, the fear of impending radicalism, and the pique of personal humiliation, gradually ebbed. Hull never changed his beliefs, but in the stead of anger there developed a reluctant, almost passive, acceptance of Mexico's actions. To Daniels' credit, it was a triumph for personal diplomacy.[14]

The keys to reciprocal trade negotiations from 1938 to 1942 continued to be the inextricable factors of geopolitics and oil. Despite Daniels' importunities and despite the various political and economic forces that prevented a complete break in relations, an oil slick still stretched from Mexico City to Washington. After September 1, 1939, however, neither country could afford the luxuries of conflict. Mexico needed oil markets and did not care where she got them. The United States, on the other hand, had no need of oil tainted with radicalism but hated to see it fall into German hands. Negotiations at last proved successful in November, 1941, when the United States and Mexico publicly agreed to a general settlement of their outstanding questions. Included in this package deal were compensation for oil and agrarian claims, United States purchase of Mexican silver, export-import credit, and assistance for stabilizing Mexico's currency.[15]

The November agreement also cleared the air for a trade treaty. Although concerned that reciprocity might destroy incipient industries, the Mexican government needed more commercial markets to defray the additional costs of the oil and agrarian compensation agreements. At first, the Mexicans sought

14. These letters can be found in Hull, papers, Personal Correspondence, Daniels to Hull, March 22, 1938, to October 18, 1938. For a good account of Daniels' influence see E. David Cronon, *Josephus Daniels in Mexico* (Madison: University of Wisconsin Press, 1960). *FTLA*, pt. 2, section 17, p. 27; section 10, p. 57.

15. Wood, p. 257.

a provisional agreement to open up American markets for oil, cattle, fruits, and vegetables, but the State Department held out for a formal reciprocal trade treaty. On December 23, 1942, Washington got its way. In return, the United States abandoned its tariff-quota limitations on Mexican oil. This concession removed all restrictions on the amount of foreign oil that might be imported at the reduced rate of $.105 per barrel. Mexico for her part bound many United States imports and made some concessions on agricultural and industrial goods. Washington also extended new credits, maintained Mexican silver prices at world market values, and continued military assistance.[16]

One of the more interesting features of the Mexican reciprocal agreement concerned the "escape clause" first introduced in this treaty. By late 1942 chaos reigned supreme in international trade. Apprehension over the consequences of a commercial agreement prompted Mexico to insist upon the following clause:

> If, as a result of unforeseen developments and of the concessions granted on any article . . . such article is being imported in such increased quantities and under such conditions as to cause or threaten serious injury to domestic producers of like or similar articles, the Government of either country shall be free to withdraw the concession, in whole or in part, or to modify it [by duty or quota].

On February 24, 1947, President Harry Truman directed by executive order that all future agreements should contain this "escape clause."[17]

Throughout the decade of the 1930s, the reciprocal trade agreements program had not served its purpose as the economic arm of the Good Neighbor policy in Mexico. Trade between the two states had increased from 1933–1937, in spite of the fact that no reciprocal treaty had been signed. Politics caused a decline after 1938. In each case, reciprocity had taken a back seat to other imperatives of diplomacy. In the trade discussions with Central America and the Caribbean the story was different. By 1941 all of the banana republics had been "lined up," but the

16. *FR*, 1940, 5: 1046–47; 1942, 6: 490–500. DS 611.1231/500C; 611.2131/630/A, NA, RG 59. Federico Gil, *Latin American–United States Relations* (New York: Harcourt Brace Jovanovich, Inc., 1971), p. 165.

17. J. M. Letiche, *Reciprocal Trade Agreements in the World Economy* (New York: King's Crown Press, 1948), p. 22.

results, as far as good neighborliness was concerned, were far from satisfying. This was the case because a great percentage of Central American exports to the United States were already on the free list. Consequently, the department could make very few tariff concessions as long as it negotiated on the basis of the doctrine of principal supplier. Problems of this sort plagued the reciprocal program throughout the 1930s. On competitive imports like oil, copper, tin, sugar, cotton, meat, wool, etc., which could have made some economic contributions to the Good Neighbor policy, the New Deal backed away.[18]

Cordel Hull claimed that the trade agreements program must look toward the industrial nations of Europe. Yet, he believed that the program could initially make more progress with the underdeveloped nations and thereby serve as an example and a testing ground for other more complicated negotiations. Hence, the department first chose to deal with Brazil, Colombia, and Argentina. As to the scale of priority values in Central America, Washington ranked them in the following order: Guatemala, Honduras, Costa Rica, Nicaragua, El Salvador, and Panama. In the Caribbean he rated Cuba first, Haiti second, and the Dominican Republic third. Roosevelt's support for these schemes remained tepid. What concerned the President was that nothing be done to jeopardize the concessions granted to American territories like Puerto Rico, the Virgin Islands, and Hawaii. For the Administration, it was the path of least resistance and most profit.[19]

18. Three books which mainly give the political history of Central America but do not deal directly with United States–Latin American trade relations are Mario Rodrígues, *Central America* (Englewood Cliffs, N. J.: Prentice-Hall, Inc., 1965); John D. Martz, *Central America: The Crisis and the Challenge* (Chapel Hill: University of North Carolina Press, 1959); Franklin D. Parker, *The Central American Republics* (London: Oxford University Press, 1964). For a brief but interesting look at the Central American economies, see DA, Foreign Agricultural Service, *Central America as a Market and Competitor for U. S. Agriculture* (GPO, 1959). Also see BFDC, *Commercial Travelers' Guide to Latin America*, TPS No. 122, 1931.

19. Franklin D. Roosevelt, papers, Franklin D. Roosevelt Library, Hyde Park, N. Y., Official File, 614–A, Trade, Box 1, FDR to Welles, November 5, 1934. DS 811.5831/63, /64; 611.2531/69, NA, RG 59. Lloyd Gardner, *Economic Aspects of New Deal Diplomacy* (Madison: University of Wis-

Increased trade also held forth certain geopolitical advantages. Controlling the political economies of Central America was uppermost. A degree of political independence had been gained for these nations at Montevideo in 1933 when Hull renounced the use of armed intervention in the region. The region also struck a blow for economic independence when some of them adopted compensation agreements with Germany and Italy. Also, Nicaragua, Costa Rica, and Honduras initiated foreign-exchange control. Both moves prompted concern, even in the White House. In addition, the region began a search for markets other than those in North America. Costa Rica, for example, negotiated commercial agreements in 1932–1933 with Great Britain, France, Italy, and Germany; she had also begun to negotiate with China and Japan. Without American marines and without trade dominance in Central America, the Administration wondered if the area might become the Achilles heel of the Open Door empire in Latin America.

Hull's main task in the trade negotiations, therefore, was to reassert American control while convincing the Central Americans that reciprocity would bestow mutual benefits to all concerned. This was all the more difficult as far as trade was concerned, since the principal exports of the region already entered the United States duty free. Eighty per cent of Costa Rican exports and 70 per cent of Nicaraguan exports to the United States were coffee and bananas and were on the free list. Over 90 per cent of Guatemala's exports to America received the same treatment. Coffee accounted for 75 per cent of El Salvador's exports to the United States and got the same benefits. Honduras' main commodity, bananas, which accounted for 75 per cent of her exports to this country, also entered the United States free of tariff restrictions. Besides the loss of this leverage, Washington by 1935 had entered into trade treaties with Haiti and Colombia, both nations having competitive economies with Central America. Since the Roosevelt Administration extended unconditional most-favored-nation treaties to all nations, the banana republics

---

consin Press, 1964), p. 44. For bilateral conventions between Central America and Germany, Italy, and the United Kingdom, see *Comercio Exterior de la America Latina*, primera parte, pp. 26–28.

were assured of all benefits derived from the former agreements.[20]

The Administration had first hoped to conclude an agreement with Guatemala. In communications with Guatemala City, Assistant Secretary of State Francis Sayre believed that a United States guarantee of continued free duty for Guatemalan products would be equivalent in value to concessions by Guatemala on the principal products imported from the United States. The Guatemalans, however, objected. The American minister, Matthew Hanna, reported the government's fear that without a better market for its coffee, the duty reductions would mean a serious loss in revenue. The oligarchy, which had no intention to offset lost revenue from imports and exports by tax reform, countered with a request for American credit. This Hull would not do. On June 7, 1935, Hanna reported that Guatemala could not understand why the United States wanted a "trifling advantage" that would impair the economy of such a small nation. "We certainly will have to lower our demand," he confessed.[21] Although some officials in the Latin American Division, like Willard Beaulac, objected, the department's economic advisers persisted. Over the next months Sayre continued to press for concessions on fresh meats, dried powdered milk and cream, cereals, brandies, cotton seed oil, varnishes, lacquers, enamels, tires and tubes, office furniture, receiving apparatus, motor cars and chassis, fish, shrimp, oysters, canned fruits, fresh apples, and tobacco. Guatemala countered by desiring concessions on wood, cattle hides, furniture, honey, pineapples, pears, dried fruits, dried beans, and industrial alcohol. Washington objected to the proposals because Guatemala was not the principal supplier of any of the items. Hull did point out that the nation might eventually receive these concessions if they were generalized in other treaties.

At this juncture, Guatemalan President Jorge Ubico Castañeda attempted to establish a dictatorship by running for re-

20. Ethel B. Dietrich, *World Trade* (New York: Henry Holt and Company, 1931), pp. 125, 226–27. Roosevelt, papers, Official File, 614, Trade, Box 1, Roper to McIntyre, March 1, 1938. *FR*, 1934, 5:86. *Comercio Exterior de la America Latina*, primera parte, p. 16.

21. *FR*, 1935, 4:588–90, 596–97. Kenneth J. Grieb, "Negotiating a Reciprocal Trade Agreement with an Underdeveloped Country: Guatemala as a Case Study," *Prologue* (Spring 1973) :25.

election, an action deemed unpermissable by the constitution. This development may help to explain Ubico's willingness to come to terms economically with the United States. Effective August 30, 1936, Ubico announced, Guatemala would denounce its unconditional most-favored-nation agreement with the United Kingdom. The Guatemalan government also initiated a maximum-minimum tariff much like El Salvador's to incur Washington's friendship. The El Salvadorian trade model adopted by Ubico allowed United States goods to enter the country at the minimum rate but imposed the higher rates on products imported from nations like Japan. The State Department made no formal protest over these actions, although they were clearly not within the letter and spirit of liberal trade. Privately, the department must have been pleased to see Japanese competition slowed by any type of action. Trade relations with Germany were also being curtailed. In 1929 Germany purchased 40 per cent of Guatemala's exports. A decade later the figure had fallen to 11 per cent. German imports, however, remained too high for the department throughout the decade. They were a constant source of irritation and worry.[22]

Ubico's trump card remained the reciprocal treaty, since it implied political approval of his regime. It was also an easy way to entice Hull away from his political scruples. In fact, the Guatemalans deferred to United States business and agricultural interests in the tariff bargaining. The commercial agreement signed on April 24, 1936 gave the United States approximately fifteen reductions and fifty-eight bindings. The reductions amounted to one-fourth to one-half of the duties in effect prior to the treaty. On the other hand, Washington made little or no concessions to Guatemala. Four bindings and five minor concessions (pineapples being the most important) were the extent of American generosity. The Guatemalan negotiations, like some of the other Central American trade discussions, clearly demonstrated: first, the limits to which United States policymakers would go to gain concessions very minimal to domestic recovery, yet crucial to nations whose existence depended upon the diminishing customs receipts; second, the reciprocal program in Guatemala was not the economic right arm of the Good Neigh-

22. *FR*, 1935, 4:602–5. *FTLA*, pt. 2, section 13, pp. 15–19. Grieb, p. 27.

bor policy; and third, the willingness of dictators like Ubico to collaborate with foreign business interests at the expense of domestic development.[23]

In the Honduran negotiations, the United States encountered a political situation similar to that in Guatemala. On February 1, 1933, General Tiburcio Carías Andino, a member of the Nationalist party, assumed the presidency. By 1936 he had annulled many of Honduras' constitutional guarantees, and had extended his own term of office until January 1, 1943. Again, the United States found that dealing with a counterrevolutionary dictator facilitated business. As in the case of Guatemala, reciprocity had political overtones. The trade agreement, reported American chargé Raleigh Gibson in May, 1935, had "political values" and "would be used as a means of attack by one division (of the Nationalist party) against the other."

Economically a reciprocity agreement offered little in the way of benefits for Carías. Bananas, which accounted for 75 per cent of the value of Honduran exports to the United States, were the dictator's main concern. The anticipated loss of revenue from reduced duties and the damage to domestic industry were other sources of anxiety. Since the value of Honduran bananas to Germany was six times the value of German exports to Honduras and four times the value of English exports to Honduras, Carías Andino did not want a reciprocity agreement to jeopardize these markets. He also feared that an agreement with Washington might put Japanese imports at a competitive disadvantage. He soon retreated on both accounts. The department allayed these fears by assuring Honduras that she would find sizeable banana markets in the United States. Hull also assured Carías that, although some Honduran duties were unnecessary for protection, the others would still be high enough to preserve his domestic industries. The mistake in this regard, Hull believed, was that Honduran duties created artificial monopolies, burdened her consumers, and actually contributed to a loss in revenue.

The American minister in Tegucigalpa, Julius G. Lay, did not share Hull's optimism over the reciprocity program. He was especially worried that it would not deter Japanese competition

23. *FTLA*, pt. 2, section 13, p. 18. *FR*, 1936, 5:584–98. Laurence Duggan, *The Americas* (New York: Henry Holt and Company, 1949), p. 156, also pp. 74–78. Grieb, p. 28.

in cotton and electrical goods. His concern was understandable, since cotton markets in Central America accounted for nearly 20 per cent of the United States exports before the Japanese moved into the area. Lay, therefore, suggested "inducing Honduras to enact a bargaining maximum-minimum tariff law" similar to the one in El Salvador. This device established discriminatory tariff rates against nations that sold sizeable quantities of goods to Honduras, such as Japan, but purchased little in return. "I understand" Lay wrote to Hull, "that the new tariff of El Salvador, has already started the recovery of our cotton goods market in that country. There seems to be no reason why a similar bargaining tariff here would not accomplish the same results."

As in the case of the Guatemalan negotiations, the *Foreign-Relations Series* made no mention of Hull or his department trying to discourage these insinuations although they violated the spirit, if not the letter, of multilateralism. Washington also moved closer to unchallenged commercial superiority in the Caribbean when Carías, in 1936, denounced most-favored-nation agreements with Germany and France. Again, the State Department offered only half-hearted remonstrances. The following year, America purchased nearly nine-tenths of her bananas.[24] Honduras was squarely within the trade orbit of the United States.

The El Salvador tariff model, however, almost became a two-headed monster. Whereas the department desired a reciprocal agreement with concessions on flour, butter, cotton shirts, lard, soap, and eggs, Honduras hoped to satisfy Washington by adopting a minimum-maximum tariff "as a sop to the United States for declining to grant many of our requests for tariff reductions." This ploy, however, did not for long delay the treaty. Washington held firm, and on December 18, 1935, Honduras signed a reciprocal agreement. As previously mentioned, Carías' actions were not calculated on the basis of national economic self-interests. Once again a Central American dictator had used economic bait to serve political ends. In the agreement, Honduras gave the United States seventeen "important" reductions and twenty bindings. The reductions ranged from 33 per cent to 75

24. *FR*, 1934, 5:372–76. *FTLA*, pt. 2, section 14, pp. 11, 25. *Comercio Exterior de la America Latina*, primera parte, p. 16.

per cent of the duties in effect before the treaty. Flour, a serious bone of contention during the negotiations, was bound. The State Department had driven a hard bargain granting virtually no concessions to Honduras. Thus, Honduras was granted an "escape clause" that would nullify the agreement in six months if a substantial loss in revenue occurred. Interestingly enough, the clause said nothing about damage to domestic producers in Honduras, a provision placed in the 1934 Reciprocal Trade Agreements Act to protect interests in this country.[25]

With the exception of El Salvador, commercial negotiations with Costa Rica were the most difficult in Central America. As in the case of the other banana republics, the United States free list took the bite out of State Department requests. Combined with this lack of leverage was the realization that Washington, in all probability, would not resort to blacklists, embargoes, discrimination tariffs or quotas to "line up" her suspicious neighbors to the south. True enough, the higher NRA price levels inhibited badly needed exports from reaching Latin America (American flour and lard to Costa Rica were the major import items affected by the NRA) and New Deal currency depreciation likewise made American tariffs more foreboding.[26] Yet those impediments to world trade were not discriminatory, in one sense, because they singled out no particular nation or bloc of nations. This freedom from fear of United States sanctions became an important factor in the Costa Rica negotiations. Also, Washington had to deal with a democracy rather than a dictatorship. Since Hull could not rely upon internal or external coercion to ensure the success of the liberal trade, he had to convince this democracy of the merits of his program. Costa Rica was an underdeveloped nation, but she was also more independent than her Caribbean neighbors.

On September 7, 1934, the two nations publicly announced their intention to negotiate a reciprocal trade treaty. In return for a guarantee of continued free duty for Costa Rican copper and bananas, Assistant Secretary Sayre informed the American minister in San José, Leo Sack, to seek reductions on over thirty important products. The treaty might also contain, Sayre told Sack, an unconditional most-favored-nation clause, provisions

25. *FR*, 1935, 4:732–38; 1936, 5:810. *FTLA*, pt. 2, section 14, p. 11.
26. DS 611.1831/10, NA, RG 59.

against quantitative restrictions and increased internal taxes on trade agreement items, and national treatment (American businessmen would receive the same treatment as Costa Ricans in Costa Rica) with respect to internal taxes.

For the most part, the Costa Ricans did not object to the additional provisions, since the nation had kept tariffs low, had not instituted quotas, and had utilized exchange control only in a minimum of cases. They did object to American requests for reductions on lard and flour so strenuously that the negotiations ground to a standstill. Even the American minister, in exasperation, notified Hull that the United States supplied 50 per cent of all Costa Rican imports, and many of the people were asking, "What more does the United States want?" Sack went on to say, "It is a difficult one to answer."

Trade negotiations continued throughout 1935 and into 1936. San José held firm on flour and agreed only to a minor reduction in duty on lard (Washington eventually agreed to a binding on flour and a rate of 55 centimos on lard). President Ricardo Jiménez Oreamuno and his administration countered American requests by seeking concessions on fruits and vegetables sold to the Panama Canal Zone as a means of offsetting the loss in customs revenue (as late as 1939 customs duties accounted for 47.5 percent of national revenue). As a ploy, Costa Rica offered to invoke the Salvadorian tariff plan against the Japanese and to delay action on the reciprocal treaty. Washington refused to "hook" up the matters. By the spring of 1936 a compromise weighted heavily in the favor of Washington began to emerge. Costa Rica "tentatively agreed" to give the United States thirty reductions and seven bindings. Yet the desire to maintain good relations with the United States and a fear of economic isolation (Honduras, Nicaragua, Guatemala, Cuba, and Haiti had all signed), did not outweigh the dangers of customs losses of up to 200,000 colónes, the damage to domestic producers, and the anticipated outcry of the Costa Rican congress. In addition to these obstacles, Costa Rica believed that it was receiving the benefits of the other reciprocal agreement and could get no other concessions from the Roosevelt Administration. The Costa Rican foreign minister frankly admitted to Sack that the United States bargaining position was not strong. Frustrated and disappointed by the stall, Sack on June 19, 1936, suggested to Hull that this country postpone the discussions until such a time as Costa Rica would negotiate in earnest. The department in a June 29 communiqué agreed with Sack, and stated that there must be "wholehearted and sincere desire" before further negotiations.

Politics more than economics again broke the impasse in the trade talks. León Cortés Castro replaced Ricardo Jiménez Oreamuno as president of Costa Rica, and the State Department quickly seized the moment. The new president, the department felt, was less nationalistic and more susceptible to United States overtures. On November 20 the American chargé in San José urged Hull to sign a reciprocal agreement before the opposition party in Costa Rica had time to organize against it. "Even a day's delay would be dangerous under the circumstances." Facing these demands, Hull agreed. The department eliminated the two major conflicts by dropping the flour concession and lowering its demands on lard. Minor concessions were retained on over thirty items that were either bound or reduced. These affected over two hundred commodities with reductions ranging from 8 per cent to 65 per cent of the previous rates. American concessions, like all that were made with Central America, were limited to "distinctively" tropical products. Coffee, bananas, and cacao were bound on the free list. But there was another political reason for the compromise. Hull wanted to finish the negotiations prior to the Buenos Aires Conference to be held later in December, 1936. Another signator nation in Central America, he thought, would lend credence to America's assertion that the Good Neighbor partnership could function in both the political and economic sphere. Many of the Costa Ricans, however, remained unconvinced.[27]

By the time of the Buenos Aires Conference, the United States had also reached a commercial agreement with Nicaragua. In these negotiations the Roosevelt Administration again encountered some initial difficulty. Sugar was the chief commodity discussed. And the government in Managua, knowing that the best defense against American trade demands was to augment its own requests, assumed the offensive. As early as 1933, the Nicaraguan government stressed the fact that over the past decade 66.6 per cent of her total imports came from the United

27. *FTLA*, pt. 2, section 11, p. 9. Parker, pp. 263–64. *FR*, 1935, 4:450–55, 459–60; 1936, 5:383–85, 395–97, 402–4, 810.

States because of "substantially reduced" duties. Therefore, the Nicaraguans believed they deserved "special concessions" (on sugar) in "compensation for the continued favorable treatment of the commerce and products of the United States." Although Sayre and Hull often stated that the Cuban reciprocal agreement was in a special category, Nicaragua still hoped that the preferential treatment given to Cuban sugar would be granted to them as well. Barring acceptance of this position, Nicaragua could then hold out against any other concessions to the United States.[28] As such, an acceptance of their nonpreferential position was tantamount to Washington's negative assurance that bananas and coffee (70 per cent of United States imports from Nicaragua) would remain on the free list. To the Nicaraguans, it was a fair trade, nothing for nothing. Other than "a matter of principle" argued Fletcher Warren, the American chargé in Nicaragua, there seemed to be little reason for an agreement.

The Nicaraguans also took a different line of attack. They offered to implement the Salvadorian tariff scheme in exchange for holding the line on United States duties. This would allow Washington to preserve her dominant trade position and to eliminate Japanese competition. In this way, Managua would still be able to collect its customs revenue. As in the other cases, Washington made no formal objection to the anti-Japanese moves and refused to suspend reciprocal talks.[29]

Until late 1934 Washington allowed trade matters to drift. Hull and the American minister in Nicaragua, Arthur Bliss Lane, realized that punitive economic measures, such as taking Nicaraguan coffee and bananas off the free list, would force the impoverished nation into the arms of America's competitors, produce an anti-American backlash, and thereby endanger direct investments, such as the United Fruit Company. There was also another reason why the discussions stalled. The negotiations in Central America were characterized by caution, ignorance, and

28. See U. S., Congress, *Congressional Record*, 74th Cong., 2d sess., 1936, 80, pt. 10: 10627–51, for statistics dealing with American exports granted concession by reciprocity agreements prior to June 15, 1936. These include Cuba, Belgium, Haiti, Sweden, Brazil, Canada, Netherlands, Switzerland, Honduras, Colombia, Guatemala, France, Finland, and Nicaragua. See also *FR*, 1934, 5:493–94, 496–97, 511–15, 519.

29. *FR*, 1934, 5:523–25.

skepticism of United States trade objectives. Arthur Bliss Lane, for example, admitted that there was a "complete lack of preparation" on the part of the Nicaraguan officials. Since the department conducted the Central American negotiations simultaneously (most of them became effective in 1936), there was no way for Latin statesmen to compare the effects of the program. Consequently, when the State Department talked about a priority of goods for which it desired reductions or bindings (flour, industrial machinery, leather, lard, medicinals, condensed milk, radios, tires and tubes, paints and varnishes, batteries, beans, fruits, vegetables, electrical equipment, hosiery, typewriters, etc.), the Nicaraguans stalled the proceedings by objecting to most American demands. They simply had not had the time to make the necessary statistical, product by product, analysis.[30]

Dismayed at Managua's refractory attitude, Hull in early 1936 quipped to Lane that United States requests were "more moderate than those we have submitted to any other Central American Republic." Hull then went to the heart of the matter. If Nicaragua did not relent, then other republics in the region would feel betrayed, and might even retreat on their concessions forthcoming to the United States. Nicaragua, therefore, must grant "a reasonable number of the concessions originally requested."

Again politics came to the rescue. General Anastasio Somoza, head of the Guardia Nacional, made a power play for the presidency that threatened to engulf Central America in war. El Salvador and Honduras backed the incumbent President Juan Sacasa and Guatemala backed Somoza. But Washington's attitude remained the most crucial. Sacasa first asked the United States to intervene to depose Somoza. Washington refused. Then Sacasa, in an eleventh-hour effort to curry favor with its big brother, went before the Nicaraguan congress to lobby for a trade agreement with the United States. On March 11, 1936, the two nations signed an agreement favorable to United States interests. The scheme partially backfired when Somoza siezed power less than two months later. He did not, however, cancel the trade treaty.[31]

Nicaragua's efforts to vitiate the trade treaty took some new

30. *FR*, 1935, 4:824, 827, 831.
31. Ibid., pp. 872–75; 1936, 5:810.

twists in the years between 1936 and 1938. Under mounting United States pressure, Managua agreed to sign a limited reciprocity agreement with the United States but then desired to establish a new tariff policy with regard to third countries by renouncing most-favored-nation treatment with them. The Nicaraguan government would give in to United States demands, but retain its flexibility vis-à-vis other nations by not automatically extending to them the benefits of the American agreement. This development was a different form of challenge to Hull's liberal trade principles since the agreement with Nicaragua was too good for the United States to pass up. On the other hand, if Nicaragua denounced the most-favored-nation clause and worked against the worldwide implications of reciprocity, then Hull had set a bad precedent while gaining little in the way of trade.

Hull expressed "regret" at Nicaragua's decision, although he added that "this Government has no intention of presuming to suggest to Nicaragua what tariff policy it should follow." In addition, he told the American minister, Lane, to be sure that reciprocity and the denunciation of most-favored-nation treatment "be handled as a separate and unrelated matter [and that they] be separated as far as possible in point of time." The trade agreements program had won a Pyrrhic victory, but at the expense of the Open Door principle.[32]

The second twist in the reciprocal knot came in early 1938 when Nicaragua sought an increase in the rate of exchange for the payment of import duties. Somoza's corrupt regime had never been happy with the agreement signed two months prior to his *coup d'état*. If there was to be a drain on the country's revenues, he wanted it to be into the hands of his family, not into American coffers. Due to shrinking revenues and a grave financial crisis, the United States and Nicaragua on February 8, 1938, modified the reciprocal agreement. It was a defeat for Hull of the first degree since reciprocity had not brought an iota of prosperity to an oligarchic nation racked with corruption. Understandably, Hull warned the Division of American Republics against "giving undue emphasis" to the proceedings. Under the final settlement there would be no increase in the basic rate of duty on American goods, but rather an increase in the rate of conversion between the paper córdoba and the gold córdoba. This financial manipu-

32. *FR*, 1935, 4:798–99.

lation had the effect of raising United States export prices and impeding their access into Nicaragua. Henceforth, Hull dropped the banana republic from the list of signatory nations.[33]

The Nicaraguan discussions highlighted the major trade problems that the United States encountered in Central America. First, the doctrine of principal supplier made few concessions from Washington possible. Hence, many nations were unwilling to discuss trade. Second, regions like Central America lacked exchange and purchasing power. Therefore, reciprocal agreements had little meaning except in the broader sense of principle, hemispheric solidarity, and the ability to dominate the political economy of neighboring states. Third, and herein lay a basic weakness of the Good Neighbor, a policy that satisfied economic self-interests ran the risk of undermining national interests in the political realm. Fourth, hard bargains in the first agreements haunted and jeopardized future agreements in Central America since the United States, in the interest of fairness, had to get approximately the same value of concessions from each nation. This point was highlighted by a fifth liability; namely, that the Central American nations were not only in an economic struggle with the United States but among themselves as well. Concessions granted to the United States, therefore, weakened each nation's economic position in relation to its neighbors. This was perhaps the chief reason Washington had tried to conduct the Central American negotiations simultaneously, and why each republic jealously watched United States negotiations with the others. And lastly, Nicaragua's modification of the reciprocal agreement in 1938 was visible proof that reciprocity was not in the best interests of underdeveloped nations. Lower tariff duties had not, as Hull contended, led to an increase in customs revenue and purchasing power by increasing the volume of international trade.[34]

Politics conditioned trade negotiations with El Salvador from the very beginning. From December, 1931, to January, 1934, the United States withheld diplomatic recognition from the regime of Maximiliano Hernández Martínez because of obligations under the 1923 Central American Treaty, which barred recognition from governments that came to power by revolution. At the

33. *FR*, 1938, 5:785–87. Diebold, p. 9.
34. *FR*, 1935, 4:842.

instigation of Sumner Welles, Washington and Central America abandoned nonrecognition and moved toward a more realistic policy within the first year of the New Deal. But until political contact was established, a reciprocal trade agreement was out of the question. In July, 1934, Sayre made his initial offer to El Salvador. Coffee, which accounted for 75 per cent of her exports to the United States and over 90 per cent of her world exports, would remain on the free list in return for equivalent concessions on the principal products imported from the United States.[35]

El Salvador, however, did not like the trade. Nationalism and a degree of anti-American sentiment had taken root during the two years of diplomatic ostracism. This semblance of independence made commercial negotiations even more difficult. Martínez, obviously, did not want to provoke a confrontation with Washington, but on the other hand he had little desire to further weaken the economy. In June, 1934, his country experimented with a discriminatory three-column tariff based on the idea of trade balancing. It was intended to handicap Japanese cotton products in an attempt to propitiate United States trade interests. The example, as we have seen, spread throughout Central America. As a result, conventional reductions frequently were not generalized but given only to most-favored-nations.

This approach did not satisfy the Department of State. On August 1, 1935, Sayre told the American minister in El Salvador, Frank Corrigan, to find out "just how far El Salvador is prepared to go in meeting our desires," although Sayre had previously stated that an ad valorem reduction on balsam from 10 per cent to 5 per cent and a binding on the free list for coffee and henequen were the only concessions the United States would give. He later admitted to Corrigan that it was difficult for the Committee on Trade Agreements to find other products of which Central America was the principal supplier. To go beyond this position would jeopardize the goodwill of the U.S. Congress. Nevertheless, Sayre informed Corrigan to seek the "best terms obtainable" for American exports. The list included sixteen items such as condensed milk, cornstarch, hog lard, wheat, cotton goods, lumber, tires, paints, and flour products designed to curry favor with domestic agricultural interests.

Martínez also did not want to endanger his own political stand-

35. *FR*, 1933, 4:685; 1934, 5:218–19, 257. *FTLA*, pt. 2, section 12, p. 6.

ing at home. In March, 1936, Corrigan informed Hull that El Salvador saw no "positive commercial advantages" from the reciprocal program. Concessions to the United States were thought to cost El Salvador from $839,000 to nearly $1,000,000 in revenue per year. In addition to this loss, a reciprocal agreement under the provisions of unconditional most-favored-nation treatment would entail even more losses to third nations (over 50 per cent of her exports went to Europe and about 90 per cent of this figure was coffee). Liberal trade would also jeopardize special markets in Germany. The most-favored-nation clause was, therefore, viewed by Salvadorians as the harbinger of economic difficulties. Besides, the political consequence of such a course of action were not hard to perceive. Dictators, too, are vulnerable to recession. And recession breeds political trouble. "As the Department is aware," wrote Corrigan, "every problem in El Salvador is considered by the Government primarily from a political angle."[36]

For most of 1936 the United States and El Salvador made little progress in the trade negotiations. The *Foreign Relations Series* for that year and the next provide few if any clues as to why the two nations were able to reach an understanding on February 19, 1937. One factor may have been smuggling. Trade agreements with Honduras, Guatemala, and Nicaragua had lowered the price of United States goods. If the duties remained high in El Salvador, there was a good chance that smuggled United States products would enter the blackmarket and deprive the country of revenue anyway. Another may have been that by this time Hull considered the political consequences of the reciprocity program to be as important as the economic. This may explain why the United States tapered its requests for concessions. Politics may also have played in Martínez's decision to reach a compromise arrangement, for shortly after the treaty, Martínez

36. *FTLA*, pt. 2, section 12, p. 12. *FR*, 1935, 4:547; 1936, 557–61. A comment made by a Salvadorian in 1933 from an unpublished doctoral dissertation by Power Yung-Chao Chu titled "A History of the Hull Trade Program, 1934–1939" written at Columbia University, 1947, page 212, deserves quoting: "If we entered into an agreement on lowering of tariffs which would undoubtedly give to North American goods free entrance to our markets, we would be considered a sort of Zollverein, a sort of customs understanding which endanger [*sic*] the sale of our raw material on the European continent."

imposed tighter control over the country and ran unconstitutionally for reelection. Sumner Welles saw to it that Washington, for its part, stayed neutral. There would be no more moral judgments like the ones made under the 1923 Central American Treaty. Whether or not a bargain was struck remains a mystery. But Corrigan, in obvious displeasure, told the Department of State that the Good Neighbor policy had become too "negative." The United States, he said, had a "moral responsibility" to aid Latin America in the struggle for democracy. Hull had his precious reciprocity agreement, and the matter was closed.[37]

New Deal trade negotiations with South America were even more trying than those conducted in Central America. As in the case of Central America, each nation was tied to the production of one or two export products for its economic survival. For Chile, the staff of life was the nitrate and copper industry. For Venezuela, it was oil. For Uruguay and Argentina, it was meat. For Peru, it was sugar and fish although petroleum, copper, gold, and silver were her principal export products. For Bolivia, it was tin. And, Colombia and Brazil were heavily dependent upon coffee. On the surface, it would then appear that Washington could have exerted enormous pressure to spur negotiations. Such was not the case. Other than coffee, each of these products competed with American items. Also in the case of Peru, Bolivia, Chile, and Venezuela, these exports were minerals as opposed to Central American agricultural products. Therefore, it may not be too surprising to find out that only in the Colombia and Brazilian negotiations did Hull accomplish his initial objective in short order. Frankly, the United States had little to offer those nations whose exports were complementary to the domestic economy, such as Central American, Brazilian, and Colombian coffee, bananas, and other items already on the free list. But the Trade Agreements Division of the Department of State had even greater difficulty and even less to offer those South American nations whose economies were competitive with the United States.

There was, of course, another important reason for the failure of New Deal economic diplomacy in South America, and that was the Great Depression and, concomitantly, the rise of economic nationalism. Chile was a case in point. Because of wild

37. *FR*, 1935, 4:547–51; 1936, 5:557–61, 565–67; 1937, 5:523–25.

price fluctuations in her exports, the Chilean government made discreet inquiries to Washington as to the possibilities of a reciprocal agreement in the summer of 1933. The Administration remained silent. These commercial overtures, however, did not preclude the government of Arturo Alessandri Palma from initiating what the American ambassador to Chile, William S. Culbertson, called a "vigorous nationalistic policy [that] has brought new and perhaps even more serious threats against our interests." Culbertson included in this list Chilean exchange control (there were four rates of exchange, although United States firms were forced to sell at the invidious official rate of 16.5 pesos to the dollar), frozen American credits totaling $21 million in 1933, and threats against the American-owned nitrate industry. Culbertson added that the country had also experimented with loan defaults, currency depreciation, and compensation agreements (the latter first signed with France and Spain). Compensation agreements, he wrote, allowed the nations to reimburse themselves for goods exported to Chile and for the payment of back commercial debts. In early 1933 the ambassador informed the Chilean minister of foreign affairs that the United States was "disturbed" that Chile was considering further compensation agreements with Germany, Belgium, Italy, and Cuba.[38] These agreements normally provide that imports from one nation to another should be in an agreed proportion to the exports of the other. Thus, trade is balanced and forced into artificial channels.

Chile's hard-line attitude on exchange matters forestalled meaningful trade discussions. Washington, for its part, demanded equal treatment in exchange and trade matters and Chile's acceptance of the unconditional most-favored-nation clause. Exchange control in fact became a paramount issue not only because it slowed down United States sales but because it inhibited credits from loan repayments and direct investments from reaching this country. In order to hasten negotiations, Culbertson suggested that Washington "create some disadvantage for Chilean commerce in the United States. Later in 1933 the ambassador badgered Hull to license Chilean nitrates and to find "some means of blocking for the benefit of our frozen credits such exchange as is created by purchases of Chilean goods in the United

38. DS 611.2531/69; 811.5831/63. *FR*, 1933, 4:103–8, 111, 114. *Comercio Exterior de la America Latina*, primera parte, pp. 14 and 71.

States." To many American businessmen, he wrote Hull, the Roca Agreement should be the model for United States–Chilean discussions.[39]

Culbertson's suggestions did not suit Cordell Hull. The Department realized that such tactics would merely precipitate open economic warfare. Such a war might endanger more important American interests than trade; namely, direct investments in copper and nitrate. Besides, the United States had unwittingly played its trump card when it shut off Chile's sale of copper ore to this country. Without copper exports to America (a political football that FDR did not want to touch), Chile's exchange position would remain very unstable. One must also remember that 75 to 80 per cent of the value of Chile's exports came from mining and even the revenue from Chilean copper sold abroad found its way back to the United States, because American firms owned the copper interests, thus exacerbating Chile's balance-of-payments problems. Copper imports had all but dried up with the Hawley-Smoot Tariff, and the very powerful copper industry in this country was intent on keeping the duties prohibitive for some time.

Consequently, Alessandri offered only to sign a compensation agreement with the United States, but to give no exchange rate lower than the current market rate. Since the Roosevelt Administration refused to remove tariff restrictions on copper imports (United States duties were also high on Chilean vegetables, fruits, wines, and wool), and Hull refused to relinquish his principles on exchange and unconditional most-favored-nation control, the chances for a reciprocity agreement remained bleak.

Throughout the years 1933 to 1938 Washington explored a variety of solutions to the exchange problem. Pending a reciprocity agreement, even a temporary settlement aimed at breaking the impasse looked fruitful. One such plan in 1933 was a provisional agreement to supplement the existing commercial agreement of September 28, 1931. The old plan was based on most-favored-nation treatment only in trade. The new plan called for most-favored-nation treatment in the allotment of exchange by one of three ways: first, by giving equal exchange to all countries; second, by exchange on the basis of each nation's exports to Chile; or third, by Chile's exports to each country. Chile rejected

39. *FR*, 1933, 4:119, 121–24.

the plan. The following year, Hull asked the new U.S. ambassador, Hal Sevier, to explore the possibilities of Chile dividing foreign countries into those which would obtain exchange solely from compensation agreements and those which would derive exchange solely from the free market, i.e., the United States. This would impede the former group from encroaching upon United States interests and, therefore, satisfy the Administration. Again Chile refused. The compensation agreements, wrote chargé R. Henry Norweb, was a "world tendency" and "too strong for any one nation to divert."[40]

Reaction of American businessmen to these restrictions was never consistent. In September, 1933, chargé Norweb expressed fear that businessmen were "about to explode." By April, 1934, Sevier communicated to Hull that it would perhaps be better to leave well enough alone. "At least," he said, "if the *de facto* situation is not entirely satisfactory to us, neither is it to compensation countries." The next year, however, in an effort to safeguard its European markets, Chile established an even more serious pattern of restrictions against American trade. Trade, reported the new U.S. ambassador, Hoffman Philip, in January, 1936, was on "a casual and uncertain basis." The only exception was that Chile received the benefits from reciprocal agreements that the United States had signed with third countries. In obvious agreement with Philip's comments, Hull cabled the ambassador to seek a *modus vivendi* to supplant the September 28, 1931, trade agreement. Hull at least hoped to get Chilean acceptance of the unconditional most-favored-nation clause, equal treatment in quotas, and a curtailment of exchange restrictions. Although the *modus vivendi* failed to gain momentum, it was admission itself that Hull's reciprocal program had died aborning in Chile. The *modus vivendi*, remarked a State Department official in 1937, would be of "relatively small benefit" and would jeopardize the negotiation of a reciprocal agreement containing safeguards against exchange control. Hull, nevertheless, persisted. In early 1938 he reached a compromise weighted heavily in the favor of the Chileans. The agreement gave the United States equality of treatment in regard to import quotas, tariffs, and exchange mat-

40. Ibid., p. 133, *FR*, 1934, 5:6–9, 20–21. For a description of Chilean exchange control see *FTLA*, pt. 2, section 4, pp. 11–14. BFDC, *Commerical Travelers' Guide to Latin America*, TPS No. 179 (1938) p. 34.

ters, but it did not prohibit even better treatment for nations having compensation agreements.[41]

Investments, more than any single reason, necessitated the commercial bargain. As to United States bonds, Chile opposed a long-term bond settlement on a fixed-charge basis. Rather, the Chilean government hoped to place them on an income basis; revenue derived from the American-owned Nitrate Sales Corporation was to be used for repayment. Chile's Law Number 5580 of January 31, 1935, further tightened service on the external loans (United States holdings of Chilean dollar bonds had a par value of $198 million at the end of 1938). Although the department made representations to obtain an equitable settlement on both trade and bond matters, the department still realized, as chargé Winthrop Scott put it, that United States–Chilean economic relations had "a distinctive character, in that there is a tremendous disproportion between the value of our current trade and the value of our capital investments in Chile." These trade figures, incidentally, stood at $15 million a year in United States exports compared to a little over a billion dollars in direct investments. Pressure against the present government, Scott added, might lead to "a period of more intense nationalism" and greater attacks on these investments. The chargé's remarks merely pointed out once again that direct investment more than trade or portfolio investment was the key to United States economic diplomacy with this Andean nation.[42]

For Hull, the 1938 *modus vivendi* was a bad bargain but one that Washington could live with. The arrangement operated in this manner: Since trade and loans took a back seat to direct investments, the United States could inflexibly adhere to its principles on the former matters. This position might do nothing to enhance United States–Chilean political relations, but unlike the Brazilian case Hull viewed the Axis powers in the Andes more as economic nuisance than geopolitical threat. The following year, Chile confirmed Hull's suspicions when she suppressed the vocal but never large Nazi elements throughout the land.

Hull also relied upon principle because he had learned by

41. *FR*, 1933, 4:133; 1934, 5:28; 1935, 4:389, 400–402; 1936, 5:314, 316–17, 322–24; 1937, 5:424–28.

42. *FR*, 1934, 5:41; 1935, 4:407–8; 1936, 5:149–50. *FTLA*, pt. 2, section 4, pp. 63–65.

1938 that trade agreements without stiff exchange clauses were ineffective instruments of American diplomacy. In 1938 Francis Sayre coyly put it this way to the American chargé, "For tactical reasons," the department had decided against initiating reciprocal talks. If Chile insisted, he said, then the United States must demand "unconditional most-favored-nation treatment [in] all forms of trade and payments control." In addition, Hull again demanded as a condition for reciprocal negotiations that Chile retreat from the essence of compensation agreements by granting the United States equal treatment. On the question of contiguous countries (Chile desired to give trade preferences to neighboring Argentina, Peru, and Bolivia), Washington opposed any exception to the unconditional most-favored-nation principle. This hard-line position stood in contradiction to the tacit permission the Department of State gave Finland and Sweden. In the latter case, Hull recognized that contiguity dictated special economic relationships.

Despite these impediments, the outbreak of war in 1939 forced the United States and Chile to put up a facade of hemispheric solidarity. It also made Chile more dependent upon the North American market. Therefore, one month after the invasion of Poland, the two nations publicly announced their intention to negotiate a reciprocal agreement. But Hull had no intention of softening his department's demands. In December, 1939, Washington removed copper "from the scope of the negotiations" by refusing to take up the matter of relaxed restrictions on this most important trade item and relegated the discussions, as Harry Hawkins, chief of the Division of Commercial Treaties and Agreements put it, to the inactive stage. Again, if principle did not prove to be profitable, it sacrificed nothing.

The department also took a hard-line approach on the issue of Chile's external debts by linking it to the question of export-import credits. Henceforth, a debt settlement became "an essential condition of any arrangement for economic cooperation." Toward this end, Hull directed that "an assurance from the Chilean government that at least the present interest payments on the external debt he continued" would be the least Washington could accept. Although the bank relented somewhat in late 1939, it was not until June 13, 1940, that the Export-Import Bank extended Chile a sizeable loan totaling $12 million and then only to buy and to transport American industrial machinery, equipment, and supplies.[43]

The outbreak of war and the need for regional security should have gotten United States–Chilean trade talks off dead center. In fact, the compensation agreements with the fascist powers ceased to have relevancy as the Allied blockade tightened. At the same time, the United States agreed to the formula submitted July 31, 1941, to the Inter-American Financial and Economic Advisory Committee that regional tariff preferences should not stand in the way of broad economic reconstruction along the lines of liberal trade. This formula thereby established an escape clause for Chile on the question of "contiguous countries." In August, 1941, the United States also backed down on the exchange issue by not demanding exchange without delay on all imports but merely seeking most-favored-nation treatment. On the matter of Chilean copper ore, Hawkins on July 1, 1941, informed Hull that domestic production was inadequate and that the nation should make a copper concession. He went on to report, "in short, an opportunity is now presented to reduce the tax on copper with the greatest economic benefit and the least potential danger." Later, as the exigencies of wartime production became greater, Washington lowered the $.04 per pound excise duty on Chilean ore.[44] In short, military requirements accomplished what years of tariff bargaining had been unable to achieve—a reduction in copper duties.

With the air cleared of several difficulties, many diplomats believed that trade negotiations would progress smoothly, but they did not. The reason for this was simple: The reciprocity program had lost its momentum. Preoccupation with the war, reliance upon stockpiling, lend-lease, and export-import loans, plus Chile's dependence upon United States exports all diverted attention from the trade program. For example, in the first quarter of 1940 as compared to the same period in 1939, her imports from

43. *FR*, 1938, 5:432–33, 443; 1939, 5:407–8, 777; 1940, 5:674–75, 679; 1941, 6:596. Edward O. Guerrant, *Roosevelt's Good Neighbor Policy* (Albuquerque: University of New Mexico Press, 1950) , p. 103. Also see "Effectos de la querra sobre el comercio exterior de la America Latina" in *Comercio Exterior de la America Latina*, primera parte, pp. 141–48.

44. *FR*, 1941, 6:597, 600–603. For U. S. opposition also to a customs union of the states bordering the Rio de la Plata see Duggan, p. 156.

Germany and Great Britain fell by 81 and 48 per cent respectively, while purchases from the United States increased 88 per cent. By this time the war had taken its toll upon Hull's program. He could give only two cheers for reciprocity. Even as late as April, 1944, a department memorandum from the Division of Commercial Policy cited the secretary's wish for the United States to take no initiative in the stalled Chilean trade discussions. The inability to bring this Andean republic into the trade fold was perhaps the most glaring failure of Hull's reciprocity program.[45]

Hull also experienced many political difficulties in the Bolivian negotiations. During the first years of the trade program, the secretary made every effort to avoid discussions with La Paz for fear of jeopardizing the negotiations with Brazil, Chile, and Argentina. As late as 1937 a U.S. minister, R. Henry Norweb, described the "marked rivalry" among the three South American powers for trade predominance in Bolivia. Therefore, he wrote, "it might perhaps be injudicious at this time for the United States to appear to be injecting itself into the triangular competition." Politics affected trade even more after March 13, 1937, when Bolivia cancelled Standard Oil's petroleum concessions.

Expropriation was symbolic of economic nationalism and the length that a military government in Latin America would go to rally internal support against both external and internal threats. Standard Oil was culpable of many of the charges levied against it, and Hull, by reading the dispatches from La Paz, knew it. He therefore did not register a formal protest to Bolivia as he did in Mexico, for fear of pushing Bolivia into the Argentine camp. Also, the government at La Paz had made assurances that no more expropriations were planned. Nevertheless, it would have been risky business to antagonize interests in the United States Congress, which sympathized with Standard Oil by concluding a trade agreement. Such an action might also be interpreted by other Latin Americans as tacit approval of nationalization schemes.

45. Diebold, pp. 88–89. DS 611.3231/1481; For prewar information on stockpiling see a memo by Herbert Feis, DS 811.24/1058, NA, RG 59. Also see BFDC, *Raw Materials General*, 060.0, Welles to Roper, December 6, 1938, NA, RG 40; and Dozer, pp. 77–78. Minutes of a special meeting, March 1, 1940 of the Board of Trustees of the Export-Import Bank can be found in R. Walton Moore, papers, Franklin D. Roosevelt Library, Hyde Park, N. Y., Box 6.

In addition to these political factors, Hull realized that in a reciprocal agreement, Bolivia would seek direct marketing of tin in the American market and a smelting industry in the United States to offset dependence on Great Britain and the Bolivian industrialist Simón Patiño (Patiño mines produced 50 per cent of Bolivia's tin). However, tin, which accounted for almost three-fourths of Bolivia's income from exports, and petroleum both competed with domestic interests, which had strong backing in the United States. Consequently, Hull urged the department to proceed cautiously if at all. In a confidential dispatch to Norweb on February 26, 1937, Hull admitted that an agreement would be "a matter of considerable difficulty, [since] there are no products on which reductions in duty could be granted to Bolivia" and only a few, he confessed, that could even be bound.

Economically, there also appeared to be no reason for hurry, since the department believed that a reciprocity agreement would do little to improve commerce because of Bolivia's lack of purchasing power. Hull also felt that Bolivia's import duties were not excessive and that her exchange restrictions did not substantially injure United States exports. Lastly, the Roosevelt Administration did not feel that its dilatory tactics would push Bolivia into the waiting arms of Germany, Italy, or Japan. Other than Great Britain, the United States still remained Bolivia's largest trading partner outside the South American continent. For these reasons, both political and economic, New Deal officials made no real effort to implement a reciprocal agreement with Bolivia throughout World War II.[46]

Hull's trade program also encountered difficulties in another Andean nation, Peru. The main problem in United States–Peruvian negotiations pertained to commodities such as copper and sugar (in the hands of foreign interests), cotton, oil, gasoline, balata, ore, wool, hides, and petroleum products (also in foreign hands). These goods equalled nearly half of Peru's exports yet most were, unfortunately, competitive with United States products. For these reasons, Peru had a history of economic semi-independence. The United States, declared the Peruvian minister of foreign affairs, Carlos Concha, had "closed its doors to every

46. Diebold, pp. 66–67. Green, pp. 25–27. *FR*, 1937, 5:271–74. For the oil expropriation matter see Wood, Chapter 7. TPS No. 179, pp. 17, 23. *FTLA*, pt. 2, section 2, pp. 3–8.

Peruvian export which permitted the country to eke out an economic existence." This, he said, was the reason Peru had been forced to maintain its British markets and to turn to Germany.

In addition, Peru had signed an agreement with Chile based on the principle of contiguous countries that constituted an exception to the unconditional most-favored-nation clause. Although Hull had previously accepted the same principle in his negotiations with Cuba, he displayed a remarkable penchant for playing inter-American situation ethics when the principle of the Open Door was violated in the Andean highlands. Insistence on unconditional most-favored-nation treatment, warned United States Ambassador Laurence Steinhardt, might be "an insuperable barrier" to negotiations in 1938. Hull, for his part, did not take sufficient cognizance of Peru's dependence upon the Chilean market. Nor did he realize the invidious connection between America's protective policies on Peruvian products competitive with United States goods, especially sugar, and his hard line attitude on contiguous countries. The Chilean market, for example, accounted for nearly 120,000 tons of sugar per year as compared to United States purchases of 50,000 tons per year. Without a greater United States market, Peru could not afford to break its special agreement with Chile. Hence, the main difficulty in the reciprocity discussions.[47]

Throughout 1938–1939 the position of both nations hardened. Peru extended its exceptions to unconditional most-favored-nation treatment to include Bolivia, Brazil, Colombia, and Ecuador. Hull opposed these extensions as vigorously as he had opposed the original exception to Chile. He feared an erosion of America's bargaining position in relation to Argentina, Uruguay, and Chile, plus the potential threat to agreements already signed with Bolivia, Colombia, and Ecuador. The only exceptions the United States might countenance, Hull wrote to Steinhardt in November, 1938, would be limited to Chile, and then only "on a limited list of specific commodities." The reason for Washington's position may be found in a June 24, 1938, memorandum from the Division of Trade Agreements stating that export trade

47. Diebold, pp. 66–67; *FR*, 1938, 5:832–37, 852, 859. For a more detailed study of United States-Peruvian relations, although weak on reciprocity, see James Carey, *Peru and the United States, 1900–1962* (Notre Dame: University of Notre Dame Press, 1964).

to Peru was in a "relatively satisfactory position." Exchange control, quotas, and other discriminatory practices were held to a minimum. Also, most of the concessions sought by the United States were in the area of bindings rather than reductions, and, therefore, an agreement would do little to increase American markets. For these reasons, the department felt no compunction to depart from the principles of the Open Door. In November, 1939, Washington informed Peru that because of the backlog of reciprocity agreements, preparations for renewal of the Trade Agreements Act, due to expire June 12, 1940, negotiations with Lima could not be undertaken in the "immediate future"[48]

The question of debt payments and credit extensions also compounded the trade difficulties. At the Panama Conference in September, 1939, Under Secretary of State Welles listened attentively to Latin America's requests for additional export-import credits. Peru, in particular, petitioned the United States for aid. A few months prior to the conference, Peruvian President Óscar Benavides, had warned that American credit to Bolivia, Colombia, and Chile would force his nation into the arms of Germany. The American chargé promptly told Benavides that he was singularly unimpressed. Peru, he said, had made no effort to meet the United States halfway on loan repayments and, therefore, did not qualify for credit.

Because of the European war, Welles cabled Hull from Panama to mollify the American position. The secretary, however, remained steadfast. If a defaulting nation such as Peru had the resources to pay its obligations but refused to do so, then the United States would not extend large sums of credit. On the other hand, Hull retreated from this position in cases where a nation in default was obviously insolvent and unable to make debt repayments. The position may have given the secretary some self-satisfaction, but it did nothing to improve United States–Peruvian relations. In fact, only a small export-import loan to stabilize exchange rates and an extension of $10 million worth of credit to facilitate purchases of American products were made before the war. Meanwhile, trade talks remained in limbo.[49]

48. *FR*, 1938, 5:844–45, 861–66; 1939, 5:769–72.
49. DS 821.51/2383, NA, RG 59, contains both Welles' September 26, 1939, cable and Hull's reply on September 29, 1939. Also see *FR*, 1939, 5:773; and 1940, 5:1142–44. Carey, p. 106.

Pearl Harbor resuscitated reciprocity discussions with Peru. Two days after the Japanese attack, Ambassador Norweb informed Hull that a trade initiative from the United States "might consolidate our improved position in Peru." Two weeks later, Lima and Washington issued a public notice stating their intention to negotiate an agreement. The Peruvian government, now headed by Manuel Prado Ugarteche, was still more interested in a cotton agreement than a trade agreement because, as Norweb put it, "the cotton interests represent probably the strongest political influence in the nation." Until Pearl Harbor, Japan had provided the largest market for long staple cotton because of the $.07 per pound duty imposed by the United States. To compound the problem, Washington in September, 1939, had established an import quota because of its subsidization of domestic cotton. The subsidy was later suspended, but the duty and the quota remained in tact. Peruvian cotton imports were thereupon limited to 4,000 bales annually—a situation Peru was intent on correcting.

The political implications of a cotton agreement, according to Harry Hawkins, chief of the Division of Commercial Policy and Agreements, were also being analyzed by the State Department. A reciprocity agreement encompassing cotton, said Norweb, would create "an attitude of confidence and cooperation" and would be "of immense value in maintaining the stability of the incumbent administration." It would also help the United States, he wrote, to achieve "a number of our anti-Axis objectives in Peru." High on this list of priorities was the goal of depriving the Axis powers of strategic raw materials and creating a better political climate between Lima and Washington. Hull realized that a retreat had to be made on the cotton issue in order to line up Peru. Unlike many of his timorous actions, the secretary braved the protective interests at home and called for a meaningful concession on cotton. Ironically, Hull had justified liberal trade less than a decade before on the grounds that it would serve as the precursor of peace and international economic cooperation. Now in 1942 the program's *raison d'être* turned out to be its usefulness in the war effort.

On April 28, 1942, Hull wrote to Roosevelt asking that Peruvian cotton be reduced in duty by 50 per cent and Section 22 of the Agricultural Adjustment Act, which limited Peru to 4,000 bales of cotton per year, be increased by consolidating "the present individual country quotas into a global amount equal to the individual quotas." This action, Hull wrote, was necessary to induce Peru to sign an agreement, to stop the impending shortage by long-staple cotton in connection with the war effort, and to "allow Peru to compete with other countries for the entire amount of whatever imports are permitted under quota." Luckily, Claude Wickard, the secretary of agriculture who opposed Hull's scheme, was out of Washington for the week and, Hull confessed, "cannot be reached." Roosevelt quietly approved the plan and set the stage for an agreement.

On the question of contiguous countries, Hull retreated again. By an exchange of notes very similar to the draft of notes formulated in the October, 1941, agreement with Argentina, Washington accepted Peru's exclusive preferences for her neighbors in the Andean highlands. With these stumbling blocks removed, Prado signed the reciprocity agreement on May 7, 1942. In addition to cotton, Washington gave Peru maximum concessions on alpaca, llama, and vicuña hair, and some tropical cabinet woods. Due to wartime conditions, Peru also received a larger market for her sugar. In return, the United States received reductions and bindings on approximately 20 per cent of its imports to Peru. The concessions, however, were academic. With European goods and markets no longer as available, Peru had no other choice but to turn to the United States. Hull had indeed won another victory for liberal trade, but under the circumstances there was little cause to cheer. [50]

Besides Brazil, Colombia, Argentina, and Peru, the Roosevelt Administration also signed trade treaties with Ecuador, Venezuela, and Uruguay (Paraguay came into the trade fold in 1946). Of the latter group, the Venezuelans proved to be the least difficult and the Ecuadorians the most difficult to handle. Problems with Ecuador arose over her insistence on the conditional most-favored-nation clause and her efforts at bilateral balancing of trade. By 1937 the government at Quito had consented to sign a secret agreement with the United States but opposed the extension of these concessions to third nations. It was a delicate problem for the State Department, since the Ecuadorian government

50. *FR*, 1941, 7:542–47. Carey, p. 105. *FR*, 1942, 6:675–76, 678, 682, 686–88, 690–92.

forced Washington to choose between principle and self-interest. "From an immediate and narrow point of view," Sayre wrote, the deal would be desirable although in the long run the "apparent advantages are both transitory and illusory." It was a question, Sayre finally resolved, that "the Ecuadorian Government itself must decide."

In August, 1938, the two nations resolved their differences when Hull accepted Article VII of the proposed treaty. This article permitted the imposition of quantitative restrictions on importation and thus insured the exchange value of the Ecuadorian currency. The proposal, however, did little to safeguard the tiny South American republic's economic viability. Ecuador granted concessions on thirty-three items that affected more than two hundred individual commodities. Reductions of 25 to 50 per cent were given on fifteen items, and eighteen tariff items were bound. America's gain was Ecuador's loss. From January, 1936, through March, 1939, this Andean republic's adverse balance of trade with the United States rose to over 36,000,000 sucres.

The severity of the crisis, in fact, forced Quito to initiate import control provisions (both higher duties and quotas) and currency depreciation to stem financial deterioration. On June 4, 1940, the Export-Import Bank extended a $1,150,000 loan. These measures were of no help, however. Throughout World War II Ecuador's economy remained as tenuous as her political structure. Even though the preceding restrictions (in 1939 United States imports were placed at 40 million sucres per year) had no effect on overall American trade, Ecuador's protest was still a haunting reminder that uninterrupted flow of international goods and services was indeed a mixed blessing. If Hull was not to blame for this situation, his program had certainly done little or nothing to correct the international economic imbalance.[51]

Although of far more economic importance, United States–Venezuelan trade negotiations were more easily concluded. This was true because Venezuela was more dependent upon a single export item, oil, than any other Latin American nation beside El Salvador. Consequently, the Venezuelan government actively

51. *FR*, 1937, 5:482–83, 490, 498–504; 1938, 5:433, 512, 522–23; 1939, 5:606; 1940, 5:862, 868–69, 875.

sought an agreement that would, as American minister at Caracas, Meredith Nicholson, explained, "safeguard oil from United States congressional legislation and open new oil markets in this country." Domestic oil interests, however, were just too strong for the secretary to challenge. Consequently, he showed little inclination to oblige the Venezuelans. There were other reasons why the department could afford to procrastinate. American investments, particularly Standard Oil, had the Venezuelan political economy sewed up. The opening of new oil fields in Venezuela also necessitated their purchase of additional American machinery and supplies. And American business profited. The exchange of both goods and money was facilitated by the commercial *modus vivendi* of May 12, 1938, granting the United States favorable trade, exchange, and import provisions. The situation in Venezuela had an obvious carryover. With trade and investments squarely in American hands, there was no chance that the Axis powers, especially Germany, could make great inroads in Venezuela. In fact, in 1938 she made a trade balancing agreement with Berlin and the following year with Italy and Japan. These agreements limited the Axis economic threat.

With the preceding observations in mind, it is clear why delay rather than outright rejection characterized United States policy. Venezuela, however, saw through the ploy. "It is becoming increasingly difficult," lamented chargé Henry Villard on December 22, 1936, "to evade a more direct reply" as to why Washington had stalled trade discussions. The comment was indicative of Hull's tactics until the advent of war in Europe. Only then did the Roosevelt Administration reassess its position. On November 6, 1939, the two nations signed an agreement which gave the United States concessions on ninety-six goods totaling 36 per cent of its exports to Venezuela. Reductions ranged from 2.5 to 62.5 per cent on thirty-five items and on sixty-one items "assurances against less favorable customs treatment were obtained." In return, Washington kept crude oil and fuel oil on the free list and lowered the import excise tax on petroleum by 50 per cent. Washington also established an oil quota "amounting to no more than 5 per cent of the total quantity of crude petroleum processed" in refineries in the continental United States during the preceding calendar year. The agreement was a significant one although it was due more to the exigencies of war than to the alacrity of the State Department.[52]

American trade negotiations with Uruguay were perhaps the most hapless. Because of the similarity in export products from Argentina and Uruguay, the State Department hoped to conclude the two agreements simultaneously. Therefore, no meat or wool concessions to one nation, Uruguay, would be automatically extended to the other, Argentina, without a consequent loss of economic leverage. In other words, if the United States and Uruguay signed an agreement, Argentina would get the benefits without making any concessions. And, if there was one thing Hull did not want, it was an even more independent and recalcitrant Argentina. There was one alternative to the stalemate. George Peek, special adviser to the President on foreign trade, suggested blacklisting those nations that discriminated against United States trade. Since Uruguay and Argentina both practiced exchange control and bilateral trade practices (Uruguay on November 9, 1934, had established an import quota system), it would be simple to extend concessions only to that country which acceded to American demands. Although Hull and Sayre rejected Peek's plan, they did use his arguments to stall the Montevideo talks until Argentina was safely in the fold. From 1934 on, Uruguayan negotiations were in a state of suspended animation.

A snag developed in this strategy in the fall of 1939. Washington had been confident that this tiny democracy would not agree to the unconditional most-favored-nation clause nor accept American demands to eliminate exchange control, trade quotas, or to alter its position on differential exchange rates. Yet a month after Hitler's invasion of Poland, Uruguay agreed to most American demands. On October 21, 1939, the two nations announced their intention to negotiate a reciprocal agreement. This unexpected turn of events forced Hull into further procrastinations.

52. See Edwin Lieuwen, *Petroleum in Venezuela: A History* (Berkeley: University of California Press, 1954) and his *Venezuela*, 2d ed. (London: Oxford University Press, 1965), pp. 47–57. Marvin Bernstein, ed., *Foreign Investment in Latin America* (New York: Alfred A. Knopf, 1966), p. 12. *SAPFT*, General Correspondence, NA, Peek to Roosevelt, November 14, 1934. Power Yung-Chao Chu, pp. 343–44. *FR*, 1936, 5:955–56, 959–63. Diebold, p. 10. *FR*, 1940, 5:1176–79. *FTLA*, pt. 2, section 10, pp. 12–13.

By 1940, however, there was no way out. Negotiations, as Hull put it, had "broken down" with Argentina, and Washington had no alternative other than to break off discussions with Montevideo.[53] This kind of guilt by association was a serious blow to the Good Neighbor policy and postponed United States–Uruguayan trade discussions for several years. Not until Washington reached an agreement with Argentina did the two nations conclude a treaty to take effect in 1943.

The agreement followed along the lines of the Argentine treaty. In Schedule I of the agreement, Uruguay gave the United States concessions covering approximately 25 per cent by value of total American exports to Uruguay in 1940. Schedule II covered American concessions on casein, tallow, canned meat, flaxseed, coarse wools, and cattle hides and accounted for concessions of about 32 per cent by value of Uruguayan imports in 1940.[54]

The conclusions drawn from the list of Latin American nations signing reciprocal trade agreements have to be evaluated from two perspectives. First, there is the viewpoint of New Deal diplomats; and second, there is the vantage point of the historian. In the first sense, Hull could take mixed pride in his program. By the advent of World War II, Cuba, Haiti, Brazil, Honduras, Colombia, Guatemala, Nicaragua, El Salvador, Costa Rica, and Ecuador had ostensibly enlisted in the crusade for liberal trade. By war's end, Hull could also include such signatory nations as Argentina, Uruguay, Peru, and Venezuela. In 1946 Paraguay joined the trade fold.

From the historical viewpoint, however, signatures are one thing; consequences are another. For Hull, the trade program sought to revitalize American trade by reducing the number of artificial barriers to international commerce. Domestic prosperity was paramount but nevertheless codependent upon world prosperity. And, prosperity brought peace. Or so Hull thought.

53. *SAPFT*, Peek to Sayre, February 8, 1935. Information on blacklisting can also be found in George N. Peek, papers, Western Historical Manuscripts Collection, State Historical Society of Missouri, Box 17. Also see *FR*, 1938, 5:89, 901, 916–19. DS 611.3231/1298; 611.3531/422, NA, RG 59. *FR*, 1939, 5:787–90, 795, 804. DS 835.5151/1087, NA, RG 59.

54. *FR*, 1942, 6:713–14. For a more detailed study of Uruguay's economic position see *FTLA*, pt. 2, section 9.

Ironically, however, it was war that tied the hemisphere in a marriage of necessity. And, it was war far more than peace that brought relief from the depression. Reciprocity also had political ramifications for Roosevelt's secretary of state. It was to be the economic arm of the Good Neighbor policy that bound the nations of the hemisphere together in the peaceful pursuit of profit. After 1941 the trade program took on a new dimension. The policy of mutual self-interests shifted from the promotion of peace to the promotion of the war effort. The role of reciprocity became one of abetting Washington's control over the political economies of Latin America. Such control would ensure the abatement of economic nationalism, the security of American investments, the curtailment of Axis subversion, and the procurement of strategic raw materials. As was the case in the Central American negotiations, Hull found it much easier to deal with dictators than with nationalists. And, when trade agreements alone failed to "line up" the Latins, Hull could always resort to other types of economic suasion.

In retrospect, even more flaws marred the armor of Hull's idealism. Mutual self-interest required mutual self-sacrifice. Yet, the Roosevelt Administration demanded much in the way of trade concessions while giving very little. In not one Latin American negotiation did the Administration challenge a major domestic industry or make any substantial sacrifice. Consequently, coffee and banana exporting nations, whose economies were complementary to the American economy, were the first to feel the pressure of negotiation. The mineral exporting nations of South America and Mexico and the meat exporting nations of Argentina and Uruguay took a back seat in the trade discussions. Reciprocity also became very much involved in the protection of American investments and, therefore, in the effort to retard economic nationalism and revolution. Expropriation of American oil interests nearly doomed a treaty with Mexico. In the case of Bolivia, expropriation no doubt contributed to the lack of an agreement. The Venezuelan case was just the opposite. Here wartime exigencies, plus the need to increase the oil quota, prompted United States investors to seek an agreement in order to forestall expropriation. As for Chile, protective interests at home militated against reciprocity. Hull also realized that a trade treaty weighted in favor of the United States might well precipitate attacks upon American direct investments. So, he left well enough alone. Treaties were also concluded with Peru and Ecuador but, here too, expediency was the order of the day. Wartime diplomacy, more than a commitment to liberal trade, characterized the American position.

Nor did principle stand in the way of profit. Hull's precepts of the Open Door conflicted with the practices of barter, clearing and compensation agreements, embargoes, import quotas, and exchange control. They also ran counter to the doctrine of contiguous countries and the efforts to spur economic integration. In each case, Hull opposed their application in Latin America. On the other hand, Washington did not discourage the El Salvadorian tariff schedule—a technique employed by the Central Americans to discourage Japanese competition. Nor did the Department of State insist that Ecuador extend unconditional most-favored-nation treatment to nations other than the United States. In the Cuban negotiations, the United States had accepted the idea that "geographical propinquity and historical considerations" merited special benefits. However, when Peru used the same rationale to sign an agreement with Chile, the Administration strenuously objected. In 1939 Washington also objected to a customs union of the nations bordering the Rio de la Plata.

Finally, the trade agreements, especially with Central America, stimulated the process of monoculture, retarded industrialization, weakened the development of an incipient bourgeoise, and deprived nations of badly needed revenue from customs. Consequently, these nations became increasingly dependent upon American financial assistance. Such conditions fostered the continuance of rightist dictators who realized it made good sense to deal with United States business. Hence, America reaped a "bitter harvest" of ill will, and Latin America suffered the pains of instability and repression. This is not to say that Hull's trade program was totally to blame, or that he fully understood these consequences. Nevertheless, a fundamental reassessment of Good Neighbor policy is surely overdue. For forces, not men, were in the saddle of state. No horseman could have reached the stirrups. The exigencies of depression and war, not policy memorandums, goodwill tours, public declarations of continental brotherhood, or even individual efforts of self-sacrifice, rode the gallop of the 1930s and the 1940s.

9

A Retreat from Liberalism

On April 7, 1937, Assistant Secretary of State Francis B. Sayre reminded the American people that the "dogs of war" would continue to plague the international community as long as nations remained in economic conflict. The assistant secretary's remarks were directed at nations like Italy and Japan, but they bore particular relevance to the mounting German–American struggle over the political economies of key South American countries.[1]

As the struggle intensified, it became apparent that a departure from economic liberalism was necessary to check the Axis threat. The solution came with the expanded use of the Export-Import Bank. Although the rhetoric of Sayre and other Administration spokesmen sometimes lacked systematic formulation, few observers doubted that Axis economic activity could serve as a barometer of even more salient political and military activities to come. To combat this subversion in target areas of Latin America, the Administration initiated and reformulated a series of political and diplomatic concessions such as the nonintervention pledge, the Anti-War pact, and gave greater recognition, ostensibly, to the sensitivities of Latin American statesmen. In return for these political concessions, the Good Neighbor policy demanded, sometimes none too tactfully, due reciprocal action by Latin America. The State Department repeatedly affirmed its position that along with increased rights and privileges accorded in the name of multilateralism came increased burdens and responsibilities.[2]

1. DS, Francis B. Sayre, "The Hull Agreements and International Trade," *CPS* No. 35 (1937) p. 1.
2. "Liberal Trade Policies: The Basis for Peace," *CPS* No. 37 (1937)

But the department also realized, as the 1930s progressed, that political concessions without a sound economic program designed to mitigate the sting of depression in Latin America seriously prejudiced the essence of good neighborliness. Hull and his subordinates expressed great confidence that the program might well serve as an effective means of promoting economic goals and the collective security of the Western Hemisphere. By 1939, however, the optimism and aspirations of the early New Dealers had given way to a more realistic but far more discouraging assessment of the program. German economic thrusts in Brazil and other selected South American nations could not be parried by reciprocity alone. A new instrument of diplomacy, the Export-Import Bank, became the surrogate for trade liberalism. For Hull's liberal trade program could only operate successfully if the world economic situation met three fundamental conditions: first, freedom in international trade without quantitative limitation; second, unhampered convertibility of currencies in the international market; and third, international currency stability. The decade of the 1930s could boast of none of these conditions.[3]

The most immediate threat to Hull's trade program and to American commercial interests in Latin America was from the Orient. By 1933 the label "Made in Japan" had become a symbol of Japanese efforts to achieve domestic recovery through a revival of export trade. In 1935 a so-called patriotic organization in Atlanta, Georgia, found much to its dismay that a rally to demonstrate "faith in America and things American" unwittingly flew American flags "Made in Japan." Other such illustrations sounded a more ominous note. In 1931 Japanese exports to

pp. 1–7. Bryce Wood, *The Making of the Good Neighbor Policy* (New York: Columbia University Press, 1961), p. 309.

3. Henry F. Grady, "The New American Commercial Policy," *Proceedings of the Institute of World Affairs*, 13th sess., 13 (Los Angeles: University of Southern California, 1936):186–87. Richard Carlton Snyder, *The Most-Favored-Nation Clause* (New York: King's Crown Press, 1948), pp. 5–11, 236–43. League of Nations, *Equality of Treatment in the Present State of International Commercial Relations: The Most-Favored-Nation Clause*, League of Nations, II, Economic and Financial, 1936, II. B. 9 (Geneva: Series of League of Nations Publications, 1937): 6. Hereafter cited as *Equality of Treatment*.

Latin America stood at 13,527,000 yen. By 1933 the figure sky-rocketed to 46,555,000 yen. For the first six months of 1934 alone, Japanese exports totaled 41,456,000 yen—a percentage increase in trade matched by few of her competitors.

Paradoxically, while Europe and the United States in the first years of the depression resorted mainly to measures of self-sufficiency and containment in the search for domestic recovery, Japanese leaders envisioned economic recovery by an active campaign to capture foreign markets. By 1935 Japan had set a new record high in total trade. The secret of her export success lay chiefly in the rationalization of industries by reduction of cost production, improvement of organization and technique, and lower wage scales. Japan further stimulated foreign trade by currency depreciation and the subsidization of exports. By the mid-1930s Japan's textiles, pottery, drugs, metals, shoes, machinery, chemicals, dyes, and paints briskly competed for Latin American markets long considered to be purviews of the United States and Europe.[4]

Barraged by a cacophony of congressional, presidential, and commercial concern over Japan's export gains, the State Department intensified its efforts to secure reciprocal trade agreements in Latin America. But the department did not remain content with multilateral trade. In Cuba, for example, trade concessions granted to American concerns did not extend to third powers. The department did little to discourage Central American nations from adopting the El Salvadorian multicolumn tariff scheme, which was aimed at depriving the Japanese of their textile markets. The department likewise discouraged Japanese efforts to secure commercial agreements in Argentina, Colombia, Brazil, and other Latin American states. As Spruille Braden wrote in 1941, "The Department will recall previous efforts of Japan to obtain trade agreements [in Colombia] have been checkmated

4. DS 611.2131/90, NA, RG 59. U. S., Congress, *Congressional Record*, 73d Cong., 2d sess., 1934, 78, pt. 7:7748. U. S., Congress, *Congressional Record*, 74th Cong., 1st sess., 1935, 79, pt. 6:6009. Maxwell S. Stewart, "Paradoxes of World Recovery," *FPR* 10:12 (August 15, 1934):156. T. A. Bisson, "Japan's Trade Boom: Does it Menace the United States?" 12:1 (March 15, 1936) :2–15; T. A. Bisson, "Japan's Trade Expansion," 10:16 (October 10, 1934) :194–99. Yamato Ichihashi, "Japan's Foreign Trade Expansion," *Proceedings of the Institute of World Affairs*, 12th sess., 12 (Los Angeles: University of Southern California, 1935) :129–31.

largely by Embassy's efforts. . . . Once in, they [Japan and Germany] will be evicted only with greatest difficulty if at all."[5]

The Japanese, however, faced more serious impediments to trade expansion in Latin America than American hostility. Because of the nature of the Japanese diet, many Latin American staple products such as beef, coffee, and cocoa did not find abundant markets in the land of the Rising Sun. Her trade gains, when examined more closely, were more relative than absolute; their percentage increase was great, but in terms of volume or value they lagged far behind Europe and America. As a consequence, Japan's export expectations far outran the realities of international trade. German and British bilateral schemes throughout South America, combined with American commercial hegemony in the Caribbean, likewise tended to retard Japanese trade expansion in the Western Hemisphere.[6]

Nor did the Japanese find economic solace in the American domestic market. By 1936 political and economic tension between the United States and Japan had sufficiently intensified to warrant an increased rate of duty on Japanese cotton textiles exported to the United States.[7] Throughout the mid-1930s, Hull steadily qualified his economic dictum that international trade promoted world peace so as to apply only when political affairs among nations created an environment favorable to increased trade. In other words, increased trade generated greater political friendship among allies, but potentially hostile powers would merely augment their warmaking capacity against the United States. Operating upon these assumptions, United States–Japanese political and economic relations continued to deteriorate. In July, 1939, the Department of State denounced its existing trade treaty with Japan by giving her the required six-month notice before termination. Notwithstanding, Hull's main concern in matters relating to the political economy of Latin America was not directed toward Japan.

5. DS 611.2131/184, /266; 621.9417/50, NA, RG 59. U. S., Congress, *Congressional Record*, 74th Cong., 2d sess., 1936, 80, pt. 1:1107–8. U. S., Congress, *Congressional Record*, 75th Cong., 3d sess., 1938, 83, pt. 1:218. Franklin D. Roosevelt, papers, Franklin D. Roosevelt Library, Hyde Park, N. Y., Official File, 614–A, Trade, Roosevelt to Hull, December 10, 1934.

6. DS 611.2131/568, NA, RG 59.

7. Roosevelt, papers, Official File, 614–A, Trade, Hull to Roosevelt, April 15, 1936; Hull to Roosevelt, May 21, 1936.

Nazi Germany offered the most serious challenge to Hull's trade program in the Western Hemisphere. The origins of German trade practices went deep into that nation's history. From the Middle Ages, the German states had failed to develop a unified system of substantive law commensurate with judicial precedent. Unable to free herself from the legal and cultural tides that swept across the continent, the German Empire built up a veritable maze of conflicting rules stemming from the laws of the separate German principalities, the laws of ancient Rome, and the legal framework of surrounding nations. These historical distinctions between German civil and commercial law remained intact on the eve of the destruction of the Weimar Republic.[8]

The Great Depression intensified the trend toward economic self-sufficiency initiated by Weimar statesmen. Confronted by the depreciation of international currencies, Germany suffered domestic price increases, declining exports, abnormal capital withdrawals, and dwindling exchange reserves. To remedy the situation, in July, 1931, Germany adopted official foreign exchange control and abrogated Article 280 of the Treaty of Versailles, which stated that the Allied and Associated powers should unconditionally and without compensation be granted most-favored-nation treatment by Germany. While other nations dabbled with temporary expedients such as currency depreciation, German statesmen turned to exchange control, barter, bilateral exchange, quota embargoes, import licenses, and clearing and compensation agreements because of the unhappy conditions that depreciation had caused after World War I.

With the advent of National Socialism, the pace of economic nationalism increased. There was, of course, another element to be considered. Combined with the long-standing confusion in matters of commercial law, National Socialism added the ruthless and dynamic energies of German industrial power. On June 9, 1933, Germany declared a moratorium on long-term loans, exclusive of the loans incurred by the Dawes and Young plans. A year later the Führer defaulted on these loans as well. His economic policy, therefore, signaled no departure from the programs

8. BFDC, H. C. Harris, "Trading Under the Laws of Germany," TPS No. 150 (1933) pp. 1–4, 58–60. See also Charles C. Abbott, "Economic Penetration and Power Politics," *Harvard Business Review* 26:4 (July 1948) :410–24.

of the Weimar Republic. Only the force and power Hitler could bring to his disposal had actually changed.[9]

Hitler's initial success in trade and financial matters lay principally in the failure of other nations to comprehend the nature of his program. Unquestionably this program placed economic viability as a preliminary to military conquests. Although the Führer spoke of a "planned economic system" as a "perilous adventure," he continually justified his actions by pointing to the exigencies of depression and the hostility of foreign powers. Ironically, in the same year that Hull's trade ideals reached legislative fruition, Hitler's regime demonstrated the Nazi obsession with economic self-sufficiency by the adoption of the "New Plan," a scheme designed basically to reorient German foreign trade and financial policies. The New Plan included a moratorium on the transfer of interest on foreign-held German obligations, the adoption of exchange priorities designed to allocate exchange to finance vital imports, and severe restrictions on those imports that Germany would have to pay in hard exchange.[10] The New Plan in essence signaled the Reich's total abandonment of world trade cooperation and, in fact, anticipated much of the political and diplomatic tension between Germany and the Allied powers. By inference, it also gave notice to the world that henceforth Germany's trade program sought the total and rapid rearmament of the Fatherland, since the priorities of the plan were directed toward military production.

Due in part to the antithetical nature of Nazi economic philosophy and his own multilateral trade principles, Secretary Hull perceived at an early date the inherent dangers of National Socialism. Yet the State Department and United States commercial interests saw the German threat principally as an attempt to

9. DS, *Documents on German Foreign Policy 1918–1945*, Series C (1933–1937), The Third Reich: First Phase, 3 (Washington: GPO, 1959):16, 344–47. TC, *Foreign Trade and Exchange Controls in Germany*, Report No. 150, 2d Series (GPO, 1942), pp. 1–13. John C. DeWilde, "Germany's Trend Toward Economic Isolation," *FPR* 10:18 (November 7, 1934):226–29.

10. Hjalmar Schacht, *My First Seventy-Six Years* (London: Allan Wingate, 1955), pp. 327–34. *Exchange Controls in Germany*, pp. 113–14, 132. For the German colonial argument and Schacht's position see Wolfe W. Schmokel, *Dream of Empire: German Colonialism, 1919–1945* (New Haven: Yale University Press, 1964), Chapter 2.

corner select markets for commercial aggrandizement and future political profit. In truth, the nature of Hitler's foreign trade policy had serious ramifications for the political economies that he exploited (for example, Eastern Europe). Nevertheless, overriding all other considerations lay the Reich's desire for national economic self-sufficiency and the importation of vital strategic materials necessary for war.[11] German exports and short term credit assumed a vital role in Nazi strategy, not as ends in themselves, but as important factors in securing, promptly and with the least drain on foreign exchange, those import products used to promote the twisted dreams of Hitler. Toward this end, the German foreign minister and Dr. Hjalmar Schacht, minister of economic affairs and president of the Reichsbank, strove for a basic reorientation of the German import market. Aided by monopoly management, these men sought to direct German purchases toward those nations buying from Germany through the establishment of import quotas supplied only to nations purchasing sufficient amounts of German goods. The Nazi's first experiment under the New Plan concerned major coffee-producing nations. The challenge to Hull's commercial policy could not have been more direct and unequivocal.[12]

On July 3, 1934, a German trade delegation sailed for the South American continent. The objectives of the mission included efforts to forestall the capture of the Latin American market by foreign competitors, to reactivate trade through clearing agreements and barter transactions, and to unfreeze German balances accrued from deliveries of goods to South America. Germany also hoped to secure vital raw materials such as wood, hides and skins, oilseeds, maize, and wheat from Argentina and Uruguay, while coffee occupied paramount importance in Brazil and Colombia. The delegation actively sought and received support from German trading circles and from large German

11. Schacht, pp. 328–29. *FTLA*, pt. 1, Report No. 136, 2d Series, 1942, p. 16. Also of note is Von Hans-Jürgen Schröder, "Die Vereinigten Staaten Und Die National Sozialistische Handelspolitik Gegenüber Lateinamerika 1937/38" in *Jahrbuch Für Geschichte*, Band 7.

12. *Documents*, Series C., 3:26–35, 409–11, 482–83, 607–8. *Exchange Controls in Germany*, pp. 11–13. Raoul de Roussy de Sales, ed., *My New Order* (New York: Reynal and Hitchcock, 1941), pp. 310, 410–11. This is a collection of Hitler's major speeches.

communities in South America. Aided in their propaganda tactics by the *Volksbund fuer das Deutshtum in Ausland*, the *Deutsches Ausland-Institut*, and the *Auslandsorganisation*, the German trade delegation gained a "thorough knowledge of the geographical and geopolitical structure of the territory visited" as well as scoring a major propaganda coup.[13]

Holding forth the olive branch, the Reich likewise threatened economic coercion. Should South America "show no understanding for our position," warned Karl Ritter, director of the German economic department, "unilateral German measures will be unavoidable." Impressed by Nazi Germany's economic bargaining position, Argentina, Brazil, Chile, and Uruguay concluded either commercial agreements or Central Bank agreements with the trade delegation. Colombia followed suit in 1937. Not even then did the German commercial thrust abate. Between 1934 and 1936 German exports to Latin America (minus Argentina) increased by nearly 250 per cent, while the percentage of German world export trade increased from 4.3 per cent in 1934 to 8.7 per cent in 1936. By 1936 Nazi Germany had effectively switched from barter and blocked marks (depreciated currency made available to any nation for certain authorized purposes, but without distinction as to the nationality of the user or the commodities for which used), to compensation agreements commonly referred to as the aski mark system (foreign exports to Germany received askis, which could only be used to purchase specified German goods) and export subsidies.[14] Latin American nations aided the operation of the aski system by the establishment of import and

13. *Documents*, Series C., 3:74–75, 930–33. Alton B. Frye, *Nazi Germany and the American Hemisphere 1933–1941* (New Haven: Yale University Press, 1967), pp. 15–21, 65–66.

14. *Documents*, Series C., 3:75. Herbert M. Bratter, "Foreign Exchange Control in Latin America," *FPR* 14:23 (February 15, 1939):277, 283. *Exchange Controls in Germany*, pp. 14–19, 137, 142–43, 174. League of Nations, *Enquiry Into Clearing Agreements*, League of Nations, II, Economic and Financial, 1935, II. B. 6 (Geneva: Series of League of Nations Publications, 1936):35. Also see League of Nations, *Review of World Trade 1936*, League of Nations, II, Economic and Financial, 1937, II. A. 9 (Geneva: Series of League of Nations Publications, 1937):37–43. United States, Congress, House, *House Report No. 1000*, 73d Cong., 2d sess., 1934, 2:4.

export exchange-control systems designed to regulate the distribution of import trade.[15]

Although the New Plan retarded the growth of German exports to areas in which German economic pressure was minimal, it did accomplish its primary mission, which was the shift away from nonessential import products and the artificial channeling of foreign trade along bilateral lines.[16] The continual decline in United States–German trade bore testimony to Hitler's design to rechannel trade to those nations buying substantial quantities of German goods. Between 1933 and 1935, United States exports to Germany fell from 482,800,000 reichmarks to 240,700,000. Further evidence of the deterioration of German–American trade came with the termination of most-favored-nation treatment on October 14, 1935. Germany, commercial attaché Douglas Miller reported, had actively engaged in a "trade war" with the United States. In June, 1936, the United States Treasury Department intensified the economic struggle by the imposition of countervailing duties on specified German imports.[17]

On November 16, 1935, the Third Reich provided further evidence that the primary purpose of her trade program did not include the promotion of foreign trade. Henceforth, Germany prohibited the exportation of essential agricultural goods, raw materials, and semifinished products.[18] By 1936 the upsurge in the German domestic economy prompted the German foreign minister to exclaim that "the most important task of German economic policy" was "the supply of indispensable foreign raw materials." Still, in order to obtain these imports and to maintain a policy of balanced trade, the Germans were forced to seek

15. *Exchange Controls in Germany*, pp. 146–47. For a brief but adequate survey of major Brazilian commercial problems see Frank D. McCann, Jr., *The Brazilian-American Alliance, 1937–1945* (Princeton: Princeton University Press, 1973), Chapter 6.

16. *Documents*, Series C., 4:38–43.

17. William Diebold, *New Directions in Our Trade Policy* (New York: Council on Foreign Relations, 1941), pp. 98–100.

18. *Documents*, Series C., 4:608–11, 810–11. *Exchange Controls in Germany*, pp. 150, 155. George N. Peek, papers, Western Historical Manuscripts Collection, State Historical Society of Missouri, Commercial Attaché Report, November 23, 1934. William Phillips, diary, 1933–1936, Vol. 3, Houghton Library, Cambridge, Mass., November 5, 1934.

greater foreign markets. To this end, Latin America served a vital function.[19]

The Nazi trade offensive throughout Latin America had a checkered success. In Colombia, for example, an adverse trade balance forced that nation's exchange control board to suspend all German goods by limiting import permits to raw materials and commodities urgently needed for Colombian industry. In part because of the reciprocal trade agreement with the United States, Washington continued to hold the dominant position in Colombian foreign trade. In June, 1937, German exchange restrictions forced Bogotá into an agreement that in effect provided for a bilateral balancing of trade. Since the United States controlled the Colombian market, and the volume of Colombian–German trade was small, the agreement merely ensured against future German trade advances. The effect of such an action forestalled any possibility of a German threat to American commercial hegemony in Colombia.[20]

In Cuba, the Germans met stern resistance from American business because of a bilateral trade agreement between the United States and Cuba. The agreement granted trade concessions solely to American concerns. American diplomats in Haiti in 1938 stated that "severe competition" came from Great Britain, the Netherlands, Japan, and Belgium. In Central America, Germany likewise faced insurmountable handicaps from United States competitors. Even the compensation marks trade had little overall effect. Germany became aware of the complementary rather than competitive nature of United States–Caribbean products. She also knew of extensive American capital investment, geographical proximity, the direction of trade routes, the availability of shipping services, large free duty lists, and the formal and informal relationship of Central American currencies to the American dollar. Germany quickly realized the futility of competition in the Caribbean.

In Mexico, recurrent efforts by Germany to secure control of Mexican oil exports also met with limited success, mainly because United States companies owned the oil tankers and the

19. *Documents*, Series C., 5:842.
20. DS 611.2131/349–50, /568; 621.9417/4, NA, RG 59. *FTLA*, pt. 2, pp. 143–57.

marketing facilities. Also, Americans were the only ones with the technological skills necessary to run the fields at top capacity in the first year after expropriation. The trade war between Mexico and the United States, after the 1938 expropriation crisis, was Hitler's biggest asset. The Nazis' portion of Mexico's aggregate imports had fallen from approximately 15.3 per cent to 14.8 per cent in the years 1936–1937. This appeared to be good evidence that a trade treaty was not necessary because, during these same years, Mexico's percentage of total imports from the United States rose steadily from 59 per cent to 64.8 per cent. In 1938, however, the trend was reversed. German exports continued to rise, while American and British trade fell off substantially.

In Chile and Peru, Hitler's trade offensive restrained any noticeable decline in German exports. For example, the U.S. Bureau of Foreign and Domestic Commerce in 1936 regretfully admitted that Germany's use of aski marks had dislodged the United States as the principal supplier of Chilean imports. The report was unduly pessimistic. The following year, America accounted for 29.1 per cent of Chilean imports and Germany 26 per cent. In 1938 the trend toward the United States was even greater. In Peru, the Axis share of imports continued to rise from 1936 throughout 1938 but at an overall rate that was not as fast as the United States'. Most German gains were made at the expense of Great Britain, not the United States.

Hitler's basic problem in Argentina remained unsolved. This nation of the Rio de la Plata could not overcome its dependence on British markets. Even the industrial might of Krupp and Rheinmetall could not dislodge British economic predominance.[21]

Hull took comfort in the fact that the damage created by British influence in the political economy of the la Plata region by no means compared to the dangers inherent in a region linked ideologically and economically with the Third Reich. Although Argentina, in particular, was the ideological bastion of fascism throughout World War II, she nevertheless remained an economic adjunct of the British Empire in Latin America.[22]

21. *Documents*, Series C., 5:910. TC, *Latin America as a Source of Strategic and Other Essential Materials*, Report No. 144, 2d Series, 1941, pp. 3–4. Schröder has done an excellent job of condensing many State Department reports from the field, see pp. 332–36.

22. Walton Moore, papers, Franklin D. Roosevelt Library, Hyde Park,

But the Third Reich's greatest economic threat to both Hull's trade program and the security of the Western Hemisphere came from South America's largest and potentially most powerful nation. Moving with great dispatch, the German trade delegation in 1934 succeeded in beating Washington to the punch by reaching a commercial agreement with the Vargas regime, which seriously prejudiced the workability of the trade agreements program in Brazil. Through a system of barter and clearing agreements with Brazil, Dr. Schacht swiftly shifted German coffee imports from Central American markets (in 1933 Germany purchased 50 per cent of her coffee imports from Central America) to the more politically and economically important nations of South America. From July 1, 1934, to October 1, 1934, Brazil bartered 766,021 sacks of coffee for German goods. Brazilian cotton exports to Germany likewise grew steadily.[23]

By 1936 Schacht had successfully shifted from barter arrangements to the more effective compensation marks system. The effects of these actions prompted such policymakers as Economic Adviser Herbert Feis to question the ability of Hull's program to withstand the German trade offensive.[24] Combined with German export subsidies and exchange advantages by the Banco do Brasil, the compensation agreement provided the National Socialist regime with trade advantages denied to American competitors. The inherently dynamic nature of the marks system required Brazil (which enjoyed a favorable balance of trade with Germany) to purchase an ever increasing quantity of German products or to face the accumulation of more compensation marks. The agreement forced the sale of German goods to absorb the volume of marks created by German purchases whether sufficient demand existed or not. The bilateral implications of such a policy precluded the use of German imports in meeting debt

N. Y., Moore to Hull, December 10, 1936. Cordell Hull, papers, General Correspondence, Library of Congress, Roosevelt to Hull, February 6, 1936. *FTLA*, pt. 1, p. 14, *FTUS*, 1936, TPS No. 174 (1938) p. 101. Francis B. Sayre, papers, Special Correspondence, Library of Congress, Sayre to Phillips, April 12, 1937. For diplomatic correspondence dealing with the pro-Axis sympathies of the Argentineans see DS 610.1131/322; 611.3531/829, /1496, /1558, for evidence of fascist leanings in Argentina see DS 610.1131/322; 611.3531/829, /1496, /1558; 832.51/1458, NA, RG 59.

23. DS 632.6231/11, /24, /28, /30; 832.5151/440, NA, RG 59.
24. DS 632.6231/48, NA, RG 59.

service and other external payments in countries other than Germany. The Department of State had ample reason for doubting the efficacy of Hull's liberal trade doctrines in the face of such German export practices.[25]

Resolute in spirit, Hull refused to surrender his lifetime dream. In a letter to E. P. Thomas dated June 19, 1936, Hull optimistically stated that "the further the trade agreements program proceeds the stronger will be the position of this government in combating restrictive trade policies."[26]

The secretary's confidence, however, was not echoed by all department officials, since German trade policy also relied on the dynamics of expansion. If Germany extended her bilateral trade system to incorporate third powers, then the United States would have little alternative but to resort to compensation and clearing agreements. The logic of this position, wrote Feis, was "beyond dispute." Laurence Duggan, chief of the Division of Latin American Republics, concurred. Harry Dexter White of the State Department also agreed. In a memorandum written to Treasury Secretary Morgenthau, White went to the heart of the problem.

> Our international trade is being forced into ever-narrowing channels. . . . The sphere of our trade agreements is contracting as the area of political and economic domination of Germany and Japan expands. . . . The value of existing trade agreements has been diminished by Germany's trade tactics. . . . Our agreement with Brazil has worked badly. . . . Likewise our trade with third countries suffers. The expansion of the aggressor nations strikes at our trade with countries who buy from us.

In conclusion, White echoed an all-too-familiar warning. German trade practices had undermined Hull's trade program. The "continuation of the present trend," he wrote, "may well see a complete disruption of the program."[27]

Further German commercial success in Brazil forced the Department of State to consider the possibility of additional methods to deter future Nazi successes. The use of foreign loans as a means of redressing the Brazilian exchange deficit and the is-

25. DS 632.6231/188, /224, /1060, /1149, /1176, /1182, /1195, /1206B; 600.0031 World Program/123, NA, RG 59.

26. DS 832.5151/837, NA, RG 59.

27. DS 632.6231/94, NA, RG 59. White's memo can be found in Schröder, pp. 322–23.

suance of a joint British–American communiqué deploring the compensation marks system merited serious consideration. The American chargé at Rio de Janeiro favored even stronger United States actions. Due in part to the fascist predilections of the Brazilian finance ministry, as well as the stranglehold of the compensation marks system on the Brazilian economy, he wrote that nothing short of an abrogation of the reciprocal treaty or an import tax on coffee could modify Brazil's foreign trade philosophy.[28]

Secretary Hull, however, refrained from taking any drastic action in regard to the German trade problem in Brazil. Perhaps the logic of his own convictions prohibited a departure from the liberal trade philosophy. Or perhaps Hull also realized that an import tax on coffee, as well as the renunciation of the United States–Brazilian commercial agreement, gave credence to foreign and domestic assertions that in the world of harsh reality no place existed for the liberal trade ideal. Hull, therefore, searched diligently for some means to checkmate German commercial predominance in Brazil without falling prey to the trade practices he consistently opposed. In June, 1937, Hull met with a Brazilian trade delegation composed of the pro-German minister of finance, Souza Costa, and the pro-American foreign minister, Oswaldo Aranha, in an attempt to stave off Hitler's designs on the political economy of Brazil. But Hull's position, which was void of retaliatory threats or substantial economic assistance, failed to move the Vargas regime. Rio continued provisionally to extend the compensation agreement with Germany.[29]

Germany for her part continued the economic pressure. United States Ambassador to Germany William Dodd reported that Schacht and Herman Göring would "not yield an inch" to American trade principles, while in Washington the German ambassador, Hans Dieckhoff, informed Under Secretary Sumner Welles that "unwarranted interference" in German–Brazilian trade

28. DS 632.6231/128, /161–163; 611.3231/1144B, NA, RG 59.

29. DS 632.6231/181, /182, /240, NA, RG 59. For the sympathies of the Brazilian Federal Foreign Trade Council see Gibson's note to the department in DS 832.5151/442½, NA, RG 59. Also see Great Britain, Foreign Office, E. L. Woodward and Rohan Butler, eds., *Documents on British Foreign Policy, 1919–1939*, 3d Series, 4 (London: His Majesty's Stationery Office, 1951) :25.

matters by the United States "irritated and annoyed" the leaders of the Third Reich and could lead to serious diplomatic difficulties.[30]

Hitler's Nürnberg Proclamation of September 6, 1938 symbolized the Führer's increasing self-assurance in matters of foreign trade. "The idea of blockading Germany," he boasted, "can even now be buried as an entirely ineffective weapon." No longer did Hitler pay lip service to international economic cooperation. Keeping "one's own economy in order," he stated, must take priority over all economic issues. The success of war prompted even more self-assurance, as Hitler reached the pinnacle of economic nationalism. Speaking at a Munich rally on February 24, 1941, the German ruler declared, "Our economic policy, I repeat, is determined solely by the interests of the German people. From this principle we shall never depart." The transition in Hitler's economic rhetoric, from a portrayal of Germany as a commercially exploited and defenseless nation in 1933–1935 to a German nation that appeared remarkably confident and independent in matters of world trade, was complete by 1941.[31]

German economic success throughout Latin America, coupled with the standstill of the trade agreement program, created a sense of frustration and disillusionment in the ability of Hull's multilateral trade schemes to promote the best interests of the United States. In 1929, for example, the United States supplied Latin America with 38.5 per cent of its total imports. The German figure stood at 9.5 per cent. By 1938 the American figure declined by approximately 4.6 per cent, while Germany, on the other hand, increased the percentage of her export trade from 9.5 per cent of total Latin American imports in 1929 to 16.2 per cent in 1938.

The State Department watched German trade developments in Chile, Argentina, Uruguay, and Brazil closely. In 1938 German exports to Chile rose by nearly 35 per cent over the 1937 figures, but United States exports increased by a little over 50 per cent during the same year. Thus, the German share of the total Chilean imports continued to decline. The same did not hold true for Argentina. There, Germany increased her percent-

30. DS 632.6231/187, /203, NA, RG 59.
31. de Sales, pp. 495–96, 570, 673, 932.

age of total Argentine imports and her volume of trade in the years 1936–1938 but so did the United States. Again, the loser was Great Britain. Washington's biggest setback in 1938 came in Uruguay. Here, Hitler's trade machine racked up an almost 120 per cent increase in its volume of trade over 1937, while the United States suffered a nearly 20 per cent loss.

Confronted by increased German trade, propaganda, and subversive activities on the South American continent, Hull turned to various economic measures designed to thwart the German menace. At the Eighth International Conference of American States held at Lima in 1938 and the Panama Conference the following year, Hull reaffirmed the economic principles of multilateralism; the department, however, turned increasingly toward other expedients to maintain hemispheric solidarity. The construction of the Pan-American highway, the disposal of Latin American export surpluses, the procurement of essential Latin American imports, and the stabilization of currencies assumed greater priority by American policymakers. But perhaps the most dynamic economic instrument in the shaping of the Latin American policy of the United States came from an institution founded in the first years of the Roosevelt Administration and resuscitated around 1938.[32]

Incorporated on February 2, 1934, under the provisions of the National Industrial Recovery Act and endowed with capital stock totalling $11,000,000, the Export-Import Bank faced an international financial community marked by chaos, frustration, and despair. In contrast to the dismal record of both private and governmental financial policies in the decade of the 1920s, the Export-Import Bank sought to impose order and stability in an area lacking in administrative technique and purpose. The

32. Monica Curtis, ed., *Documents on International Affairs, 1938*, Vol. 1 (London: Oxford University Press, 1942), pp. 379–91. For the Declaration of American Principles adopted at Lima see Curtis, pp. 390–91. Cordell Hull, *The Memoirs of Cordell Hull*, Vol. 1 (New York: Macmillan Company, 1948) pp. 601–10. Donald M. Dozer, *Are We Good Neighbors?* (Gainesville: University of Florida Press, 1961), pp. 49, 74–76. *FTLA*, pt. 1, pp. 22–23, 34. Frye, p. 109. DS 811.516 Export-Import Bank/178; 611.3231/1263, NA, RG 59. German airlines in Latin America were one example of subversion as was the integralista movement in Brazil. For 1936–1938 figures on United States–German competition in Latin America see Schröder, pp. 332–34.

Wall Street collapse of 1929 and the failure of the Credit Anstalt of Vienna created an ambience of fear and distrust toward all forms of national and international lending by private banking concerns.

To some extent Roosevelt sought the bank's participation in the extension of credit as a device to spur the liberalization of foreign credit, the lifeblood of international commerce. Toward this end, the first Export-Import Bank began lending operations with the USSR in February, 1934, while a second Export-Import Bank assumed identical functions with Cuba the following month. Neither scheme, however, enjoyed marked success. The Russian experiment was doomed to failure because the Soviet Union would not settle its war debts, and because her foreign minister, Maxim Litvinov, did not want to spend all of the credits in the United States. The Cuban scheme was void of substantial funds and imaginative purpose. The bank had helped neither the Cuban people nor American business.

Still, the Administration had little recourse but to continue the project. Other methods of financing long-term credit, such as the floatation of foreign bonds, appeared sidetracked by the Johnson Act, which prohibited the purchase or sale of foreign obligations in the United States by any nation in debt default to the American government. The bill, however, excluded Export-Import Bank credit transactions. The bank also came into existence as a response to the same type of measures incorporated into the trade promotion activities of many European powers. Since the depression, public assistance in foreign trade had become a world fact. Roosevelt and Hull realized this fact, and they realized also that unless a governmental agency was established in this country as well the United States' share of world trade would probably continue to fall. Thus, in July, 1935, the Roosevelt Administration merged the capital stock of the two separate banks and extended lending operations to third powers. But certain basic problems continued to plague the formulation of policy by the bank.[33]

33. Peek, papers, Box 17, Chester Davis to Peek, May 23, 1935. DS 811.516 Export-Import Bank/1, /42, /83, /217; 800.51/W 39 U.S.S.R./23, NA, RG 59. DS, Eleanor Lansing Dulles, "The Export-Import Bank of Washington: The First Ten Years," *CPS* No. 75 (1944) pp. 6–7. Edward O. Guerrant, *Roosevelt's Good Neighbor Policy* (Albuquerque: University of

Characterized by "hesitation and experimentation" in 1934–1935, the Export-Import Bank appeared as a less-than-valuable adjunct of American commercial expansion abroad. Nor was it an effective means of promoting the national interests. Although the purpose and powers of Export-Import Bank, as stated in the certificate of incorporation, permitted that institution "to aid in financing trade, to facilitate exports and imports and the exchange of commodities between the United States and other nations or agencies," the results were meager. In fact, had the bank not served "as a basis for later expansion" to meet diplomatic and military exigencies, it might have had "little lasting importance" in New Deal literature.[34]

Under the initial direction of George Peek, special adviser to the President on foreign trade, the bank sought the facilitation of export trade by means of barter, extension of intermediate and long-term credit, and assistance to private firms hampered by foreign exchange control restrictions that, under normal circumstances, would be lost to American commerce. Partly because of the export proclivities of Hull and the State Department, the protective and antiliberal views of Peek, as well as the fear of domestic criticism toward any scheme that smacked of aid to United States imports, Roosevelt devoted the activities of the bank to export credit arrangements. Legally, however, the bank was empowered to aid in the development of both import and export trade.[35]

In defense of the bank's activities before congressional appropriations committees, the State Department continually stressed "that almost 'every dollar' was spent in the United States." The types of loans actively promoted by the Export-Import Bank during the early New Deal years practically omitted all types of developmental projects in favor of schemes designed to export surplus American goods. This policy, of course, worked a serious

---

New Mexico Press, 1950) , pp. 100–104. Ethel B. Dietrich, *World Trade* (New York: Henry Holt and Company, 1939) , pp. 294–95.

34. *CPS* No. 75, p. 11. Charles R. Whittlesey, "Five Years of the Export-Import Bank," *The American Economic Review* 29:3 (September 1939) :487. DS 811.516 Export-Import Bank/9, NA, RG 59.

35. *SAPFT*, NA, RG 40, Export-Import Bank File, Box 4, Peek's Radio Discussion No. 4, April 5, 1934; Charles E. Stuart's address, April 26, 1935. Whittlesey, p. 500.

hardship on underdeveloped areas such as Latin America whose desperate need of developmental capital found no recourse from United States private or public sources. The bank also went on record as opposed to the financing of arms, ammunition, and implements of war. The possibility of future Nye Committees implanted certain visions of horror long sustained in government and business circles.[36]

Nor did Roosevelt envision the Export-Import Bank as a rival of private banking interests, at least not in the area of short-term credit. To allay such concerns, the Export-Import Bank agreed to a proposition endorsed by the American Bankers Association that all proposed Export-Import Bank transactions must "have been studied and the cooperation of the commercial bankers has [sic] been obtained," before any action would be taken by the bank. The bank held no deposits and customarily worked through the banking firm of the exporter. In many cases the local bank not only acted as an agent for the exporter but participated in the loan itself. The domestic criticism of such a government agency engaged in risks considered "attractive" for private enterprise could likewise divert attention from New Deal domestic priorities—a prospect considered an anathema to the President. For these and other reasons later examined, the funds available for Export-Import Bank activities remained minimal throughout the years prior to 1938. As late as January, 1935, Roosevelt reportedly wanted "to circumscribe further lending activities by the Government as rapidly as possible."[37]

The most significant factor impeding the bank revolved around the basic clash of personalities and foreign trade policies as exemplified by the Department of State's Cordell Hull and the president of the Export-Import Bank, George Peek. Of all the areas of New Deal diplomacy, the Export-Import Bank created the most jurisdictional and administrative confusion. Less than two weeks after the conception of the first Export-Import Bank, Herbert Feis prophetically remarked, "I imagine it would be

36. *Operation*, June, 1934, to April, 1948, pt. 1, Summary (1948), p. 51 DS 810.796/54, NA, RG 59. *CPS* No. 75, pp. 8–9, 23.

37. Whittlesey, p. 490. Peek, papers, Box 16, Circular of American Bankers Association, December 3, 1934; Box 17, Memorandum (Pierson to Peek), January 9, 1935. *CPS* No. 75, pp. 18–20. DS 811.516 Export-Import Bank/73, NA, RG 59.

very awkward if a difference of judgement should arise as between the two Cabinet officers controlling the stock [Hull and Roper] and the president of the trustees [Peek]."

As the bilateral and protective intentions of Peek became evident to the Department of State, Hull and other members of his staff realized the dangers inherent in any cooperative undertaking with George Peek. The power and responsibilities of the special adviser had already assumed ominous proportions. Few doubted that Peek perceived the Export-Import Bank as a "real opportunity" to promote the artificial stimulation of export trade, barter, and other bilateral and protective devices deemed heretical by liberals in the State Department. Any effort, therefore, by Hull to endorse and sustain the bank's activities implied further threats to the doctrine of multilateralism. Before the State Department could ever utilize the economic resources of the bank as an instrument of foreign policy, the lines of communication between the agencies required serious mending.[38]

Peek's own trade philosophy also hampered his efforts to challenge multilateralism. Initially, he opposed business efforts to finance United States exports through foreign loans as much as he disliked the issuance of capital "for wildcat promotional developments" in foreign lands. Peek opposed the idea of "playing Santa Claus" for American exporters and foreigners alike. The job of the bank, he wrote to Welles on March 24, 1934, included the possible extension of credit to the sellers of American products but not to foreign corporations or governments.[39]

Peek's bilateral trade philosophy also stressed the importance of selective exports and imports achieved preferably by barter agreements and sustained by assistance from the Export-Import Bank. As a result, the special adviser did not readily perceive the possibility of such bank credit for the purpose of thawing frozen credits. Nevertheless, by 1935 Peek realized some of the potential capabilities of the Export-Import Bank as a means of offsetting

38. William S. Culbertson, papers, Library of Congress, Culbertson to J. W. Mailliard, December 19, 1934. DS 811.516 Export-Import Bank/9, NA, RG 59. Peek, papers, Box 15, Peek to Colonel House, June 30, 1934. Whittlesey, pp. 497–98.

39. Whittlesey, p. 498. George N. Peek, *Why Quit Our Own?* (New York: D. Von Nostrand Company, 1936), pp. 193–94. Peek, papers, Box 14, Peek to Welles, March 24, 1934. DS 811.516 Export-Import Bank/58, NA, RG 59.

the momentum of the trade agreement program. Consequently, Latin America assumed a larger role in the formulation of policy, since it offered, as the State Department suggested, "the best market for American capital goods."[40] As Peek intensified his attacks on multilateralism, he stressed the fact that the expansion of American blocked funds abroad could not come from the pious hopes and rhetoric of liberal traders. Thereupon, Peek insisted that the bank become involved in the liquidation of such blocked funds.

The State Department did not approve of Peek's extended activities, his expanded functional responsibilities for the bank, or of the 1935 Reconstruction Finance Corporation bill, which authorized an increase in funds and also granted the bank the right to borrow funds subject to the approval of the secretary of the treasury. The State Department most assuredly was cool toward any scheme that tended to increase the bank's power and perhaps eventually prejudice the workings of the reciprocal trade agreement program. Therefore, the department showed a marked reluctance to agree to any export-import loans with a foreign power until the conclusion of a reciprocal trade agreement.

Throughout 1934–1935 Hull also opposed any bank plan that discounted without recourse the obligations of foreign governments to American holders of blocked exchange. The department maintained that such an arrangement would make the United States government a creditor of foreign powers and prejudice American diplomatic relations with nations not receiving bank credit. The department also contended that any default on obligations to the bank would make it appear to the American public that the government had become a tool of American business. If, on the other hand, a foreign power feared the consequences of default on a semi-public loan, an Export-Import Bank obligation would be no assurance that they would not default on obligations held by American bondholders. Finally the department reasoned that liquidation of blocked exchange, even if necessary for the growth of export trade, would not stimulate American commerce until this country also increased proportionately its share of import trade. This development, they reasoned, had not sufficiently materialized. Although the depart-

40. DS 811.516 Export-Import Bank/73, NA, RG 59.

ment's logic seemed at times to defy the very arguments used in defense of the reciprocity program, Hull and his advisers firmly opposed any such innovations by the Export-Import Bank as long as George Peek remained at its helm.[41]

Even Peek's resignation from the Administration in late 1935 did not signal the final victory of Hull's trade program or the revivification of the Export-Import Bank. The elimination of Peek merely allowed the department an opportunity to appraise honestly the efficacy of both reciprocal trade agreements and the bank without the fear of direct reprisals by Peek. Hard international reality, however, gave little moral support to Hull's optimism.

American commercial expansion abroad had failed to relieve United States surpluses or to ameliorate significantly the domestic employment situation. Reciprocal trade agreements had likewise done little or nothing to improve the position of American holders of defaulted foreign securities. The Department of State also at times had reason to believe that certain Latin American nations used reciprocity agreements as a means of obtaining export-import funds with little faith in the program itself. Vested interests both at home and abroad, as well as the timidity of the Administration, hamstrung all efforts to break down the protective walls surrounding American agricultural and industrial enterprises. Exchange controls, quotas, and a copious supply of other foreign trade restrictive devices dotted the international landscape. No doubt such assaults on the principle of multilateralism dampened Hull's ebullience.

In the midst of an international structure shaken by political and economic cataclysms, the trade program more and more appeared as a brief aberration swept irrevocably aside by a world intoxicated with blind and destructive nationalism. The cessation of American private capital investment and the increasing importance of the state as the principal instrument of trade development, gave credence to those who contended that the multilateral spirit had become defunct in both international political

41. Recourse obviated the possibility of the United States government becoming a creditor of a foreign government or firm. Peek, papers, Box 18, Roosevelt to Peek, July 17, 1935; Thomas to James Edwards, June 18, 1935; Box 17, Peek to Sayre, April 12, 1935. DS 832.5151/707; 811.516 Export-Import Bank/62, /99, NA, RG 59.

and economic practice. More important still, and present in Hull's mind, was the haunting visualization of Nazi Germany progressively menacing the political and economic destiny of the Western Hemisphere. No longer could the secretary of state or the nation afford to rely upon pallid nostrums. The time had come for some very basic modifications in the commercial policy of the United States.[42]

Under the direction of George Peek's successor, Warren Lee Pierson, the Export-Import Bank slowly began to play a more vital role in the shaping of American foreign policy. In Pierson, Hull had a man whom he could at least trust. In a letter to Jesse Jones, chairman of the Reconstruction Finance Corporation, the secretary deemed the extension of the bank "of high importance in our whole program of sustaining and developing American commerce."[43]

Profit and peril dictated that Latin America would have a high priority for the bank. Partly as a result of Hitler's economic offensive in Latin America as well as market considerations, the bank turned steadily toward its southern neighbors as an outlet for capital. As Pierson remarked to Hull in February, 1938, "the most logical field for increasing the activities of the Bank, in my opinion, is throughout Latin America." By the spring of 1939 the Export-Import Bank had arranged for the extension of credit totaling 90 per cent of its $100,000,000 lending power limit. By June, 1940, increased lending authority allowed the bank to make loans approximating $157,000,000, of which $73,000,000 went to Latin America.

The problem, however, revolved primarily around the fact that Pierson looked toward the extension of sound credit risks regardless of political and diplomatic considerations. Pierson, Feis remarked to Secretary Hull, showed an "insufficient recognition of the considerations which the Department has to take into account."[44] This difference in perspective and criteria inhibited the Department of State from setting up general princi-

42. DS 835.5151/992; 811.516 Export-Import Bank/126½, /129, /209A, NA, RG 59.

43. DS 811.516 Export-Import Bank/207A. The date of this memo is February 20, 1939.

44. DS 810.51/1655. *CPS* No. 75, p. 14; 811.516 Export-Import Bank/44.

ples or guidelines for administration of the bank. A Division of Latin American Affairs memorandum confessed that the State Department and the bank acted "as if every new case were without precedent." Feis admitted that the department continued "to proceed from case to case at the risk of inconsistency and irritation."

As a result, the department blocked Pierson's designs for credit assistance to Colombia on account of bond defaults but permitted export-import loans to Brazil, also in dollar default. In regard to Mexico, the department first prohibited all bank credit because of the oil controversy but then slowly relented under mounting pressure by American interests, such as the International Telephone and Telegraph Company. The department on at least four occasions condoned the extension of bank credit to the Cuban government to assist in the coinage of additional silver pesos, yet increasingly conditioned further credit on Cuba's willingness to settle her debt obligations, to conclude a supplemental trade agreement, and to initiate monetary and banking reforms. "It is confusing [and] embarrassing to both the Department and the Bank," Pierson confessed to Hull, that no definite guidelines existed for the administration of the bank.[45]

The bank, notwithstanding, performed admirable work in offsetting the German economic threat in Latin America, particularly in Brazil. By 1939 it had become obvious to most State Department officials that Hull's multilateral trade doctrines alone could hardly offset Germany's bilateral agreements with the Vargas government. To retain the trade offensive and to maintain the viability of the Brazilian political economy, the Export-Import Bank granted credit totaling some $19,200,000 to Brazil in the March, 1939, Aranha Agreement. American credit thereby freed the Brazilian exchange market and safeguarded American external dollar debts. The bank's funds also aided Brazil's transportation program and assumed a large role in the building of a steel plant deemed vital to the Brazilian economy. Furthermore, the bank discounted a larger percentage

45. In 1939 Brazil, Colombia, Peru, Mexico, Panama, and Bolivia, were in default of their external funded obligations; see DS 821.51/2352; 837.51/2458; 837.515/473; 837.512/2311; 812.75/94; 812.77/1304; 811.516 Export-Import Bank/145, /153½.

of the $10,000,000 worth of notes used for the purchase of heavy American equipment.[46]

The success of the Brazilian experience galvanized the State Department into moving along the same lines with other Latin American nations. It also impressed Pierson. In June, 1940, the bank made available to the Central Bank of Argentina credit totaling $20,000,000 for the purpose of financing purchases of United States industrial and construction material and transportation equipment. But the loan failed to produce the same results as the Brazilian experiment. Argentina took the money and ran. Never for a moment did the loan deter her from pursuing an anti-American policy. Nevertheless, by the advent of Pearl Harbor the Export-Import Bank, in conjunction with the Department of State, had undertaken numerous financial schemes in Central America, Cuba, Chile, Haiti, Colombia, Ecuador, and Paraguay. Most brought political as well as economic remuneration.

It is also important to remember that in a large sense, the extension of government credit without full recourse pointed to the fact that in the area of government-business cooperation, the New Deal initiated new fields of economic endeavor considered far too radical for previous administrations. Even the neomercantilism of Hoover had never ventured into the area of granting public capital to private business for fear of a concentration of power in the hands of the government. FDR had no such compunction. In addition, the experience gained from such ventures proved very fruitful in the development of postwar financial institutions.[47] Of more immediate importance, however, was the fact that the bank's politico-economic success produced greater cooperation and harmony between Hull and Pierson; so much so that the guidelines of the bank and the department crystalized into a national policy.

Far from being altruistic, the motives of the Export-Import Bank and the department lay firmly rooted in the concept of national self-interest. At times these concepts violated the spirit if not the letter of multilateralism. A case in point occurred in

46. *FTLA*, pt. 2, p. 105. DS 611.3231/1426, /1428; 832.51/1406, /1508½, NA, RG 59.

47. DS 811.516 Export-Import Bank/314; 832.51/1508½, NA, RG 59. *CPS* No. 75, p. 10. *FTLA*, pt. 2, p. 42.

September, 1938, when the president of the Export-Import Bank recommended to the bank of Brazil that export-import credit to the Vargas regime must "be utilized exclusively to provide exchange" for American imports. In reaction, some Administration spokesmen viewed the agreement with shock and displeasure. One such official was Daniel C. Roper, secretary of commerce. Obviously distraught at such a maneuver, Roper, in a communiqué to Hull, blasted these bilateral arrangements as being contrary to the general trade-agreement principles and similar in nature to German economic policy. Not surprisingly, Hull appeared singularly unimpressed by Roper's logic and did not countermand Pierson's decision. As Roper soon gathered, the Open Door in Latin America, as perceived by Hull and Pierson and implemented by the liberal trade program, applied only to those transactions narrowly defined as commercial. Financial transactions, the end purpose of which ran "contrary" to the trade agreement guidelines, were not viewed with the same degree of disapproval.[48]

Conceived as an instrument in the promotion of American export trade in 1934, the bank had become a tool of diplomacy, wielded freely and sometimes severely upon those Latin American nations that took Hull's dictums too lightly. Peru, Colombia, Cuba, Chile, and Mexico knew what this meant. By 1939 the resources of the bank attacked the problem of German economic penetration of the South American continent and successfully stifled Hitler's main thrust in Brazil.

What the bank started, the war helped finish. In 1940 Congress twice extended the scope of the bank by increasing its lending power to $500,000,000 credit outstanding at any single time. To a proportionately greater extent than geography or population dictated, the State Department earmarked these funds for Latin America. The major reasons for such action included the increasing importance of hemispheric defense and the protection of American trade and investment from the contagion spread by the Mexican and Bolivian expropriation of American property.[49] A department memorandum submitted to Feis and Welles

48. DS 832.51 Bank of Brazil/1, NA, RG 59.
49. Wood, p. 311. R. Walton Moore, papers, Box 6, Special Meeting of the Board of Trustees of the Export-Import Bank, March 1, 1940. Diebold, p. 97; *CPS* No. 75, pp. 7–14, 24–25.

in 1939 entertained the belief that the solution of commercial and financial problems in Latin America by the United States amounted to the surest protection of American national interests. The memo deserves closer scrutiny.

> There are very important American investment and trade interests to be considered. Many of those investments and part of that trade relate to industries and materials in which continued American control or participation is of great importance to our own national interest. Finally, any constructive assistance that the United States can give to the other American republics during this critical period may serve to check the growing tendency toward expropriation of foreign (largely American) property in those countries.[50]

Although the European war checkmated Germany's designs on the political economies of the nations of the Western Hemisphere, it also helped to stave off a rising tide of Latin American nationalism principally directed toward American investments. (During the war Latin Americans were also too busy expropriating German investments and exporting their products to the United States to worry about American investments.) Judged by the lack of further expropriation of American investments as well as the demise of German bilateral methods of trade, the bank made a considerable contribution to foreign policy and, in fact, became one of the most dynamic instruments in American economic diplomacy. It, along with the Anglo-American economic vise on the South American continent, spoiled many Axis designs. The bank's importance and prestige throughout the war continued to impress both executive and legislative branches of government. Again in 1945 Congress recognized the success of the bank by shifting its source of funds from the Reconstruction Finance Corporation to the Department of Treasury and raising the capital stock to $1,000,000,000, with the limitation that at no time could the bank have outstanding loans amounting to more than $3,500,000,000. The precedent as well as the success of the bank served as a forerunner for later financial institutions such as the Inter-American Bank, the World Bank, and the Alliance for Progress.[51]

50. DS 811.516 Export-Import Bank/217, NA, RG 59.
51. Guerrant, p. 101.

10

Postscript and Conclusion

Conceived in Wilsonian thinking but born during the trauma of the Great Depression, Hull's trade program in Latin America had achieved some semblance of success before the advent of war in Europe. The secretary faced congressional and presidential skepticism and public ignorance. He also had to contend with the protective sentiments of segments of industry and agriculture, led by such economic nationalists as George Peek. In his efforts to overcome bilateralism and to educate as well as to lead the country toward freer trade, Hull and his subordinates expanded the powers of the Department of State far beyond the bounds set by previous administrations. Although the trade agreements remained essentially a Democratic program, Hull elicited some bipartisan support. Hull's role in the decisionmaking process of New Deal diplomacy, therefore, needs a thorough revision. The secretary was a more powerful figure and a greater force in shaping United States foreign policy than has been previously recognized.

The enlarged scope of New Deal diplomacy is frequently as obscure as the probusiness patina of its architects. The Roosevelt Administration, far from sharing an antipathy toward American business, represented the culmination of a half century of growing government-business involvement. The reckless foreign lending that was so characteristic of the 1920s was now replaced by more cautious and careful planning. As the New Deal assumed a larger role in international economic affairs, it stimulated trade and protected American investments through the Export-Import Bank, the Trade Agreement Division of the Department of State, and the Foreign Bondholders Protective Council. It also increased executive responsibility in matters of trade, tariffs, and warmaking. In essence it extended the scope of New Deal authority in foreign affairs to a degree commensurate with Roosevelt's domestic legislation.[1]

In matters of hemispheric trade, Hull faced the suspicion of those Latin American nations designated as the first recipients of American commercial benevolence. It was no simple task to persuade these nations that America's self-interests remarkably coincided with their own national interests. Throughout the years from 1934 to 1936, the reciprocal trade program in Latin America included few if any enthusiastic signatories. At times, politics worked to the disadvantage of New Deal diplomats, but more often than not politics and American power came to the rescue. This was particularly true in Cuba, Haiti, and Central America.

Throughout the decade of the 1930s, Hull's program continued to make progress. By January 1, 1940, the following Latin American nations had signed reciprocal agreements: Cuba, Brazil, Haiti, Colombia, Honduras, Nicaragua, Guatemala, Costa Rica, El Salvador, Ecuador, and Venezuela. The list, however, was more telling not by virtue of the signatories but the leading Latin American nations not included among the ranks. Argentina, Mexico, Peru, and Chile, as well as other strategically important powers in Latin America, remained outside the trade program.[2] As Laurence Duggan later said, "The political achievements of the Good Neighbor Policy prior to the war were not matched in the economic field. . . . Only a handful of officials in responsible positions in Washington were prepared to pitch in and work hard to overcome indifference and opposition to eco-

1. DS, Eleanor Lansing Dulles, "The Export-Import Bank of Washington: The First Ten Years," *CPS* No. 75 (1944) p. 1–2. For an analysis of how previous administrations shied away from government guaranteed loans to business, see Joan Hoff Wilson, *American Business and Foreign Policy, 1920–1933* (Boston: Beacon Press, 1971) and Carl P. Parrini, *Heir to Empire: United States Economic Diplomacy, 1916–1923* (Pittsburgh: University of Pittsburgh Press, 1969).

2. William Diebold, *New Directions in Our Trade Policy* (New York: Council on Foreign Relations, 1941), pp. 66–74. Edward O. Guerrant, *Roosevelt's Good Neighbor Policy* (Albuquerque: University of New Mexico Press, 1950), p. 96. *FTLA*, pt. 1, Report No. 146, 2d Series, 1942, p. 54. DS 837.51/2106½, NA, RG 59.

nomic help for Latin America."[3] In addition to public and private protective sentiments, the State Department also encountered German, Japanese, and British methods of bilateral trade that operated to retard the development of the program. Belatedly, Hull realized that unconditional most-favored-nation clauses and equality of treatment operated effectively only if foreign powers regulated trade primarily by tariffs.[4] Quotas, embargoes, barter, currency depreciation, and clearing and compensation agreements increasingly assumed a role far more important than Hull and his advisers had imagined they would. As a result, the State Department, while maintaining the rhetoric of liberal trade and unconditional most-favored-nation treatment, resorted to various devices designed to promote American trade and to prevent the subversion of the political economies of Latin America by foreign powers. As indicated in the previous chapter, by the late 1930s the Export-Import Bank had become the most dynamic instrument in American foreign trade policy, while reciprocity lost much of its momentum. When war began in Europe the program ground to a standstill.

For the first months of the European war, American commercial policy drifted. Slowly, the State Department realized the impracticality of freer trade in a world shackled by war. Although Hull did not abandon the liberal trade rhetoric, the department made much greater use, especially in Latin America, of strategic stockpiling, embargoes on vital exports, the utilization of lend-lease for political purposes, and the pursuit of national interests by means of investments and loans. The department began to

3. Laurence Duggan, *The Americas: The Search for Hemispheric Security* (New York: Henry Holt and Company, 1949), pp. 74–78, 156.

4. Material previously cited, such as League of Nations, *Enquiry Into Clearing Agreements*, League of Nations, II, Economic and Financial, 1935, II. B. 6 (Geneva: Series of League of Nations Publications, 1936); League of Nations, *Equality of Treatment in the Present State of International Commercial Relations: The Most-Favored-Nation Clause*, League of Nations, II, Economic and Financial, 1936, II. B. 9; Diebold, pp. 27–33. For a treatment of the effects of the Ottawa Agreements on British possessions in the Caribbean see TF, *Commercial Policies and Trade Relations of European Possessions in the Caribbean Area*, Report No. 151, 2d Series (1943), pp. 3–196. Also see James Carey, *Peru and the United States 1900–1962* (Notre Dame: University of Notre Dame Press, 1964), 102–3.

realize that assistance to underdeveloped nations in promoting industrial development did not necessarily retard American export trade.[5]

World War II, however, created problems far too complex for the reciprocal trade program alone to solve. From the outbreak of the European war in September, 1939, to the early months of 1941, Latin American foreign trade suffered serious setbacks especially in continental Europe, an area that had accounted for roughly one-third of both exports and imports. Prices on such vital export products as coffee, cocoa, bananas, sugar, copper, nitrates, meats, corn, and wheat experienced drastic reductions.[6]

Great Britain's wartime economic policy also contributed to Latin America's troubles through the imposition of blocked sterling exchange and stepped-up purchases from her Empire. As a result, the lands south of the Rio Grande turned increasingly toward the United States for both imports and exports. By 1940 United States imports from Latin America totaled $620,000,000, an increase of 37 per cent from 1938, while United States exports to Latin America in 1940 totaled $727,000,000, which was an increase of 45 per cent compared with 1938. Even the credit side of Latin America's balance of trade proved deceptive, because it overstated the amount of exchange available to Latin America by the amount of profits earned by American enterprises.

In comparing United States import and export figures in 1940 and 1938 with the rest of the world (excluding Latin America), one finds slighter increases of 33 per cent and 27 per cent respectively. Because of these factors, Washington's southern neighbors experienced severe exchange shortages that jeopardized not only the existing trade agreements but the economic and political stability of the hemisphere as well. The year 1939, therefore, marked

5. *BFDC*, Raw Materials-General, 060.0, NA, RG 40, Welles to Roper, December 6, 1938. Diebold, pp. 41–47, 103–4, 112–13, 141. Guerrant, p. 99. Donald M. Dozer, *Are We Good Neighbors?* (Gainesville: University of Florida Press, 1961), pp. 71–72, 77–78. DS 811.24/1085, NA, RG 59. Samuel F. Bemis, *The Latin American Policy of the United States* (New York: Harcourt, Brace and World, Inc., 1943), p. 351–54.

6. DS 611.3231/1435, NA, RG 59. *FTLA*, pt. 1, pp. 58–60.

the last date to gauge accurately the effects of the reciprocal trade program in Latin America, as indeed with the rest of the world.[7]

President Roosevelt, in his April, 1937, Pan-American Day address, had promised to increase the level of United States support in order to combat any trend toward the deterioration of Latin America's economy. With the exception of additional export-import credits, little else had been done to implement his pledges. The European war now provided the necessary incentive. At the Panama Conference in 1939 Under Secretary of State Sumner Welles pledged the expansion of United States shipping lines to Latin America and promised to assist in the development of new fields of production of the region through the establishment of an Inter-American Bank. Toward this end, Washington established the Inter-American Financial and Economic Advisory Committee for the purpose of relieving market surpluses.

Concomitant with this change of attitude was an increased role for the Export-Import Bank as a principal means of providing both capital to Latin America and safeguards for United States investments. Stockpiling of strategic war materials, increased export-import loans, and the stimulation of inter-American trade and finance through the handling of unexportable surpluses all helped to mitigate the adverse economic effects of the European conflict. The department, likewise, became less belligerent toward the expropriation of United States investments throughout Latin America. Tolerance, however, was tempered by Hull's formula for compensation in instances of expropriation. The secretary believed that a nation must provide "adequate, effective and prompt" compensation for expropriated property. The problem hinged on the fact that countries which resorted to these methods were usually the nations least likely to meet Hull's standards.[8]

7. Dozer, p. 70. *FTLA*, pt. 1, pp. 27, 60–62. *Operation*, June, 1934, to April, 1948, pt. 3 (1948), p. 6. *New York Times*, February 4, 1940, 4:6. Also see TC, *Recent Developments in the Foreign Trade of Colombia*. Series of Reports on Recent Development in the Foreign Trade of the American Republics (GPO, 1946), p. 5.

8. Dozer, p. 71. Bryce Wood, *The Making of the Good Neighbor Policy* (New York: Columbia University Press, 1961), pp. 310–14. Lloyd C. Gardner, *Economic Aspects of New Deal Diplomacy* (Madison: University

With the collapse of the western front by Hitler's blitzkrieg in the spring of 1940, the Department of State increased its efforts to build a viable continental defense system in both the military and economic spheres. The United States had to legitimatize its claim to leadership as war approached. The question focused principally on the most expedient means of implementing such policies.

In the area of hemispheric trade, the Administration searched for a more positive program than reciprocal trade to offset Axis propaganda and economic depression in Latin America. Toward this end, in June, 1940, Washington devised a cartel plan designed as a joint marketing effort by the United States and Latin America for the more important staple exports of the American republics. The plan envisioned an Inter-American Trading Corporation with capital of $2,000,000,000 capable of purchasing the exportable surpluses of Western Hemisphere nations and marketing these products in Europe. Thus, it would prevent Axis pressure on individual Latin American states. The corporation was to serve as a central planning and action agency to control the trade of the Western Hemisphere with the outside world. The very nature of such a plan demonstrated the need to find alternative schemes to the reciprocal trade program in a world at war.

The cartel plan failed to materialize. This was not so much because of the criticism of New Deal liberal traders but because of the suspicion and hostility among the Latin American states, which suspected that the plan would further subordinate their economies to the United States. Argentina led the opposition forces in South America; American domestic interests and many European powers also voiced their opposition. By the July, 1940, Foreign Ministers' Consultative Conference in Havana, Hull realized the impracticality of the plan and reaffirmed the principles of liberal trade. American economic diplomacy did not change until the United States entered World War II.[9]

of Wisconsin Press, 1964), pp. 127–32. *New York Times*, February 6, 1940, p. 29. Harry C. Hawkins, *Commercial Treaties and Agreements: Principles and Practice* (New York: Rinehart and Company, Inc., 1951), pp. 213–14. Also see DS, Sumner Welles, "On the Need for a Spirit of Tolerance in Inter-American Relationships," *LAS* No. 15, pp. 3–6.

9. Diebold, pp. 127–29. Dozer, pp. 72–73. *New York Times*, July 6,

To many a Latin American, the Japanese attack at Pearl Harbor contributed more to the economic solutions of the hemisphere than any of Washington's programs. As a total participant in the war effort, the Roosevelt Administration now sought to increase the importation of vital Latin American raw materials such as Bolivian tin; Chilean copper and nitrates; Venezuelan and Mexican oil; Brazilian rubber, cocoa, and manganese; Cuban sugar; and Argentine flaxseed. Washington, furthermore, restricted the availability of American exports to Latin America, which in turn led once again to a more favorable balance of trade with the United States. The effects on American economic diplomacy were not alarming, since Latin America could more readily meet interest payments on United States dollar bonds (having, as of 1937, a par value of about $1,000,000,000 or 30 per cent of total United States holdings of foreign dollar bonds) and remittances on United States direct investments in Latin America (valued at about $2,800,000,000 or 43 per cent of total United States direct investments abroad).[10]

War accelerated the accretion of exchange credits in the Americas while it retarded the purchase of vital import products from the United States and Europe. To meet the challenge, Latin America increased both the rate of technological development and the rate of industrialization. As a result, the area made marked progress in the diversification of its export trade. Again, it should be remembered that it was war, not liberal trade, that encouraged diversification. In 1932, for example, coffee accounted for 85 per cent of the total value of Brazil's export trade, while the figure during the 1940s stood at less than 45 per cent. Other prominent nations such as Argentina, Mexico, Chile, and Peru, likewise witnessed agricultural diversification and increased industrialization on account of wartime shortages.[11] Brazil's escape from the perils of monoculture was in large part a result of the establishment of the Inter-American Coffee Board.

1940, p. 46; pp. 13–14; July 7, 1940, pp. 14; section 3, p. 3. Joseph Tulchin, ed., *Problems in Latin American History* (New York: Harper and Row, 1973), p. 461.

10. *FTLA*, pt. 1, pp. 26–27, 61.

11. Rollie E. Poppino, *Brazil: The Land and People* (New York: Oxford University Press, 1968), pp. 152–53. *FTLA*, pt. 1, pp. 25–26. Also see fn 6.

As it accelerated the rate of industrialization throughout Latin America, the war changed many of the preconceptions upon which Hull had founded the reciprocal trade agreement program. And to a large degree, Hull's trade program failed to take cognizance of these changing economic realities throughout Latin America. Conceived basically as an instrument for the promotion of the Open Door commerce throughout the Western Hemisphere, Hull's program envisioned Latin America primarily as a readily available source of raw materials vital to the domestic economy as well as a market capable of absorbing sizable amounts of American surpluses.[12]

But Hull's economic philosophy, which was devoted to the democratic ideals of decent, honorable, and fair commercial relations and buttressed by the principles of classical economics, failed to adjust rapidly enough to meet the challenges posed by the war and its aftermath. Hull's foreign trade assumptions too often took the form, if not the substances, of dogma rather than the spirit of experimentation. By war's end, Latin America, along with much of the underdeveloped world, no longer accepted the economic dictums of American "experts." The international specialization of labor and capital and the principles of comparative advantage sounded like sophist pronouncements to nations obsessed by ideologies of revolution and national self-sacrifice.

Hull and his department also had to contend with numerous assertions at home that the trade program was unconstitutional, un-American, and the precursor of destruction for domestic industries. Serious critics of the trade program repeatedly charged that increased United States total export trade figures failed to provide an adequate analysis of individual commodity figures. For example, they argued, the European war drastically curtailed the exportation of certain United States agricultural products. From September to November, 1940, cotton exports declined by 80 per cent compared with the same months for the previous ten-year average. The quantity of agricultural exports other than cotton fell by 53 per cent during the same period.[13]

12. Gardner, pp. 44–45.
13. U. S., Congress, Senate, *Extension of Reciprocal Trade Agreements Act: Hearing Before the Committee on Finance*, 76th Cong., 3d sess., 1940,

(Henry Wallace argued that agricultural exports to trade agreement nations in the fiscal year 1938–1939 were 15 per cent higher than in 1935–1936, while agricultural exports to nonagreement nations declined 19 per cent from 1935–1936.)

During the 1940 congressional hearings over the extension of the 1934 reciprocity act, both the advocates and opponents of reciprocity manipulated facts and trade figures with slight regard to objectivity.[14] In relation to United States–Latin American export and import trade, critics argued that the New Deal agreements merely continued a trend begun in 1931 toward a favorable balance of trade for the United States. Although the substance of the argument deserved merit, the fact remained that the reciprocity program accelerated this development and put much of Latin America squarely within the trade orbit of the United States. It also contributed to Latin America's greater reliance on the United States as the primary source of her imports. In 1933 the United States supplied Latin America with 12.9 per cent of her total imports, or approximately $215,680,000. By 1938 the value of American exports had risen to $726,770,000 or 18.1 per cent of Latin America's total imports.[15]

But the pattern of increased trade advantages for American commerce was not limited solely to trade agreement nations in the Western Hemisphere. The value of American exports to all trade agreement nations increased by 62.8 per cent between 1934–1935 and 1938–1939, while United States imports from agreement nations for the same years increased 21.6 per cent. The figures for United States exports and imports with nonagreement nations, comparing 1934–1935 with 1938–1939, showed increases of 31.7 per cent and 12.5 per cent respectively. In the prewar years American exports, subject to duties reduced by trade agreements, accounted for 23 per cent of total American exports. Of the sixteen nations that signed trade agreements with the United

---

pp. 47–50. Hereafter cited as *Extension. Operation*, pt. 4, p. 34. Diebold, pp. 2–3.

14. For the pertinent testimony of Peek see U. S., Congress, House, *Extension of Reciprocal Trade Agreements Act: Hearings Before the Committee on Ways and Means*, 73d Cong., 3d sess., 1940, 2:1427–93. Hereafter cited as *Hearings*. For John Coulter's testimony see *Extension*, pp. 363–90, and *Hearings*, 3: 2757–59.

15. *FTUS*, 1934, TPS No. 162 (1935) p. 66. *FTLA*, pt. 1, p. 36.

States by 1938, the percentage of their total imports from America increased from 12.2 per cent in 1933 to 19.7 per cent in 1938. But the percentage of total imports from the United States to twenty of the most important non-trade agreement nations increased only from 12.1 per cent in 1933 to 14.5 per cent in 1938. By 1939 88.2 per cent of the total dutiable import trade of the United States had been covered by trade agreement concessions. In 1933 the ratio of total duties collected to total value of dutiable imports stood at 53.6 per cent. By 1946 the figure had decreased to 25.5 per cent.[16]

But to a large degree, the effects of the trade program defy accurate investigation. The problem relates to the statistician's inability to measure American commercial gains or losses had there been no trade agreements at all. Although the Tariff Commission cited actual reductions in duty as the largest single class of concessions by foreign trade agreement countries, one must remember that bindings of continued free entry by trade agreements equalled 13 per cent of total American exports in the prewar years. Bindings of existing rates of duty against foreign increases approximated 19 per cent of total American exports in the prewar years. It is difficult to determine to what degree the United States would have continued to hold these foreign markets without the trade program. To a lesser extent, the general provisions of trade agreements dealing with quotas, exchange, internal taxations, licenses, and fines also retarded non-tariff restrictions on American commerce. But these also escape precise analysis.[17]

This concluding chapter would perhaps be the best place to reassess briefly the motif of the Good Neighbor policy. Much of the early literature, like that of Samuel F. Bemis, unequivocally praised Roosevelt's renunciation of imperialism while later research flatly denied this thesis.

Explicit in many contemporary analyses is the notion that New Deal imperialistic motivations were conscious and preor-

16. *Hearings*, 1: 7–8. *Extension*, pp. 105, 121, 131–32. *Operation*, pt. 3, pp. 3, 7; *Hearings*, 4:20. Raymond L. Buell, *The Hull Trade Program and the American System* (New York: Foreign Policy Association, 1938), p. 36. Henry J. Tasca, *The Reciprocal Trade Policy of the United States* (Philadelphia: University of Pennsylvania Press, 1938), Chapter 12.

17. *Operation*, pt. 1, pp. 33, 52; pt. 4, pp. 13, 20.

dained. Such was not altogether the case with Cordell Hull or Francis Sayre. These men sought the ends of an international capitalistic order by means of shrewd national bargaining. But with the very tragic exception of Cuba, the records of the Department of State show no covert attempt on their part to subjugate consciously the economies of Latin America or to keep them in a state of agricultural backwardness. These men sincerely, though mistakenly, believed that a harmony of interests could be forged between the diverse economies of the hemisphere. If their intentions had been imperialistic, in the sense used by Lenin, then Hitler's New Plan or Peek's bilateralism could have served the purpose much better. Nor would it have been necessary to expand the activities of the Export-Import Bank for the purpose of financing such projects as Brazil's steel plant, Volta Redonda.

On the other hand, as an idealist promoting the national interests of the United States, Hull sought "a reversal of existing relations" in the area of economics. The United States badly needed to regain lost markets and financial respectability in Latin America. The economic health of all the Americas demanded it. To this extent American "imperial" objectives were consistent, although the formulation of policies was not. Hull, as would any good diplomat, made a variety of concessions to national self-interests. To have done less would have incurred the wrath of FDR, Congress, and the capitalist interests. Hull's success can be measured by the fact that for the next four decades the theory of liberal trade, although never fully implemented, was not seriously challenged in the United States.[18] His failure was also the failure of the Good Neighbor policy.

Most New Deal trade theories were based on sound principles of self-interests for the developed world. And, they have become the working basis for present-day policies. Few international

18. For an analysis of imperialism see Donald J. Puchala, *International Politics Today* (New York: Dodd, Mead and Co., 1971) , pp. 95–119. William L. Langer, *The Diplomacy of Imperialism, 1890–1902*, 2d edition (New York: Alfred A. Knopf, 1956) . Joseph Schumpeter, "Imperialism" in *Two Essays by Joseph Schumpeter* (Cleveland: The World Publishing Co., 1955) . Vladimir Lenin, *Imperialism the Highest Stage of Capitalism* (New York: International Publishers, 1939) . Hans J. Morgenthau, *Politics Among Nations*, 4th edition (New York: Alfred A. Knopf, 1967) .

economists today would quarrel with Hull's assertion that resorting to exclusive bilateral trade agreements and methods designed artificially to rechannel foreign trade destroyed triangular trade and, therefore, the very basis for increased world commerce. The resort to economic warfare did nothing to further better political relations among nations.[19] Nor would many students of New Deal economic diplomacy deny that Hull's trade policies substantially promoted the commercial interests of American business. Few, if any, nations literally "outbargained" the American State Department in tariff negotiations.[20]

Nevertheless, the program fostered a reservoir of ill will toward the United States by those South American nations whose principal mineral exports competed with American domestic products. Argentina, Uruguay, Chile, Bolivia, Peru, and Mexico all questioned the New Deal's desire to put real economic teeth in the Good Neighbor. In no Latin American commercial agreement did the New Deal make a concession that threatened a domestic enterprise. Sacrifices were made but not by Uncle Sam.

With good cause, Hull's trade agreements sought to promote the self-interests of the United States. Hull referred to reciprocity as "enlightened nationalism," and Francis Sayre appropriately called the program "enlightened self-interest." At the same time the State Department maintained, contrary to all facts, that reciprocity increased the prosperity of all the Americas in equal

19. Tasca, p. 114.
20. Professor Bemis, in *The Latin American Policy of the United States*, in particular failed to see the long-range consequences of American commercial hegemony in the Western Hemisphere. Praisingly he wrote, "Another way of summing up the apparent results of the reciprocal trade agreements program in the years before the Second World War is that the balance of trade of the United States with Latin American nations has been more 'favorable' with the agreement countries than with the non-agreement countries." Bemis, p. 310. Graham H. Stuart, *The Department of State* (New York: Macmillan Company, 1949), p. 318. Holbert N. Carroll, *The House of Representatives and Foreign Affairs* (Pittsburgh: University of Pittsburgh Press, 1958), pp. 16–17. Raymond A. Bauer, Ithiel de Sola Pool, and Lewis Anthony Dexter, *American Business and Public Policy* (New York: Atherton Press, 1963), pp. 36–38, 84–85. Tasca argues that the educational program undertaken by the State Department to explain why lower tariffs do not harm domestic industries neglected the most important feature of reciprocity, i.e., a means of safeguarding United States investments abroad. Tasca, p. 290.

proportion. Not surprisingly, critics in Latin America attacked the secretary's program from all sides. To many of these nationalists reciprocity appeared as a subtle maneuver by the United States to stifle incipient industrialization, to retard economic self-sufficiency, and to keep Latin America in a state of colonial dependence. For these opponents, the Open Door in matters of inter-American trade signaled the industrial and commercial hegemony of the United States in the Western Hemisphere rather than mutual prosperity. Ironically, as historian David Green has pointed out, the nation that least cooperated with the United States, Argentina, witnessed the greatest degree of economic recovery south of the Rio Grande. This was a bitter pill for Cordell Hull to swallow.[21]

Perhaps Hull failed to perceive the paradox inherent in the tremendous recuperative powers of American capitalism, a system too dynamic and self-assertive to conform to his own ideals. Although reciprocal trade agreements produced more equal commercial opportunities for American business and assured the maintenance of Hull's unique conception of the Open Door in Latin America, the program failed to promote the harmony of interests among nations as conceived by liberal trade economists. Still, Hull's error could be best considered one of omission more than commission.

In brief, Hull never realized that the principles of self-determination, mutual gain, and equality of nations were unobtainable when confronted by the vast economic powers of the American business system.[22] Nor could he understand why shortly after the war, Mexico, Colombia, Brazil, Nicaragua, Ecuador, and other Western Hemisphere nations were forced to modify drastically the provisions of the trade agreements. The reasons for such modification were sound. There were steady reductions in gold reserve, adverse balances of trade and payments, and an inability to promote industrialization in the face of American competition; but for Hull these smacked a little of betrayal.[23]

21. Cordell Hull, "Foreign Trade, Farm Prosperity and Peace," *CPS* No. 44 (1938), p. 15. Francis B. Sayre, "To World Peace Through World Trade," *CPS* No. 43 (1938), p. 2. David Green, *The Containment of Latin America* (Chicago: Quadrangle Books, 1971), chapters 2–3.

22. William A. Williams, *The Tragedy of American Diplomacy* (New York: Dell Publishing Company, Inc., 1962), pp. 165–66. Diebold, p. 25.

23. *Operation*, pt. 4, p. 27. Lincoln Gordon and Engelbert L. Grommers,

In his memoirs, which were published in 1948, Hull looked back on the foreign trade philosophy developed in the prewar years of the New Deal. No doubt, the ex-secretary had cause for reflection. The buoyancy and hope visibly demonstrated in 1933 had given way to sobering afterthoughts tempered by the hindsights of history. In 510 bilateral conventions, treaties, and exchanges of notes between foreign powers from 1931 to 1939, only 42 per cent incorporated the most-favored-nation clause. Moreover, quotas, exchange provisions, and barter arrangements continued to increase in number. Fifty-nine such agreements had been made that resorted to bilateral trade balancing. International specialization, price differentials, and other economic considerations gave way to more government control of foreign trade for political and national purposes.[24] To a larger degree Hull's dream of world trade based on the principles of equality of treatment and the elimination of excessive trade barriers failed to materialize. The trade program had not been able to escape from politics, nor had it promoted that harmony among nations for which Hull had so passionately labored.

In 1939 war had again revisited a troubled world that was unable to realize its horror. Reluctantly, America too was drawn into the conflict. Nearly a decade later, Hull searched for an explanation for war, and America's inability to deter it.

Throughout his memoirs, however, one finds little to suggest that Hull ever seriously doubted the efficacy of his own approach to the vexations of international politics. With a naiveté deeply rooted in a moral and idealistic vision of the world that placed

---

United States Manufacturing Investment in Brazil (Boston: Center for International Affairs, 1962), p. 14. Also see Sanford A. Mosk, *Industrial Revolution in Mexico* (Berkeley: University of California Press, 1950), p. 116. International Bank for Reconstruction and Development, *Report on Cuba* (Baltimore: Johns Hopkins Press, 1951), p. 132. Also see Werner Baer, *Industrialization and Economic Development in Brazil* (Homewood, Illinois: Richard D. Irwin, Inc., 1965) and Aldo Ferrer, *The Argentine Economy* (Berkeley: University of California Press, 1967). TC, *Recent Developments in the Foreign Trade of Argentina*, Series of Reports on Recent Developments in the Foreign Trade of the American Republics (GPO, 1950).

24. Richard C. Snyder, "Commercial Policy as Reflected in Treaties from 1931 to 1939," *The Amrican Economic Review* 30:4 (Dcember 1940): 787–802. Guerrant, p. 98.

economic justice and liberal trade as the indispensable exponents of peace, Hull found the answer to war.

> If, as I urged in my speeches during the First World War, something like the Trade Agreement Act could have been passed instead of the Fordney-McCumber Act of 1922 and other nations had seen fit to follow suit at once, the story might have been different.[25]

Indeed, Hull never seriously challenged the assumptions of his nineteenth-century liberal beliefs. Operating on the dictum that "the political line-up followed the economic line-up," Hull failed to assess clearly the widespread use of commercial policy for non-economic purposes—a characteristic of international relations in the decade of the 1930s. This was true even at times when the secretary himself countenanced violations of the Open Door philosophy. These political exigencies, in fact, sometimes dictated economic policies not in keeping with Hull's own philosophy, but he was unwilling or unable to see the contradictions. The Roosevelt Administration, for example, never came to a commercial *détente* with Nazi Germany, Japan, or Italy mainly because of political considerations.[26]

When war came in 1939, Hull merely shifted the justification for the renewal of the Trade Agreements Act from its ability to promote peace and prosperity to its future role in the foundation of peace in the postwar world. In fact, both Hull and Roosevelt argued that the United States possessed no alternative save the disastrous return of Hawley-Smoot. Without the Trade Agreements Act, Hull said, "The other countries would walk off with it. They would organize the trade of the world and leave us high and dry."[27] In the 1940 congressional hearings concerning the extension of the act, Hull argued passionately and effectively that it must become "an indispensable part of the foundation of any stable and durable peace."[28] To foresake the reciprocity

---

25. Cordell Hull, *The Memoirs of Cordell Hull*, Vol. 1 (New York: Macmillan Company, 1948), p. 364.

26. Ibid., p. 365. Diebold, pp. 91–95, 111.

27. *Extension*, pp. 11, 35. Cordell Hull, "War, Peace, and the American Farmer," *CPS* No. 63 (1939), pp. 7–8. For a treatment of the politics of trade policy see Joe R. Wilkinson, *Politics and Trade Policy* (Washington: Public Affairs Press, 1960), Chapter 1.

28. *Extension*, p. 5.

agreements in 1940, Hull added, would give testimony to the world that the United States intended to return to economic nationalism and political isolationism at the end of the war. Moreover, a rejection of the trade program implied a return to protectionism and the loss of markets abroad. The secretary also stressed the importance of the 10 per cent of United States products sold abroad that vitally affected the price and stability of the other 90 per cent. "We are living in a period in which our vast home market must be supplemented by foreign markets for our ever-increasing surpluses."[29]

Hull never abandoned his hostility toward state planning, nor his belief that reciprocal agreements could effectively check the tendency toward increased regimentation, bureaucracy, and totalitarianism. As he stated in 1940:

> This is the crux of the whole issue. The question of the survival or disappearance of free enterprise in our country and in the world is bound up with the continuation or abandonment of the trade-agreements program.[30]

Hull's protégé, Francis Sayre, most succinctly described the dialectical conflict between regimentation and economic liberalism when he remarked in 1939, "There is not room in the world for both . . . since neither system is self-contained within a single nation."[31]

No doubt Hull's attempts to seek a better postwar world through the elimination of excessive trade barriers was a noble and lasting contribution to better international understanding. By 1947 the United States had signed a total of twenty-nine reciprocity agreements and had successfully laid the groundwork for the General Agreements on Trade and Tariffs, which met the same year in Geneva.[32] The Geneva agreements, incorporating as they did the multilateral principles of liberal traders, demonstrated the increased international stature given to the ideals and

29. Ibid., pp. 8–9, 26–28, 33.

30. Ibid., p. 12.

31. Francis B. Sayre, "The Special Significance of the Trade-Agreements Program Today," *CPS* No. 60 (1939), p. 8.

32. *Operation*, pt. 1, p. 6. At Geneva the United States made concessions to twenty-two nations. With about half of them the United States had previously signed reciprocity agreements. As a result, the reciprocal agreements were superseded by the GATT agreements.

persuasiveness of men such as Cordell Hull. The 1930s had indeed been the watershed of economic diplomacy.

What the secretary's theories and asssumptions lacked in sophistication and insight were in good measure compensated by the sincerity of his ideals. Yet, in his later years, he shared the disenchantment of the Cold War. Postwar trade once again had failed to produce a world truly at peace. Perhaps the limitations inherent in any venture undertaken with crusading zeal and a sense of national purpose must, by the very nature of its own expectations, experience only partial fulfillment and painful reassessment. Yet Hull's failure, as with indeed his success, lay not so much with the cause he espoused as the consequences he was unable to perceive. The economic system in which he placed unlimited trust and that he strove to keep free from government regulation proved incapable of bridging the hiatus between American self-interests and the aspirations of the underdeveloped nations of the world—an ideal still unattained today.

Bibliography

I. Public Manuscript Materials

A. *Houghton Library, Cambridge, Mass.*
William Phillips diary.

B. *State Historical Society of Missouri, Columbia, Mo.*
Western Historical Manuscripts Collection. George N. Peek papers.

C. *Franklin D. Roosevelt Library, Hyde Park, N.Y.*
R. Walton Moore papers.
Franklin D. Roosevelt papers.
Charles W. Taussig papers.

D. *Library of Congress, Manuscripts Division*
William S. Culbertson papers.
Cordell Hull papers.
Francis B. Sayre papers.

E. *National Archives*
U.S. Department of Agriculture. Record Group 16, "Records of the Secretary of Agriculture."
———. Department of Commerce. Record Group 40, "General Correspondence of the Bureau of Foreign and Domestic Commerce."
———. Department of State. Record Group 59, "General Correspondence of the Department of State."
———. General Correspondence, "File of the Special Adviser to the President on Foreign Trade."

II. Foreign Government Documents

A. *Colombia*
Anales de la Cámara de Representativos: Sesiónes Extraordinaria. Serie 2.a. Número 151–66. Bogotá: Imprenta Nacional, 1936.
Anales del Senado: Sesiónes Extraordinaria. Serie 6.a. Número 256–66. Bogotá: Imprenta Nacional, 1936.
Diario Oficial. Número 23186. Bogotá: Imprenta Nacional, 1936.
"Proyecto de ley por la Cualse Aprueba un Convenio Comercial entre la República de Colombia y los Estados Unidos de América." Bogotá: Imprenta Nacional, 1935.

B. *Cuba*

Gaceta Oficial de la República de Cuba. Número 54, tomo III. Habana: Administración de la Imprenta, 1934.

Gaceta Oficial de la República de Cuba: Edición Extraordinaria. Número 79. Habana: Administración de la Imprenta, 1934.

C. *Great Britain*

Department of Overseas Trade. E. Murray Harvey. *Report on Economic and Commercial Conditions in Brazil.* London: His Majesty's Stationery Office, 1939.

Foreign Office. E. L. Woodward and Rohan Butler, eds. *Documents on British Foreign Policy, 1919–1939.* 2d–3d Series. 16 volumes. London: His Majesty's Stationery Office, 1946–1960.

III. League of Nations, United Nations Publications

A. *League of Nations*

Economic and Financial, Considerations on the Present Evolution of Agricultural Protectionism. 1935. II. B.7. Geneva: Series of League of Nations Publications, 1936.

Enquiry Into Clearing Agreements. 1935. II. B.6. Geneva: Series of League of Nations Publications, 1936.

Equality of Treatment in the Present State of International Commercial Relations: The Most-Favored-Nation Clause. 1936. II. B.9. Geneva: Series of League of Nations Publications, 1937.

Monetary and Economic Conference. 1933. II. Spec. I. Geneva: Series of League of Nations Publications, 1934.

Remarks on the Present Phase of International Economic Relations. 1937. II. B.9. Geneva: Series of League of Nations Publications, 1938.

Review of World Trade 1934–1936. 1935–1937. II. A.8. Geneva: Series of League of Nations Publications, 1935–1937.

World Economic Survey, Fourth Year, 1934–1935. 1935. II. A.14. Geneva: Series of League of Nations Publications, 1935.

B. *United Nations*

Department of Economic and Social Affairs. *Foreign Capital in Latin America.* New York: United Nations, 1955.

United States. Committee for Reciprocity Information. *Stenographer's Minutes of the Hearings Before the Committee for Reciprocity Information in Connection with the Negotiations of a Reciprocal Trade Agreement with Brazil, Guatemala, Nicaragua, El Salvador, Honduras, and Costa Rica.* Vol. 1. Washington: Government Printing Office, 1934.

IV. United States Government Publications

A. *Congress*

Congressional Record. Vol. 78–87, 1934–1941.

House of Representatives. *Comparison of Tariff Acts of 1909, 1913, and 1922.* 68th Cong., 1st sess., 1924.

Extension of Reciprocal Trade Agreements Act: Hearings Before the Committee on Ways and Means. 73d Cong., 3d sess., Vol. 1–3, 1940.

House Report No. 1000. 73d Cong., 2d sess., 1934.

Senate. *Extension of Reciprocal Trade Agreements Act: Hearings Before the Committee of Finance.* 76th Cong., 3d sess., 1940.

Sale of Foreign Bonds or Securities in the United States. Hearings Before the Committee of Finance, 72d Cong., 1st sess., 1931.

World Trade Barriers in Relation to American Agriculture. Document No. 70. Washington: GPO, 1933.

B. *Department of Agriculture, Foreign Agricultural Service*

Central America as a Market and Competitor for United States Agriculture. Washington: GPO, 1959.

C. *Department of Commerce, Bureau of Foreign and Domestic Commerce*

The Coffee Industry in Colombia. Trade Promotion Series No. 127. Washington: GPO, 1931.

Commercial Travelers' Guide to Latin America. Trade Promotion Series No. 122, 179. Washington: GPO, 1938.

F. R. Eldridge. *Export and Import Practice.* Trade Promotion Series No. 175. Washington: GPO, 1938.

H. C. Harris. *Trading Under the Laws of Germany.* Trade Promotion Series No. 150. Washington: GPO, 1933.

United States Trade with Latin America in 1930. Trade Promotion Series No. 124. Washington: GPO, 1931.

Grace A. Witherow. *Foreign Trade of the United States, 1932–1936.* Trade Promotion Series No. 151, 156, 162, 166, and 174. Washington: GPO, 1933–1938.

D. *Department of State*

Commercial Policy Series. No. 20–73. Washington: GPO, 1936–1943.

Conference Series. No. 16. Warren Kelchner. "Inter-American Conference for the Maintenance of Peace." Washington: GPO, 1936.

————. No. 43. Cordell Hull. "Addresses and Statements by the Honorable Cordell Hull." Washington: GPO, 1940.

————. No. 25. Cordell Hull. "Opening Address to the Inter-American Conference for the Maintenance of Peace." Washington: GPO, 1936.

————. No. 44. "Report of the Delegate of the United States of America to the Meeting of the Foreign Ministers of the American Republics Held at Panama, September 23–October 3, 1939." Washington: GPO, 1940.

————. No. 33. "Report of the Delegation of the United States of America to the Inter-American Conference for the Maintenance of Peace." Washington: GPO, 1937.

————. No. 19. "Report of the Delegates of the United States of America to the Seventh International Conference of American States." Washington: GPO, 1934.

————. No. 26. Sumner Welles. "The Accomplishments of the Inter-American Conference for the Maintenance of Peace." Washington: GPO, 1937.

————. No. 29. Sumner Welles. "The Practical Accomplishments of the Buenos Aires Conference." Washington: GPO, 1937.

Documents on German Foreign Policy, 1918–1945. Series C (1933–1937), Vol. 1–5. Washington: GPO, 1959–1962.

The Department of State Bulletin. Vol. 1–5. Washington: GPO, 1939–1941.

Executive Agreement Series. No. 311. Washington: GPO, 1943.

Latin American Series. No. 4–22. Washington: GPO, 1931–1942.

Papers Relating to the Foreign Relations of the United States, 1933–1940. Washington: GPO, 1952–1961.

Peace and War: United States Foreign Policy, 1931–1941. Washington: GPO, 1943.

Reciprocal Trade Agreement Between the United States of America and Argentina. Executive Agreement Series, No. 277, Washington: GPO, 1943.

Reciprocal Trade Agreement Between the United States of America and Brazil. Executive Agreement Series, No. 78. Washington: GPO, 1942.

Reciprocal Trade Agreement Between the United States of America and Colombia. Executive Agreement Series, No. 89. Washington: GPO, 1936.

Reciprocal Trade Agreement Between the United States of America and the Republic of Cuba. Washington: GPO, 1942.

E. *Tariff Commission*

Comercio Exterior de la America Latina. Primera parte. Washington: GPO, 1941.

Commercial Policies and Trade Relations of European Possessions in the Caribbean Area. 2d Series. Report No. 151. Washington: GPO, 1943.

Computed Duties and Equivalent Ad Valorem Rates on Imports into the United States from Principal Countries, Calendar Years 1929–1931, and 1935. Richmond: W.P.A. Statistical Project 265–31–7000, 1937.

Digest of Trade Data with Respect to Products on which Concessions were Granted by the United States–Brazilian Trade Agreement. Washington: GPO, 1935.

Economic Controls and Commercial Policy in Argentina. Series of Reports on Economic Controls and Commercial Policy in the American Republics. Washington: GPO, 1948.

Economic Controls and Commercial Policy in Colombia. Series of Reports on Economic Controls and Commercial Policy in the American Republics. Washington: GPO, 1948.

Economic Controls and Commercial Policy in Cuba. Series of Reports on

Economic Controls and Commercial Policy in the American Republics. Washington: GPO, 1946.

The Effects of the Cuban Reciprocity Treaty of 1902. Washington: GPO, 1929.

Foreign-Trade and Exchange Controls in Germany. 2d Series. Report No. 150. Washington: GPO, 1942.

The Foreign Trade of Latin America. Part II. Washington: GPO, 1940.

The Foreign Trade of Latin America. In 3 parts. 2d Series. Washington: GPO, 1942.

Imports, Exports, Domestic Production, and Prices. Washington: GPO, 1937.

Iron and Steel. 2d Series. Report No. 128. Washington: GPO, 1938.

Hogs and Hog Products. 2d Series. Report No. 143. Washington: GPO, 1941.

Latin America as a Source of Strategic and Other Essential Materials. 2d Series. Report No. 144. Washington: GPO, 1941.

Method of Valuation. 2d Series. Report No. 70. Washington: GPO, 1933.

Operation of the Trade Agreements Program, June, 1934, to April, 1948. In 5 parts. Washington: GPO, 1948.

Recent Developments in the Foreign Trade of Argentina. Series of Reports on Recent Developments in the Foreign Trade of the American Republics. Washington: GPO, 1950.

Recent Developments in the Foreign Trade of Colombia. Series of Reports on Recent Developments in the Foreign Trade of the American Rpublics. Washington: GPO, 1946.

Regulation of Imports by Executive Action in Countries with Independent Tariff Jurisdiction. Miscellaneous Series. Washington: GPO, 1941.

Regulation of Tariffs in Foreign Countries by Administrative Action. Miscellaneous Series. Washington: GPO, 1934.

Sugar: Report to the President of the United States. 2d Series. Report No. 73. Washington: GPO, 1934.

The Tariff and Its History. Miscellaneous Series. Washington: GPO, 1934.

V. Interviews

Dana G. Munro. January 29, 1968. Washington, D. C.

VI. Dissertations

Chu, Power Yung-Chao. "A History of the Hull Trade Program, 1934–1939." Ph.D. dissertation, Columbia University, 1957.

VII. Periodicals

A. Articles

Abbott, Charles C. "Economic Penetration and Power Politics." *Harvard Business Review* 26 (July 1948): 410–24.

"Argentine–Brazilian Rapprochement." *Bulletin of the Pan American Union* 58:1 (January 1934) : 39–49.

Ballagh, Thomas C. "Bargains in Tariffs." *The American Mercury* 34:134 (February 1935) : 192–201.

Berglund, Abraham. "The Reciprocal Trade Agreements Act of 1934." *The American Economic Review* 25:3 (September 1934) : 411–25.

Bidwell, Percy. "The Yankee Trader in 1936." *The Yale Review* 25:4 (June 1936) : 702–23.

Bisson, T. A. "Japan's Trade Boom: Does it Menace the United States?" *Foreign Policy Reports* 12:1 (March 15, 1936) : 2–16.

———. "Japan's Trade Expansion." *Foreign Policy Reports* 10:16 (October 10, 1934) : 194–208.

Bratter, Herbert M. "Foreign Exchange Control in Latin America." *Foreign Policy Reports* 14:23 (February 15, 1939) : 274–88.

Buell, Raymond L. "The Caribbean Situation: Cuba and Haiti." *Foreign Policy Reports* 9:8 (June 21, 1933) : 82–92.

Caro, Julio. "Economic Progress in the Americas, 1935: Colombia." *Bulletin of the Pan American Union* 70:2 (February 1936) : 180–83.

Chalmers, Henry. "The Depression and Foreign Trade Barriers." *The Annals of the American Academy of Political and Social Science* 174: Supp. (July 1934) : 88–100.

Clemen, Rudolf A. "Economics in Latin-American Relations." *Proceedings of the Institute of World Affairs*, 14th Session. 14 (December 13–18, 1936) : 133–38.

Collings, Harry T. "Tariff Problems of the United States." *The Annals of the American Academy of Political and Social Science* 141:230: Supp. (January 1929) : 1–10.

Colon, José L. "How Colombia is Improving Agricultural Production." *Bulletin of the Pan American Union* 68:1 (January 1934) : 51–59.

"Cordell Hull, Secretary of State." *American Foreign Service Journal* 10:4 (April 1933) : 121–22.

"Cotton in Brazil." *Bulletin of the Pan American Union* 59:10 (October 1935): 746–62.

Cronon, E. David. "Interpreting the New Good Neighbor Policy: The Cuban Crisis of 1933." *Hispanic American Historical Review* 39:4 (November 1959): 538–67.

Cullberston, William S. "Wandering Between Two Worlds." *The Annals of the American Academy of Political and Social Science* 174: Supp. (July 1934): 81–87.

Davies, J. B. "Economic Progress in the Americas, 1935: Argentina." *Bulletin of the Pan American Union* 70:2 (February 1936) : 166–68.

Davis, Horace B. "Brazil's Political and Economic Problems." *Foreign Policy Reports* 11:1 (March 13, 1935) : 2–12.

de Rycke, Laurence J. "International Commodity Control." *Proceedings of the Institute of World Affairs*, 11th Session. 11 (December 10–15, 1933) : 132–39.

de Wilde, John C. "Germany's Controlled Economy." *Foreign Policy Reports* 14:24 (March 1, 1939) : 290–304.

———. "Germany's Trend Toward Economic Isolation." *Foreign Policy Reports* 10:18 (November 7, 1934) : 226–36.

———. "Sugar: An International Problem." *Foreign Policy Reports* 9:15 (September 27, 1933) : 162–72.

Deimel, Henry L., Jr. "Commercial Policy Under the Trade Agreements Program." *The Annals of the American Academy of Political and Social Science* 186 (July 1936) : 16–23.

Dietrich, Ethel B. "The New Model Trade Agreements." *The Journal of Political Economy* 42:5 (October 1934) : 595–612.

Feiler, Arthur. "Current Tendencies in Commercial Policy." *The American Economic Review* 27:1: Supp. (March 1937) : 28–42.

Feis, Herbert, "The Open Door at Home." *Foreign Affairs* 13:4 (July 1935) : 600–11.

Fogg, Philip S. "International Implications of the War Debts." *Proceedings of the Institute of World Affairs*, 11th Session. 11 (December 10–15, 1933): 149–56.

Fuller, George G. "Convention Commends Reciprocal Trade Agreements." *American Foreign Service Journal* 13:1 (January 1936): 12, 44.

Gantenbein, James W. "The Causes and Effects of Governmental Control of Foreign Exchange." *American Foreign Service Journal* 13:2 (February 1936): 61–63, 92–99.

Grady, Henry F. "The New American Commercial Policy." *Proceedings of the Institute of World Affairs*, 13th Session. 13 (December 14–20, 1934): 185–89.

Grieb, Kenneth J. "Negotiating a Reciprocal Trade Agreement with an Underdeveloped Country: Guatemala as a Case Study." *Prologue* (Spring 1973): 22–29.

Harding, Gardner L. "American-Owned Imports Help Our Trade." *American Foreign Service Journal* 9:12 (December 1932): 481.

Hasslocher, Paulo G. "Economic Progress in the Americas, 1935: Brazil." *Bulletin of the Pan American Union.* 70:2 (February 1936) : 172–74.

Hull, Cordell. "Secretary of State Sends Message to the Foreign Service." *American Foreign Service Journal* 10:5 (May 1933) : 165.

Ichihashi, Yamato. "Japan's Foreign Trade Expansion." *Proceedings of the Institute of World Affairs*, 12th Session. 12 (December 9–14, 1934) : 125–31.

Kelbaugh, Paul R. "Recent Trends and Events in the Agriculture of Latin America." *Bulletin of the Pan American Union* 59:3 (March 1935) : 212–29.

Magee, J. D. "Some Aspects of Tariffs and Trade in South America." *The Tariff Review* 81:1 (January 1930) : 2–13.

Munro, William B. "Hitler and the New Deal in Germany." *Proceedings of the Institute of World Affairs*, 11th Session. 11 (December 10–15, 1933) : 5–10.

"National Foreign Trade Council's Review of World Export Trade." *American Foreign Service Journal* 10:1 (January 1933) : 10–11, 29.

"Pan American Commercial Conference." *American Foreign Service Journal* 12:9 (September 1935) : 507, 518.

Popper, David H. "The Hull Trade Program." *Foreign Policy Reports* 12:15 (October 15, 1936) : 190–200.

———. "Progress of American Tariff Bargaining." *Foreign Policy Reports* 11:6 (May 22, 1935) : 58–68.

Skinner, Macy M. "The Outlook for Inter-American Trade." *Proceedings of the Institute of World Affairs*, 11th Session. 11 (December 10–15, 1933) : 99–109.

Smith, H. Gerald. "Economic Ties Linking the United States and Latin America." *Bulletin of the Pan American Union* 70:3 (March 1936): 269–75.

Stinebower, Leroy D. "Proposed Foreign Trade Agreements." *American Foreign Service Journal* 11:4 (April 1934) : 196–97.

Stewart, Maxwell S. "Paradoxes of World Recovery." *Foreign Policy Reports* 10:12 (August 15, 1934) : 146–56.

———. "Tariff Bargaining Under the New Deal." *Foreign Policy Reports* 10:6 (May 23, 1934) : 70–84.

———. "Tariff Issues Confronting the New Administration." *Foreign Policy Reports* 9:2 (March 29, 1933) : 14–24.

Stuart, Graham H. "Cuba and the Platt Amendment." *Proceedings of the Institute of World Affairs*, 10th Session. 10 (December 11–16, 1932) : 55–58.

Suro, Guillermo A. "Forty Years of Trade with the Latin American Republics." *Bulletin of the Pan American Union* 57:10 (October 1933) : 760–68.

———. "Trade Agreements Between the United States and Latin America." *Bulletin of the Pan American Union* 58:11 (November 1934) : 780–89.

"Survey of the Financial and Trade Problems of Colombia in Their Relation to the United States of America." *National Foreign Trade Council*, No. 3 (1933).

Snyder, Richard C. "Commercial Policy as Reflected in Treaties from 1931 to 1939." *The American Economic Review* 30:4 (December 1940) : 787–802.

Taussig, F. W. "Necessary Changes in Our Commercial Policy." *Foreign Affairs* 11:3 (April 1933) : 397–405.

Thomson, C. A. "The Cuban Revolution: Fall of Machado." *Foreign Policy Reports* 11 (December 18, 1935) : 250–60.

———. "The Seventh Pan-American Conference." *Foreign Policy Reports* 10:7 (June 6, 1934) : 86–96.

———. "Toward a New Pan-Americanism." *Foreign Policy Reports* 12:16 (November 1, 1936) : 202–12.

Wallace, Henry. "America Must Choose." *American Foreign Service Journal* 11:4 (April 1934) : 182–83, 201–4.

————. "The World Cotton Drama." *Foreign Affairs* 13:4 (July 1935):
543–56.

Wertheimer, Mildred S. "Aims of Hitler's Foreign Policy." *Foreign Policy Reports* 11:7 (June 5, 1934): 70–84.

————. "Forces Underlying the Nazi Revolution." *Foreign Policy Reports* 9:10 (July 19, 1933): 106–16.

White, John W. "Secretary Hull Wins South American Good Will." *American Foreign Service Journal* 12:7 (July 1935): 408.

Whittlesey, Charles R. "Five Years of the Export-Import Bank." *The American Economic Review* 29:3 (September 1939): 487–502.

Zier, Julian G. "Commercial Interdependence of the Americas." *Bulletin of the Pan American Union* 67:3 (March 1933): 197–202.

B. Newspapers and Newsletters

Argentina
Buenos Aires Herald
La Prensa
La Nación
El Mundo
Review of the River Plata
La Razón
The Standard
La Acción

Brazil
Jornal do Commércio
O Jornal
Correio da Manhá

Colombia
Union Liberal
El Tiempo
El Espectador
El País
Mundo al Día
La Razón

Cuba
Noticiero Mercantil
Diario de la Marina
Acción
El Mundo
El País
Havana Post
Hoy

United States
American Manufacturers Export Association Newsletter
National Foreign Trade Council Newsletter, New York Times

VIII. Books

Allen, William R. "Cordell Hull and the Defense of the Trade Agreements Program, 1934–1940." In *Isolation and Security*. Edited by Alexander DeConde. Durham: Duke University Press, 1957.

Baer, Werner. *Industrialization and Economic Development in Brazil*. Homewood, Ill.: Richard D. Irwin, Inc., 1965.

Batista, Fulgencio. *The Growth and Decline of the Cuban Republic*. New York: Devin-Adair Company, 1964.

Barager, Joseph, ed. *Why Perón Came to Power*. New York: Alfred A. Knopf, 1968.

Bauer, Raymond A., Pool, Ithiel de Sola, and Dexter, Lewis Anthony. *American Business and Public Policy*. New York: Atherton Press, 1963.

Beard, Charles A. *American Foreign Policy in the Making, 1932–1940*. New York: Harper and Brothers, 1944.

———, and Smith, G. H. E. *The Idea of National Interest*. New York: Macmillan Company, 1934.

———, and Smith, G. H. E. *The Open Door at Home*. New York: Macmillan Company, 1935.

Bello, José Maria. *A History of Modern Brazil: 1889–1964*. Stanford: Stanford University Press, 1966.

Bemis, Samuel Flagg. *The Latin American Policy of the United States*. New York: Harcourt, Brace and World, Inc., 1943.

Bernstein, Harry. *Venezuela and Colombia*. Englewood Cliffs: Prentice-Hall, Inc., 1964.

Bernstein, Marvin, ed. *Foreign Investment in Latin America*. New York: Alfred A. Knopf, 1966.

Buell, Raymond I. *The Hull Trade Program and the American System*. New York: Foreign Policy Association, 1938.

Burr, Robert N. *Our Troubled Hemisphere: Perspectives on United States–Latin American Relations*. Washington: Brookings Institution, 1967.

Carey, James. *Peru and the United States: 1900–1962*. Notre Dame: University of Notre Dame Press, 1964.

Carr, E. H. *The Twenty Years' Crisis, 1919–1939*. New York: Macmillan and Company, 1939.

Carroll, Holbert N. *The House of Representatives and Foreign Affairs*. Pittsburgh: University of Pittsburgh Press, 1958.

Cline, Howard F. *The United States and Mexico*. Rev. ed. New York: Atheneum Press, 1963.

Cronon, E. David. *Josephus Daniels in Mexico*. Madison: University of Wisconsin Press, 1960.

Culbertson, William S. *Reciprocity*. New York: McGraw-Hill Book Company, Inc., 1937.

Cumberland, Charles C. *Mexico: The Struggle for Modernity*. London: Oxford University Press, 1968.

Curtis, Monica, ed. *Documents on International Affairs, 1938*. London: Oxford University Press, 1942.

Daniels, Josephus. *Shirt-Sleeve Diplomat.* Chapel Hill: University of North Carolina Press, 1947.

De Roussy de Sales, Raoul, ed. *My New Order.* New York: Reynal and Hitchcock, 1941.

Diebold, William. *New Directions in Our Trade Policy.* New York: Council on Foreign Relations, 1941.

Dietrich, Ethel B. *World Trade.* New York: Henry Holt and Company, 1939.

Dodd, William E., Jr., and Dodd, Martha, eds. *Ambassador Dodd's Diary, 1933–1938.* New York: Harcourt, Brace and Company, 1941.

Dozer, Donald M. *Are We Good Neighbors?* Gainesville: University of Florida Press, 1961.

Drummond, Donald F. "Cordell Hull." In *An Uncertain Tradition: American Secretaries of State in the Twentieth Century.* Edited by Norman Graebner. New York: McGraw-Hill Book Company, Inc., 1961.

Duggan, Laurence. *The Americas: The Search for Hemisphere Security.* New York: Henry Holt and Company, 1949.

Farrell, Robert H. *American Diplomacy in the Great Depression.* New Haven: Yale University Press, 1957.

Ferrer, Aldo. *The Argentine Economy.* Berkeley: University of California Press, 1967.

Feis, Herbert. *1933: Characters in Crisis.* Boston: Little Brown and Company, 1966.

⸻. *The Diplomacy of the Dollar.* Baltimore: Johns Hopkins Press, 1950.

Fite, Gilbert. *George Peek and the Fight for Farm Parity.* Norman: University of Oklahoma Press, 1954.

Fitzgibbon, Russell H. *Cuba and the United States 1900–1935.* Menasha, Wis.: George Banta Publishing Company, 1935.

Friedel, Frank. *Franklin D. Roosevelt: Launching the New Deal.* Boston: Little, Brown and Company, 1973.

Frye, Alton B. *Nazi Germany and the American Hemisphere: 1933–1941.* New Haven: Yale University Press, 1967.

Fusfield, Daniel R. *The Economic Thought of Franklin D. Roosevelt and the Origins of the New Deal.* New York: Columbia University Press, 1956.

Gardner, Lloyd C. *Economic Aspects of New Deal Diplomacy.* Madison: University of Wisconsin Press, 1964.

Gordon, Lincoln, and Grommers, Engelbert L. *United States Manufacturing Investment in Brazil.* Boston: Center for International Affairs, 1962.

Gordon, Wendell. *The Political Economy of Latin America.* New York: Columbia University Press, 1965.

Green, David. *The Containment of Latin America.* Chicago: Quadrangle Books, 1971.

Gross, Bertram M. *The Legislative Struggle: A Study in Social Combat.* New York: McGraw-Hill, 1953.

Guerrant, Edward O. *Roosevelt's Good Neighbor Policy.* Albuquerque: University of New Mexico Press, 1950.

Haberler, G. V. *The Theory of International Trade.* London: W. Hodges and Sons, Ltd., 1936.

Hawkins, Harry C. *Commercial Treaties and Agreements: Principles and Practices.* New York: Rinehart and Company, Inc., 1951.

Heald, Stephen, and Wheeler-Bennett, John W., eds. *Documents on International Affairs, 1933–1936.* London: Oxford University Press, 1934–1937.

Herring, Hubert. *A History of Latin America.* 3d. ed. New York: Alfred A. Knopf, 1967.

Hilgert, Folke. "The Case for Multilateral Trade." In *Foreign Trade and Finance,* edited by W. R. Allen and C. L. Allen. New York: Macmillan Company, 1949.

Hinton, Harold B. *Cordell Hull, A Biography.* Garden City: Doubleday, Doran and Company, Inc., 1942.

Hull, Cordell. *The Memoirs of Cordell Hull.* 2 vols. New York: Macmillan Company, 1948.

Ickes, Harold L. *The Secret Diary of Harold L. Ickes: The First Thousand Days, 1933–1936.* New York: Simon and Schuster, 1953.

International Bank for Reconstruction and Development. *Report on Cuba.* Baltimore: Johns Hopkins Press, 1951.

Jobim, José. *Brazil in the Making.* New York: Macmillan Company, 1943.

Langley, Lester D. *The Cuban Policy of the United States: A Brief History.* New York: John Wiley and Sons, 1968.

Letiche, J. M. *Reciprocal Trade Agreements in the World Economy.* New York: King's Crown Press, 1948.

Levin, N. Gordon, Jr. *Woodrow Wilson and World Politics: America's Response to War and Revolution.* New York: Oxford University Press, 1968.

Lieuwen, Edwin. *Petroleum in Venezuela: A History.* Berkeley: University of California Press, 1954.

———. *U. S. Policy in Latin America.* New York: Frederick A. Praeger, 1965.

———. *Venezuela.* London: Oxford University Press, 1965.

Lowenstein, Karl. *Brazil Under Vargas.* New York: Macmillan Company, 1942.

McCann, Frank D., Jr. *The Brazilian–American Alliance, 1937–1945.* Princeton: Princeton University Press, 1973.

McGann, Thomas F. *Argentina, the United States and the Inter-American System: 1880–1914.* Cambridge: Harvard University Press, 1957.

McGaffey, Wyatt, and Barnett, Clifford R. *Twentieth-Century Cuba: The Background of the Castro Revolution.* Garden City: Doubleday and Company, 1965.

Martz, John D. *Central America: The Crisis and the Challenge.* Chapel Hill: University of North Carolina Press, 1959.

Mecham, John Lloyd. *The United States and Inter-American Security, 1889–1960.* Austin: University of Texas Press, 1961.

Moley, Raymond. *After Seven Years.* New York: Harper and Brothers, 1939.

Mosk, Sanford A. *Industrial Revolution in Mexico.* Berkeley: University of California Press, 1950.

Palmer, Thomas W., Jr. *Search for a Latin American Policy.* Gainesville: University of Florida Press, 1957.

Parker, Franklin O. *The Central American Republics.* London: Oxford University Press, 1964.

Parrini, Carl P. *Heir to Empire: United States Economic Diplomacy, 1916–1923.* Pittsburgh: University of Pittsburgh Press, 1969.

Peek, George N. *Why Quit Our Own?* New York: D. Van Nostrand Company, 1936.

Perkins, Dexter. *The United States and Latin America.* Baton Rouge: Louisiana State University Press, 1961.

Peterson, Harold F. *Argentina and the United States, 1810–1960.* Albany: State University of New York, 1964.

Phillips, William. *Ventures in Diplomacy.* Boston: Beacon Press, 1953.

Poppino, Rollie E. *Brazil: The Land and People.* New York: Oxford University Press, 1968.

Pratt, Julius. *Cordell Hull: 1933–1944.* 2 vols. New York: Cooper Square Publishers, Inc., 1964.

The Public Papers and Addresses of Franklin D. Roosevelt, Vol. II. New York: Random House, 1938.

Rippy, J. Fred. *British Investment in Latin America, 1822–1949: A Case Study in the Operations of Private Enterprise in Retarded Regions.* Minneapolis: University of Minnesota Press, 1959.

Robinson, James A. *Congress and Foreign Policymaking.* Homewood, Ill. Dorsey Press, 1962.

Rodrígues, Mário. *Central America.* Englewood Cliffs: Prentice-Hall, Inc., 1965.

Roper, Daniel. *Fifty Years of Public Life.* Durham: Duke University Press, 1941.

Roosevelt, Elliott, ed. *F.D.R.: His Personal Letters, 1928–1945.* New York: Duell, Sloan and Pearce, 1950.

Roosevelt, Franklin D. *Looking Forward.* New York: John Day Company, 1933.

Sayre, Francis B. *The Way Forward: The American Trade Agreements Program.* New York: Macmillan Company, 1939.

Schacht, Hjalmar. *My First Seventy-Six Years.* London: Allan Wingate, 1955.

Schmokel, Wolfe W. *Dream of Empire: German Colonialism, 1919–1945.* New Haven: Yale University Press, 1964.

Schattschneider, E. E. *Politics, Pressures and the Tariff*. New York: Prentice-Hall, Inc., 1935.

Schlesinger, Arthur M., Jr. *The Age of Roosevelt: The Coming of the New Deal*. Boston: Houghton Mifflin Company, 1959.

Scholes, Walter V., ed. *United States Diplomatic History*, Vol. II. Boston: Houghton Mifflin Company, 1973.

Scobie, James R. *Argentina: A City and a Nation*. New York: Oxford University Press, 1964.

Smith, Robert F. *The United States and Cuba: Business and Diplomacy 1917–1960*. New Haven: College and University Press, 1960.

———. *The United States and Revolutionary Nationalism in Mexico, 1916–1932*. Chicago: University of Chicago Press, 1972.

Snyder, Richard Carlton. *The Most-Favored-Nation Clause*. New York: King's Crown Press, 1948.

Spiegel, Henry W. *The Brazilian Economy*. Philadelphia: Blakiston Company, 1949.

———. "Brazil: The State and Economic Growth." In *Economic Growth: Brazil, India, Japan*. Edited by Simon Kuznets, Wilbert E. Moore, and Joseph J. Spencer. Durham: Duke University Press, 1955.

Steward, Dick. "It Actually Costs Us Nothing." In *United States Diplomatic History*, Vol. II. Edited by Walter V. Scholes. Boston: Houghton Mifflin Company, 1973.

Strackbein, C. R. *American Enterprise and Foreign Trade*. Washington: Public Affairs Press, 1965.

Stuart, Graham H. *The Department of State*. New York: Macmillan Company, 1949.

Tasca, Henry J. *The Reciprocal Trade Policy of the United States*. Philadelphia: University of Pennsylvania Press, 1938.

Taussig, F. W. *Free Trade, The Tariff and Reciprocity*. New York: Macmillan Company, 1924.

———. *The Tariff History of the United States*. New York: G. P. Putnam's Sons, 1931.

Tulchin, Joseph S. *The Aftermath of War: World War I and U. S. Policy Toward Latin America*. New York: New York University Press, 1971.

Weinberg, Gerhard. *The Foreign Policy of Hitler's Germany*. Chicago: University of Chicago Press, 1970.

Welles, Sumner. *Time for Decision*. New York: Harper and Brothers. 1944.

Whitaker, Arthur P. *Argentina*. Englewood Cliffs, N. J.: Prentice-Hall, Inc., 1964.

———. *The Western Hemisphere Idea: Its Rise and Decline*. Ithaca: Cornell University Press, 1954.

———, and Jordon, David C. *Nationalism in Contemporary Latin America*. New York: Free Press, 1966.

Wilkinson, Joe R. *Politics and Trade Policy*. Washington: Public Affairs Press, 1960.

Williams, William A. *The Tragedy of American Diplomacy*. New York: Dell Publishing Company, Inc., 1962.

Wood, Bryce. *The Making of the Good Neighbor Policy*. New York: Columbia University Press, 1961.

Wilson, Joan Hoff. *American Business and Foreign Policy, 1920–1933*. Boston: Beacon Press, 1971.

————. *Ideology and Economics: U. S. Relations with the Soviet Union, 1918–1933*. Columbia: University of Missouri Press, 1974.

Wyeth, George. "Brazil: Trends in Industrial Development," In *Economic Growth: Brazil, India, Japan*. Edited by Simon Kuznets, Wilbert E. Moore, and Joseph J. Spencer. Durham: Duke University Press, 1955.

Abbreviations and Shortened Expressions in Footnotes

AFSJ—American Foreign Service Journal

BFDC—United States Department of Commerce, Bureau of Foreign and Domestic Commerce

CPS—Commercial Policy Series, United States Department of State

DA—United States Department of Agriculture

DC—United States Department of Commerce

DS—United States Department of State

FPR—Foreign Policy Reports

FR—Papers Relating to the Foreign Relations of the United States, 1933– 1940, United States Department of State

FTLA—The Foreign Trade of Latin America, United States Tariff Commission

FTUS—Foreign Trade of the United States, 1932–1936, United States Department of Commerce, Bureau of Foreign and Domestic Commerce

GPO—United States Government Printing Office

LAS—Latin American Series, numbers 4–22, United States Department of State

NA, RG—National Archives, Record Group

Operation—Operation of the Trade Agreements Program, United States Tariff Commission

SAPFT—File on the Special Adviser to the President on Foreign Trade, National Archives

TC—United States Tariff Commission

TPS—Trade Promotion Series, United States Department of Commerce, Bureau of Foreign and Domestic Commerce

Index